Language
Network

Grammar • Writing • Communication

McDougal Littell
A HOUGHTON MIFFLIN COMPANY

Language
Network

- Grammar, Usage, and Mechanics
- Essential Writing Skills
- Writing Workshops
- Communicating in the Information Age

McDougal Littell
A HOUGHTON MIFFLIN COMPANY

ISBN 0-395-96736-8

2004 Impression.

Acknowledgments begin on page 621.

12 13 14 15 – DCI – 09 08 07 06 05

Teacher Panels

The teacher panels helped guide the conceptual development of *Language Network*. They participated actively in shaping and reviewing prototype materials for the pupil edition, determining ancillary and technology components, and guiding the development of the scope and sequence for the program.

Gloria Anderson, Campbell Junior HIgh School, Houston, TX
Luke Atwood, Park Junior HIgh School, LaGrange, IL
Donna Blackall, Thomas Middle School, Arlington Heights, IL
Karen Bostwick, McLean Middle School, Fort Worth, TX
Rebecca Hadavi, Parkland Middle School, El Paso, TX
Sandi Heffelfinger, Parkland Junior High School, McHenry, IL
Diane Hinojosa, Alamo Middle School, Pharr, TX
Patricia Jackson, Pearce Middle School, Austin, TX
Sue Kazlusky, Lundahl Middle School, Crystal Lake, IL
Tom Kiefer, Cary Junior High School, Cary, IL
Keith Lustig, Hill Middle School, Naperville, IL
Joanna Martin, Haines Middle School, St. Charles, IL
Sandy Mattox, Coppell Middle School, Lewisville, TX
Susan Mortensen, Deer Path Junior High School, Lake Forest, IL
Adrienne Myers, Foster Middle School, Longview, TX
Kathy Powers, Welch Middle School, Houston, TX
Patricia Smith, Tefft Middle School, Streamwood, IL
Frank Westerman, Jackson Middle School, San Antonio, TX
Bessie Wilson, Greiner Middle School, Dallas, TX
Kimberly Zeman, Hauser Junior High School, Riverside, IL

Content Specialists

Dr. Mary Newton Bruder, former Professor of Linguistics at University of Pittsburgh; (creator of the Grammar Hotline Web site)
Rebekah Caplan, High School and Middle Grades English/Language Arts Specialist for the New Standards Project, National Center on Education and the Economy, Washington, D.C.
Dr. Sharon Sicinski Skeans, Assistant Professor, University of Houston–Clear Lake
Richard Vinson, Retired Teacher, Provine High School, Jackson, Mississippi

Technology Consultants

Dr. David Considine, Media Studies Coordinator, Appalachian State University, Boone, NC (author of *Visual Messages: Integrating Imagery into Instruction*)

Heidi Whitus, Teacher, Communication Arts High School, San Antonio, Tex.

Anne Clark, Riverside-Brookfield High School, Riverside, Ill.

Pat Jurgens, Riverside-Brookfield High School, Riverside, Ill.

Ralph Amelio, Former teacher, Willowbrook High School, Villa Park, Ill.

Cindy Lucia, Horace Greeley High School, New York, N.Y.

Aaron Barnhart, Television writer for the *Kansas City Star* and columnist for *Electronic Media,* Kansas City, Mo.

ESL Consultants

Dr. Andrea B. Bermúdez, Professor of Studies in Language and Culture; Director, Research Center for Language and Culture; Chair, Foundations and Professional Studies, University of Houston-Clear Lake, Clear Lake, Tex.

Inara Bundza, ESL Director, Kelvyn Park High School, Chicago, Ill.

Danette Erickson Meyer, Consultant, Illinois Resource Center, Des Plaines, Ill.

John Hilliard, Consultant, Illinois Resource Center, Des Plaines, Ill.

John Kibler, Consultant, Illinois Resource Center, Des Plaines, Ill.

Barbara Kuhns, Camino Real Middle School, Las Cruces, N.M.

Teacher Reviewers

Gloria Anderson, Campbell Junior High School, Houston, TX

Patricia Jackson, Pearce Middle School, Austin, TX

Sandy Mattox, Coppell Middle School, Lewisville, TX

Adrienne Myers, Foster Middle School, Longview, TX

Frank Westerman, Jackson Middle School, San Antonio, TX

Bessie Wilson, Greiner Middle School, Dallas, TX

Student Reviewers

Saba Abraham, Chelsea High School

Julie Allred, Southwest High School

Nabiha Azam, East Kentwood High School

Dana Baccino, Downington High School

Christianne Balsamo, Nottingham High School

Luke Bohline, Lakeville High School

Nathan Buechel, Providence Senior High School

Melissa Cummings, Highline High School

Megan Dawson, Southview Senior High School

Michelle DeBruce, Jurupa High School

Brian Deeds, Arvada West High School

Ranika Fizer, Jones High School

Ashleigh Goldberg, Parkdale High School

Jacqueline Grullon, Christopher Columbus High School

Dimmy Herard, Hialeah High School

Sean Horan, Round Rock High School

Bob Howard, Jr., Robert E. Lee High School

Rebecca Iden, Willowbrook High School
Agha's Igbinovia, Florin High School
Megan Jones, Dobson High School
Ed Kampelman, Parkway West High School
David Knapp, Delmar High School
Eva Lima, Westmoor High School
Ashley Miers, Ouachita High School
Raul Morffi, Shawnee Mission West High School
Sakenia Mosley, Sandalwood High School
Sergio Perez, Sunset High School
Jackie Peters, Westerville South High School
Kevin Robischaud, Waltham High School
Orlando Sanchez, West Mesa High School
Selene Sanchez, San Diego High School
Sharon Schaefer, East Aurora High School
Mica Semrick, Hoover High School
Julio Sequeira, Belmont High School
Camille Singleton, Cerritos High School
Solomon Stevenson, Ozen High School
Tim Villegas, Dos Pueblos High School
Shane Wagner, Waukesha West High School
Swenikqua Walker, San Bernardino High School
Douglas Weakly, Ray High School
Lauren Zoric, Norwin High School

Student Writers

Trilly Bagwell, Nichols Middle School
Gabrielle Davis, Chute Middle School
Katie Delbecq, Hauser Junior High
Lydia Eickstaedt, Arizona School for the Arts
Lynnette Michelle Fisher, Monforton School
Alec McMullen, Holmes Junior High
Luke Pendry, Churchill Junior HIgh
Ryan Powell, Foster Middle School
Heidi Wiendenheft, Glasgow Middle School

Contents Overview

Grammar, Usage, and Mechanics

1 The Sentence and Its Parts — 4

2 Nouns — 34

3 Pronouns — 52

4 Verbs — 86

5 Adjectives and Adverbs — 120

6 Prepositions, Conjunctions, Interjections — 146

7 Subject-Verb Agreement — 164

8 Capitalization — 184

9 Punctuation — 204

Diagramming Sentences — 232

Quick-Fix Editing Machine — 238

Essential Writing Skills

10 Writing Process — 263

11 Building Sentences — 277

12 Building Paragraphs — 289

13 Organizing Paragraphs — 301

14 Building Compositions — 311

15 Elaboration — 323

16 Revising Sentences — 335

17 Effective Language — 347

Writing Workshops: Writing for Different Purposes

18 Personal Experience Essay   358

19 Describing a Place   366

20 Response to Literature   374

21 Process Description   382

22 Problem-Solution Essay   390

23 Opinion Statement   398

24 Short Story and Poem   406

25 Research Report   418

Communicating in the Information Age

26 Finding Information   437

27 Study and Test-Taking Skills   451

28 Thinking Clearly   467

29 Listening and Speaking Skills   481

30 Examining Media   497

31 Building Your Vocabulary   511

Student Resources

Exercise Bank   528
Additional Exercises for Chapters 1–9

Model Bank   562

Rules and Guides   568

Quick-Fix Spelling Machine   568

Commonly Misspelled Words   576

Commonly Confused Words   578

MLA Citation Guidelines   582

Glossary for Writers   590

Grammar, Usage, and Mechanics

1 **The Sentence and Its Parts** 4

    Diagnostic Test *What Do You Know?*   5

Complete Subjects and Predicates   6

Simple Subjects   8

Simple Predicates, or Verbs   10

Verb Phrases   12

Compound Sentence Parts   14

Kinds of Sentences   16

    LITERARY MODEL *Words on a Page* by Keith Leckie   16

Subjects in Unusual Order   18

Complements: Subject Complements   21

    LITERARY MODEL "The Boy Who Flew" by Anne Rockwell   22

Complements: Objects of Verbs   23

Fragments and Run-Ons   25

Grammar in Literature "Arachne" by Olivia E. Coolidge   28

    Mixed Review   30

    Mastery Test *What Did You Learn?*   31

    Student Help Desk   32

The Sentence at a Glance

    Subjects and Predicates *Story Line*

    Complements *Finishing Touches*

    Kinds of Sentences *Different Voices*

    The Bottom Line *Checklist for Editing Sentences*

2 **Nouns** 34

    Diagnostic Test *What Do You Know?*   35

What Is a Noun?   36

Singular and Plural Nouns   38

    LITERARY MODEL "The Dog of Pompeii" by Louis Untermeyer   39

Possessive Nouns   41

Nouns and Their Jobs   43

Grammar in Science *Diagram*   46

We are learning how to use computers and now I can use the mouse and paste.

Mixed Review	48
Mastery Test *What Did You Learn?*	49

Student Help Desk   50

Nouns at a Glance

    Quick-Fix Spelling Machine *Plurals of Nouns*

    Quick-Fix Spelling Machine *Possessives*

    Nouns and Their Jobs *What's in the Desert?*

    The Bottom Line *Checklist for Nouns*

3 Pronouns

52

Diagnostic Test *What Do You Know?*	53
What Is a Pronoun?	54
LITERARY MODEL "The Southpaw" by Judith Viorst	55
Subject Pronouns	57
Object Pronouns	59
LITERARY MODEL *The Story of My Life* by Helen Keller	60
Possessive Pronouns	61
Reflexive and Intensive Pronouns	64
Interrogatives and Demonstratives	66
Pronoun-Antecedent Agreement	69
Indefinite Pronoun Agreement	72
Pronoun Problems	75
More Pronoun Problems	77
Grammar in Literature *Damon and Pythias* retold by Fan Kissen	80
Mixed Review	82
Mastery Test *What Did You Learn?*	83

Student Help Desk   84

Pronouns at a Glance

    Pronoun-Antecedent Agreement *Me and My Shadow*

    Types of Pronouns *"I'm Nobody. Are You Nobody Too?"*

    Pronoun Problems *Friends by the Case*

    The Bottom Line *Checklist for Pronouns*

All for One

One for All

4 Verbs 86

   Diagnostic Test *What Do You Know?*   87

What Is a Verb?   88

   LITERARY MODEL "My First Dive with the Dolphins"   90
      by Don C. Reed

Action Verbs and Objects   91

Linking Verbs and Predicate Words   94

Principal Parts of Verbs   96

Irregular Verbs   98

   LITERARY MODEL adapted from *Taking Flight, My Story*
      by Vicki Van Meter with Dan Gutman   100

Simple Tenses   101

Perfect Tenses   104

   LITERARY MODEL "The Dog of Pompeii" by Louis Untermeyer   105

Using Verb Tenses   107

Troublesome Verb Pairs   111

Grammar in Physical Education *Instructions*   114

   Mixed Review   116

   Mastery Test *What Did You Learn?*   117

Student Help Desk   118

Verbs at a Glance

   Principal Parts of Regular Verbs

   Keeping Tenses Straight *Travel Time*

   The Bottom Line *Checklist for Verb Usage*

5 Adjectives and Adverbs 120

   Diagnostic Test *What Do You Know?*   121

What Is an Adjective?   122

   LITERARY MODEL "Scout's Honor" by Avi   124

Predicate Adjectives   125

   LITERARY MODEL "Oh Broom, Get to Work" by Yoshiko Uchida   125

Other Words Used as Adjectives   127

   LITERARY MODEL "The All-American Slurp" by Lensey Namioka   128

What Is an Adverb?   130

Making Comparisons   133
Adjective or Adverb?   136
Avoiding Double Negatives   138
Grammar in Literature "Ghost of the Lagoon" by Armstrong Sperry   140
Mixed Review   142
    LITERARY MODEL "The Sand Castle" by Alma Luz Villanueva 142
    Mastery Test *What Did You Learn?*   143

Student Help Desk   144

Adjectives and Adverbs at a Glance
    Modifiers in Comparisons *Zoom Lens*
    Double Forms *Double Take*
    Modifier Problems *Field Guide*
    The Bottom Line *Checklist for Adjectives and Adverbs*

6 Prepositions, Conjunctions, Interjections 146

    Diagnostic Test *What Do You Know?*   147
What Is a Preposition?   148
    LITERARY MODEL *The Hobbit* by J. R. R. Tolkien,
        dramatized by Patricia Gray   150
Using Prepositional Phrases   151
Conjunctions   154
Interjections   157
Grammar in Social Studies *Map*   158
    Mixed Review   160
    Mastery Test *What Did You Learn?*   161

Student Help Desk   162

Prepositions, Conjunctions, Interjections at a Glance
    Prepositions, Conjunctions, Interjections *Summary*
    Prepositional Phrases *What Do They Do?*
    Interjections! *Just a Few Ideas . . .*
    The Bottom Line *Checklist for Prepositions, Conjunctions, and*
        Interjections

Wow! Awesome!

7 Subject-Verb Agreement 164

Diagnostic Test *What Do You Know?*	165
Agreement in Number	166
Compound Subjects	169
Phrases Between Subjects and Verbs	171
Indefinite Pronouns as Subjects	173
Subjects in Unusual Positions	176
LITERARY MODEL *Damon and Pythias* retold by Fan Kissen	177
Grammar in Literature "Scout's Honor" by Avi	178
Mixed Review	180
Mastery Test *What Did You Learn?*	181

Student Help Desk	182

Subject-Verb Agreement at a Glance
  Indefinite Pronouns *One for All*
  Compound Subjects *All for One*
  Tricky Sentences *Make Them Get Along*
  The Bottom Line *Checklist for Subject-Verb Agreement*

8 Capitalization 184

Diagnostic Test *What Do You Know?*	185
People and Cultures	186
First Words and Titles	189
LITERARY MODEL "All That Is Gold" by J. R. R. Tolkien	189
Mixed Review	192
Places and Transportation	193
Organizations and Other Subjects	196
Grammar in Math *Tables and Bar Graphs*	198
Mixed Review	200
Mastery Test *What Did You Learn?*	201

Student Help Desk	202

Capitalization at a Glance
  Do Capitalize *Upper Case Ursula*
  Don't Capitalize *Lower Case Larry*
  The Bottom Line *Checklist for Capitalization*

9 Punctuation 204

Diagnostic Test *What Do You Know?*	205
Periods and Other End Marks	206
Commas in Sentences	209
Commas: Dates, Addresses, and Letters	212
Punctuating Quotations	214
LITERARY MODEL "All Summer in a Day" by Ray Bradbury	216
Semicolons and Colons	218
Hyphens, Dashes, and Parentheses	220
Apostrophes	222
Punctuating Titles	224
Grammar in Literature "The Quarrel" by Eleanor Farjeon	226
Mixed Review	228
Mastery Test *What Did You Learn?*	229

Student Help Desk
230

Punctuation at a Glance
  Punctuating Titles *Long or Short*
  Punctuation with Commas *Separating Ideas*
  Punctuation with Quotation Marks *In or Out*
  The Bottom Line *Checklist for Punctuation*

Diagramming: Sentence Parts	232
Diagramming: Complements	234
Diagramming: Prepositional Phrases	236
Diagramming: Compound Sentences	237

Hey, kids!
Learn to snowboard
with
Powder Hound
Club for Teen Skiers

Personal instruction and supervision by trained professionals who put safety first.

The best value and experience in town. Payment plans available.

Join the club at Snow Dog's Ski Hut 2500 N. Mercer Rd.

Quick-Fix Editing Machine

Fixing Errors

1. Sentence Fragments	240
2. Run-On Sentences	241
3. Subject-Verb Agreement	242
4. Pronoun Reference Problems	244
5. Incorrect Pronoun Case	245
6. *Who* and *Whom*	246
7. Confusing Comparisons	247
8. Verb Forms and Tenses	248
9. Missing or Misplaced Commas	249

Improving Style

10. Improving Weak Sentences	250
11. Avoiding Wordiness	251
12. Varying Sentence Structure	252
13. Varying Sentence Length	253
14. Adding Supporting Details	254
15. Avoiding Clichés and Slang	255
16. Using Precise Words	256
17. Using Figurative Language	257
18. Paragraphing	258

Essential Writing Skills

10 Writing Process 263

Power Words *We're Not All Sprinters*
Prewriting   264
   Finding a Topic
   Focusing a Topic
   Finding and Organizing Information
Drafting   267
   Making a Plan
   Using Peer Response
Revising   269
   Six Traits of Good Writing
   Traits in Action
Editing and Proofreading   271
Publishing and Reflecting   272
   Ways to Present Your Work
   Reflecting on Your Writing

Student Help Desk   274

Writing Process at a Glance
   Finding Ideas *Write Until the Light Goes On!*
   Tips for Drafting *Get the Words Out*
   Editing Hints *Watch for Word Traps!*
   Proofreading Tips *Keep an Eye Out for Errors*
   The Bottom Line *Checklist for Writing*

11 Building Sentences 277

Power Words *A Change for the Better*
Improving Your Sentences   278
   Checking for Completeness
   Expanding with Modifiers
Growing Sentences   280
   LITERARY MODEL "Matthew Henson at the Top of the World"
     by Jim Haskins   280

Adding Sentence Openers

Adding to the Middle

Sentence Closers

Combining Complete Sentences   282

Combining with *And, But,* and *Or*

LITERARY MODEL "Nadia the Willful" by Sue Alexander

Combining with Other Conjunctions

Combining Sentence Parts   284

Creating Compound Parts

Inserting Words and Phrases

Student Help Desk   286

Building Sentences at a Glance

Finding Fragments *Check for Completeness*

Expanding with Modifiers *Add Some Color!*

Expanding Sentences *Help It Grow!*

The Bottom Line *Checklist for Building Sentences*

12 Building Paragraphs

289

Power Words *For a Limited Time Only!*

Creating Good Paragraphs   290

What Is a Good Paragraph?

What Is a Good Topic Sentence?

Focusing Your Paragraphs   292

Unity: Fitting the Parts into a Whole

Logical and Smooth: Making the Parts Connect

Paragraphs: Descriptive and Narrative   294

Paragraphs that Describe

LITERARY MODEL *The House of Dies Drear* by Virginia Hamilton

Paragraphs that Tell a Story

Paragraphs: Informative and Persuasive   296

Student Help Desk 298

Building Paragraphs at a Glance
> Tips for Terrific Topic Sentences *Light the Way*
> Test for Paragraph Unity *All for One, and One for All*
> Types of Paragraphs *Does It Fit the Part?*
> Transition Words *Make It Flow*
> The Bottom Line *Checklist for Building Paragraphs*

13 Organizing Paragraphs 301

Power Words *The Main Event*
Sequential Order 302
> **LITERARY MODEL** "The Circuit" by Francisco Jiménez 302

Spatial Order 304
> **LITERARY MODEL** "Why Monkeys Live in Trees" retold by
> Julius Lester 304

Compare-and-Contrast Order 306
> Showing Similarities and Differences

Student Help Desk 308

Organizing Paragraphs at a Glance
> Paragraph Organization *Patterns and Purpose*
> Transition Words and Phrases *Hold Them Together*
> The Bottom Line *Checklist for Organizing Paragraphs*

14 Building Compositions 311

Power Words *Building for the Future*
What Is a Composition? 312
Writing an Introduction 314
> Main Idea
> Types of Introductions
Writing the Body 316
> Unity in a Composition
> Coherence in a Composition
Writing the Conclusion 319

Student Help Desk 320

Building Compositions at a Glance
The Introduction *Off to a Good Start*
Transitions Words *Making Clear Connections*
The Conclusion *Finishing with a Flourish*
The Bottom Line *Checklist for Writing*

15 Elaboration 323

Power Words *Seven Pairs of Socks?*
Introducing Elaboration 324
What Is Elaboration?
Methods of Elaboration
Using Sensory Details 326
Sight, Smell, Taste, Touch, and Sound
LITERARY MODEL "Oh Broom, Get to Work" by Yoshiko Uchida 326
Adding Facts 328
Facts Help You Make Your Point
LITERARY MODEL "My First Dive with the Dolphins"
by Don C. Reed 328

Facts Can Support Your Opinions
Creating Visuals 330
Photographs and Illustrations
Charts and Graphs

Student Help Desk 332

Elaboration at a Glance
Sensory Words Generator *Sense-O-Matic*
Sense Doctor *Fix It with Facts*
Using Visuals *Seeing Is Believing*
The Bottom Line *Checklist for Elaboration*

16 Revising Sentences 335

Power Words *Highways and Byways*
Fixing Empty Sentences 336
LITERARY MODEL "My First Dive with the Dolphins"
by Don C. Reed 337

Fixing Stringy Sentences 338
   Creating Separate Ideas
Varying Sentence Length 340
   Adding Sentence Variety
   Combining Choppy Sentences
Varying Sentence Structure 342
   Rearranging Phrases
   Varying Sentence Types

Student Help Desk 344

Revising Sentences at a Glance
   Filling Empty Sentences *Ask Questions*
   Smoothing Choppy Sentences
   Rearranging Phrases
   The Bottom Line *Checklist for Revising Sentences*

17 Effective Language

.... 347

Power Words *Hey, Look at Me!*
Levels of Language 348
   Formal or Informal?
Using Exact Language 350
   Just the Right Words
   Kinds of Meaning
Imagery and Figurative Language 352
   Say It with Similes
   LITERARY MODEL "Tuesday of the Other June"
      by Norma Fox Mazer 352
   LITERARY MODEL "The Bamboo Beads" by Lynn Joseph 352
   Metaphors Make It Marvelous

Student Help Desk 354

Effective Language at a Glance
   Formal Language/Informal Language
   Precise Words *What Do You Mean by That?*
   Figurative Language *Paint Some Word Pictures*
   Connotations *Words with Strong Feelings*
   The Bottom Line *Checklist for Effective Language*

Writing Workshops

Personal Writing

18 Personal Experience Essay 358

Basics in a Box—Elements and Rubric 358

    STUDENT MODEL *Theater* 359

Prewriting 361

Drafting 361

Revising *Using Sensory Details* 362

Editing and Proofreading *Correcting Fragments* 362

Sharing and Reflecting 362

Speak for Yourself *Monologue* 363

  Student Help Desk 364

Personal Experience Essay at a Glance

  Idea Bank

  Detail Generator *Little Things Count*

  Friendly Feedback *Questions for Your Peer Reader*

  Publishing Options

  The Bottom Line *Checklist for Personal Experience Essay*

Descriptive Writing

19 Describing a Place 366

Basics in a Box—Elements and Rubric 366

    STUDENT MODEL *My Place* 367

Prewriting 369

Drafting 369

Revising *Strong Conclusions* 370

Editing and Proofreading *Fixing Comma Errors* 370

Sharing and Reflecting 370

Speak for Yourself *Guided Tour* 371

Student Help Desk 372

Describing a Place at a Glance
> Idea Bank
> **Friendly Feedback** *Questions for Your Peer Reader*
> **Publishing Options**
> **The Bottom Line** *Checklist for Describing a Place*

Literary Analysis

20 Response to Literature 374

Basics in a Box—Elements and Rubric 374
> **STUDENT MODEL** *"All Summer in a Day"* 375
Prewriting 377
Drafting 377
Revising *Effective Introductions* 378
Editing and Proofreading *Subject-Verb Agreement* 378
Sharing and Reflecting 378
Speak for Yourself *Readers Theater* 379

Student Help Desk 380

Response to Literature at a Glance
> Idea Bank
> **Including Quotations** *A Shower of Quotes*
> **Friendly Feedback** *Questions for Your Peer Reader*
> **Publishing Options**
> **The Bottom Line** *Checklist for Response to Literature*

Informative/Explanatory

21 Process Description 382

Basics in a Box—Elements and Rubric 382
> **STUDENT MODEL** *How to Make Yourself a Suit of Armor* 383
Prewriting 385
Drafting 385
Revising *Making the Sequence Clear* 386
Editing and Proofreading *Correcting Run-Ons* 386
Sharing and Reflecting 386
Speak for Yourself *Demonstration* 387

Table of Contents **xxiii**

Student Help Desk   388

Process Description at a Glance
    Idea Bank
    What's Next *Logic Checklist*
    Friendly Feedback *Questions for Your Peer Reader*
    Publishing Options
    The Bottom Line *Checklist for Process Description*

Informative/Explanatory

22 Problem-Solution Essay 390

    Basics in a Box—Elements and Rubric   390
        STUDENT MODEL   *How Racism Affects Children*   391
    Prewriting   393
    Drafting   393
    Revising *Considering Audience*   394
    Editing and Proofreading *Avoiding Confusing Comparisons*   394
    Sharing and Reflecting   394
    Speak for Yourself *Persuasive Speech*   395

    Student Help Desk   396

    Problem-Solution Essay at a Glance
        Idea Bank
        Friendly Feedback *Questions for Your Peer Reader*
        Publishing Options
        The Bottom Line *Checklist for Problem-Solution Essay*

Persuasive Writing

23 Opinion Statement 398

    Basics in a Box—Elements and Rubric   398
        STUDENT MODEL *School Schedule*   399
    Prewriting   401
    Drafting   401
    Revising *Supporting an Opinion with Reasons*   402
    Editing and Proofreading *Shifting Verb Tense*   402
    Sharing and Reflecting   402
    Speak for Yourself *Discussion*   403

Student Help Desk

404

Opinion Statement at a Glance

Idea Bank

Charting Your Ideas

Friendly Feedback *Questions for Your Peer Reader*

Publishing Options

The Bottom Line *Checklist for Opinion Statement*

Narrative/Literary Writing

24 Short Story and Poem 406

Basics in a Box—Elements and Rubric: Short Story   406

STUDENT MODEL   *Lion and the Peculiar Purple Peach*   407

Prewriting   409

Drafting   409

Revising *Using Dialogue*   410

Editing and Proofreading *Punctuating Dialogue*   410

Sharing and Reflecting   410

Basics in a Box—Elements and Rubric: Poem   411

STUDENT MODEL   *Who*   412

Prewriting   413

Drafting   413

Revising *Choosing Precise Words*   414

Editing and Proofreading *Avoiding Forced Rhyme*   414

Sharing and Reflecting   414

Speak for Yourself *Skit*   415

Student Help Desk

416

Short Story and Poem at a Glance

Idea Bank

Friendly Feedback *Questions for Your Peer Reader*

Publishing Options

The Bottom Line *Checklists for Short Story and Poem*

Research Report

25 Research Report 418

   Basics in a Box—Elements and Rubric   418
      STUDENT MODEL *Greek and Roman Gods*   419
   Developing a Research Plan   421
      Narrowing Your Topic
      Developing Research Questions
   Finding Information   422
      Evaluating Sources
      Making Source Cards
   Taking Notes   424
      Paraphrasing
      Quoting
      Avoiding Plagiarism
   Organizing and Outlining   426
      Planning Your Report
      Making an Outline
   Drafting   427
      Using Your Notes to Write Your Paper
   Documenting Information   428
      Preparing a Works Cited List
   Revising *Varying Sentence Beginnings*   430
   Editing and Proofreading *Avoiding Shifts in Verb Tense*   430
   Sharing and Reflecting   430
   Speak for Yourself *Oral Report*   431

   Student Help Desk   432

   Research Report at a Glance
      Idea Bank
      Friendly Feedback *Questions for Your Peer Reader*
      Publishing Options
      The Bottom Line *Checklist for Research Report*

Communicating in the Information Age

Inquiry and Research

26 Finding Information 437

Power Words *Facing the Mountain*
The Library and Media Center   438
  Library Collection
  Special Services
  Fiction and Nonfiction
Using Library Catalogs   440
  The Computer Catalog
  The Card Catalog
Finding Magazine Articles   442
  Using a Magazine Index
Using Reference Materials   444
  Reference Books
  Electronic Reference Sources
The World Wide Web   446
  Smart Searching
  Judging Search Results

Student Help Desk   448
Finding Information at a Glance
  Dewey Decimal System *Dewey Leads the Way!*
  The Web *Traps and Truths*
  The Bottom Line *Checklist for Finding Information*

Classroom Skills

27 Study and Test-Taking Skills 451

Power Words *The Game of Life*
Reading for Information   452
  Using Aids to Reading
Understanding Visuals   454
  Types of Graphic Aids

Taking Notes   456
   Taking Notes for Studying
   Taking Notes for Research
   Organizing Note Cards
Creating an Outline   459
   Creating a Formal Outline
Taking Objective Tests   460
   Common Formats
Writing for Tests   463
   Understanding the Question
   Writing the Response

Student Help Desk   464
Study Skills at a Glance
   Study Tips
   Preparing for a Test
   Types of Essay Questions You May Need to Answer
   The Bottom Line Checklist for Study and Test-Taking Skills

Critical Thinking

28 Thinking Clearly

467

Power Words Whose Idea Was That?
How Ideas Are Related   468
   Main Idea and Supporting Details
   Cause and Effect
   LITERARY MODEL "The Wolf and the House Dog" by Aesop   469
   Similarities and Differences
Separating Facts from Opinions   470
   Identifying Facts
   Identifying Opinions
Going Beyond the Facts   472
   Making Inferences
   Drawing Conclusions
Avoiding Errors in Reasoning   474
   Overgeneralization
   Circular Reasoning
   Either/Or Thinking

Recognizing Emotional Appeals   476
    Loaded Language
    Name-Calling
    Bandwagon and Snob Appeal

Student Help Desk   478

Thinking Clearly at a Glance
    Related Ideas *Similarities and Differences*
    Fact or Opinion *Where's the Proof?*
    Errors in Thinking *What I Meant to Say Was . . .*
    The Bottom Line *Checklist for Thinking Clearly*

Speaking and Listening

29 Listening and Speaking Skills   481

    Power Words *It Takes Two*
    Listening Actively   482
        Listening with a Purpose
        Strategies for Active Listening
        Judging What You Hear
    Interviewing   485
        Planning an Interview
        Conducting and Following Up on an Interview
    Speaking Informally   487
        Everyday Speaking
        Speaking in Groups
    Preparing an Oral Report   489
        From Writing to Speaking
        Presentation Skills
    Presenting an Oral Interpretation   492
        Choosing a Selection
        Practicing Your Delivery

Student Help Desk   494

Listening and Speaking Skills at a Glance
    Tips for Effective Listening *Lend an Ear*
    Speaking Tips *You Said It!*
    Letter for an Interview *Dear Expert*
    The Bottom Line *Checklist for Listening and Speaking Skills*

Viewing and Representing

30 Examining Media 497

Power Words *Media Messages*

The Elements of Media   498
     Print Media
     Video and Film
     World Wide Web

Understanding Media Influence   500
     What's the Purpose of the Message?
     Who Sends the Message?
     Who Receives the Message?

Analyzing Media   502
     Film
     Magazine Feature Story
     World Wide Web Site ·

Creating a Class Newspaper   505
     Choose Your Medium
     Understanding Newspapers
     Planning and Creating
     One Classroom's Newspaper

Student Help Desk   508
Examining Media at a Glance
     Media Influence *Hitting the Target*
     Questions for Media Literacy *Asking the Right Questions*
     Creating a Newspaper
     The Bottom Line *Checklist for Learning About Media*

Expanding Literacy

31 Building Your Vocabulary 511

Power Words *These Words Are All Legit!*

Using Vocabulary Strategies   512
     Strategies for Understanding New Words
     Strategies for Remembering New Words

Using Context Clues   514
     Definitions and Restatements
     Examples

Comparisons and Contrasts
General Context
LITERARY MODEL "Chinatown" by Lawrence Yep 516

Analyzing Word Parts 517
Base Words
Prefixes and Suffixes
Word Roots
Understanding Related Words 520
Word Families
Synonyms
Using References 522
Dictionaries
Thesauruses

Student Help Desk 524
Building Your Vocabulary at a Glance
Pull Apart Puzzling Words
Spot Specific Context Clues
Interpret Suffix Signals
The Bottom Line Checklist for Developing Vocabulary

Student Resources (See page 1.) 526

Special Features

Grammar Across the Curriculum

Science: Diagram 46
Physical Education: Instructions 114
Social Studies: Map 158
Math: Tables and Bar Graphs 198

Grammar in Literature

"Arachne" 28
Damon and Pythias 80
"Ghost of the Lagoon" 140
"Scout's Honor" 178
"The Quarrel" 226

Power Words: Vocabulary for Precise Writing

We're Not All Sprinters 262
A Change for the Better 276
For a Limited Time Only! 288
The Main Event 300
Building for the Future 310
Seven Pairs of Socks? 322
Highways and Byways 334
Hey, Look at Me! 346
Facing the Mountain 436
The Game of Life 450
Whose Idea Was That? 466
It Takes Two 480
Media Messages 496
These Words Are All Legit! 510

Quick-Fix Editing Machine

Sentence Fragments 240
Run-On Sentences 241
Subject-Verb Agreement 242
Pronoun Reference Problems 244
Incorrect Pronoun Case 245
Who and Whom 246
Confusing Comparisons 247
Verb Forms and Tenses 248

Missing or Misplaced Commas 249
Improving Weak Sentences 250
Avoiding Wordiness 251
Varying Sentence Structure 252
Varying Sentence Length 253
Adding Supporting Details 254
Avoiding Clichés and Slang 255
Using Precise Words 256
Using Figurative Language 257
Paragraphing 258

Student Resources

Exercise Bank 528

Model Bank 562
    Book Review 562
    Editorial 563
    Letter of Complaint 564
    Thank–You Letter 564
    Comparison-and-Contrast Essay 565
    Cause-and-Effect Essay 566
    Analyzing a Subject 567

Quick-Fix Spelling Machine 568

Commonly Misspelled Words 576

Commonly Confused Words 578

MLA Citation Guidelines 582

Glossary for Writers 590

Index 598

Acknowledgments 621

Grammar, Usage, and Mechanics

1 The Sentence and Its Parts   4

2 Nouns   34

3 Pronouns   52

4 Verbs   86

5 Adjectives and Adverbs   120

6 Prepositions, Conjunctions, Interjections   146

7 Subject-Verb Agreement   164

8 Capitalization   184

9 Punctuation   204

Diagramming Sentences   232

Quick-Fix Editing Machine   238

Writing Machine

A machine doesn't run unless all of it's parts work together. If even one part stops working, the machine can break down. Your writing won't make sense unless your words work together. Use the rules of grammar to avoid breakdowns in your writing.

The Sentence and Its Parts

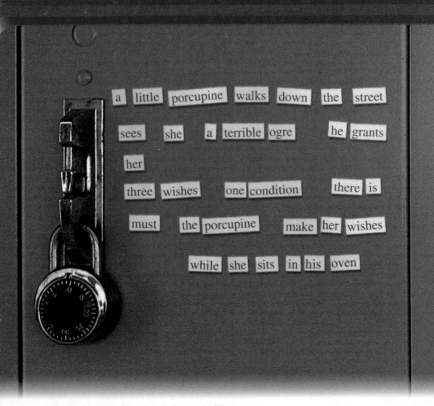

Theme: Stories and Storytelling

Putting the Pieces Together

How would you arrange the words and phrases above to tell a story? Magnetic word blocks are fun because they let you group words together in any order. However, the words will only make sense if they are arranged in complete sentences. Sentences allow you to express complete thoughts. You can use different types of sentences to tell stories.

Write Away: Story Time

What do you think will happen to the porcupine? Write a brief story based on the words and phrases in the photograph. Place your completed story in your 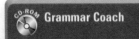 **Working Portfolio.**

Grammar Coach

For each underlined item, choose the letter of the term that correctly identifies it.

All societies have storytellers. In the Songhai Empire of West
    (1)
Africa, griots traveled from village to village. These storytellers
                   (2)
informed people about historical and current events. Songhai kings
   (3)
greatly valued their work. Some modern griots have continued this
                    (4)   (5)
tradition. Troubadours were European storytellers who performed
                                        (6)
a similar role during the Middle Ages. From their songs and stories

flowed all kinds of information. Sometimes they would tell funny
       (7)   (8)
tales, other times they would explain herbal medicine. They

enlightened and entertained audiences in market places and
           (9)
palaces. At one royal wedding, 426 troubadours performed!
                          (10)

1. A. simple subject
   B. simple predicate
   C. complete subject
   D. complete predicate

2. A. simple subject
   B. simple predicate
   C. complete subject
   D. complete predicate

3. A. simple subject
   B. simple predicate
   C. complete subject
   D. complete predicate

4. A. predicate noun
   B. predicate adjective
   C. direct object
   D. indirect object

5. A. compound predicate
   B. verb phrase
   C. helping verb
   D. main verb

6. A. predicate noun
   B. predicate adjective
   C. direct object
   D. indirect object

7. A. fragment
   B. run-on sentence
   C. declarative sentence
   D. exclamatory sentence

8. A. fragment
   B. run-on sentence
   C. inverted sentence
   D. exclamatory sentence

9. A. complete subject
   B. complete predicate
   C. compound subject
   D. compound verb

10. A. exclamatory sentence
    B. interrogative sentence
    C. imperative sentence
    D. declarative sentence

SENTENCE PARTS

Complete Subjects and Predicates

❶ Here's the Idea

In order to share ideas and information successfully, you need to use complete sentences.

▶ **A sentence is a group of words that expresses a complete thought.**

Here is a group of words.

lost   her   slipper   Cinderella

These words cannot get a message across unless they have a structure. Here is a sentence made from the same words. Notice that the sentence communicates a complete idea.

Cinderella   lost   her   slipper

▶ **Every complete sentence has two basic parts: a subject and a predicate.**

1. The **complete subject** includes all the words that tell whom or what the sentence is about.

COMPLETE SUBJECT

The glass slipper fits only one person.

2. The **complete predicate** includes the verb and all the words that tell about the verb.

COMPLETE PREDICATE

The glass slipper fits only one person.

Here's How Finding Complete Subjects and Predicates

The prince searches for its owner.

1. **To find the complete subject, ask who or what does something (or is something).**
   Who searches for its owner? **The prince**

2. **To find the complete predicate, ask what the subject does (or is).**
   What does the prince do? searches for its owner

---

❷ Why It Matters in Writing

You need to write complete sentences to share your ideas with others. When you revise your writing, make sure that each sentence has both a subject and a predicate.

> **STUDENT MODEL**
>
> There are over 500 European versions of "Cinderella."
> *Storytellers*
> ∧Probably passed them around by word of mouth for
>   *appeared*
> centuries. The first written version∧in 1634.

❸ Practice and Apply

CONCEPT CHECK: Complete Subjects and Predicates

Draw two columns on a sheet of paper. Label one "Complete Subjects" and the other "Complete Predicates." Write the complete subject and complete predicate for each sentence.

Cinderella in Asia
1. People around the world tell Cinderella stories.
2. The oldest version of all comes from China.
3. The main character's name is Yeh-Shen.
4. This lovely young woman lives with a cruel stepmother and a selfish stepsister.
5. Yeh-Shen receives help from a wise old man and a dead goldfish.
6. The bones of the dead goldfish grant the unlucky maiden's wish.
7. She goes to a party in a beautiful cloak and a beautiful pair of slippers.
8. One of the slippers falls off Yeh-Shen's foot.
9. A king seeks the slipper's owner.
10. You probably know the rest of the story.

➜ For a SELF-CHECK and more practice, see the EXERCISE BANK, p. 528.

LESSON 2 Simple Subjects

❶ Here's the Idea

You have learned that one basic part of a sentence is the complete subject. Now you will learn about the key part of the complete subject.

▶ **The simple subject is the main word or words in the complete subject.** Descriptive words are not part of the simple subject.

COMPLETE SUBJECT

Oral tales are important in Pueblo culture.
↑
SIMPLE SUBJECT

This tradition has inspired Pueblo potters.
↑
SIMPLE SUBJECT

HOT TIP

When a proper name is used as a subject, all parts of the name make up the simple subject.

SIMPLE SUBJECT
Mary Trujillo makes clay storyteller figures.

❷ Why It Matters in Writing

The simple subject gives important information. It tells the reader whom or what the sentence is about. When you revise your work, look out for unclear words used as simple subjects. Notice how a change in wording improves the sentence below.

Example: The clay object holds children on his lap.

Revision: The clay storyteller holds children on his lap.

CHAPTER 1

❸ Practice and Apply

A. CONCEPT CHECK: Simple Subjects

On a separate sheet of paper, write the simple subject of each sentence. Remember, descriptive words are not part of the simple subject.

Example: Desert tortoises are sneaky.
Simple subject: tortoises

A Traditional Pueblo Tale
1. A slow tortoise lived in the desert long ago.
2. A nimble rabbit crossed his path one day.
3. The rabbit challenged the tortoise to a race.
4. Immediately, his tricky neighbor accepted the challenge.
5. The mismatched animals agreed to hold the race four days later.
6. The confident rabbit crossed the finish line.
7. A big surprise awaited the rabbit.
8. A smiling tortoise greeted him.
9. The unsuspecting rabbit was the victim of a trick.
10. His opponent's twin brother met him at the finish line!

➜ **For a SELF-CHECK and more practice, see the EXERCISE BANK, p. 528.**

B. WRITING: Creating Complete Sentences

Create four sentences by combining complete subjects with complete predicates from the table below. Underline the simple subject in each sentence.

Clay Storytellers	
Complete Subject	**Complete Predicate**
The storyteller figures	come from natural substances
Each Pueblo potter	pay thousands of dollars for some storyteller figures
The colors on the storyteller figures	are handmade and hand painted
Collectors	works in a different style

LESSON 3 Simple Predicates, or Verbs

❶ Here's the Idea

You have learned about the simple subject of a sentence. You also need to know about the simple predicate.

▶ **The simple predicate, or verb, is the main word or words in the complete predicate.**

COMPLETE PREDICATE

Hercules battles the nine-headed Hydra.

SIMPLE PREDICATE

His nephew helps him in the struggle.

SIMPLE PREDICATE

▶ **A verb is a word used to express an action, a condition, or a state of being.** A **linking verb** tells what the subject *is*. An **action verb** tells what the subject *does,* even when the action cannot be seen.

Hercules arrived in a foreign city. (action you can see)

The ruler disliked Hercules. (action you cannot see)

Greek myths are timeless. (linking)

❷ Why It Matters in Writing

The verb is the most important word in a complete predicate because it tells what the subject does or is. When describing an event, choose powerful verbs that will help your readers imagine the action.

PROFESSIONAL MODEL

The Hydra **lunged** at Hercules with one of its deadly heads. Hercules **swung** his club. He **crushed** the skull. Two new heads quickly **sprouted** in its place.

—Dee Stiffler

❸ Practice and Apply

A. CONCEPT CHECK: Simple Predicates, or Verbs

On a separate sheet of paper, write the simple predicate, or verb, for each sentence.

The Labors of Hercules

1. Hercules is the hero of many Greek myths.
2. He served King Eurystheus for 12 years.
3. The cowardly king hated Hercules.
4. He assigned the hero a series of dangerous tasks.
5. The Greeks called these tasks the labors of Hercules.
6. Hercules once captured a gigantic wild boar.
7. He also battled a flock of monstrous birds.
8. The birds showered Hercules with sharp bronze feathers.
9. Hercules held the sky on his shoulders during one of his labors.
10. The king was furious over Hercules' successes.

➡ For a **SELF-CHECK** and more practice, see the **EXERCISE BANK, p. 529.**

B. WRITING: Summarizing Information

The first column of this chart lists five gods and goddesses from Greek mythology. The second column lists a responsibility or role that each is known for. Use the information to write a sentence about each character. When you have finished, underline each simple predicate. Some possible verbs include the following: *protects, commands, represents, delivers.*

Mythic Figures	
God or Goddess	**Known As or For . . .**
Athena	goddess of wisdom and warfare
Demeter	protection of farmers and their crops
Hermes	delivery of important messages
Poseidon	command of the seas
Zeus	most powerful of the Greek gods

Athena

Verb Phrases

LESSON 4

❶ Here's the Idea

The simple predicate, or verb, may consist of two or more words. These words are called a verb phrase.

▶ **A verb phrase is made up of a main verb and one or more helping verbs.**

VERB PHRASE

The princess had yawned loudly.

HELPING VERB ↗   ↖ MAIN VERB

Main Verbs and Helping Verbs

A **main verb** can stand by itself as the simple predicate of a sentence.

Her visitor talked for hours. (action)

MAIN VERB

The tale was endless. (linking)

MAIN VERB

Helping verbs help the main verb express action or show time.

VERB PHRASE

The tale might be endless.

HELPING VERB ↗   ↖ MAIN VERB

Her visitor had been talking for hours.

He will have been talking all day.

Notice that sometimes the main verb changes form when used with helping verbs. For more on these changes, see pages 96–106.

Common Helping Verbs	
Forms of *be*	is, am, was, are, were, be, been
Forms of *do*	do, does, did
Forms of *have*	has, have, had
Others	may, might, can, should, could, would, shall, will

❷ Why It Matters in Writing

You can use verb phrases to show when an action or event takes place. Notice how the verb phrases in this model move the action from the past to the present and the future.

> **PROFESSIONAL MODEL**
>
>   Different versions of "The Endless Tale" have originated in various parts of the world. The hero of an English version can talk endlessly about locusts stealing corn. In Japanese folklore, you will find a similar hero who tells a never-ending story about rats.
>
>   —Etta Worthington

PAST

PRESENT

FUTURE

❸ Practice and Apply

CONCEPT CHECK: Verb Phrases

Write the verb phrase in each sentence below. Be sure to include all the helping verbs.

An Endless Tale
1. A beautiful princess was searching for a husband.
2. Her perfect suitor should be a good storyteller.
3. He must tell an endless tale to the royal family.
4. A poor young man did appear at the castle one day.
5. He would share a story about a well-built barn full of corn.
6. Just a single locust may fit through the barn's only hole.
7. The first locust could grab only a single grain of corn.
8. Soon a second locust has stolen another grain, and so on.
9. This man's boring story might have continued forever.
10. Fortunately, his marriage to the princess will interrupt it.

➔ **For a SELF-CHECK and more practice, see the EXERCISE BANK, p. 529.**

Compound Sentence Parts

LESSON 5

CHAPTER 1

❶ Here's the Idea

Sentences can have **compound subjects** and **compound verbs**.

▶ **A compound subject is made up of two or more subjects that share the same verb.** The subjects are joined by a conjunction, or connecting word, such as *and, or,* or *but.*

COMPOUND SUBJECT

Caroline and Suzanne are looking for fables.
SUBJECT   SUBJECT

The library or bookstore will have **a collection.**

▶ **A compound verb is made up of two or more verbs that share the same subject.** The verbs are joined by a conjunction such as *and, or,* or *but.*

COMPOUND VERB

Fables entertain and teach.
     VERB   VERB

The animal characters speak and behave **like people.**

❷ Why It Matters in Writing

You can use compound subjects and verbs to get rid of unnecessary words. Notice how the writer of this paragraph combined sentences.

STUDENT MODEL

>   *or retold*
>   Aesop probably created ‸some of the stories that made
> him famous. ~~He probably retold some others.~~ However, he
>   *and myths*
> did not write any of them down. In his day, fables‸were
> part of the oral tradition. They were passed along by word
> of mouth. ~~Myths were also part of the oral tradition.~~

❸ Practice and Apply

A. CONCEPT CHECK: Compound Sentence Parts

On a separate sheet of paper, write the compound subject or compound verb for each sentence.

The Ant and the Grasshopper
1. An ant and a grasshopper were in a field on a fine summer day.
2. The grasshopper hopped and sang.
3. The ant gathered and hauled seeds all day long.
4. The grasshopper relaxed or played in the meantime.
5. Cold winds and icy rains arrived in the winter.
6. The ant ate and enjoyed plenty of food.
7. The grasshopper starved and suffered.
8. His foolishness and laziness taught him a lesson.
9. Readers and listeners will probably guess what it is.
10. Discipline and hard work bring rewards in the future.

➡ **For a SELF-CHECK and more practice, see the EXERCISE BANK, p. 530.**

B. REVISING: Combining Sentences

This version of a fable by Aesop is a little wordy. Make it flow better by using compound subjects and verbs to combine sentences.

> The belly enjoyed food. So did the other body parts. Yet all meals went into the belly. Snacks also wound up there. One day the body parts decided to strike. The hands no longer obtained food. They didn't cook it either. The mouth refused to chew. The teeth stopped chewing as well. Soon the entire body grew uncomfortable. Now the body parts understood digestion. They appreciated digestion too. The strike was canceled. From then on, the body parts never blamed the belly. They also stopped complaining about it.

The Sentence and Its Parts **15**

Kinds of Sentences

❶ Here's the Idea

▶ A sentence can be used to make a statement, to ask a question, to make a request or give a command, or to show strong feelings.

Four Kinds of Sentences

	What It Does	Examples
Declarative .	Makes a statement; always ends with a period.	Funny stories are popular everywhere. People from all cultures enjoy humor.
Interrogative ?	Asks a question; always ends with a question mark.	Do you know any jokes? Which one is your favorite?
Imperative . or !	Tells or asks someone to do something; usually ends with a period but may end with an exclamation point.	Listen carefully. Stop interrupting me!
Exclamatory !	Shows strong feeling; always ends with an exclamation point.	You're really funny! That joke is a lot older than I am!

❷ Why It Matters in Writing

The four kinds of sentences enable you to express different feelings and attitudes in your writing. Notice the variety of sentence types used in this dialogue, or conversation, between a teacher and her student, who is a promising writer.

LITERARY MODEL

> **Miss Walker.** What's wrong? I don't understand.
> **Lenore.** I don't want to read my story. And I don't want to go to Thunder Bay!

INTERROGATIVE
DECLARATIVE
EXCLAMATORY

—Keith Leckie, *Words on a Page*

CHAPTER 1

❸ Practice and Apply

A. CONCEPT CHECK: Kinds of Sentences

Identify each of the following sentences as declarative (D), interrogative (INT), exclamatory (E), or imperative (IMP).

Shoe Trouble

1. I found an amusing story in a book of folk humor.
2. Was it about a well-known judge who lived in China?
3. That's the one!
4. Remind me how the story goes.
5. One morning, the judge noticed that he was walking with a limp.
6. What could the cause be?
7. He was wearing two completely different shoes!
8. He asked his servant to run home and fetch a replacement.
9. The servant told him that there was no point in changing shoes.
10. The pair at home was exactly like this one!

➜ For a SELF-CHECK and more practice, see the EXERCISE BANK, p. 530.

B. WRITING: Creating Dialogue

When writers rewrite stories for the stage, they often use all four types of sentences. For example, imagine what the hedgehog might say when he discovers the creature in the stove. Different types of sentences help writers show the different feelings and attitudes of their characters. In your 📁 **Working Portfolio,** find the story that you wrote for the **Write Away** on page 4. Write a brief skit based on this story. Use each type of sentence at least once in the dialogue.

Subjects in Unusual Order

❶ Here's the Idea

In most declarative sentences, subjects come before verbs. In some kinds of sentences, however, subjects can come between verb parts, follow verbs, or not appear at all.

Questions

▶ **In most questions, the subject comes after the verb or between parts of the verb phrase.**

Is the story suspenseful?

VERB
⌒ PHRASE ⌐
Did you find it scary?
↑ SUBJECT

To find the subject, turn the question into a statement. Then ask who or what is or does something.

Did the ending surprise you?

The ending did surprise you. (What did surprise you? *the ending*)

Commands

▶ **The subject of a command, or imperative sentence, is usually you.** Often, *you* doesn't appear in the sentence because it is understood.

(You) Turn down the lights.
↑ SUBJECT

(You) Sit perfectly still.

Inverted Sentences

In inverted sentences, the subject comes after the verb. Their usual order is reversed.

Inverted Subject and Verb	
Normal	A scratching **sound** came from the other side of the door.
Inverted	From the other side of the door came a scratching **sound**.
Normal	A large black **cat** rushed into the room.
Inverted	Into the room rushed a large black **cat**.

Sentences Beginning with *Here* or *There*

▶ **In some sentences beginning with *here* or *there*, the subject follows the verb.** To find the subject, look for the verb and ask *who?* or *what?*

WHAT COMES?

Here comes the scariest part.
    VERB   SUBJECT

WHAT GOES?

There goes our flashlight.
    VERB   SUBJECT

❷ Why It Matters in Writing

Most people would grow tired of eating the same meal every day. Variety is also important in writing. You should look for opportunities to vary the order of subjects and verbs in sentences. Notice how inverting a sentence in the model makes the paragraph more interesting to read.

STUDENT MODEL

DRAFT

    Miranda cautiously approached the abandoned barn. The hinges creaked and groaned as she opened the door. A pair of squeaking bats flew out. She ducked just in time.

REVISED

    Miranda cautiously approached the abandoned barn. The hinges creaked and groaned as she opened the door. **Out flew a pair of squeaking bats.** She ducked just in time.

❸ Practice and Apply

A. CONCEPT CHECK: Subjects in Unusual Order

In two columns on a separate sheet of paper, write the simple subject and verb (or verb phrase) of each sentence.

> **What a Nightmare!**
> **1.** Are your friends bored?
> **2.** Tell a scary story.
> **3.** Speak softly at first.
> **4.** Then shock your listeners with a timely scream.
> **5.** There are many scary stories.
> **6.** Will you set yours in a cemetery?
> **7.** In the shadows appear strange figures.
> **8.** There is a mournful cry behind a tomb.
> **9.** Are your friends afraid now?
> **10.** At the end of the story is a terrible surprise.

➜ For a **SELF-CHECK** and more exercises, see the **EXERCISE BANK, p. 531.**

B. REVISING: Adding Variety

Follow the instructions to revise the model sentence.

Model: A headless man appears in the window.

1. Turn the sentence into a question.
2. Rewrite the sentence to begin with *There is.* (Hint: Remove the verb *appears.*)
3. Invert the sentence without using *there* so that the subject comes after the verb.

Now decide how your revisions affect the mood of the model sentence.

4. Which revisions could you use to give information?
5. Which revision asks for information?
6. Which revision seems the scariest?

CHAPTER 1

❶ Here's the Idea

A **complement** is a word or a group of words that completes the meaning of a verb. Two kinds of complements are **subject complements** and **objects of verbs**.

▶ **A subject complement is a word or group of words that follows a linking verb and renames or describes the subject.** A linking verb links the subject with a noun or adjective that tells more about it.

LINKING VERB
Cowboy poetry is a Western tradition.
SUBJECT ⬦ ⬦ COMPLEMENT

Common Linking Verbs	
Forms of *be*	am, is, are, was, were, being, been
Other linking verbs	appear, feel, look, sound, seem, taste

Predicate Nouns and Predicate Adjectives

Both nouns and adjectives can serve as subject complements.

▶ **A predicate noun follows a linking verb and defines or renames the subject.**

RENAMES
A popular cowboy poet is Rudy Gonzales.
SUBJECT ⬦ ⬦ PREDICATE NOUN

▶ **A predicate adjective follows a linking verb and describes a quality of the subject.**

DESCRIBES
Most cowboy poetry is humorous.
SUBJECT ⬦ ⬦ PREDICATE ADJECTIVE

Some of the poems are sad. (describes)

SENTENCE PARTS

❷ Why It Matters in Writing

Subject complements tell the reader much more about the subject.

LITERARY MODEL

One of Athene's pupils was a man called Daedalus. Even though he was mortal, he was almost as remarkable an inventor and craftsman as the god Hephaestus. He became famous throughout the world.

PREDICATE NOUN

PREDICATE ADJECTIVE

—Anne Rockwell, "The Boy Who Flew"

❸ Practice and Apply

A. CONCEPT CHECK: Subject Complements

Write the italicized word in each sentence and identify it as either a predicate noun (PN) or a predicate adjective (PA).

Poems on the Range
1. The cattle drives of the 1800s are *legendary*.
2. Life was *difficult* on the Western frontier.
3. It was also *colorful*.
4. Cowboy poets were the *storytellers* of the Old West.
5. Horses, hard work, and the cowboy life were their *themes*.
6. Their poems still seem so *vivid*.
7. The cowboy life remains an irresistible *subject*.
8. The stories of the Old West are *popular* once again.
9. Cowboy-poetry festivals are big *events* these days.
10. The future looks *bright* for this uniquely American art form.

➜ For a SELF-CHECK and more practice, see the EXERCISE BANK, p. 531.

B. REVISING: Using Subject Complements

Choose one of the following words to supply each missing subject complement below: *cowboys, veterinarian, authentic.*

It's no wonder that cowboy poets often sound so **(1)** (predicate adjective). Many of them are real **(2)** (predicate noun). The famous poet Baxter Black used to be a **(3)** (predicate noun) who treated livestock.

Complements: Objects of Verbs

❶ Here's the Idea

In addition to subject complements, there are objects of verbs. Action verbs often need complements called direct objects and indirect objects to complete their meaning.

Direct Objects

▶ **A direct object is a word or group of words that names the receiver of the action.** A direct object answers the question *what* or *whom*.

CLIMBED WHAT?

Jack climbed **the beanstalk.**
DIRECT OBJECT

The giant's wife protected **Jack.** (protected whom? *Jack*)

Indirect Objects

▶ **An indirect object is a word or group of words that tells to whom or what (or for whom or what) an action is performed.** An indirect object usually comes between a verb and a direct object.

TO WHOM?

Jesse told his little **cousins** the story.
INDIRECT OBJECT   DIRECT OBJECT

Verbs that are often followed by indirect objects include *bring, give, hand, lend, make, offer, send, show, teach, tell, write,* and *ask.*

> **Here's How** **Finding Direct and Indirect Objects**
>
> **Jack showed his mother the magic beans.**
>
> **1.** Find the action verb in the sentence. *showed*
> **2.** To find the direct object, ask, *Showed what? beans*
> **3.** To find the indirect object, ask, *Showed to whom? mother*

❷ Why It Matters in Writing

When you describe events, you can use direct objects and indirect objects to help readers understand relationships.

PROFESSIONAL MODEL

A strange-looking man offered Jack five beans for his cow. Jack immediately rejected this offer. Yet he changed his mind when he heard that the beans were magical. Jack's mother gave him a fierce scolding when he came home with the beans.

DIRECT OBJECT

INDIRECT OBJECT

—Eric Scholl

❸ Practice and Apply

CONCEPT CHECK: Objects of Verbs

For each sentence below, write each object and identify it as a direct object (DO) or an indirect object (IO).

Climbing the Beanstalk

1. Jack's mother tossed the beans away.
2. The boy saw a huge beanstalk outside his window the next morning.
3. He discovered a giant's castle at the top.
4. The giant's wife served Jack some breakfast.
5. She could have brought her hungry husband the boy.
6. Instead she offered Jack her oven for a hiding place.
7. The giant counted his gold coins.
8. This task gave him a great weariness.
9. Jack stole a bag of gold after the giant fell asleep.
10. He showed his delighted mother the gold at home.

➡ **For a SELF-CHECK and more practice, see the EXERCISE BANK, p. 532.**

Fragments and Run-Ons

LESSON 10

❶ Here's the Idea

Sentence fragments and run-on sentences are writing errors that can make your writing difficult to understand.

Sentence Fragments

▶ **A sentence fragment is a part of a sentence that is written as if it were a complete sentence.** A sentence fragment is missing a subject, a predicate, or both.

FRAGMENTS

The Bayeux Tapestry in an ancient French town.
(missing a predicate)

Tells the story of the Norman victory in England.
(missing a subject)

From the 11th century. (missing subject and predicate)

To make a complete sentence, add a subject, a predicate, or both.

REVISION

The Bayeux Tapestry hangs in an ancient French town. It tells the story of the Norman victory in England. The tapestry dates from the 11th century.

SENTENCE PARTS

Run-On Sentences

▶ **A run-on sentence is two or more sentences written as though they were a single sentence.**

RUN-ON

The English lost the historic battle, Duke William of Normandy became their new king.

REVISION

The English lost the historic battle. Duke William of Normandy became their new king.

REVISION

The English lost the historic battle, and Duke William of Normandy became their new king.

When combining two sentences with a conjunction, use a comma before the conjunction.

❷ Why It Matters in Writing

When you take notes or do prewriting, you often jot down ideas as fragments or run-on sentences. It is important to change your notes into complete sentences when you write your draft.

STUDENT MODEL

NOTES

Consists of 72 scenes and a fancy border. Over 1,500 people, animals, and other figures in it. Scholars value the tapestry as a great work of art, it is also an important historical document.

DRAFT

The Bayeux Tapestry consists of 72 scenes and a fancy border. Over 1,500 people, animals, and other figures appear in it. Scholars value the tapestry as a great work of art. It is also an important historical document.

❸ Practice and Apply

A. CONCEPT CHECK: Sentence Fragments and Run-Ons

On a separate sheet of paper, identify each of the following items as a fragment (F), run-on (RO), or complete sentence (CS).

A Storytelling Tapestry

1. William of Normandy led the Norman invasion of England in 1066.
2. In those days, Normandy was a small dukedom, today it is a region of France.
3. Bishop Odo of the town of Bayeux.
4. Was William's half-brother.
5. His teams of craftspeople made the enormous piece of needlework.
6. The tapestry is 231 feet long, it is only 20 inches wide.
7. This magnificent work tells the story of the invasion.
8. Is in many ways like a movie.
9. The thousands of details within the tapestry.
10. Have taught us a great deal about life in the Middle Ages.

→ For a SELF-CHECK and more practice, see the EXERCISE BANK, p. 532.

Rewrite the exercise as a paragraph. Fix any fragments or run-on sentences.

B. REVISING: Fixing Fragments and Run-Ons

You and a classmate are working together on a presentation about the Bayeux Tapestry. You have taken the following notes. Correct any fragments or run-ons so that your partner will understand your notes.

SECTION 21 OF THE BAYEUX TAPESTRY

Shows soldiers from Duke William's army. They have just landed on the English coast, some are just getting out of their ships. One interesting detail the long oars within the ships. The Norman ships always fairly small in the tapestry. Historians tell us that they were actually around a hundred feet long.

SENTENCE PARTS

Grammar in Literature

Using Different Types of Sentences

Whenever you ask a question, make a request, or express your excitement, you use different types of sentences. In writing, you need these types of sentences to show emotion and give information. Notice the types of sentences that Olivia E. Coolidge uses in retelling the Greek myth of Arachne.

ARACHNE
retold by Olivia E. Coolidge

*a*rachne was used to being wondered at, and she was immensely proud of the skill that had brought so many to look on her. Praise was all she lived for, and it displeased her greatly that people should think anyone, even a goddess, could teach her anything. Therefore, when she heard them murmur, she would stop her work and turn round indignantly to say, "With my own ten fingers I gained this skill, and by hard practice from early morning till night.... As for Athena's weaving, how could there be finer cloth or more beautiful embroidery than mine? If Athena herself were to come down and compete with me, she could do no better than I."

DECLARATIVE SENTENCE

INTERROGATIVE SENTENCE

One day when Arachne turned round with such words, an old woman answered her. "... Take my advice and ask pardon of Athena for your words."

IMPERATIVE SENTENCE

Illustration by Arvis Stewart, from *The Macmillan Book of Greek Gods and Heroes* by Alice Low. Copyright © 1985 Macmillan Publishing Company, reprinted with the permission of Simon & Schuster Books for Young Readers, an imprint of Simon & Schuster Children's Publishing Division.

Practice and Apply

WRITING: Using Different Types of Sentences

Retell your favorite fable, myth, fairy tale, or folktale, using at least three types of sentences. If you like, you can rewrite one of the following fables:

The Lion and the Mouse

One day a big lion caught a tiny mouse. The mouse pleaded with the lion to let her go and promised to return his kindness one day. The lion, of course, didn't believe the mouse could ever help him, but he let her go anyway. A few days later, he walked into a trap whose net closed tightly around him. The mouse heard the lion roar in frustration and hurried to him. She quickly began to gnaw through the net until the lion was able to escape. Moral: Even a small friend can be a great friend.

The Hare and the Tortoise

The hare was always making fun of the tortoise. He would laugh at the tortoise's short legs and call him slowpoke. One day, the tortoise claimed that even though he was slow, he could still beat the hare in a race. The hare thought the tortoise was joking, but he accepted the challenge to race. From the starting line, the hare far outdistanced the tortoise. But the tortoise kept going, slowly and steadily. The hare got so far ahead that he soon grew tired. Thinking he had lots of time, he ate some clover, sipped water from a stream, and sat down under a tree to rest. While the hare was fast asleep, the tortoise kept going, not stopping for food, water, or rest. Just before the tortoise reached the finish line, the hare woke up. He hurried down the road, but he was too late. The tortoise had won. Moral: Slow and steady wins the race.

Mixed Review

A. Subjects, Predicates, and Compound Sentence Parts Read the passage; then write the answers to the questions below it.

A Cunning Spider

(1) Picture the following scene. (2) A king has discovered a crime in his household. (3) The guilty one climbs and escapes as a spider. (4) Who is this slippery trickster figure? (5) Folklore fans will recognize him as Anansi. (6) Stories about Anansi originated in West Africa. (7) Storytellers and listeners are quite fond of him. (8) This humorous character always tries to trick people. (9) He succeeds most of the time. (10) Sometimes he himself is the victim of a practical joke or a clever trick.

1. What kind of sentence is sentence 1?
2. What is the main verb of sentence 2?
3. What is the compound part of sentence 3?
4. What kind of sentence is sentence 4?
5. What is the helping verb of sentence 5?
6. What is the simple subject of sentence 6?
7. What is the compound part of sentence 7?
8. What is the complete subject of sentence 8?
9. What is the simple predicate of sentence 9?
10. What is the complete predicate of sentence 10?

B. Complements Identify each underlined word as a predicate noun, a predicate adjective, a direct object, or an indirect object.

> **PROFESSIONAL MODEL**
>
> An incident in "Anansi and the Crabs" is an **(1)** example of Anansi's trickery. At the end of the story, Anansi fears a harsh **(2)** punishment from Alligator. He tells **(3)** Alligator the lie that they are cousins. Alligator is **(4)** suspicious. He gives **(5)** Anansi this test. Supposedly, all alligators can drink boiling water. Therefore, Anansi must drink some boiling **(6)** water. Only then will Alligator believe him. Anansi seems **(7)** cooperative. He makes one **(8)** suggestion, however. According to Anansi, the water will become even **(9)** hotter after a long rest in the sun. Alligator agrees. Of course, the water becomes cooler instead. Anansi drinks the **(10)** water with ease!

For each underlined item, choose the letter of the term that correctly identifies it.

Have you considered storytelling as a hobby? Many students are
(1)   (2)
showing interest in this ancient art. Even a shy person could tell
(3)
stories before an audience. The following suggestions may be

helpful for beginners. You should consider the age of your
(4)   (5)
listeners. Myths and legends are good stories for younger
(6)
audiences. Practice telling the story over and over. Some
(7)
storytellers record their practice sessions on audiotape or
(8)
videotape. Speak clearly and directly, use appropriate gestures and
(9)
facial expressions. Look for a good location for your performance.

Schools, parks, libraries, and community centers often attract

enthusiastic crowds.
(10)

---

1. A. run-on sentence
   B. inverted sentence
   C. interrogative sentence
   D. declarative sentence

2. A. complete subject
   B. simple subject
   C. complete predicate
   D. simple predicate

3. A. complete subject
   B. simple subject
   C. complete predicate
   D. simple predicate

4. A. predicate adjective
   B. predicate noun
   C. direct object
   D. indirect object

5. A. complete predicate
   B. compound predicate
   C. helping verb
   D. verb phrase

6. A. compound subject
   B. compound verb
   C. direct object
   D. run-on sentence

7. A. declarative sentence
   B. interrogative sentence
   C. imperative sentence
   D. exclamatory sentence

8. A. complete subject
   B. simple subject
   C. complete predicate
   D. simple predicate

9. A. fragment
   B. run-on sentence
   C. inverted sentence
   D. declarative sentence

10. A. predicate noun
    B. predicate adjective
    C. indirect object
    D. direct object

SENTENCE PARTS

Student Help Desk

The Sentence at a Glance

A sentence has two parts: a complete subject and a complete predicate.

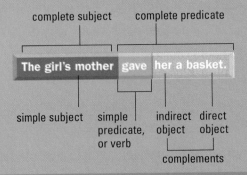

complete subject   complete predicate

The girl's mother | **gave** | **her a basket.**

simple subject   simple predicate, or verb   indirect object   direct object

complements

Subjects and Predicates   Story Line

Sentence Part	Example	How to Find It
Complete subject	**The sly wolf** slipped into the bed.	Ask who or what is or does something.
Simple subject	**wolf**	Find the main word(s) in the complete subject.
Complete predicate	Little Red Riding Hood **knocked on the door.**	Ask what the subject is or does.
Simple predicate	**knocked**	Find the verb(s) or verb phrase(s).

Complements Finishing Touches

Type of Complement		Example	What It Does
Linking verbs	Predicate noun	The wolf is a **killer.**	Renames or defines the subject
	Predicate adjective	His teeth are **big.**	Describes the subject
Action verbs	Direct object	He ate the **grandmother.**	Completes the verb's action
	Indirect object	She gave the **wolf** indigestion.	Tells to whom/what or for whom/what the action is done

Kinds of Sentences Different Voices

Declarative sentence	The story has a happy ending.
Interrogative sentence	How does it end?
Imperative sentence	**(You)** Tell me how it ends.
Exclamatory sentence	What a happy ending!

The Bottom Line

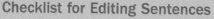

Checklist for Editing Sentences

Have I . . .

____ made sure that each sentence has a subject and a predicate?

____ corrected any fragments or run-on sentences?

____ combined any sentences with similar ideas by using compound subjects or verbs?

____ used different kinds of sentences and subject-verb order for variety?

____ used complements to make the meaning of sentences clear?

Nouns

Carmen's Diary
Thursday, July 23, 2001
On our trip Dad and I got lost
on the Greek island of Crete.
We wandered in the ruins looking
for the mosaic of the minotaur.
Because of the kindness of a
stranger, we finally found it.

Theme: Lost Cities and Civilizations

Finding Your Way

Poor Carmen! She and her father lost their way while exploring the ruins of a lost civilization on the island of Crete. Look at the different nouns in her diary. Which name people? Which name a place? Which name things? Which names an idea?

As you can see, nouns are an important part of language. You need nouns to name the people, places, things, or ideas you write about. Nouns are the signposts in your sentences. They keep you from getting "lost."

Write Away: Missing Out

Think about a time when you lost something important to you. You may have misplaced a treasured item, lost a contest or competition, or missed a big opportunity. Write a paragraph that describes this important event.

Save your writing in your 📁 **Working Portfolio.**

 **Grammar Coach**

For each numbered item, choose the letter of the term that correctly identifies it.

> <u>Plato</u> was a Greek philosopher. He wrote about an ancient
> (1)
> <u>civilization</u> called Atlantis. Long ago, he said, Atlantis had
> (2)
> disappeared beneath the <u>waves</u>. <u>Plato's</u> words have caused many
> (3)   (4)
> people to wonder about this lost place. Some people think <u>Atlantis</u>
> (5)
> was only a <u>legend</u>. Other <u>people</u> think it was indeed a real place.
> (6)   (7)
> There may be a very simple explanation for Atlantis. About 3,500
>
> <u>years</u> ago, a volcano erupted on Thera, an island near Greece.
> (8)
> The explosion completely destroyed the <u>center</u> of the island. So
> (9)
> <u>Thera</u> may be remembered as Atlantis, a civilization lost to a
> (10)
> natural disaster.

1. A. plural noun
   B. possessive noun
   C. common noun
   D. proper noun

2. A. singular noun
   B. proper noun
   C. possessive noun
   D. plural noun

3. A. noun as subject
   B. noun as direct object
   C. noun as object of preposition
   D. noun as predicate noun

4. A. common noun
   B. possessive noun
   C. predicate noun
   D. plural noun

5. A. plural noun
   B. possessive noun
   C. common noun
   D. proper noun

6. A. noun as subject
   B. noun as direct object
   C. noun as object of preposition
   D. noun as predicate noun

7. A. noun as direct object
   B. noun as subject
   C. noun as predicate noun
   D. noun as object of preposition

8. A. singular noun
   B. plural noun
   C. proper noun
   D. possessive noun

9. A. noun as subject
   B. noun as direct object
   C. noun as predicate noun
   D. noun as object of preposition

10. A. noun as predicate noun
    B. noun as direct object
    C. noun as object of preposition
    D. noun as subject

What Is a Noun?

❶ Here's the Idea

> ▶ **A noun is a word that names a person, place, thing, or idea.**

PERSONS
archaeologist
Theresa

PLACES
site
Colorado

THINGS
pail
shovel

IDEAS
exploration
excitement

Common and Proper Nouns

A **common noun** is a general name for a person, place, thing, or idea. Common nouns are not capitalized.

A **proper noun** is the name of a particular person, place, thing, or idea. Proper nouns are always capitalized.

Common	people	home	state
Proper	Pueblo Indians	Cliff Palace	Colorado

Proper nouns make writing clear and precise.

COMMON NOUNS

People abandoned their home in the state.

PROPER NOUNS

Ancient Pueblo Indians abandoned the Cliff Palace in Colorado.

❷ Why It Matters in Writing

Sentences without proper nouns are often too general. Notice how proper nouns make the following description more colorful and specific.

DRAFT

I saw **the man** slowly hike up **the road** with **his students** to see the **houses** last **month.**

REVISION

I saw **Mr. DeLalo** slowly hike up **Ruins Road** with **Rick and Theresa** to see the **Cliff Palace** last **August.**

❸ Practice and Apply

CONCEPT CHECK: What Is a Noun?

Write each noun, and label it as common or proper.

Quickly Lost, Slowly Found
1. Sometimes a place disappears quickly.
2. This happened to Pompeii, in Italy.
3. A volcano called Mount Vesuvius erupted almost 2,000 years ago.
4. Hot lava and ash shot out of the volcanic mountain.
5. The material rained down on the buildings of Pompeii.
6. Families were sitting down to eat bread and fish.
7. Some people ran to the sea and escaped in small boats.
8. Ash completely covered the town, and it was forgotten.
9. Pompeii was finally excavated in recent times.
10. Giuseppe Fiorelli found blackened rolls in a bakery.

Label each noun that you wrote above as a person, place, thing, or idea.

➡ **For a SELF-CHECK and more practice, see the EXERCISE BANK, p. 533.**

Singular and Plural Nouns

❶ Here's the Idea

▶ **A singular noun names one person, place, thing, or idea. A plural noun names more than one person, place, thing, or idea.**

A **tourist** walked down the cobbled **street.** (singular nouns)

Tourists walked down the cobbled **streets.** (plural nouns)

To make sure you spell plural nouns correctly, follow the rules in the Quick-Fix Spelling Machine.

QUICK-FIX SPELLING MACHINE: PLURALS OF NOUNS

	SINGULAR	RULE	PLURAL
❶	ruin building	Add -s to most nouns.	ruins buildings
❷	trench dish	Add -es to a noun that ends in s, sh, ch, x, or z.	trenches dishes
❸	volcano	Add -s to most nouns that end in o.	volcanos
	echo	Add -es to a few nouns that end in o.	echoes
❹	city	For most nouns ending in y, change the y to an i and add -es.	cities
	stairway	When a vowel comes before the y, just add -s.	stairways
❺	shelf knife	For most nouns ending in f or fe, change the f to v and add -es or -s.	shelves knives
	chief	Just add -s to a few nouns that end in f or fe.	chiefs
❻	deer buffalo	For some nouns, keep the same spelling.	deer buffalo

CHAPTER 2

▶ **The plurals of some nouns are formed in irregular ways.**

Singular	child	woman	man	foot
Plural	children	women	men	feet

❷ Why It Matters in Writing

Plural nouns are the cause of many spelling errors in writing. When you proofread, pay special attention to this challenge. Notice how plural nouns are spelled correctly in the model below.

> **LITERARY MODEL**
>
> Suddenly it seemed too late for Tito. The red hot **ashes** blistered his skin; the stinging **vapors** tore his throat. He could not go on.... In a moment Bimbo was beside him.... He licked Tito's **hands,** his **feet,** his face.
>
> —Louis Untermeyer, "The Dog of Pompeii"

❸ Practice and Apply

A. CONCEPT CHECK: Singular and Plural Nouns

Rewrite the nouns in parentheses in their plural forms.

Have You Seen My Mummy?

1. The (priest) of Egypt put the (body) of dead kings in tombs.
2. (Egyptian) believed that a body had to be preserved in order to have life after death.
3. For this reason, they prepared their dead to be (mummy).
4. At first, only dead (king) and (queen) were wrapped in cloth.
5. After many (century), ordinary people were also mummified.
6. The mummies were buried with precious (object).
7. (Scientist) study mummies to learn about (disease).
8. They have found (rash) and (sore) caused by (parasite).
9. Egyptians with many (rich) often had short (life).
10. Perhaps the (story) about a mummy's curse got started because (archaeologist) were infected by ancient germs.

➡ **For a SELF-CHECK and more practice, see the EXERCISE BANK, p. 533.**

B. PROOFREADING: Spelling Plural Nouns

Ten plural nouns in the following passage are misspelled. Find them and write their correct spellings.

Garbage In, Knowledge Out!

Can you imagine archaeologists going through your trash? People who excavate, or dig up, lost citys do exactly that! They find artifacts that provide us with echos of the past. An artifact is any object mans, womans, and childs use in their daily lifes. Today's scientists examine pottery, tools, and other objects used by ancient communities. A future scientist may examine your mattresses, your toothbrushs, or your baby toys! A scientist today may look at bones to see which animals people ate, such as deers or buffalo. A future excavator may examine the leftover tomatos in your salad! Here's a hint. Keep your old dishs clean, in case they're ever seen!

C. WRITING: Describing Artifacts

On a social studies field trip, you saw the student archaeologist below. Write a description of the tools he used and the artifacts he found. Be sure to spell plural nouns correctly.

Social Studies Field Trip Notes

tools	artifacts
brush	bone
pick	pot

Possessive Nouns

❶ Here's the Idea

▶ **The possessive form of a noun shows ownership or relationship.**

The divers waited outside the archaeologist's tent.
OWNERSHIP

The archaeologist's family had come to visit.
RELATIONSHIP

You may use possessive nouns in place of longer phrases.

The divers used a robot to find the ~~location of the ship.~~ *ship's location.*

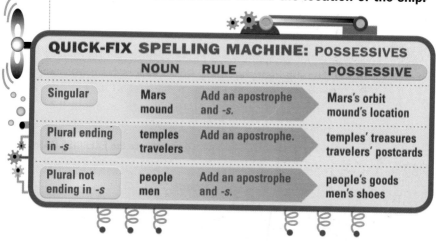

QUICK-FIX SPELLING MACHINE: POSSESSIVES

	NOUN	RULE	POSSESSIVE
Singular	Mars mound	Add an apostrophe and -s.	Mars's orbit mound's location
Plural ending in -s	temples travelers	Add an apostrophe.	temples' treasures travelers' postcards
Plural not ending in -s	people men	Add an apostrophe and -s.	people's goods men's shoes

❷ Why It Matters in Writing

When you write, be sure you have formed the possessive correctly. A misplaced apostrophe can confuse the reader. Notice how the revision in the model below clears up whether one or more people made the discovery.

> When the archaeologists opened the wooden chests, they found priceless relics. The explorer's discovery made headlines in newspapers across the country.

NOUNS

❸ Practice and Apply

A. CONCEPT CHECK: Possessive Nouns

Write the possessive form of each noun in parentheses. Then label each possessive noun singular or plural.

Risen from a Watery Grave

1. The *Mary Rose* was one of (England) finest warships.
2. She sank near the Portsmouth (Harbor) seabed during a battle with the French fleet in 1545.
3. Many (eyewitnesses) accounts told of her sad end.
4. The *Mary Rose* quickly became covered with the (seabed) mud and sand.
5. Alexander McKee located the (wreck) position in 1967.
6. In 1982 the ship was raised and stored in the (city) dry dock.
7. Bows, arrows, and other (archers) equipment were found on the gun deck.
8. Other weapons were found in the (sailors) cabins.
9. Netting kept the (*Mary Rose*) sailors from escaping when the ship sank.
10. The *Mary Rose* and its artifacts tell us about the (seamen) lives on board the ship.

➡ For a SELF-CHECK and more practice, see the EXERCISE BANK, p. 534

B. REVISING: Using Possessive Nouns

Use possessive nouns to make these phrases short enough to fit on labels for a social studies project.

Example: The Cliff Houses of Mesa Verde
Answer: Mesa Verde's Cliff Houses

1. The Capital City of the Aztecs
2. The Ruins of Pompeii
3. The Earth Mounds of Cahokia
4. The Royal Tomb of King Tut

Mesa Verde's Cliff Houses

Nouns and Their Jobs

LESSON 4

① Here's the Idea

You use nouns every time you talk or write. Nouns name the people you meet, the places you visit, the sights and sounds you experience, and the ideas you have. Because nouns have many jobs, they are found in different places in sentences.

Nouns as Subjects

A **subject** tells whom or what the sentence is about. Notice the following sentences in which nouns act as subjects.

The Aztec Empire **was located in the area now known as Mexico.**

Tenochtitlán **was the capital of the Aztec Empire.**

Invaders **entered Tenochtitlán in 1519.**

Spanish soldiers **destroyed Tenochtitlán during their conquest of Mexico.**

Nouns as Complements

A **complement** is a word that completes the meaning of a verb. When a noun is a complement, it may be a predicate noun, a direct object, or an indirect object.

Nouns as Complements		
Predicate noun	renames or defines the subject after a linking verb	The Aztecs were fierce **warriors.**
Direct object	names the receiver of the action of the verb	Spanish soldiers defeated the **Aztec Empire** in 1521.
Indirect object	tells *to whom or what* or *for whom or what* an action is done	The Aztecs gave the **Spanish** gold and other precious goods.

NOUNS

Nouns **43**

Nouns as Objects of Prepositions

An **object of a preposition** is the noun or pronoun that follows the preposition. Nouns often appear in sentences as objects of prepositions.

The Aztec people settled in central Mexico.

PREPOSITION   OBJECT OF PREPOSITION

Aztec merchants traded with distant lands.

Among their valuable goods were gold and silver.

❷ Why It Matters in Writing

Using nouns in their various jobs can help you write a detailed explanation of any subject. Notice how the highlighted nouns in the model below add information to the sentences.

STUDENT MODEL

The Aztecs had many enemies. For this reason, they built their capital on an island. Long causeways led from the mainland to the island. Causeways are raised roads built across water. Aztec warriors guarded the ends of the causeways. In this way causeways provided the Aztec people protection.

SUBJECT
DIRECT OBJECT
INDIRECT OBJECT
PREDICATE NOUN
OBJECT OF PREPOSITION

❸ Practice and Apply

A. CONCEPT CHECK: Nouns and Their Jobs

Identify each underlined noun as a subject, a complement, or an object of a preposition.

Roadbuilders in the Sky
1. The Inca lived in the Andes Mountains in South America.
2. Cuzco was their capital.
3. The Inca were excellent record keepers.
4. They invented the quipu to keep track of their goods.

5. The <u>quipu</u> was a long <u>cord</u> with many <u>strings</u>.
6. Clerks tied <u>knots</u> in the strings in different patterns.
7. The Inca also built excellent <u>roads</u>.
8. Their <u>system</u> of roads carried <u>runners</u> across deep <u>gorges</u>.
9. <u>Officials</u> gave <u>runners</u> <u>messages</u> to carry hundreds of miles.
10. Some <u>roads</u> are still used today by Andean people.

➡ **For a SELF-CHECK and more practice, see the EXERCISE BANK, p. 534.**

Identify each complement in the exercise above as a predicate noun, a direct object, or an indirect object.

B. WRITING: Creating a Caption

Quetzalcoatl: Feathered-Serpent God
The photograph below shows Quetzalcoatl, a god worshiped by the Aztecs. Write a caption for a museum exhibit based on the information provided. Include nouns as subjects, complements, and objects of prepositions.

1. Quetzalcoatl = both snake and bird
2. Quetzal = brightly colored bird found in forests of Central and South America
3. long emerald feathers of quetzal highly valued
4. Quetzalcoatl = god of learning
5. Aztecs worshiped Quetzalcoatl

📂 **Working Portfolio: Revising** Find your **Write Away** paragraph from page 34. Revise your paragraph by adding specific complements that add to your explanation.

Grammar in Science

Using Nouns in Science

When you label diagrams, or identify specimens for science, chances are you use nouns. For example, nouns label the parts of the coniferous tree in the illustration. Some parts, or structures, are common to most plants. The illustrations show two types of plants; one coniferous plant (a pine tree) and one flowering plant (a rosebush). Notice the nouns used to label the pine tree.

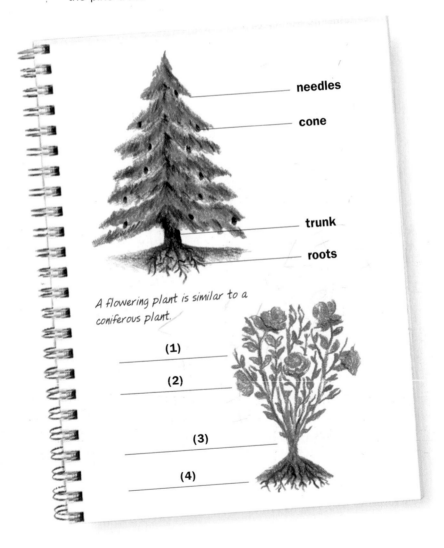

needles

cone

trunk

roots

A flowering plant is similar to a coniferous plant.

(1) _____

(2) _____

(3) _____

(4) _____

Practice and Apply

A. USING NOUNS

Look at the diagrams of the pine tree and the rosebush. Copy the diagram of the rosebush on a separate sheet of paper. Then use the nouns below to write the words that label the rosebush. Use the labels on the pine tree diagram as a guide.

stem holds the plant upright, like the trunk of a pine tree

roots hold the plant in the soil and absorb water and nutrients from the soil to feed the plant

flower holds the seed of the plant, like the cone of the pine tree

leaves make plant food from sunlight and chlorophyll, like the needles on a pine tree

B. WRITING: Compare and Contrast in Science

A flowering plant carries its seeds in its flowers. A cone-bearing plant carries seeds in its cones. Write a paragraph in which you compare and contrast a pine tree and a rosebush. How are they alike? How are they different? Use the nouns you have learned in this lesson to refer to the parts that are alike and different.

NOUNS

A. Kinds of Nouns Look at the cartoon, and answer the questions.

THE FAR SIDE   By GARY LARSON

© 1985 FarWorks, Inc. All Rights Reserved

PALEONTOGOL
DEPT.

"Cummings! Schneider! You've got plenty of research to work on ... and for the last time, stop playing with those plastic models!"

1. Which of the following is a proper noun?

   Cummings,
   research,
   time

2. Which of the following is a common noun?

   Schneider,
   Cummings,
   work

3. Which of the following is a plural noun?

   Cummings,
   time,
   models

4. Which of the following is the correct possessive?

   Cummings's chair,
   Cumming's chair,
   Cummings' chair

5. Write a sentence telling what is going on in the cartoon. Underline the nouns, and identify how they are used.

B. Nouns and Their Jobs In each group of sentences, the same underlined noun is used in different ways. Label each noun as a subject, direct object, indirect object, predicate noun, or object of a preposition.

1. The <u>dinosaurs</u> had no cities or civilizations.
2. What happened to the <u>dinosaurs</u>?
3. The most popular animals in museums are <u>dinosaurs</u>.
4. We must give <u>dinosaurs</u> credit for surviving 160 million years.
5. Did an asteroid or other disaster kill the <u>dinosaurs</u>?
6. Other animals on Earth were <u>mammals</u>.
7. Ancient <u>mammals</u> were much smaller than the huge dinosaurs.
8. Finding food was easier for these <u>mammals</u>.
9. An earth without dinosaurs gave <u>mammals</u> much more space.
10. However, no blockbuster movie features small <u>mammals</u>!

For each numbered item, choose the letter of the term that correctly identifies it.

Roanoke Island lies off the coast of <u>North Carolina</u>. In 1587
(1)
English <u>colonists</u> started a colony on the island. John White was
(2)
the <u>leader</u> of the colony. <u>White's</u> ship *Hopewell* returned to
(3)   (4)
England in 1587 to get more supplies. In 1590 the ship was

bringing <u>supplies</u> to the new colony. However, White found no
(5)
colonists, only the <u>colonists'</u> possessions. A tree near the <u>fort</u> had
(6)   (7)
the name CROATOAN scratched in its bark. A storm prevented

the <u>ship</u> from reaching Croatoan Island. The disappearance of the
(8)
colony is a great <u>mystery</u>. Some <u>historians</u> believe the colonists
(9)   (10)
went to live with local Native American people in their villages.

1. A. proper noun
   B. common noun
   C. possessive noun
   D. plural noun

2. A. possessive noun
   B. plural noun
   C. singular noun
   D. proper noun

3. A. noun as direct object
   B. noun as predicate noun
   C. noun as object of preposition
   D. noun as indirect object

4. A. common noun
   B. plural noun
   C. possessive noun
   D. predicate noun

5. A. noun as subject
   B. noun as indirect object
   C. noun as direct object
   D. noun as object of preposition

6. A. singular noun
   B. proper noun
   C. possessive noun
   D. predicate noun

7. A. noun as object of preposition
   B. noun as predicate noun
   C. possessive noun
   D. noun as direct object

8. A. proper noun
   B. plural noun
   C. common noun
   D. possessive noun

9. A. noun as direct object
   B. noun as indirect object
   C. noun as object of preposition
   D. noun as predicate noun

10. A. noun as subject
    B. noun as direct object
    C. noun as indirect object
    D. noun as predicate noun

Student Help Desk

Nouns at a Glance

A noun names a person, place, thing, or idea.

Archaeologists in Egypt discovered a cemetery filled with mummies' tombs.

Common Noun	Proper Noun	Singular Noun	Possessive Noun	Plural Noun

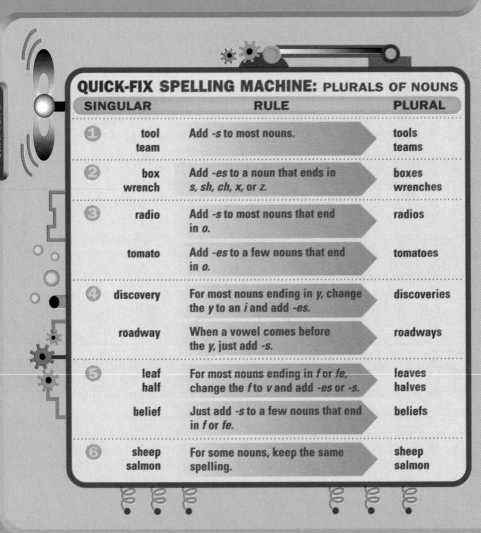

QUICK-FIX SPELLING MACHINE: PLURALS OF NOUNS

	SINGULAR	RULE	PLURAL
❶	tool team	Add -s to most nouns.	tools teams
❷	box wrench	Add -es to a noun that ends in s, sh, ch, x, or z.	boxes wrenches
❸	radio	Add -s to most nouns that end in o.	radios
	tomato	Add -es to a few nouns that end in o.	tomatoes
❹	discovery	For most nouns ending in y, change the y to an i and add -es.	discoveries
	roadway	When a vowel comes before the y, just add -s.	roadways
❺	leaf half	For most nouns ending in f or fe, change the f to v and add -es or -s.	leaves halves
	belief	Just add -s to a few nouns that end in f or fe.	beliefs
❻	sheep salmon	For some nouns, keep the same spelling.	sheep salmon

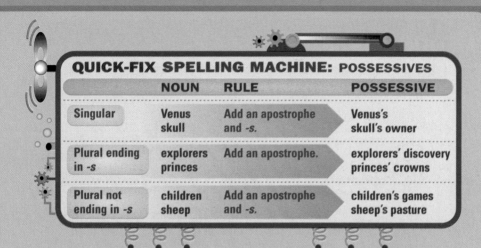

QUICK-FIX SPELLING MACHINE: POSSESSIVES

	NOUN	RULE	POSSESSIVE
Singular	Venus skull	Add an apostrophe and -s.	Venus's skull's owner
Plural ending in -s	explorers princes	Add an apostrophe.	explorers' discovery princes' crowns
Plural not ending in -s	children sheep	Add an apostrophe and -s.	children's games sheep's pasture

What's in the desert?

Nouns and Their Jobs

Nouns as . . .	Examples
Subject	The **cemetery** is more than 2,000 years old.
Predicate Noun	Dr. Salwah is an **archaeologist.**
Direct Object	He visited a **tomb.**
Indirect Object	He handed his **assistant** a flashlight.
Object of a Preposition	There were rows of **mummies.**

The Bottom Line

Checklist for Nouns

Have I . . .

____ chosen specific nouns?

____ spelled plural nouns correctly?

____ used possessives to show ownership or relationship?

____ used complements to provide specific details in explanations?

Pronouns

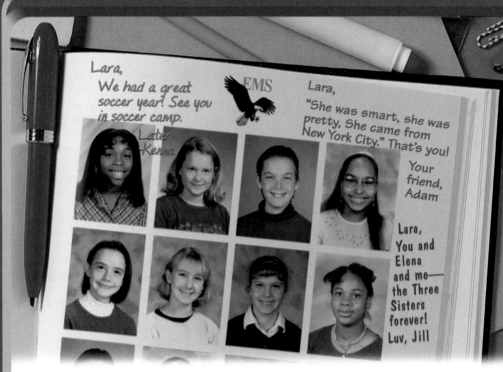

Theme: Friendship

A Little Help from My Friends

A good friend has asked you to sign her yearbook. You have a writing space about the size of a large postage stamp. What if you couldn't use pronouns, like *I, we, you,* and *she,* but had to use everybody's name instead? Could you make your message fit?

Pronouns are little words that make a big difference. Be careful how you use them, though. Otherwise, your friends may misunderstand your messages.

Write Away: Thanks for the Memories!
Write a brief yearbook message for one or more of your friends. Use pronouns to make the most of your limited space. Place your work in your  **Working Portfolio.**

Grammar Coach

Choose the letter of the best revision for each underlined word or group of words.

Kevin and me did a report on peer pressure. Our teacher Mrs.
(1)
Lourdes asked him and me to do an oral presentation in class.
(2)
Peer means "equal in age or rank." Peer pressure is the influence

that people in you're own age group have on you. People want to
(3)
be accepted by their peer group. This here is why peer pressure is
(4)   (5)
so powerful. Peer pressure can be negative, but it's positive too.
(6)
One boy we interviewed said, "My buddy signed up for the

basketball team. Him and Daniel pressured me to sign up too.
(7)
Us buddies always do things together." Whom can resist the
(8)   (9)
pressure of two friends? "I'm glad I joined the team. The coach,

like the rest of us, is enjoying ourselves!"
(10)

---

1. A. Kevin and I
   B. Me and Kevin
   C. Us
   D. Correct as is

2. A. he and me
   B. him and I
   C. he and I
   D. Correct as is

3. A. yours
   B. youre
   C. your
   D. Correct as is

4. A. there
   B. theirs
   C. they're
   D. Correct as is

5. A. That there
   B. This
   C. These
   D. Correct as is

6. A. its
   B. its'
   C. it
   D. Correct as is

7. A. Daniel and him
   B. Daniel and them
   C. He and Daniel
   D. Correct as is

8. A. Them buddies
   B. We buddies
   C. Me and them buddies
   D. Correct as is

9. A. Who
   B. Which
   C. Whose
   D. Correct as is

10. A. himself
    B. theirselves
    C. myself
    D. Correct as is

What Is a Pronoun?

❶ Here's the Idea

▶ **A pronoun is a word that is used in place of a noun or another pronoun.** Like a noun, a pronoun can refer to a person, place, thing, or idea. The word that a personal pronoun refers to is called its **antecedent.**

REFERS TO

Alexis is a great friend. She is so funny!

REFERS TO

Alexis read her jokes to the class.

Personal Pronouns

▶ **Pronouns such as *we, I, he, them,* and *it* are called personal pronouns.**

Unlike nouns, personal pronouns change their forms to reflect **person, number,** and **case.**

Person and Number Personal pronouns have different forms for first person, second person, and third person. Pronouns can be singular or plural in number.

	Singular	Plural
First person:	I went out.	We left early.
Second person:	You left too.	You are all leaving.
Third person:	He came by bus.	They came by car.

Case Personal pronouns change their forms, or cases, depending on how they are used in a sentence. Each pronoun has three cases: subject, object, and possessive.

Subject:	He just started middle school.
Object:	Scott met him on the first day.
Possessive:	Now Scott is his best friend.

In the chart on the next page, notice how personal pronouns change according to their person, number, and case. You'll learn more about each case in the next three lessons.

Personal Pronouns			
	Subject	**Object**	**Possessive**
Singular			
First person	I	me	my, mine
Second person	you	you	your, yours
Third person	he, she, it	him, her, it	his, her, hers, its
Plural			
First person	we	us	our, ours
Second person	you	you	your, yours
Third person	they	them	their, theirs

❷ Why It Matters in Writing

Without personal pronouns, the narrator of the passage below
would need to repeat her friend's name and her own name
several times! Instead, she uses forms of *I* and *you*.

LITERARY MODEL

Don't invite **me** to **your** birthday party because **I**'m
not coming. And give back the Disneyland sweat shirt **I**
said **you** could wear. If **I**'m not good enough to play on
your team, **I**'m not good enough to be friends with.

—Judith Viorst, "The Southpaw"

❸ Practice and Apply

A. CONCEPT CHECK: What Is a Pronoun?

List the personal pronoun(s) in each sentence.

Definition of a Friend
1. Did you ever see the statue in front of
   Boys Town?
2. It shows one boy carrying a smaller boy.
3. Its caption says, "He ain't heavy, Father,
   . . . he's m' brother."
4. True friends are not burdens when they
   need help.

5. I interviewed my classmates about friendship.
6. "What is a friend?" I asked them.
7. They gave me different answers—all of them good.
8. "A friend stands by you no matter what," said Rachel.
9. "My friends want to be with me, and I want to be with them," Lenny said.
10. Sue said, "For me, friends are loyal, or they aren't friends."

➡ **For a SELF-CHECK and more practice, see the EXERCISE BANK, p. 535.**

B. REVISING: Substituting Pronouns for Nouns

Rewrite this student's draft of a social studies report. Change the underlined nouns to pronouns.

In ancient times, the idea of friendship was foreign to many people. **(1)** <u>Many people</u> didn't even have a word for "friend." In Old English, though, the word *friend* did exist. **(2)** <u>The word *friend*</u> first appeared in English in A.D. 1018.

Most ancient people lived in close communities. **(3)** <u>Most ancient people</u> had little contact with outsiders. These people did have a word for "stranger." **(4)** <u>The word for "stranger"</u> meant "enemy."

Today, we meet "strangers" all the time. Are these strangers enemies? Most of **(5)** <u>these strangers</u> are not. In fact, many strangers will become our friends.

C. WRITING: Dialogue

Write a dialogue between you and a friend of yours. In the dialogue, ask your friend for advice. When you're finished, underline all the personal pronouns you used.

Example:

You: Can <u>you</u> help <u>me</u>? <u>I</u> have a problem.
Friend: What is <u>it</u>? If <u>I</u> can help <u>you</u>, <u>I</u> will.

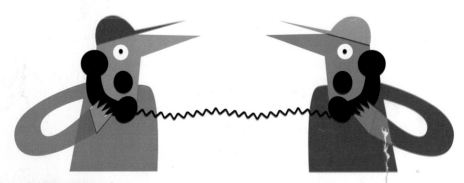

Subject Pronouns

❶ Here's the Idea

▶ **A subject pronoun is used as the subject of a sentence or as a predicate pronoun after a linking verb.**

Singular	Plural
I	we
you	you
he, she, it	they

Pronouns as Subjects

Use the subject case of a pronoun when the pronoun is the subject of a sentence. Remember, a pronoun can be part of a compound subject.

Friends often play on opposing teams. They compete hard against each other. (*They* replaces noun subject *Friends.*)

Charlene and I play on different teams.

We stay friends no matter what.

Predicate Pronouns

A predicate pronoun follows a linking verb and renames, or refers to, the subject. Use the subject case for predicate pronouns.

SUBJECT ▸ RENAMES

Mrs. Sands is the coach. The coach is she.

PREDICATE PRONOUN

RENAMES

The best players are Aaron and I.

RENAMES

The toughest opponents are Teresa and he.

Remember, the most common linking verbs are forms of the verb *be;* they include *is, am, are, was, were, been, has been, have been, can be, will be, could be,* and *should be.*

❷ Why It Matters in Writing

Sometimes subject pronouns may sound strange even though they are correct. As many writers have discovered, you can't rely on "sound" to choose the correct case.

STUDENT MODEL

Michael Jordan is a close friend of Charles Barkley. However, on court the fiercest competitors were ~~him~~ *he* and Charles. Off the court, Hermano and ~~me~~ *I* saw them laughing and playing golf together.

❸ Practice and Apply

CONCEPT CHECK: Subject Pronouns

Write the correct form of the pronoun to complete each sentence.

Friends across the (Tennis) Net

1. I read about Martina Navratilova and Chris Evert. (Them, They) were the top two women tennis players in the early 1980s.
2. Martina and (her, she) played each other 80 times.
3. Rulers of the tennis courts were (they, them)!
4. My friend Elana and (me, I) are tennis rivals, too.
5. (We, Us) like to win but stay friends, just like Martina and Chris.
6. If Martina won, (she, her) would go over and comfort Chris.
7. Sometimes (they, them) would leave each other notes, like "Sorry," or "I'm sure you'll get me next time."
8. My brother is different. (He, Him) hates his rivals.
9. He's not like me and my friends. Best friends and tennis players are (us, we)!
10. Martina and (we, us) agree—be rivals on the court but stay close off the court.

➡ For a SELF-CHECK and more practice, see the EXERCISE BANK, p. 535.

Object Pronouns

❶ Here's the Idea

▶ **Object pronouns are personal pronouns used as direct objects, as indirect objects, or as the objects of prepositions.**

Object Pronouns	
Singular	**Plural**
me	us
you	you
him, her, it	them

Direct Object: receives the action of a verb and answers the question *whom or what?*

True animal stories fascinate Jen. (fascinate whom? *Jen*)
DIRECT OBJECT

Do you like them too? (like what? *them*)

Indirect Object: tells *to whom or what* or *for whom or what* an action is performed.

TO WHOM?
Jen gave me a book about a dolphin who guided ships.
INDIRECT OBJECT

People gave him a hero's welcome.

Object of a Preposition: follows a preposition (such as *to, from, for, against, by,* or *about*).

We'd like to hear more about him.
PREPOSITION   OBJECT

Can you tell the story to her and me?
PREPOSITION   OBJECT   OBJECT

Always use an object pronoun after the preposition *between*.

The books were divided between Mike and me. (Not between Mike and I)

❷ Why It Matters in Writing

Using the pronouns *I* and *me* allows the writer to be up close and personal. In the passage below, Helen Keller uses these pronouns to describe when she first felt loved.

> **LITERARY MODEL**
>
> I stretched out my hand. . . . Someone took it, and I was caught up and held close in the arms of her who had come to reveal all things to me, and, more than all things else, to love me.
>
> —Helen Keller, *The Story of My Life*

❸ Practice and Apply

CONCEPT CHECK: Subject and Object Pronouns

Write the correct pronoun(s) for each sentence. Label each pronoun *subject* or *object*.

The Sailors' Friend

1. Jen told (we, us) a true story about a dolphin.
2. People gave (he, him) the name Pelorus Jack.
3. (He, Him) guided ships through the dangerous Cook Strait near New Zealand.
4. No one trained (he, him) to do this.
5. It was (he, him) who decided to guide ships.
6. Ships would come to the strait, and (he, him) would lead (they, them) out of danger.
7. Sailors watched (he, him) leaping through the waves.
8. Pelorus Jack swam swiftly in front of (they, them) and brought their ships through the strait.
9. (He, Him) was protected from harm by New Zealand law.
10. A movie was even made about (he, him)!

➜ For a SELF-CHECK and more practice, see EXERCISE BANK, p. 536.

Identify how each object pronoun you chose is used in the sentence: as a direct object, an indirect object, or an object of a preposition.

LESSON 4 · Possessive Pronouns

① Here's the Idea

▶ **Possessive pronouns are personal pronouns used to show ownership or relationship.**

Possessive Pronouns	
Singular	**Plural**
my, mine	our, ours
your, yours	your, yours
her, hers, his, its	their, theirs

The possessive pronouns *my, your, her, his, our,* and *their* come before nouns.

RELATIONSHIP

Some of my best friends live in other countries.

OWNERSHIP

All our correspondence is by e-mail.

OWNERSHIP

Even their old computers are on-line now.

The possessive pronouns *mine, ours, yours, his, hers,* and *theirs* can stand alone in a sentence.

The blue mouse pad is theirs. Ours is red.

Is that video game yours? Mine is broken.

Is his any good? Or should we play hers?

Possessive Pronouns and Contractions

Some possessive pronouns sound like contractions (*its/it's, your/you're, their/they're*). Because these pairs sound alike, writers often confuse possessive pronouns and contractions.

Remember, possessive pronouns *never* use an apostrophe. Contractions *always* use an apostrophe. Look at the examples in the Quick-Fix Spelling Machine on the following page.

PRONOUNS

QUICK-FIX SPELLING MACHINE

POSSESSIVE PRONOUNS		CONTRACTIONS	
its	Its modem is fast!	it's	It's fun to get new mail.
your	Your e-mails are funny.	you're	You're a good writer.
their	Their smiles are sideways! :-)	they're	They're full of funny faces.

❷ Why It Matters in Writing

Proofread your work carefully to be sure you haven't confused contractions and possessive pronouns. A computer spell checker will not catch these mistakes.

STUDENT MODEL

A circle of mountains lies deep under the Pacific Ocean between Japan and North America. It is known as the "ring of fire." If ~~your~~ *you're* wondering why, it's because the mountains are part of a circle of active volcanoes.

A volcanic eruption at sea can cause tsunami waves. ~~They're~~ *Their* danger is hard to see at first. A tsunami crossing the ocean is barely a ripple. But when it nears land, a tsunami can travel nearly 500 miles an hour and reach a height of over 100 feet. It destroys everything in ~~it's~~ *its* path.

In 1993 a tsunami struck Okushiri, Japan, and destroyed its wharf.

❸ Practice and Apply

A. CONCEPT CHECK: Possessive Pronouns

Write the correct pronoun or contraction for each sentence.

Cyber Friends

1. (Its, It's) now possible for schools throughout the world to be linked on the Internet.
2. A school can partner with a "Sister School" overseas to learn about (its, it's) land and culture.
3. If (your, you're) interested, contact the Society for International Sister Schools (SISS).
4. (Your, You're) school can correspond with schools in Russia, Mexico, Korea, Ireland—almost anywhere!
5. Your international Web pals write from (their, they're) computers, and you write from yours.
6. Within minutes, (their, they're) sending you e-mails through cyberspace.
7. Some schools post on-line surveys for (their, they're) Sister Schools to answer.
8. *Hablo Español?* You can sharpen (your, you're) Spanish or other language writing skills.
9. There are many native speakers in the program, and (their, they're) happy to help you!
10. Maybe someday SISS will even have (its, it's) own virtual classroom!

➜ **For a SELF-CHECK and more practice, see the EXERCISE BANK, p. 536.**

B. PROOFREADING: Using Possessive Pronouns

For each sentence, write the correct form of the possessive pronoun or contractions. If a sentence contains no error, write *Correct*.

(1) Hey, Josie,
Your probably amazed finally to hear from me! I meant to answer your e-mail right away, but its been a crazy time. **(2)** Our class is doing a climate project for the Science Fair, and I am in charge of gathering data! **(3)** Our Sister School in Hirosaki, Japan, is helping us. **(4)** Its so great having a Sister School! **(5)** Their sending us information about their climate. **(6)** It's perfect because **(7)** their latitude is about the same as ours in Baltimore. **(8)** Your invited to see the exhibit when its done.

LESSON 5 · Reflexive and Intensive Pronouns

❶ Here's the Idea

Pronouns that end in *-self* or *-selves* are either **reflexive** or **intensive** pronouns.

Reflexive and Intensive Pronouns		
myself	yourself	herself, himself, itself
ourselves	yourselves	themselves

Reflexive Pronouns

▶ **A reflexive pronoun refers to the subject and directs the action of the verb back to the subject.** Reflexive pronouns are necessary to the meaning of a sentence.

REFLECTS

The winners considered themselves lucky.

REFLECTS

How do you prepare yourself for a game?

Notice that if you drop the reflexive pronoun, you change the meaning of the sentence. (*The winners considered lucky.*)

Intensive Pronouns

▶ **An intensive pronoun emphasizes the noun or pronoun in the same sentence.** Intensive pronouns are not necessary to the meaning of the sentence.

EMPHASIZES

I myself just keep saying, "We'll win!"

EMPHASIZES

The players themselves designed their uniforms.

Notice that when you drop the intensive pronoun, the sentence still makes sense. (*I just keep saying, "We'll win!"*)

Hisself and *theirselves* may look like real words, but they are not in the dictionary. Use *himself* and *themselves* instead.

❷ Why It Matters in Writing

Notice how the student sportswriter uses reflexive and intensive pronouns to emphasize key words and ideas.

> **STUDENT MODEL**
>
> The U.S. women's soccer team won the 1999 World Cup in a final shootout. At the end, the players **themselves** were screaming for joy. Injured player Michelle Akers said: "I found **myself** hobbling out to the field to join my team. The 90,185 fans were going crazy. I was struggling to soak it all in and keep **myself** together."

INTENSIVE
REFLEXIVE

PRONOUNS

❸ Practice and Apply

CONCEPT CHECK: Reflexive and Intensive Pronouns

For each sentence, write the reflexive or intensive pronoun. Then label it *reflexive* or *intensive*.

All for One and One for All

1. My sister Emmy never pictured herself playing team sports.
2. Now Emmy herself admits that her best friends are her soccer teammates.
3. The players have to get themselves in step with the team.
4. One player can't win a match all by himself or herself!
5. Pro athletes themselves encourage young people to join teams.
6. Olympic soccer player Mia Hamm said: "Don't worry about how well you play; just enjoy yourself."
7. As a teen, pro basketball player Cynthia Cooper found herself imitating how the pros played.
8. She herself didn't try out for a team until she was 16.
9. I myself will never forget Sammy Sosa embracing Mark McGwire—his home-run rival!
10. Team players think of others besides themselves.

➔ For a SELF-CHECK and more practice, see the EXERCISE BANK, p. 537.

Interrogatives and Demonstratives

❶ Here's the Idea

Interrogative Pronouns

▶ **An interrogative pronoun is used to introduce a question.** Interrogative pronouns include *who, whom, what, which,* and *whose.*

> **Who** has an animal for a friend?
> **What** do you like best about animals?

Writers often confuse *who* and *whom.* The following guidelines can help you decide which form to use in your sentences.

Using *Who* and *Whom*

▶ ***Who*** **is always used as a subject or a predicate pronoun.**

> Subject: **Who** gave you the parakeet?
> Predicate pronoun: **It was who?**

Don't confuse *who's* with *whose. Who's* is a contraction that means *who is* or *who has. (Who's missing?) Whose* is an interrogative or possessive pronoun. *(Whose is this?)*

▶ ***Whom*** **is always used as an object.**

> Direct object: **Whom** do you ask about pet stores?
> Indirect object: **You gave whom a turtle?**
> Object of preposition: **From whom did you buy it?**

Here's How Choosing *Who* or *Whom* in a Question

(Who, Whom) did you see at the store?

1. If necessary, rewrite the question to put the subject first.
   You did see (who, whom) at the store?

2. Decide whether the pronoun is used as a subject or an object.
   You is already the subject. *Whom* is used as an object.
   You did see whom at the store? (direct object of *did see*)

3. Use the correct pronoun in the question.
   Whom did you see at the store?

Demonstrative Pronouns

▶ **A demonstrative pronoun points out a person, place, thing, or idea.**

Demonstrative pronouns—*this, that, these,* and *those*—are used alone in a sentence, as shown below.

Singular

This is my parakeet Newton.

That is his new cage.

Plural

These are his chewed-up toys.

Those are his favorite treats.

This and *these* mean that something is near, or here. *That* and *those* mean that something is far away, or there. Never use *here* or *there* with a demonstrative pronoun. The pronoun already points out which one; it doesn't need help.

This ~~here~~ is our cat.

That ~~there~~ is our crazy dog.

❷ Why It Matters in Writing

Knowing when to use *who* and *whom* can be tricky because many people use these pronouns incorrectly. Be careful to use the correct pronouns when you create questionnaires or surveys, like the one below.

STUDENT MODEL

Questionnaire for Friends

• Who is your oldest friend?

• Who talks more—you or your best friend?

• With whom would you share your deepest secret?

• Whom would you trust for advice?

SUBJECT

OBJECT OF PREPOSITION

DIRECT OBJECT

❸ Practice and Apply

A. CONCEPT CHECK: Interrogatives and Demonstratives

Write the correct pronoun to complete each sentence. Then identify it as an *interrogative* or *demonstrative* pronoun.

Four-Legged Versus Two-Legged Friends

1. **Aretha:** (Who, Whose) is your best friend?
2. **Cindy:** (That, That there) is easy: either Marsha Hanks or my dog Bandit.
3. **Aretha:** (Which, What) is it?
4. Besides, (who, whom) would prefer dogs as best friends?
5. **Cindy:** (Those, That) are the best kind.
6. (Who, Whom) loves you all the time? Only a dog.
7. (Who, Whom) can you play with anytime? A dog!
8. **Aretha:** (Those, Those there) are good arguments. I hadn't thought about it that way.
9. **Cindy:** By the way, your best friend is (who, whom)?
10. **Aretha:** (Who, Whom) would I choose? My parakeet Newton. I can talk to him about anything, and he talks back!

➜ For a SELF-CHECK and more practice, see the EXERCISE BANK, p. 537.

B. WRITING: Science Questions and Answers

Write a five-question quiz based on the article below. Use each of these interrogative pronouns at least once: *who, whom, what,* and *which.* Underline the interrogative pronouns you use.

Example: <u>Who</u> learned sign language first—Koko or Michael?

In July 1972, Penny Patterson first met her good friend Koko. Penny was a graduate student at a major university. Koko was a one-year-old female lowland gorilla. Penny taught Koko sign language. Today, Koko knows more than 1,000 signs. She uses them to "talk" to humans and to her friend Michael, another lowland gorilla. Koko and Penny taught Michael to use sign language as well.

LESSON 7

Pronoun-Antecedent Agreement

❶ Here's the Idea

▶ **The antecedent is the noun or pronoun that a pronoun replaces or refers to.** The antecedent can be in the same sentence or in a different sentence from the pronoun.

REFERS TO

Maria shared her favorite book, *The Friends*.
⬆ ANTECEDENT ⬆ PRONOUN

REFERS TO

The story is set in Harlem. It tells about young girls growing up.

Pronouns must agree with their antecedents in number, person, and gender.

Agreement in Number

▶ **Use a singular pronoun to refer to a singular antecedent.**

REFERS TO

At first Phyllisia doesn't like her new classmate.

▶ **Use a plural pronoun to refer to a plural antecedent.**

REFERS TO

Later the girls share their dreams together.

Agreement in Person

▶ **The person of a pronoun must be the same as the person of the antecedent.**

3RD PERSON

The author is Rosa Guy. She was born in Trinidad.

2ND PERSON

Do you write stories about your life?

PRONOUNS

Avoid switching from one person to another in the same sentence or paragraph.

Incorrect:
> Students like strong plots. We want to know what happens. (*Students* is third person; *we* is first person.)

Correct:
> Students like strong plots. They want to know what happens. (*Students* and *they* are both third person.)

Agreement in Gender

▶ **The gender of a pronoun must be the same as the gender of its antecedent.**

Personal pronouns have three gender forms: masculine (*he, his, him*), feminine (*she, her, hers*), and neuter (*it, its*).

> Anne is mad because she lost her book.

> Jim gave his extra copy to Anne.

Don't use only masculine or only feminine pronouns when you mean to refer to both genders.

DRAFT:
> Every student has his own opinion.
> (Student could be male or female.)

There are two ways to correct this sentence.

1. Use the phrase *his or her*.
   > Every student has his or her own opinion.

2. Rewrite the sentence using a plural antecedent and a plural pronoun. Be careful! Other words in the sentence may also need to be made plural.
   > Students have their own opinions.

❷ Why It Matters in Writing

It's easy to make mistakes with person or number. Proofread your writing carefully. Avoid the common errors that the student writer made in the model on the following page.

Best **friends** come in all shapes and sizes.

They

~~You~~ may be opposites of each other. For

instance, you might not like **someone** at first.

he or she

Then later on ~~they~~ become͜ your best friend.

Friends is third person plural.

Someone is singular and could be male or female.

❸ Practice and Apply

CONCEPT CHECK: Pronoun-Antecedent Agreement

For each sentence, write the personal pronoun and its antecedent.

Number the Stars

1. This story is by Lois Lowry. It is set in Denmark during World War II.
2. Annemarie Johansen and her best friend Ellen Rosen live happily—until the Nazis come.
3. Then the girls are scared as their lives turn upside down.
4. Ellen is in special danger because her family is Jewish.
5. The Nazis have targeted all Jews as their enemies.
6. Annemarie's parents hide Ellen in their home.
7. The Johansens know that they must also try to protect Ellen's family.
8. Uncle Henrik uses his boat to carry some Jews to safety.
9. When Annemarie is asked to go on this dangerous ride, she agrees.
10. She must find the strength to save her best friend's life.

➜ **For a SELF-CHECK and more practice, see the EXERCISE BANK, p. 538.**

Write the number and person of each pronoun.

PRONOUNS

Indefinite Pronoun Agreement

❶ Here's the Idea

▶ **An indefinite pronoun does not refer to a specific person, place, thing, or idea.**

Indefinite pronouns often do not have antecedents.

Everyone should know about the men of the *Endurance*.

Anybody would be amazed by the story of this shipwreck.

▶ **Indefinite pronouns can be singular, plural, or either singular or plural.**

Indefinite Pronouns			
Singular		**Plural**	**Singular or Plural**
another	neither	both	all
anybody	nobody	few	any
anyone	no one	many	most
anything	nothing	several	none
each	one		some
either	somebody		
everybody	someone		
everyone	something		
everything			

Pronouns containing *-one, -thing,* or *-body* are always singular.

Singular Indefinite Pronouns

▶ **Use a singular personal pronoun to refer to a singular indefinite pronoun.**

REFERS TO

Anyone in trouble depends on his or her friends.
(*Anyone* could be masculine or feminine.)

REFERS TO

On the *Endurance*, everybody had to keep up his spirits while waiting for rescue. (There were only men on the ship.)

Plural Indefinite Pronouns

▶ **Use a plural personal pronoun to refer to a plural indefinite pronoun.**

REFERS TO

Many shared their food and clothing.

REFERS TO

None realized they would not return home for 20 months.

Singular or Plural Indefinite Pronouns

▶ **Some indefinite pronouns can be singular or plural.**
Often the phrase that follows the indefinite pronoun will tell you whether the pronoun is singular or plural.

Most of the mast had lost its sail.
♦ SINGULAR INDEFINITE PRONOUN   ♦ SINGULAR PERSONAL PRONOUN

Most of the masts had lost their sails.
♦ PLURAL INDEFINITE PRONOUN   ♦ PLURAL PERSONAL PRONOUN

❷ Why It Matters in Writing

Agreement can help keep your facts and ideas clear. Make sure that all pronouns agree with their indefinite antecedents in number.

STUDENT MODEL

Many wonder how well ~~he~~ *they* would do in a crisis. The men aboard the ship *Endurance* had a chance to find out. Everyone did ~~their~~ *his* best to keep up hope. The leaders and crew battled wind, ice, and darkness. No one wanted to let ~~their~~ *his* friends down.

PRONOUNS

❸ Practice and Apply

A. CONCEPT CHECK: Indefinite-Pronoun Agreement

Choose the pronoun that agrees with the indefinite pronoun antecedent.

The Ordeal of the *Endurance*
1. In 1915, all of the men became trapped with (his, their) ship in the Antarctic ice.
2. No one could send (his, their) family a message.
3. Few of them were able to avoid sleeping on the ice in (his, their) wet clothes.
4. When spring came, all the men had to board three lifeboats. (He, They) sailed toward a splinter of land.
5. Each was relieved when (he, they) reached the land safely.
6. Shackleton chose a few of the men and asked (him, them) to row 800 icy miles to get help.
7. Each was chosen for (his, their) special courage.
8. One used (his, their) carpentry skills to make new boat parts from packing crates!
9. Some of the waves were 50 feet high. The men had to face (it, them) in only a lifeboat!
10. Incredibly, nobody in Shackleton's crew lost (his, their) life during the voyage.

➜ **For a SELF-CHECK and more practice, see the EXERCISE BANK, p. 538.**

B. PROOFREADING: Agreement Errors

This paragraph contains four pronoun-antecedent errors. Rewrite the sentences to correct the errors.

Rescue in the Antarctic!
Ernest Shackleton chose five men to sail with him on a fearsome journey to find help. Many left on the island had his troubles too. Everyone had to eat penguins and seals for their daily diet. Several men had frostbite. One needed medical attention for his infected wound. Everyone in the remaining crew anxiously awaited their rescue. Nearly five months after Shackleton left, all of the men had his dream come true. Shackleton and the others came back for them!

Pronoun Problems

① Here's the Idea

We and *Us* with Nouns

The pronouns *we* and *us* are sometimes followed by a noun that identifies the pronoun (*we students, us students*).

▶ **Use *we* when the noun is a subject or a predicate noun. Use *us* when the noun is an object.**

We volunteers like to help out.
　　　↖SUBJECT

Do you have work for us volunteers?
　　　　　　　　　↖OBJECT OF PREPOSITION

Here's How Choosing *We* or *Us*

You can join (we, us) students tomorrow.

1. Drop the identifying noun from the sentence.

You can join (we, us) tomorrow.

2. Decide whether the pronoun is used as a subject or an object. In this sentence, the pronoun is the object of the verb *join.*

You can join us tomorrow.

3. Use the correct pronoun with the noun.

You can join us students tomorrow.

Unclear Reference

▶ **Be sure that each personal pronoun refers clearly to only one person, place, or thing.** If there is any chance your reader will be confused by whom or what you are talking about, use a noun instead of a pronoun.

Confusing:

　Noah and Rodrigo came to the work site, but he didn't stay. (Who didn't stay? Noah or Rodrigo?)

Clear:

　Noah and Rodrigo came to the work site, but Noah didn't stay.

❷ Why It Matters in Writing

When you write instructions or directions, make sure you use the right case and keep your pronoun references clear. You don't want to confuse your readers, as this writer did.

Heads up! Hands out!

~~Us~~ *We* youth volunteers need help. Can you join us? Call Nicki at 555-2222 or Ann at 555-0000. ~~She~~ *Nicki* has an answering machine, so leave a message!

> Use *we* as the subject.

> *She* could mean either Nicki or Ann. Name the person to avoid confusion.

❸ Practice and Apply

A. CONCEPT CHECK: Pronoun Problems

Write the correct pronoun or noun.

Helping Hands
1. (We, Us) students help out in lots of ways.
2. That garden was planted by (we, us) volunteers.
3. Carlos worked with Joe to clean the river, even though (he, Carlos) had never done that kind of work before.
4. Some of (we, us) athletes offered to coach youngsters.
5. Stacey always beats Terese to work, but (she, Terese) still gets there on time.

➡ For a SELF-CHECK and more practice, see the EXERCISE BANK, p. 539.

B. REVISING: Correcting Pronoun Errors

Correct the four pronoun errors in the following paragraph.

Cleaning up on the River!
Us swimmers are determined to clean up the riverbanks. The garbage there has disgusted we kids for a long time. For months, the mayor and the parks commissioner talked about doing something, but he didn't take any action. Danielle worked with Margo to pick up junk along the shore. She filled three trash bags in one hour!

More Pronoun Problems

❶ Here's the Idea

Using Pronouns in Compounds

People often make mistakes when they use pronouns as parts of compound subjects and compound objects.

▶ **Use the subject pronouns *I, she, he, we,* and *they* in a compound subject or a compound predicate pronoun.**

Shawn and he are on the same study team.

The leaders of the team are he and I.

▶ **Use the object pronouns *me, her, him, us,* and *them* in a compound object.**

Our friends saw Darlene and me at the library.

The librarian gave Shawn and her some books.

To choose the correct case of a pronoun in a compound subject or object, mentally screen out the other noun or pronoun. Then choose the correct case.

Shawn gave an article to ~~Darlene and~~ (I, me). (*Me* is the object of the preposition *to*—therefore, *to Darlene and me* is correct.)

Phrases that Interfere

Sometimes words and phrases come between a subject and a pronoun that refers to it. Don't be confused by the words in between.

REFERS TO

Darlene, ~~like the others,~~ is working on her report.
(*Her* agrees with *Danielle* and not with *others.*)

REFERS TO

Harriet Tubman, ~~unlike many people,~~ risked her life to free slaves. (*Her* agrees with *Harriet Tubman* and not with *people.*)

PRONOUNS

❷ Why It Matters in Writing

Some people think *I* sounds more correct than *me* in a compound object. "I" is only correct when used as a subject or predicate pronoun. Watch out for this common mistake when you write.

> **STUDENT MODEL**
>
> You and I make great study partners. It's easy to divide the work between you and ~~I~~ *me*. I ask the questions. You find the answers!

❸ Practice and Apply

A. CONCEPT CHECK: More Pronoun Problems

Choose the correct pronoun to complete each sentence.

A Friend to Her People

1. Our social studies teacher asked Danielle and (I, me) to do a report on Harriet Tubman.
2. The librarian helped (her, she) and me with the research.
3. Both (she, her) and I knew that Tubman led slaves to freedom on the Underground Railroad.
4. Many facts about Tubman were new to (she, her) and me.
5. More than 300 slaves, including Harriet's own sister, owed (their, her) freedom to Tubman.
6. (She, Her) and the runaways had to move secretly from one house to another along the Underground Railroad.
7. Tubman, like other conductors, wouldn't let any of (her, their) runaways turn back.
8. Slave owners placed a $40,000 reward on her head. That fact surprised Danielle and (me, I).
9. John Brown, another of the freedom fighters, praised Tubman in (his, their) letters and speeches.
10. The librarian gave copies of some letters to Danielle and (I, me).

➡ **For a SELF-CHECK and more practice, see the EXERCISE BANK, p. 540.**

B. PROOFREADING: Correct Use of Pronouns

On a separate sheet of paper, correct the underlined pronoun errors.

> <u>Darren and me</u> read about the Underground Railroad. <u>Him and I</u> soon realized that it was not "underground" and it was not a "railroad." Instead, it was a secret network of escape routes for slaves. This network of escape routes had <u>their</u> beginning in the South. The paths of the Underground Railroad crisscrossed <u>its</u> way through the North. Eventually, many routes ended in Canada. Canada, unlike the United States, had outlawed slavery within <u>their</u> borders.
>
> The Underground Railroad was a hard journey for runaway slaves. Abolitionists and <u>them</u> were tracked by slave hunters. Anyone caught could be tried and sentenced to death!

C. WRITING: SOCIAL STUDIES: Drafting from a Time Line

Read the following biographical time line. Then write a paragraph about Harriet Tubman, based on the information. Underline any pronouns you use.

Example: Harriet Tubman was born around 1820 in Dorchester County, Maryland. <u>She</u> ran away for the first time when <u>she</u> was about six or seven years old.

1820?
Born in Dorchester County, Maryland.

1849
Harriet flees to Pennsylvania and freedom. Many people help Harriet along the Underground Railroad.

1820 1830 1840 1850 1860

1827?
Runs away for the first time, but goes back. Is punished by the farm owners Harriet worked for.

1844
Marries John Tubman. Wants John to run away with her. John refuses and stays in Maryland.

1850–1860s
Serves as a conductor on the Underground Railroad. Brings more than 300 people out of slavery. People admire Harriet. People call Harriet "Moses."

Grammar in Literature

Using Pronouns in Dialogue

You can use **dialogue,** or conversation, in stories and plays to show what your characters think and feel. Pronouns can make your dialogue sound more natural and make your characters seem more realistic. As you read this excerpt from *Damon and Pythias: A Drama,* notice how the use of pronouns makes the conversation between the two friends seem real.

DAMON
AND
PYTHIAS

RETOLD BY FAN KISSEN

Damon. Oh, Pythias! How terrible to find you here! I wish I could do something to save you!

Pythias. Nothing can save me, Damon, my dear friend. I am prepared to die. But there is one thought that troubles me greatly.

Damon. What is it? I will do anything to help you.

Pythias. I'm worried about what will happen to my mother and my sister when I'm gone.

Damon. I'll take care of them, Pythias, as if they were my own mother and sister.

Pythias. Thank you, Damon. I have money to leave them. But there are other things I must arrange. If only I could go to see them before I die! But they live two days' journey from here, you know.

Damon. I'll go to the king and beg him to give you your freedom for a few days. You'll give your word to return at the end of that time. Everyone in Sicily knows you for a man who has never broken his word.

Practice and Apply

WRITING: Using Pronouns in Dialogue

When actor Clifton Davis was a boy in the 1950s, he was the only African American in his middle school class. For graduation, the class was going to Glenn Echo Amusement Park in Maryland. Then Clifton learned that he would not be allowed into the park because he was black. He went back to his room, crying.

When he told his friend Frank what was wrong, Frank said he wouldn't go to the park either. Clifton knew how badly Frank wanted to go, but his friend was firm. Frank also told the other boys, and they all refused to go to the park. Clifton felt proud that he had such loyal friends.

Write a dialogue between Clifton and Frank that dramatizes this story. When you are finished, underline the pronouns you used. How did they help make the dialogue sound more realistic?

Frank: Hey Clifton, why do you seem down?

Clifton: I just found out that I can't go with the rest of you to the amusement park.

A. Pronouns Choose the correct pronoun for each sentence.

1. Everyone in our class had to write (his or her, their) report on a myth.
2. Shirell and I worked together. (We, Us) chose a myth about Damon and Pythias.
3. Between you and (I, me), this myth turned out to be really good.
4. Damon and Pythias, each from a noble family, had vowed (his, their) undying loyalty to each other.
5. Pythias, sentenced to death by Dionysius, asked permission to leave the city to put (his, their) affairs in order.
6. Damon promised to die in place of Pythias if (he, Pythias) did not return on time.
7. Pythias, unexpectedly delayed, almost failed to keep (his, their) word.
8. Damon was nearly killed in (his, their) place.
9. Pythias saved (him, he) by arriving just in time.
10. Dionysius marveled at their friendship. He pardoned Pythias and asked the two to become (his, their) friends.

B. Revising: Using Pronouns Correctly This passage contains six errors in pronoun usage. Rewrite the paragraph to correct the errors.

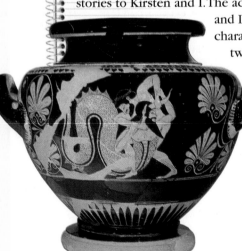

STUDENT MODEL

Between you and I, the idea of reading "ancient stories" sounded boring to me. Then us students read a few Greek myths in class. It was the first time a teacher explained the stories to Kirsten and I. The action kept us interested. Her and I really liked the heroic characters Hercules and Jason. The two of they were always doing something exciting, like fighting monsters. Some of my friends like to act out his or her favorite characters. These myths would make great TV movies!

Choose the correct replacement for each underlined word in the passage, or indicate if it is correct as is.

<u>Whom</u> knows the story of Sacajawea? Ellen, Terri, and <u>me</u> saw
(1)   (2)
a movie about <u>she</u>. Sacajawea befriended Lewis and Clark in 1804
(3)
and helped guide <u>they</u> to the Pacific Ocean. In the early 1800s,
(4)
most of the land west of the Mississippi River was unexplored. The
idea to map the territory was <u>who's</u>? President Jefferson was the
(5)
one who ordered the expedition.

<u>Us students</u> couldn't believe how lucky Lewis and Clark were.
(6)
<u>Them</u> and their men crossed icy rivers and traveled through
(7)
hostile lands. Only one of the travelers lost <u>his</u> life. Sacajawea and
(8)
her husband even took <u>they're</u> baby on the trail! Ellen, along with
(9)
the rest of us, couldn't believe <u>our</u> ears when Sacajawea asked
(10)
Clark to raise her son as his own in St. Louis.

1. A. What
   B. Who
   C. Whose
   D. Correct as is

2. A. us
   B. I
   C. Me, Ellen, and Terri
   D. Correct as is

3. A. her
   B. we
   C. hers
   D. Correct as is

4. A. him
   B. he
   C. them
   D. Correct as is

5. A. whose
   B. who
   C. whom
   D. Correct as is

6. A. Us
   B. Them students
   C. We students
   D. Correct as is

7. A. Him
   B. They
   C. He
   D. Correct as is

8. A. their
   B. her
   C. his or her
   D. Correct as is

9. A. they
   B. their
   C. them
   D. Correct as is

10. A. her
    B. my
    C. their
    D. Correct as is

Student Help Desk

Pronouns at a Glance

Subject Case

I	we
you	you
he	they
she	
it	

Use this case when
- the pronoun is a **subject**
- the pronoun is a **predicate pronoun**

Object Case

me	us
you	you
him	them
her	
it	

Use this case when
- the pronoun is a **direct object**
- the pronoun is an **indirect object**
- the pronoun is the **object of a preposition**

Possessive Case

my, mine	our, ours
your, yours	your, yours
his	their, theirs
her, hers	
its	

Use this case for
- pronouns that show **ownership or relationship**

Me
and
my
Shadow

Pronoun-Antecedent Agreement

A pronoun should agree with its antecedent in number, person, and gender.

A singular antecedent takes a singular pronoun.

Tanya says **her** best friend is a yo-yo champ. (singular)

A plural antecedent takes a plural pronoun.

The **friends** stick together through **their** ups and downs. (plural)

At times the reference will include both genders.

Each has **his or her** special talent.

They have **their** special talents.

Types of Pronouns

"I'm Nobody. Are You Nobody too?"

Intensive & Reflexive
myself
herself
himself
itself
yourself
ourselves
yourselves
themselves

Interrogative
who
whom
what
which
whose

Demonstrative
this
that
these
those

Indefinite
someone
anyone
each
several
many
all
most
none

For a list of indefinite pronouns, see p. 72.

Pronoun Problems

Friends by the Case

We:	Subject/predicate pronoun	**We** guys stick together.
Us:	Object	Nothing comes between **us** guys.
Who:	Subject/predicate pronoun	**Who** is your oldest friend?
Whom:	Object	For **whom** would you do anything?

PRONOUNS

The Bottom Line

Checklist for Pronouns

Have I . . .

____ used the subject case for pronouns that are subjects and predicate pronouns?

____ used the object case for pronouns that are objects?

____ used the possessive case to show ownership or relationship?

____ made sure that pronouns agree with their antecedents in number, person, and gender?

____ used who and whom correctly?

____ used the correct cases in compound subjects and objects?

Verbs

WE MOVE YOU

Theme: On the Move

Moving Words

Verbs make sentences move. Just as a truck can't go anywhere without an engine, a sentence can't go anywhere without a verb. In this chapter, you will learn how to use verbs to move your sentences.

Write Away: Getting There

In a paragraph, describe your favorite way to get around. You can describe any form of transportation—your own two feet, a bike, rollerblades, a train, a car, or even a spaceship. Put the paragraph in your 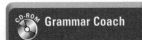 **Working Portfolio.**

Grammar Coach

Choose the best way to rewrite each underlined word or group of words.

For more than a hundred years, science fiction writers <u>will predict</u> new ways of transportation. In 1865 Jules Verne <u>wrote</u> a
(1)   (2)
novel called *From the Earth to the Moon*. Verne <u>is getting</u> many
(3)
scientific details right. Science fiction writers today <u>had described</u>
(4)
journeys to other galaxies. Someday we <u>are traveling</u> to those
(5)
distant places, just as we really <u>did travel</u> to the moon more than 30
(6)
years ago. Science fiction <u>will contribute</u> to transportation on Earth
(7)
as well. In 1903 H. G. Wells <u>maked</u> up military tanks in his short
(8)
story "The Land Ironclads." A decade later, during World War I,
Winston Churchill remembered that story and <u>began</u> the research
(9)
that led to tanks. Surely other fictional means of transportation
<u>are becoming</u> realities in the future.
(10)

1. A. have predicted
   B. predict
   C. are predicting
   D. Correct as is

2. A. writed
   B. have written
   C. will write
   D. Correct as is

3. A. will get
   B. got
   C. getted
   D. Correct as is

4. A. were describing
   B. will describe
   C. have described
   D. Correct as is

5. A. will travel
   B. have traveled
   C. travel
   D. Correct as is

6. A. should travel
   B. will travel
   C. do travel
   D. Correct as is

7. A. should contribute
   B. is contributing
   C. has contributed
   D. Correct as is

8. A. made
   B. will make
   C. is making
   D. Correct as is

9. A. will begin
   B. has begun
   C. beginned
   D. Correct as is

10. A. became
    B. will become
    C. have become
    D. Correct as is

VERBS

What Is a Verb?

❶ Here's the Idea

▶ **A verb is a word used to express an action, a condition, or a state of being.** The two main types of verbs are **action verbs** and **linking verbs.** Both kinds can be accompanied by helping verbs.

Action Verbs

An **action verb** tells what its subject does. The action it expresses can be either **physical** or **mental.**

Early humans moved constantly. (physical action)

They carried their few possessions with them. (physical action)

These people worried about survival. (mental action)

They feared large animals. (mental action)

Linking Verbs

A **linking verb** links its subject to a word in the predicate. The most common linking verbs are forms of the verb *be.*

Linking Verbs	
Forms of *be*	be, am, is, are, was, were, been, being
Verbs that express condition	appear, become, feel, grow, look, remain, seem, smell, sound, taste

LINKS

Early humans were food gatherers.

LINKING VERB

They often felt hungry.

CHAPTER 4

Some verbs can serve as either action or linking verbs.

Animals appeared at their campsites.
       ACTION VERB
          LINKS

Some animals appeared friendly.
          LINKING VERB

Helping Verbs and Verb Phrases

Helping verbs help main verbs express action or precise shades of meaning. The combination of one or more helping verbs with a main verb is called a **verb phrase.**

VERB PHRASE
Animals could carry the humans' heavy loads farther.
HELPING   MAIN

Then people would travel farther.

Some verbs can serve both as **main verbs** and as **helping verbs.** For example, *had* stands alone in the first sentence below but is a helping verb in the second sentence.

People had tools now.
      MAIN VERB

They had mastered many skills.
     HELPING VERB

Common Helping Verbs	
Forms of *be*	be, am, is, are, was, were, been, being
Forms of *do*	do, does, did
Forms of *have*	have, has, had
Other	could, should, would, may, might, must, can, shall, will

VERBS

❷ Why It Matters in Writing

When writing, use verbs that are strong and lively. Notice this author's use of *soared, rushed,* and *swirled,* which are more specific than some other verbs, like *dived, went,* and *flowed.*

> **LITERARY MODEL**
>
> We **soared**. The water **rushed** past my face and **swirled** around my body, and I felt the streaking lines of speed.
>
> —Don C. Reed, "My First Dive with the Dolphins"

❸ Practice and Apply

A. CONCEPT CHECK: What Is a Verb?

Write the verb or verb phrase in each of the following sentences.

They Got Around
1. Transportation developed along with civilization.
2. Half a million years ago, humans traveled frequently.
3. They searched for food like nuts and berries.
4. They hunted animals on foot.
5. Later they used beasts of burden.
6. They must have invented sledges about 5000 B.C.
7. These sledlike vehicles could move tons of weight.
8. Around 3500 B.C., someone created the wheel.
9. With wheels on vehicles, people could travel long distances.
10. The wheel was one of the most important inventions ever.

Label each verb above as *Action* or *Linking*.

➜ **For a SELF-CHECK and more practice, see the EXERCISE BANK, p. 540.**

B. REVISING: Using More Specific Verbs

Write a more specific verb to replace each underlined verb in the paragraph below.

Animal Travel

Most animals travel. Dolphins <u>swim</u> through the water. Eagles <u>fly</u> in the sky. Horses can <u>move</u> for great distances. Snakes <u>go</u> through the grass. Butterflies <u>fly</u> from flower to flower.

Action Verbs and Objects

❶ Here's the Idea

Action verbs are often accompanied by words that complete their meaning. These **complements** are called direct objects or indirect objects.

Direct Objects

▶ **A direct object is a noun or pronoun that names the receiver of a verb's action.** The direct object answers the question *what* or *whom.*

LOVE WHAT?

Americans love the automobile.
   ACTION VERB   DIRECT OBJECT

Cars changed our society.

Indirect Objects

▶ **An indirect object tells *to what* or *whom* or *for what* or *whom* an action is done.** Verbs that often take indirect objects include *bring, give, hand, lend, make, send, show, teach, tell,* and *write.*

Sue gave a ride. (gave to whom?)

TO WHOM?

Sue gave her sisters a ride.
         INDIRECT   DIRECT
         OBJECT   OBJECT

TO WHOM?

Sue gave them a ride.

If the preposition *to* or *for* appears in a sentence, the word that follows it is *not* an indirect object. It is the object of the preposition.

Martin's mother taught the rules of the road to him.
                              OBJECT OF PREPOSITION

Martin's mother taught him the rules of the road.
                    INDIRECT OBJECT

VERBS

Transitive and Intransitive Verbs

An action verb that has a direct object is called a **transitive verb.** A verb that does not have a direct object is called an **intransitive verb.**

Good drivers avoid accidents.

TRANSITIVE VERB ⬈ ⬉ DIRECT OBJECT

They stay alert.

⬉ INTRANSITIVE VERB (No object)

Sometimes an intransitive verb is followed by a word that looks like a direct object but is really an adverb. An adverb tells where, when, how, or to what extent; a direct object answers the question whom or what.

DRIVE WHAT?

Some people drive trucks.

TRANSITIVE VERB ⬈ ⬉ DIRECT OBJECT

DRIVE HOW?

Some people drive carelessly.

INTRANSITIVE VERB ⬈ ⬉ ADVERB

❷ Why It Matters in Writing

The correct use of direct objects will help you make it clear to your readers exactly who did what. Notice how the model below uses a direct object to show what the automobile provides.

> **PROFESSIONAL MODEL**
>
> Today the automobile provides convenient, relatively inexpensive, and enjoyable transportation for people from all walks of life.
>
> —*Understanding Science & Nature: Transportation*

VERB

DIRECT OBJECT

❸ Practice and Apply

A. CONCEPT CHECK: Action Verbs and Objects

Identify the action verbs in these sentences. Then write
15 complements and label them as direct or indirect objects.
Identify each as a direct object or an indirect object.

The First Accidents

1. Experience tells us the risks of different vehicles.
2. In 1769 Nicolas-Joseph Cugnot showed the world the
first automobile.
3. His vehicle had three wheels.
4. Steam power gave the vehicle a speed of about three
miles an hour.
5. The auto had difficulties, however.
6. This fact gave Cugnot another place in history.
7. His car hit a wall in the world's first car accident.
8. In 1865 Pierre Lallemont made a test of his bicycle in
Connecticut.
9. He hadn't given it brakes.
10. He hit a surprised team of horses in the first bike
accident ever.

➡ For a SELF-CHECK and more practice, see the EXERCISE BANK, p. 541.

B. REVISING: Finding Direct Objects

Read the paragraph below. From the list of words at the top,
select a direct object to fill each blank.

passengers, rumble seats, luggage, seat, name

Rumble Seats

   In the 1930s many cars had no back ___**(1)**___ . A
rider unfolded the ___**(2)**___ at the rear of the car.
A rumble seat held only one
or two ___**(3)**___ . Sometimes
people carried ___**(4)**___ in
a rumble seat. The bumpy
ride in these little seats
explains the ___**(5)**___ .

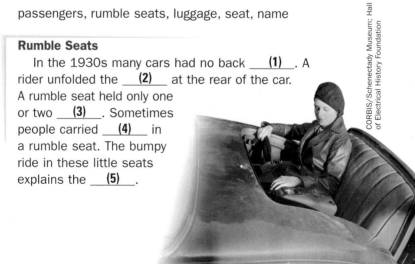

Linking Verbs and Predicate Words

LESSON 3

❶ Here's the Idea

The complement that a linking verb connects its subject to is called a **subject complement**. The subject complement identifies or describes the subject. Some common linking verbs are *is, feel, seem,* and *look.*

IDENTIFIES

Barnstormers were **stunt** **pilots in the 1910s and 1920s.**
SUBJECT   VERB   SUBJECT COMPLEMENT

DESCRIBES

Their job looked dangerous.
SUBJECT   VERB   SUBJECT COMPLEMENT

Predicate Nouns and Predicate Adjectives

A subject complement can be a **predicate noun** or a **predicate adjective.**

▶ **A predicate noun is a noun that follows a linking verb and identifies, renames, or defines the subject.**

IDENTIFIES

Harriet Quimby was **a drama** critic.
SUBJECT   VERB   PREDICATE NOUN

She became **a stunt** pilot **in 1911.**

▶ **A predicate adjective is an adjective that follows a linking verb and modifies the subject.**

MODIFIES

Quimby was natural **at the controls.**
SUBJECT   VERB   PREDICATE ADJECTIVE

She felt happy **in the air.**

CHAPTER 4

❷ Why It Matters in Writing

BLACK HERITAGE

USA
32
BESSIE COLEMAN

You can use a predicate noun to tell more about your subject. Notice how the predicate nouns add information about the subjects.

Bessie Coleman was an African-American pilot who broke barriers of racial prejudice. She once said "The air is the only place free from prejudices."

❸ Practice and Apply

VERBS

CONCEPT CHECK: Linking Verbs and Predicate Words

Identify each linking verb, predicate noun, and predicate adjective in the sentences below.

A Flying First
1. The first African-American woman pilot was a Texan.
2. Her name was Bessie Coleman.
3. She became a pilot in 1921.
4. Coleman seemed an unlikely candidate.
5. She was a poor girl from Texas.
6. World War I pilots became her heroes.
7. American flying schools were too biased to let her in.
8. She seemed more welcome in France.
9. Coleman became an expert at stunt flying and parachuting.
10. Her goal became equality in the air.

➡ For a SELF-CHECK and more practice, see the EXERCISE BANK, p. 541.

Principal Parts of Verbs

❶ Here's the Idea

▶ **Every verb has four basic forms called its principal parts: the present, the present participle, the past, and the past participle.** These principal parts are used to make all of the forms and tenses of the verb. Here are some examples.

We live in a mobile society.
PRESENT

People are traveling more all the time.
PRESENT PARTICIPLE

Automobiles lent travelers more freedom.
PAST

Drivers have enjoyed this freedom for years.
PAST PARTICIPLE

The Four Principal Parts of a Verb			
Present	**Present Participle**	**Past**	**Past Participle**
move	(is) mov**ing**	mov**ed**	(has) mov**ed**
travel	(is) travel**ing**	travel**ed**	(has) travel**ed**

Notice that helping verbs are used with the present participle and the past participle.

Regular Verbs

There are two kinds of verbs: regular and irregular.

▶ **A regular verb is a verb whose past and past participle are formed by adding -ed or -d to the present.** The present participle is formed by adding -ing to the present.

Present	**Present Participle**	**Past**	**Past Participle**
walk	(is) walk + **ing**	walk + **ed**	(has) walk + **ed**

You will learn about irregular verbs in the next lesson.

CHAPTER 4

❷ Why It Matters in Writing

The principal parts allow you to form verbs that show changes in time. In the news report below, notice how the writer uses the past and the present to show a shift in time.

> **PROFESSIONAL MODEL**
>
> Yesterday's Auto Expo showcased all the new cars plus some futuristic models. The sports models remain the most popular exhibit at the car show.

PAST

PRESENT

❸ Practice and Apply

CONCEPT CHECK: Principal Parts of Verbs

For each underlined verb in the paragraph below, name the principal part.

Gas, Food, Lodging

Henry Ford Museum in Dearborn, Michigan, **(1)** has showcased transportation since its early stages. For years, its exhibit "Automobile in American Life" **(2)** has appealed to visitors. The exhibit **(3)** started with more than 100 historic cars. The 15-millionth Model T **(4)** stands there. The exhibit **(5)** features a 1946 diner. Jukeboxes in the diner **(6)** are playing old songs. The exhibit also **(7)** shows a 1960s motel room. The details of a camper's cabin **(8)** make it special. Plastic ants **(9)** are crawling across the bureau. An open suitcase **(10)** is sitting on a rumpled bed.

➡ **For a SELF-CHECK and more practice, see the EXERCISE BANK, p. 542.**

Irregular Verbs

LESSON 5

❶ Here's the Idea

▶ **Irregular verbs are verbs whose past and past participle forms are not made by adding -ed or -d to the present.**

The following chart shows you how to form the past and past participle forms of many irregular verbs.

Common Irregular Verbs			
	Present	**Past**	**Past Participle**
Group 1 The forms of the present, past, and past participle are all the same.	burst cut hit hurt let put set split spread	burst cut hit hurt let put set split spread	(has) burst (has) cut (has) hit (has) hurt (has) let (has) put (has) set (has) split (has) spread
Group 2 The forms of the past and the past participle are the same.	bring buy catch dig feel flee have keep lay lead leave lose make say sell sit sleep teach think win wind	brought bought caught dug felt fled had kept laid led left lost made said sold sat slept taught thought won wound	(has) brought (has) bought (has) caught (has) dug (has) felt (has) fled (has) had (has) kept (has) laid (has) led (has) left (has) lost (has) made (has) said (has) sold (has) sat (has) slept (has) taught (has) thought (has) won (has) wound

Common Irregular Verbs *(continued)*

	Present	Past	Past Participle
Group 3 The past participle is formed by adding *-n* or *-en* to the past.	**bite** break choose lie speak steal tear wear	**bit** broke chose lay spoke stole tore wore	(has) **bitten or bit** (has) broken (has) chosen (has) lain (has) spoken (has) stolen (has) torn (has) worn
Group 4 The past participle is formed from the present, often by adding *-n* or *-en*.	**blow** do drive eat fall give go know ride rise see take throw write	**blew** did drove ate fell gave went knew rode rose saw took threw wrote	(has) **blown** (has) done (has) driven (has) eaten (has) fallen (has) given (has) gone (has) known (has) ridden (has) risen (has) seen (has) taken (has) thrown (has) written
Group 5 The last vowel changes from *i* in the present to *a* in the past and to *u* in the past participle.	**begin** drink ring shrink sing sink swim	**began** drank rang shrank sang sank swam	(has) **begun** (has) drunk (has) rung (has) shrunk (has) sung (has) sunk (has) swum

The Irregular Verb *Be*

	Present	Past	Past Participle
The past and past participle do not follow any pattern.	**am, are, is**	**was, were**	(has) **been**

❷ Why It Matters in Writing

Writers must use the correct irregular verb forms to make their writing sound right. The best way to avoid mistakes is to memorize the principal parts of the most common irregular verbs. Notice the irregular forms used in this pilot's account of her first transatlantic flight.

LITERARY MODEL

I **brought** Harmony down to 7,000 feet, and then 5,000 feet, but the air **was** thick with clouds. I **came** down to 3,000 feet, then 2,000 feet, then 1,000 feet. Still there **were** clouds—and a real danger of crashing.

—Vicki Van Meter with Dan Gutman, adapted from *Taking Flight, My Story*

❸ Practice and Apply

CONCEPT CHECK: Irregular Verbs

In the sentences below, choose the correct forms of the verbs in parentheses.

Moving Through History
1. Transportation (beginned, began) before civilization.
2. For centuries, people walked and (runned, ran) everywhere.
3. They first (rode, rided) in dugout canoes and reed boats nearly 10,000 years ago.
4. They (letted, let) animals carry their loads by 3000 B.C.
5. They (drived, drove) chariots with solid wheels by 2500 B.C.
6. They (dug, digged) canals for ship traffic soon thereafter.
7. Spoked wheels (maked, made) their appearance around 2000 B.C.
8. The Greeks (built, builded) light, fast ships around 400 B.C.
9. The Roman Empire (saw, seen) advances in road building.
10. In A.D. 80, Roman gladiators in the Colosseum (rose, raised) to the arena on elevator-like lifting platforms.

➡ For a SELF-CHECK and more practice, see the EXERCISE BANK, p. 542.

Simple Tenses

❶ Here's the Idea

▶ **A tense is a verb form that shows the time of an action or condition.** Verbs have three **simple tenses:** the present, the past, and the future.

Understanding Simple Tenses

Simple Tenses

One biker pedals faster than anyone else.	The present tense shows an action or condition that occurs now.
She sped past the pack 50 feet ago.	The past tense shows an action or condition that was completed in the past.
Soon she will cross the finish line alone.	The future tense shows an action or condition that will occur in the future.

A **progressive form** of a tense expresses an action or condition in progress.

Progressive Forms

The crowd is cheering.	Present Progressive
The winner's parents were holding their breath.	Past Progressive
They will be celebrating later.	Future Progressive

Forming Simple Tenses

The present tense of a verb is the present principal part. The past tense is the past principal part. To form the future tense, add *will* to the present principal part.

Forming Simple Tenses

	Singular	Plural
Present (present principal part)	I skate you skate he, she, it skates	we skate you skate they skate
Past (present part + *ed/d*)	I skated you skated he, she, it skated	we skated you skated they skated
Future (*will* + present part)	I will skate you will skate he, she, it will skate	we will skate you will skate they will skate

To make the progressive form of one of these tenses, add the present, past, or future form of *be* to the present participle.

Present Progressive: **I am skating.**

Past Progressive: **I was skating.**

Future Progressive: **I will be skating.**

❷ Why It Matters in Writing

When you are stating a sequence of events, change tenses to show clearly when things happen in relation to each other. Notice how this student has revised the model to change from past to present to future tense.

STUDENT MODEL

Yesterday I ~~ride~~ *rode* my bike to my friend Lynn's house. I often walk to her house on weekends. She lives two miles away. Next Saturday, we *will* bike together along the lakefront.

❸ Practice and Apply

A. CONCEPT CHECK: Simple Tenses

Identify the tense of each underlined verb below by labeling it *Present, Past,* or *Future.*

Move Over, Superman

1. Long ago, people <u>walked</u> everywhere.
2. They <u>covered</u> three or four miles an hour on foot.
3. Later, people <u>rode</u> horses.
4. They <u>traveled</u> up to 30 miles in an hour.
5. Now most adults <u>drive</u> everywhere.
6. Many other adults as well as most kids <u>bike</u> around town.
7. In the future, <u>will</u> people <u>travel</u> on high-speed monorails?
8. An early monorail <u>carried</u> people in Lyons, France, in 1872.
9. Maybe we <u>will fly</u> through the airways in vehicles like cars in the future.
10. In any case, we <u>will find</u> other ways for faster, more efficient travel.

➜ **For a SELF-CHECK and more practice, see the EXERCISE BANK, p. 542.**

B. REVISING: Correcting Simple Tenses

Revise the following paragraph by correcting the verb tenses.

Rocket Belts

In A.D. 1280, the Syrian writer al-Hasan al-Rammah **(1)** <u>will give</u> instructions for making rockets. In the 1960s the U.S. Army **(2)** <u>tests</u> rocket belts. They **(3)** <u>will carry</u> a soldier 360 feet forward in each hop. Some experts say that someday we **(4)** <u>saw</u> rocket belts in wide use. In the future, some people **(5)** <u>travel</u> only in virtual reality through their computers.

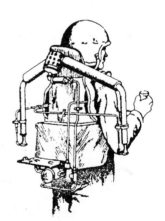

🗀 **Working Portfolio:** Find your **Write Away** from page 86 or a sample of your most recent work. Identify any errors in using simple tenses and correct them.

Perfect Tenses

❶ Here's the Idea

Understanding Perfect Tenses

The **present perfect tense** places an action or condition in a stretch of time leading up to the present.

Hot-air balloons have existed for 300 years.	Balloons existed in the past; they still exist.

The **past perfect tense** places a past action or condition before another past action or condition.

After scientists had used weather balloons for years, people discovered them for sport.	Had used is farther back in the past than discovered.

The **future perfect tense** places a future action or condition before another future action or condition.

However, many more people will have tried the sport before it becomes ordinary.	Will have tried will occur before it becomes ordinary.

This balloon has finished first.

This balloon will have finished before dark.

Forming Perfect Tenses

To form the present perfect, past perfect, and future perfect tenses, add *has, had, have,* or *will have* to a past participle of the verb.

Forming Perfect Tenses		
	Singular	**Plural**
Present perfect (*has* or *have* + past participle)	I have floated you have floated he, she, it has floated	we have floated you have floated they have floated
Past perfect (*had* + past participle)	I had floated you had floated he, she, it had floated	we had floated you had floated they had floated
Future perfect (*will* + *have* + past participle)	I will have floated you will have floated he, she, it will have floated	we will have floated you will have floated they will have floated

In a perfect form, the tense of the helping verb *have* shows the verb's tense.

We often have seen balloons in the Arizona skies.

❷ Why It Matters in Writing

When writing about an event, you can use perfect tenses to help your readers understand when the event occurred in relation to other events. In the model, notice the effective use of the past perfect tense in relation to the past tense.

> **LITERARY MODEL**
>
> By a miracle the two companions has escaped — **PAST PERFECT**
> the dangerous side streets and were in a more
> open space. It was the forum. They rested here — **PAST**
> awhile—how long he did not know.
>
> —Louis Untermeyer, "The Dog of Pompeii"

❸ Practice and Apply

A. CONCEPT CHECK: Perfect Tenses

Write the tense of each underlined verb: present perfect, past perfect, or future perfect.

Up, Up, and Away

1. People <u>had wanted</u> flight for hundreds of years, even though they were flightless.
2. The Montgolfier brothers <u>had launched</u> small balloons in 1782 before they sent up a balloon carrying a sheep, a duck, and a rooster in 1783.
3. Now pilots <u>have circled</u> the world nonstop in a balloon.
4. In March 2009 it <u>will have been</u> ten years since Brian Jones and Bertrand Piccard's historic flight.
5. Piccard's grandfather <u>had piloted</u> a balloon to a height of nearly 52,000 feet in 1931, almost 70 years before his grandson's feat.
6. Weather scientists <u>have learned</u> much about the earth's atmosphere from balloon flights.
7. They <u>have taken</u> air samples around the globe.
8. Plant scientists <u>have used</u> balloon rafts for exploration of the trees in the rain forest.
9. Their discoveries <u>have inspired</u> new medicines.
10. About 75,000 weather balloons <u>will have gone</u> up by the end of this year.

➜ For a SELF-CHECK and more practice, see the EXERCISE BANK, p. 543.

B. WRITING: Using Perfect Tenses

Rewrite each underlined verb in the tense named in parentheses.

Airships

By the time of the first airplane, airships <u>fly</u> (past perfect) for years. The first engine-powered balloon <u>take</u> (past perfect) to the air on September 24, 1852, over 50 years before the first successful engine-powered airplane flight. Engineers <u>build</u> (present perfect) different types of airships. Rigid airships <u>see</u> (present perfect) better days. Nonrigid airships, or blimps, <u>soar</u> (future perfect) over many sports events before their era ends.

Using Verb Tenses

❶ Here's the Idea

A good writer uses different verb tenses to show that events occur at different times. If you do not need to show a change of time, do not switch from one tense to another.

Writing About the Present

▶ **The present tenses show actions and conditions that occur in the present.** You can write about the present using the present tense, the present perfect tense, and the present progressive form.

Bullet trains are common in Japan. **They reach speeds of more than 130 miles per hour.**	The **present tense** places the action in the present.
Subways have carried commuters to work for decades. **They have given workers a fast trip to work.**	The **present perfect tense** places the actions in a period of time leading up to the present.
Traffic engineers are improving mass transportation. **They are making subways more pleasant.**	The **present progressive forms** show the actions or conditions in progress now.

VERBS

Writing About the Past

▶ **The past tenses show actions and conditions that came to an end in the past.** When you write about the past, you can use past verb forms to indicate the order in which events occurred.

> In the 1850s batteries propelled some tram railways.
>
> The first cable cars appeared in San Francisco in 1873.

The **past tense** shows action that began and was completed in the past.

> Until subways made commutes easy, workers had lived near their jobs.
>
> People had crowded Boston's streets before its subway opened.

The **past perfect tense** places the actions before other past actions.

> Officials were encouraging mass transit for years before highways got too crowded.
>
> They were preparing cities for worse traffic as the population grew.

The **past progressive forms** show that the actions in the past were in progress.

CHAPTER 4

Writing About the Future

▶ **The future tenses show actions and conditions that are yet to come.** By using the future verb forms, you can show how future events are related in time.

People always will need to get from home to work. **But many of them will commute fewer than five days a week.**	The **future tense** shows that the actions are yet to come.
Home offices will have become popular before subways are overloaded. **By the time subways are full, workers will have learned to "commute" by computer.**	The **future perfect tense** places the actions or conditions before other future actions or conditions.
More people will be working at home several days a week. **Telecommuters will be sending their work to the office by computer.**	The **future progressive forms** show that the action or condition in the future will be continuing.

❷ Why It Matters in Writing

When you are writing for social studies, use tenses correctly to show that you know the sequence of important events.

1880	**1900**	**Today**	**2025**
Steam provided power for trains.	Electricity provided power for subways.	Electromagnetic energy provides power for high-speed trains.	What kind of energy will move vehicles in the future?

③ Practice and Apply

A. CONCEPT CHECK: Using Verb Tenses

In each sentence, choose the correct verb form in parentheses.

It's Off to Work They Go

1. Commuters (have used, will use) mass transit since the 1800s.
2. The first electric subway (opens, opened) in London, England, in 1890.
3. In 1897 Boston (will become, became) the first U.S. city with a subway.
4. After subways (had run, ran) for a few decades, they improved.
5. They (ran, will run) faster and were better ventilated.
6. Now many cities (had enjoyed, enjoy) computer-controlled trains.
7. These automatic commuter trains (carry, had carried) millions of people every day.
8. Bullet trains like those in Japan now (have traveled, travel) around 160 miles per hour over long distances.
9. The next generation of subway trains (had moved, will move) without engines or rails.
10. These "maglev" trains (will float, were floating) on a magnetic cushion at 300 miles per hour.

Name the tense of each verb you chose in part A.

➡ **For a SELF-CHECK and more practice, see the EXERCISE BANK, p. 544.**

B. EDITING: Arranging Verb Tenses

The following sentences tell about a commuter train ride. List the sentence numbers in a logical order so that the tenses of the verbs make sense. (Hint: Read all the sentences before you begin.)

1. The train started before Mrs. Bakiloff had sat down.
2. "Are you hurt?" said Mrs. Bakiloff.
3. "Ouch! That's hot!" he exclaimed.
4. After the train had stopped, 12 passengers rushed up the train steps to get the best seats.
5. She fell toward Mr. Indigo, spilling her coffee.

Troublesome Verb Pairs

❶ Here's the Idea

Some pairs of verbs seem similar, but are actually different words with different meanings. Troublesome verb pairs include *lie* and *lay*, *rise* and *raise*, *sit* and *set*, and *learn* and *teach*.

Lie and *Lay*

Lie means "to recline." It does not take an object.
Lay means "to put or place." It does take an object.

Pat lies on the floor with her model cars.

She lays a van on top of a carrier truck.

Lie and *Lay*		
Present	**Past**	**Past Participle**
lie Pat **lies** down.	lay Pat **lay** down.	lain Pat has **lain** down.
lay Pat **lays** the car down.	laid Pat **laid** the car down.	laid Pat has **laid** the car down.

Lie and *lay* are confusing because the present principal part of *lay* is the same as the past principal part of *lie*.

Rise and *Raise*

Rise means "to move upward" or "to go up." It does not take an object. *Raise* means "to lift up." It usually takes an object.

Helicopters rise above the trees.

The pilot raises the flaps on the airplane's wings.

Rise and *Raise*		
Present	**Past**	**Past Participle**
rise The plane **rises**.	rose The plane **rose**.	risen The plane has **risen**.
raise Jo **raises** the car's hood.	raised Jo **raised** the hood.	raised Jo has **raised** the hood.

VERBS

Sit and Set

Sit means "to be seated." It does not take an object.

Set means "to put or place." It does take an object.

Jeff sits next to the flat tire.

He sets the lug wrench on the ground.

Sit and Set

Present	Past	Past Participle
sit Let's sit up front.	sat We sat up front.	sat We have sat up front.
set Bob sets down the keys.	set Bob set down the keys.	set Bob has set down the keys.

Learn and Teach

Learn means "to gain knowledge or skill."

Teach means "to instruct" or "to help someone learn."

Sam learned to skateboard.

Leisha taught Sam to skateboard.

Learn and Teach

Present	Past	Past Participle
learn Maria learns to ski.	learned Maria learned to ski.	learned Maria has learned to ski.
teach Mr. Lu teaches math.	taught Mr. Lu taught math.	taught Mr. Lu has taught math.

❷ Practice and Apply

A. CONCEPT CHECK: Troublesome Verb Pairs

Choose the correct word in parentheses in each of the following sentences.

Going Up?

1. The origin of modern elevators (lies, lays) in the invention of skyscrapers.
2. Only elevators could (raise, rise) to the upper floors.
3. Engineers (learned, taught) how to build hydraulic elevators.
4. These elevators (raised, rose) only freight, not people.
5. Workers (sat, set) the goods on the elevator floor and sent them up or down.
6. People were afraid to (sit, set) in boxes held up only by ropes.
7. Then Elisha Graves Otis (lay, laid) their fears to rest.
8. Otis (learned, taught) builders how to make elevators safe.
9. In 1857 he installed the world's first passenger elevator, which (rose, raised) five stories at 40 feet per minute.
10. For many years, elevators had cushioned places where riders (sat, set).

➔ For a SELF-CHECK and more practice, see the EXERCISE BANK, p. 544.

B. PROOFREADING: What Do They Mean?

List the five verbs that are used incorrectly in the following paragraph. Then change them to the correct verb forms.

Escalator Up

In St. Petersburg, Russia, the subway lays far underground. Passengers set in subway trains. When they get out, an escalator rises the passengers 195 feet up. As they raise, they may be distracted sometimes. But they teach quickly to pay attention when they step off the escalator at the top.

Grammar in Physical Education

Using Action Verbs to Describe Motion

Whether you watch the playoffs on TV, read the sports page, or learn how to play a sport in gym class, you need verbs to express what is happening. Verbs explain physical movement, tell what something is, or link ideas. What verbs might you use to describe the following cheerleading jumps?

J-U-M-P!

Split

Herky

Full "C"

Pike

Bambi

Banana

Practice and Apply

A. USING VERBS IN INSTRUCTIONS

Hooray! You got through tryouts and made the cheerleading squad. There's only one hitch—the coach's handout of basic jumps does not have any written directions. Study the illustration on page 114. Then write five steps explaining how to do one of these jumps. Use verbs from the list below that precisely describe the motion of your arms, legs, body, and head.

Action Verbs

raise	shake	straddle	thrust	leap
lower	land	clench	kick	squat
bend	hop	twist	split	crouch
straighten	cross	lift	drop	bounce
extend	lunge	push	point	vault
turn	twirl	roll	spin	swing
clasp	wrap	step	scoop	touch
pivot	move	jump	switch	lock
grab	place	stretch	stand	pull

B. USING VERBS IN A PLAY-BY-PLAY

With a partner, role-play two radio sports announcers. Do a play-by-play broadcast, or a running account of the action of a sports event as it unfolds, for the class. Narrate the action of one of the following sports highlights or another of your choice.

• a winning goal in a soccer match
• a home run in a tie softball game
• a record-breaking finish in a race

Use precise, vivid verbs that describe the action that takes place. Remember that you want your classmates to be able to picture in their minds what is happening.

VERBS

A. Revising Incorrect Verb Parts Find and correct the 10 incorrect verbs and verb forms in the following sentences. Watch out for irregular verbs and troublesome verb pairs.

Space: The Final Frontier

1. Fifty years ago, scientists will wonder whether humans could survive in outer space.
2. So they sended a dog named Laika up in a rocket in 1957.
3. Yuri Gagarin becomes the first person in space in 1961.
4. Just eight years later, astronauts are landing on the moon.
5. Today they had traveled in the space shuttle.
6. Unlike the older spacecraft, the shuttle was being reused again and again, like an airplane.
7. Some experts predict that we had a base on the moon in the 21st century.
8. Rockets will sit down tourists and businesspeople every day.
9. Some say we flew beyond our solar system someday.
10. Who knows where the human race has gone after that?

B. Using Tenses Using the ideas in the phrases listed below, write five sentences about the picture. Tell what happened before the scene shown in the picture, what is happening in it, and what might happen next.

puts on spacesuit

steps out into space

locks feet into foot holder on robot arm

rides robot arm to repair location

returns to the shuttle after fixing the problem

CHAPTER 4

Choose the best way to rewrite each underlined word or group of words.

> We now <u>are living</u> in the age of the automobile, but some people
> (1)
> <u>had worried</u> about that fact for a while. Cars give us freedom and
> (2)
> mobility, but they also <u>gave</u> us pollution, accidents, and road rage.
> (3)
> Before the automobile age, there <u>will be</u> almost no pavement in
> (4)
> the United States. Now we have 2.4 million miles of paved roads,
> which <u>costed</u> $200 million per day to keep up and add to. Some
> (5)
> futurists believe that as roads get more crowded, more people <u>have</u>
> (6)
> <u>turned</u> to mass transit. Even now, subways, trains, and buses
> <u>pollute</u> less per person than automobiles do. Other people predict
> (7)
> that communities <u>had become</u> more self-sufficient. After people
> (8)
> finally work near their homes, they <u>abandoned</u> their cars. The air
> (9)
> will be cleaner, and people <u>will have been</u> healthier.
> (10)

1. A. will live
   B. have lived
   C. will be living
   D. Correct as is

2. A. worry
   B. will worry
   C. have worried
   D. Correct as is

3. A. had given
   B. will give
   C. give
   D. Correct as is

4. A. had been
   B. are
   C. have been
   D. Correct as is

5. A. will cost
   B. cost
   C. will have costed
   D. Correct as is

6. A. turn
   B. had turned
   C. will turn
   D. Correct as is

7. A. had polluted
   B. will pollute
   C. polluted
   D. Correct as is

8. A. have become
   B. will become
   C. are becoming
   D. Correct as is

9. A. will abandon
   B. have abandoned
   C. are abandoning
   D. Correct as is

10. A. were
    B. have been
    C. will be
    D. Correct as is

Student Help Desk

Verbs at a Glance

A verb expresses action, condition, or state of being.

The two main kinds of verbs are **action verbs** and **linking verbs**.

Many people **drive** cars.
ACTION VERB

Cars **are** very handy.
LINKING VERB

Principal Parts of Regular Verbs

Present	Present Participle	Past	Past Participle
present	helping verb + present + *-ing*	present + *-ed* or *-d*	helping verb + present + *-ed* or *-d*
bike	**(is) biking**	**biked**	**(has) biked**
blast	(is) blasting	blasted	(has) blasted
dive	(is) diving	dived	(has) dived
float	(is) floating	floated	(has) floated
gallop	(is) galloping	galloped	(has) galloped
lift	(is) lifting	lifted	(has) lifted
move	(is) moving	moved	(has) moved
roll	(is) rolling	rolled	(has) rolled
travel	(is) traveling	traveled	(has) traveled
walk	(is) walking	walked	(has) walked

Keeping Tenses Straight | Travel Time

Tense	Definition	Example
Present	Action or condition occurring in the present	We **travel** everywhere.
Past	Action or condition occurring in the past	We **traveled** to Maine.
Future	Action or condition occurring in the future	We **will travel** to California next year.
Present perfect	Action or condition occurring in the period leading up to the present	We **have traveled** often.
Past perfect	Past action or condition coming before another past action or condition	We **had traveled** to Washington, D.C., before I turned 12.
Future perfect	Future action or condition coming before another future action or condition	We **will have traveled** to every state before I'm 21.

The Bottom Line

Checklist for Verb Usage

Have I . . .

____ used action verbs to express an action?

____ used linking verbs with predicate nouns and predicate adjectives?

____ used direct objects and indirect objects to answer the questions *whom, what, to whom,* and *to what*?

____ used the correct principal parts of irregular verbs?

____ used tenses correctly to express the time of actions and conditions?

____ used *sit* and *set, lie* and *lay, rise* and *raise,* and *learn* and *teach* correctly?

Adjectives and Adverbs

Dear Alice,

We hiked and camped. We saw flowers and climbed trails.

—Gomez

GRAND TETON NATIONAL PARK, WYOMING

Theme: The Great Outdoors

Tell Me More

What would you think if you received the postcard message above? It's kind of boring, isn't it? To give a better sense of what it was like to be there, the writer could add words describing what he saw and did.

> **We hiked *endlessly* and camped *late*. We saw *mountain* flowers and *carefully* climbed *steep* trails.**

The words writers use to describe people, places, and things are adjectives. The words they use to describe actions are adverbs. What adjectives and adverbs would you use to describe the picture on the postcard above?

Write Away: Wish You Were Here!

Create a postcard of one of your favorite outdoor places. On one side, describe the place and what you did there. Illustrate the other side with a picture of what you have described. Save your postcard in your 📁 **Working Portfolio.**

 **Grammar Coach**

Diagnostic Test: What Do You Know?

For each underlined item, choose the letter of the term that correctly identifies it.

Yellowstone National Park is the oldest <u>national</u> park in the
(1)
United States. Opened on March 1, 1872, <u>this</u> park attracts
(2)
millions of people each year. Visitors are <u>wild</u> about the hot
(3)
springs, mud pots, and geysers. Old Faithful is popular because it
erupts <u>more regularly</u> than other geysers in the park. One of the
(4)
<u>neatest</u> sights is the colorful rainbow in Grand Prismatic Spring
(5)
that is made by algae. Tourists also enjoy <u>the</u> animals, including
(6)
bison, elk, <u>large</u> bears, and bighorn sheep. Although fires <u>badly</u>
(7)   (8)
burned many acres of the park in 1988, this <u>American</u> treasure is
(9)
now <u>healthier</u> than ever. Yellowstone will continue to delight
(10)
generations of visitors.

---

1. A. adverb modifying *oldest*
   B. adverb modifying *is*
   C. adjective modifying *Idaho*
   D. adjective modifying *park*

2. A. pronoun used as adjective
   B. adverb
   C. proper adjective
   D. article

3. A. proper adjective
   B. demonstrative pronoun
   C. predicate adjective
   D. comparative adjective

4. A. comparative adverb
   B. superlative adverb
   C. comparative adjective
   D. superlative adjective

5. A. adjective modifying *one*
   B. adjective modifying *rainbow*
   C. adjective modifying *sights*
   D. adverb modifying *is*

6. A. proper adjective
   B. article
   C. demonstrative pronoun
   D. adverb

7. A. adjective modifying *bears*
   B. adverb modifying *including*
   C. adverb modifying *enjoy*
   D. adjective modifying *animals*

8. A. adverb telling how
   B. adverb telling when
   C. adverb telling where
   D. adjective telling how much

9. A. possessive adjective
   B. superlative adjective
   C. proper adjective
   D. noun used as adjective

10. A. comparative adjective
    B. comparative adverb
    C. superlative adverb
    D. superlative adjective

ADJ. & ADV.

What Is an Adjective?

❶ Here's the Idea

CHAPTER 5

▶ **An adjective is a word that modifies, or describes, a noun or a pronoun.**

MODIFIES

A **heavy** rainstorm soaked the campsite.

ADJECTIVE ↗   ↖ NOUN

Adjectives help you see, feel, taste, hear, and smell all the experiences you read about. Notice how adjectives make the second sentence in this pair more descriptive.

Coyotes startled the campers.

Noisy coyotes startled the sleepy campers.

Adjectives answer the questions *what kind, which one, how many,* and *how much.*

Adjectives			
What kind?	**green** backpack	**sturdy** tent	**spicy** stew
Which one or ones?	**last** hamburger	**third** hike	**every** lantern
How many or how much?	**two** flashlights	**many** insects	**little** moonlight

What kind?
waterproof floor
round roof

Which one or ones?
only door
each window

How many?
several stakes
two people

Articles

The most commonly used adjectives are the **articles** *a, an,* and *the. A* and *an* are used with singular nouns. Use *a* before a word beginning with a consonant sound.

a tent   **a candle**   **a lamp**

Use *an* before a word beginning with a vowel sound.

an axe   **an elephant**   **an unusual night**

The is an article that points to a particular person, place, thing, or idea. You can use *the* with singular or plural nouns.

The hiker tripped on the trail and dropped the cameras.

Use *the* when you want to refer to a specific person, place, thing, or idea. Use *a* and *an* when you want to be less specific.

Did the team leader bring a first-aid kit?
    ↑ ONE SPECIFIC LEADER   ↑ ANY FIRST-AID KIT

ADJ. & ADV.

Proper Adjectives

Many adjectives are formed from common nouns.

Nouns and Adjectives	
Noun	**Adjective**
rain	rainy
scene	scenic
beauty	beautiful

A proper adjective is formed from a proper noun. Proper adjectives are always capitalized.

Proper Nouns and Proper Adjectives	
Proper Noun	**Proper Adjective**
China	Chinese
Ireland	Irish
Mars	Martian

❷ Why It Matters in Writing

Adjectives provide important details about the nouns they describe. Imagine this description without adjectives.

> **LITERARY MODEL**
>
> Max came last. He was lugging a **new** knapsack that contained a **cast-iron** frying pan, a packet of hot dogs, and a box of **saltine** crackers—plus **two** bottles. **One** bottle was mustard, the other, **celery** soda. He also had a bag of Tootsie Rolls and a **shiny** hatchet. "To build a lean-to," he explained.
>
> —Avi, "Scout's Honor"

❸ Practice and Apply

CONCEPT CHECK: What Is an Adjective?

Write each adjective and the noun or pronoun it modifies. Do not include articles when you write the adjectives.

Urban Wilderness
1. Central Park is now an American landmark.
2. It was once a dirty swamp that was filled with ugly shacks and much garbage.
3. In 1858 there was a national competition for a plan to turn the spot into an attractive park.
4. People tried to imagine a place where New Yorkers could enjoy the great outdoors.
5. The park took the builders sixteen years to complete.
6. The landscape includes green meadows, lakes, ponds, woods, and beautiful gardens.
7. There is also an Egyptian statue.
8. Other attractions include a colorful carousel and a zoo.
9. The zoo features an African exhibit with birds and monkeys.
10. Many monuments are scattered throughout the park.

➜ For a SELF-CHECK and more practice, see the EXERCISE BANK, p. 545.

 Write the proper adjectives that appear in sentences 1, 7, and 9.

Predicate Adjectives

❶ Here's the Idea

▶ **A predicate adjective is an adjective that follows a linking verb and describes the verb's subject.** The linking verb connects the predicate adjective with the subject.

DESCRIBES

A volcanic eruption is violent.
SUBJECT ↗   ↖ LINKING VERB

DESCRIBES

It is explosive.

Predicate adjectives can follow linking verbs other than forms of *be*. Forms of *taste, smell, feel, look, become,* and *seem* are often used as linking verbs.

DESCRIBES

The lava looks thick.
LINKING VERB ↗   ↖ PREDICATE ADJECTIVE

DESCRIBES

Lava becomes hard when it cools.

For more about linking verbs, see page 94.

❷ Why It Matters in Writing

Writers often use predicate adjectives to tell more about a person's character, as in this author's description of her parents.

> **LITERARY MODEL**
>
> Both my parents had grown up poor, and they also knew what it was to be **lonely.** They cared deeply about other people and were always **ready** to lend a helping hand to anyone. Mama couldn't bear to think of her children ever being less than **kind** and **caring.**
> "Don't ever be **indifferent,**" she would say to Keiko and me. "That is the worst fault of all."
>
> —Yoshiko Uchida, "Oh Broom, Get to Work"

ADJ. & ADV.

❸ Practice and Apply

A. CONCEPT CHECK: Predicate Adjectives

Write each predicate adjective in these sentences, along with the noun or pronoun it modifies.

> **Look Out!**
> **1.** For more than 120 years, Mount St. Helens, a volcano in Washington, was inactive.
> **2.** Then the volcano became dangerous.
> **3.** In 1980 eruptions were responsible for widespread damage.
> **4.** The blasts were thunderous.
> **5.** After hot ash started fires, the air smelled smoky.
> **6.** The sky became very dark as ash fell like snow.
> **7.** Long after the eruption, pumice, a kind of volcanic rock, still felt hot.
> **8.** Following the blast, tall forests looked very flat.
> **9.** Thick, fast mudslides seemed deadly.
> **10.** The volcanic eruptions of Mount St. Helens were very destructive.

➡ For a **SELF-CHECK** and more practice, see the **EXERCISE BANK, p. 546.**

B. WRITING: Creating Riddles

On a piece of paper, write three sentences about yourself, using linking verbs and predicate adjectives. Underline each predicate adjective. Then fold the paper and put your sentences into a hat along with those of your classmates. Take turns drawing a piece of paper out of the hat. Try to guess the name of the author.

Example: I am <u>female</u> and very <u>tall</u>, and my hair is <u>red</u>. It is also extremely <u>long</u> and <u>curly</u>. To many people, I seem <u>quiet</u>, but often I feel <u>adventurous</u>.

In your ✉ **Working Portfolio,** find the postcard you wrote for the **Write Away** on page 120. Add or change predicate adjectives to make your description clearer.

Other Words Used as Adjectives

LESSON 3

❶ Here's the Idea

Many pronouns and nouns can be used as adjectives. They can modify nouns to make their meanings more specific.

Pronouns as Adjectives

Demonstrative Pronouns *This, that, these,* and *those* are demonstrative pronouns. They can be used as adjectives.

This canoe is made of wood and leather.

MODIFIES

These canoes are made of aluminum.

Possessive Pronouns *My, our, your, her, his, its,* and *their* are possessive pronouns. They are used as adjectives.

MODIFIES   MODIFIES

My skateboard is newer than your bicycle.

Indefinite Pronouns Indefinite pronouns such as *all, each, both, few, most,* and *some* can be used as adjectives.

MODIFIES

Most people in my family enjoy exploring caves.

MODIFIES

All members of my family enjoy picnicking.

Nouns as Adjectives

Like pronouns, nouns can be used as adjectives. In the expression "mountain climber," for example, the word *mountain* (normally a noun) modifies *climber*. Notice the nouns used as adjectives in the sentences below.

MODIFIES

Rock climbers practice indoors on winter nights.

MODIFIES   MODIFIES

They use a rock wall made from construction materials.

MODIFIES

Climbing an indoor rock wall

❷ Why It Matters in Writing

By using nouns as adjectives, a writer can pack a lot of important information into just a word or two. Notice what information the nouns that are used as adjectives add to the passage below.

LITERARY MODEL

In the same week, my brother made the **baseball** team of his junior high school, Father started taking driving lessons, and Mother discovered **rummage** sales. We soon got all the furniture we needed, plus a **dart** board and a 1,000-piece **jigsaw** puzzle (fourteen hours later, we discovered that it was a 999-piece **jigsaw** puzzle).
—Lensey Namioka, "The All-American Slurp"

❸ Practice and Apply

A. CONCEPT CHECK: Other Words Used as Adjectives

Write each noun or pronoun that is used as an adjective in these sentences. Then write the word it modifies.

Climb Every Mountain

1. Most climbers climb mountain formations.
2. "Urban climbers" scale city buildings.
3. Many climbers participate in skill training.
4. Gyms allow these people to train on rock walls.
5. My friends prefer to test their skills on mountains.
6. Some climbs occur on glacier ice.
7. Those climbers want to enjoy a mountaintop view.
8. Their equipment includes this harness and that helmet.
9. Our goal is to learn correct body positions.
10. Each skill involves muscle strength and concentration.

➡ For a SELF-CHECK and more practice, see the EXERCISE BANK, p. 546.

B. REVISING: Adding Nouns as Adjectives

Make this message more detailed by adding nouns from the list below to modify each of the nouns in boldface type.

mud   steel   neighborhood   park   safety

> Dear Tammi,
>
> You won't believe what happened today! I was roller-blading on a **sidewalk**, and a **kid** on a **skateboard** lost his balance and fell. The skateboard flew into my **helmet,** and I fell into a **puddle.**

C. WRITING: Creating a Safety Poster

Using the information below, create a safety poster about bicycle helmets. Include adjectives to show how helmets can protect bike riders from injury.

Liner absorbs shock of fall

Outer shell protects skull from impact

Chin strap holds helmet firmly in place

ADJ. & ADV.

What Is an Adverb?

❶ Here's the Idea

▶ **An adverb is a word that modifies a verb, an adjective, or another adverb.**

MODIFIES

Explorers eagerly chase adventure.
  ADVERB   VERB

MODIFIES

Some explorers visit amazingly beautiful places.
  ADVERB   ADJECTIVE

MODIFIES

Others quite bravely explore the unknown—space.
  ADVERB ADVERB

Adverbs answer the questions *how, when, where,* or *to what extent.*

Adverbs	
How?	suddenly, carefully, sadly
When?	now, later, soon
Where?	there, up, ahead
To what extent?	completely, totally, fully

Adverbs can appear in different positions in sentences.

The tourists boarded the bus eagerly. (after verb)

The tourists eagerly boarded the bus. (before verb)

Eagerly, the tourists boarded the bus. (at beginning)

Adverbs that modify adjectives or other adverbs usually come directly before the words they modify. They usually answer the question *to what extent.*

MODIFIES

Marco Polo told really wonderful tales of China.

People were very eager to hear his stories.

MODIFIES

They nearly always hung on every word.

MODIFIES

Forming Adverbs

Many adverbs are formed by adding the suffix *-ly* to adjectives. Sometimes a base word's spelling changes when *-ly* is added.

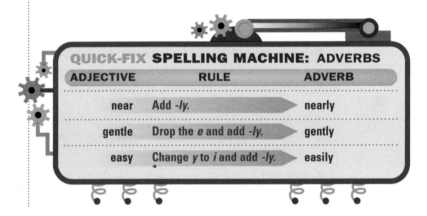

QUICK-FIX **SPELLING MACHINE:** ADVERBS

ADJECTIVE	RULE	ADVERB
near	Add *-ly.*	nearly
gentle	Drop the *e* and add *-ly.*	gently
easy	Change *y* to *i* and add *-ly.*	easily

❷ Why It Matters in Writing

Use adverbs to record what you observe in science. Notice how one scientist used adverbs to record details about the behavior of spiders.

> PROFESSIONAL MODEL
>
> The spider can remain **perfectly** still for hours, waiting for its prey. When an insect does **accidentally** stumble into the web, the spider can move **swiftly,** injecting poison **rapidly** into its prey and wrapping it **tightly** in spider silk.

❸ Practice and Apply

A. CONCEPT CHECK: What Is an Adverb?

Write each adverb and the word it modifies. Identify the modified word as a verb, an adjective, or an adverb. There may be more than one adverb in a sentence.

The Wild West

1. Thomas Jefferson became very curious about the West after he took office as president.
2. He studied maps and explorers' journals quite often.
3. He soon asked Meriwether Lewis to explore the new territory of the 1803 Louisiana Purchase.
4. In preparation for the trip, Lewis quickly learned many skills.
5. On May 14, 1804, Lewis, William Clark, and a team of explorers headed west.
6. Team members gathered truly valuable information.
7. Their remarkably complete journals told what they saw.
8. Sometimes, the explorers sent specimens, such as live prairie dogs, to President Jefferson.
9. Finally, in 1806, the difficult 8,000-mile expedition ended.
10. Because the journey was so completely successful, Lewis and Clark became famous.

➡ **For a SELF-CHECK and more practice, see the EXERCISE BANK, p. 547.**

Write the adjectives from which the adverbs in sentences 4, 6, 7, 9, and 10 are formed.

B. WRITING: Adding Adverbs

Choose one adverb from the list to fill in each of the blanks.

carefully   soon   rather   often   upward

Starstruck

As a young child, Maria Mitchell gazed **(1)** (<u>answers where</u>) at the sky. **(2)** (<u>answers when</u>), she visited her father's observatory in Nantucket, Massachusetts. At the age of 12, she **(3)** (<u>answers how</u>) recorded information about an eclipse. On October 1, 1847, the grown-up Mitchell, an astronomer, made a **(4)** (<u>answers to what extent</u>) rare discovery—a new comet. She was **(5)** (<u>answers when</u>) elected to the American Academy of Arts and Sciences, the first woman to be so honored.

Making Comparisons

❶ Here's the Idea

Adjectives and adverbs can be used to compare people or things. Special forms of these words are used to make comparisons.

▶ **Use the comparative form of an adjective or adverb when you compare a person or thing with one other person or thing.**

Mt. Rainier is higher than Mt. Hood.

Mountain climbing is more dangerous than skydiving.

▶ **Use the superlative form of an adjective or adverb when you compare someone or something with more than one other person or thing.**

Mt. Everest is the highest of the three mountains.

I think Mt. Fuji is the most beautiful mountain of all.

Regular Forms of Comparison

For most one-syllable modifiers, add -er to form the comparative. Add -est to form the superlative.

One-Syllable Modifiers			
	Base Form	**Comparative**	**Superlative**
Adjectives	thin brave	thinner braver	thinnest bravest
Adverbs	slow soon	slower sooner	slowest soonest

You can also add -er and -est to some two-syllable adjectives. With others, and with two-syllable adverbs, use *more* and *most*.

Two-Syllable Modifiers			
	Base Form	**Comparative**	**Superlative**
Adjectives	shallow awful	shallower **more** awful	shallowest **most** awful
Adverbs	calmly briskly	**more** calmly **more** briskly	**most** calmly **most** briskly

ADJ. & ADV.

With adjectives and adverbs having three or more syllables, use *more* and *most*.

Modifiers with More than Two Syllables

	Base Form	Comparative	Superlative
Adjectives	beautiful	**more** beautiful	**most** beautiful
	dangerous	**more** dangerous	**most** dangerous
Adverbs	gracefully	**more** gracefully	**most** gracefully
	dangerously	**more** dangerously	**most** dangerously

Use only one sign of comparison at a time. Don't use *more* and *-er* together or *most* and *-est* together.

INCORRECT: **That beach has the most whitest sand.**

CORRECT: **That beach has the whitest sand.**

Irregular Forms of Comparison

The comparative and superlative forms of some adjectives and adverbs are completely different words. You don't need to add *-er* or *-est* to an irregular comparison.

Irregular Modifiers

	Base Form	Comparative	Superlative
Adjectives	good	better	best
	bad	worse	worst
Adverbs	well	better	best
	much	more	most
	little	less	least

❷ Why It Matters in Writing

Comparative and superlative forms are used to compare and contrast things with each other.

> **STUDENT MODEL**
>
> Last year I thought math was the **most difficult** subject. This year I think English is **more difficult** than math.

❸ Practice and Apply

A. CONCEPT CHECK: Making Comparisons

Choose the correct comparative or superlative form to complete each sentence.

World's Eighth Natural Wonder

1. Australia's Great Barrier Reef is the (larger, largest) coral reef in the world.
2. The reef is also the (richer, richest) of all marine resources.
3. Biologists can (better, more better) study sea life near a reef than in open water.
4. The (biggest, most biggest) of all polyps, the animals that form a coral reef, are a foot in diameter.
5. Coral grows (better, best) of all in warm, shallow water.
6. During cold weather, vacationers visit the reef's northern islands (less, least) frequently than the southern ones.
7. A scuba dive is (more daring, most daring) than a glass-bottom-boat tour of the reef.
8. The Great Barrier Reef is (more fragile, most fragile) than a large rock formation would be.
9. The crown-of-thorns starfish is the reef's (deadlier, deadliest) enemy.
10. These starfish can devour polyps (more, most) quickly than the average starfish.

➡ For a SELF-CHECK and more practice, see the EXERCISE BANK, p. 547.

B. WRITING: Comparing and Contrasting

Study the three pictures of sharks. Write a paragraph in which you compare and contrast them. Use comparative and superlative forms in your writing.

Great white shark

Whale shark

Hammerhead shark

ADJ. & ADV.

LESSON 6 Adjective or Adverb?

❶ Here's the Idea

Some pairs of adjectives and adverbs are often confused.

Good and Well *Good* is always an adjective; it modifies a noun or pronoun. *Well* is usually an adverb, modifying a verb, an adverb, or an adjective.

MODIFIES

That was a good documentary about Mt. Everest.
ADJECTIVE   NOUN

MODIFIES

The filmmaker presented the information well.
         VERB   ADVERB

Well is an adjective when it refers to health.

MODIFIES

After the film, I didn't feel well.
    PRONOUN   ADJECTIVE

Real and Really *Real* is always an adjective; it modifies a noun or pronoun. *Really* is always an adverb; it modifies a verb, an adverb, or an adjective.

MODIFIES

She prefers real mountains to paintings of mountains.
ADJECTIVE   NOUN

MODIFIES

The Grand Canyon is really beautiful in the morning.
      ADVERB   ADJECTIVE

Bad and Badly *Bad* is always an adjective; it modifies a noun or pronoun. *Badly* is always an adverb; it modifies a verb, an adverb, or an adjective.

MODIFIES   MODIFIES

That wasn't a bad hike, even though we planned it badly.
    ADJECTIVE   NOUN   VERB   ADVERB

MODIFIES

I often feel bad about staying indoors so much.
 PRONOUN   ADJECTIVE

❷ Why It Matters in Writing

People make many mistakes using *good, real,* and *bad*. In your writing, check the word being modified to see if you need an adjective or an adverb.

Hiking at night is not a good idea if you can't see ~~good~~ *well* in

the dark. I had a ~~real~~ *really* scary experience once doing that. It was

a real nightmare. I saw so ~~bad~~ *badly* in the dark that I stumbled off

a hill and fell into a cactus patch.

❸ Practice and Apply

CONCEPT CHECK: Adjective or Adverb?

Choose the correct word in parentheses. Then identify it as an adjective or an adverb.

London's *Call of the Wild*
1. American author Jack London described nature (good, well).
2. Much of his fiction is based on (real, really) experiences.
3. In his teens, he had (real, really) adventures as a sailor.
4. In 1897 he was (real, really) curious about a gold rush.
5. In Canada's Yukon Territory, he lived in a tiny cabin and struggled to survive in (bad, badly) weather.
6. Unfortunately, London felt (bad, badly) because he had scurvy, a disease caused by a lack of vitamin C.
7. Although he never found gold, London discovered a (good, well) subject for his stories and novels.
8. His first Yukon tales were received (good, well).
9. London's novel, *The Call of the Wild*, is based on a (real, really) dog he had known in the Yukon.
10. In "To Build a Fire," London tells the story of a young man facing a (bad, badly) problem.

➡ **For a SELF-CHECK and more practice, see the EXERCISE BANK, p. 548.**

Avoiding Double Negatives

LESSON 7

❶ Here's the Idea

A **negative word** is a word that says "no." Contractions that end in *n't* are negative words. Remember, *n't* means *not*. A word like *can't* means "cannot." Some common negative words are listed below.

Common Negative Words			
barely	neither	nobody	nothing
hardly	never	none	nowhere

If two negative words are used together, the result is a **double negative.** Avoid double negatives in speaking and writing.

INCORRECT

I don't want no slackers on this hike.

CORRECT

I don't want any slackers on this hike.

I want no slackers on this hike.

❷ Why It Matters in Writing

Some writers accidentally create a double negative when they try to make a strong negative statement. However, a double negative makes a writer sound careless.

STUDENT MODEL

The largest cactus in North America is the saguaro. It
doesn't grow ~~nowhere~~ *anywhere* but in the deserts of southern

Arizona, southeastern California, and northwestern Mexico.
Saguaros ~~don't hardly need no~~ *need hardly any* water to survive. It almost

~~doesn't~~ never rain~~s~~ where saguaros live, but these plants can

store water in their stems for a long time.

❸ Practice and Apply

A. CONCEPT CHECK: Avoiding Double Negatives

Write the word in parentheses that correctly completes each sentence.

Beat the Heat

1. Desert dwellers live where there's barely (no, any) relief from high temperatures.
2. Many (don't have, have) no air conditioning.
3. They can't build with (nothing, anything) that gets too hot.
4. Some North Africans live underground in rock houses that don't (ever, never) get hot.
5. Adobe keeps houses cool but (can, can't) never be used in a damp climate.
6. In Syria, mud houses shaped like beehives may not be uncomfortable (either, neither).
7. Nobody (would, wouldn't) mind using solar-powered air conditioning to keep cool.
8. In Fiji, people who live in houses with thatched roofs (could, couldn't) hardly find a better design.
9. Houses that have shutters and tile floors stay cooler than those that don't have (none, any).
10. If you scarcely (ever, never) suffer from the heat, a desert home might be comfortable after all.

➡ For a SELF-CHECK and more practice, see the EXERCISE BANK, p. 549.

B. PROOFREADING: Eliminating Double Negatives

Find and correct five double negatives in the paragraph below. (There is more than one way to correct each double negative.)

Sand, Sand Everywhere

    Without sand, no one couldn't build sandcastles or walk on a beach. Sand is made of fine pieces of rock and minerals that aren't barely larger than clay or silt. In a desert, sand doesn't lie nowhere near water but covers the land. On a beach, sand isn't never always soft and white. For example, tourists visiting Hawaii can't hardly believe they are seeing black sand, which comes from volcanic lava.

Grammar in Literature

Using Adjectives and Adverbs

When you write about the great outdoors—or about any other topic—use adjectives and adverbs to make your descriptions vivid and enjoyable for readers. You can also use nouns and pronouns as adjectives. Notice the words Armstrong Sperry uses to describe a boy paddling a canoe in a tropical lagoon.

from
Ghost of the Lagoon
by Armstrong Sperry

A school of fish swept by like silver arrows. He saw scarlet rock cod with ruby eyes and the head of a conger eel peering out from a cavern in the coral. The boy thought suddenly of Tupa, ghost of the lagoon. On such a bright

day it was hard to believe in ghosts of any sort. The fierce sunlight drove away all thought of them. Perhaps ghosts were only old men's stories, anyway! ...

As the canoe drew away from shore, the boy saw the coral reef that, above all others, had always interested him. It was of white coral—a long slim shape that rose slightly above the surface of the water. It looked very much like a shark. There was a ridge on the back that the boy could pretend was a dorsal fin, while up near one end were two dark holes that looked like eyes!

ADJECTIVES

ADVERBS

© Cheryl Cooper, 1995.

140

Practice and Apply

ACROSS the CURRICULUM
LITERATURE

WRITING: Using Adjectives and Adverbs to Describe

Working with a partner, fill in the blanks in the following poem with an appropriate adjective or adverb. Save your poem in your ▭ **Working Portfolio.**

Because it was a *(adjective)* day,
And everything was *(adverb)* gray,
We were getting *(adverb)* *(adjective)*,
even though we're *(adverb)* lazy.

Just then all the lights went *(adverb)*
And everyone began to shout.
"Who is that?" "It's me; I'm *(adverb)*."
"I loudly shouted out in fear."

So, cautiously we crept outside
(Adverb), *(adverb)*, eyes open *(adverb)*.
And what we saw, did not seem *(adjective)*,
But it *(adverb)* was, we say to you.

(Adjective) penguins, an *(adjective)* duck,
(Adjective) socks, a hockey puck;
(Adjective) fish and *(adjective)* cats
(Adjective) balls and *(adjective)* bats.

Then the wind just died away.
The sun came *(adverb)*, a *(adjective)* ray.
We looked around, a *(adverb)* pale,
And went *(adverb)* to write this tale.

ADJ. & ADVERBS

A. Using Adjectives and Adverbs Read this passage. Then write the answers to the questions below it.

LITERARY MODEL

(1) "Have you dressed yet?" their grandmother called. **(2)** "Once a month in the sun and they must almost be forced," she muttered. **(3)** "Well, poor things, they've forgotten the warmth of the sun on their little bodies, what it is to play in the sea, yes...." **(4)** Mrs. Pavloff reached for her protective sun goggles that covered most of her face. **(5)** It screened all ultraviolet light from the once life-giving sun; now, it, the sun, scorched the Earth, killing whatever it touched.

—Alma Luz Villanueva, "The Sand Castle"

1. In sentence 1, what possessive pronoun is used as an adjective?
2. In sentence 2, what adverb tells *to what extent?*
3. In sentence 3, what two adjectives help you better picture the children in the story?
4. In sentence 4, what noun is used as an adjective?
5. In the last sentence, name one adjective.

B. Choosing the Right Modifier Choose the correct words from those given in parentheses.

Clever Coyotes
1. Coyotes don't have (no, any) problem with survival.
2. The coyote is (most adaptable, more adaptable) than many other animals in North America.
3. In the past, coyotes didn't live (nowhere, anywhere) but in the western part of North America and in Mexico.
4. Today, coyotes live (good, well) in many different places.
5. According to some wildlife experts, coyote populations are (more, most) widespread now than during the pioneer days.
6. First of all, coyotes hunt (real, really) efficiently.
7. If they can't find (no, any) mice, then they'll eat nearly anything, including bugs, fish, berries, watermelon, and garbage.
8. Also, their (deadlier, deadliest) enemy of all, the wolf, has vanished in many areas.
9. The coyote behaves (more cleverly, most cleverly) than people imagine.
10. Although coyotes in stories often act (bad, badly), real ones just fight to survive.

CHAPTER 5

For each underlined item, choose the letter of the term that correctly identifies it.

> Rachel Carson, a marine biologist, <u>certainly</u> influenced people to
> (1)
> protect the environment. In 1962 she published *Silent Spring,* a
> book about the <u>harmful</u> effects of pesticides. She agreed that <u>these</u>
> (2)   (3)
> chemicals killed insects and rodents. But they also <u>badly</u> poisoned
> (4)
> <u>our</u> food and wildlife. Carson's book woke up <u>ordinary</u> people.
> (5)   (6)
> Even President John F. Kennedy became very <u>anxious</u>. He called
> (7)
> for a <u>government</u> study of pesticide use. The pesticide DDT was
> (8)
> finally banned in 1972. *Silent Spring* helped make the world safer.
> An <u>American</u> Supreme Court judge said that the book was "the
> (9)
> <u>most important</u> chronicle of this century for the human race."
> (10)

ADJ. & ADV.

1. A. adverb modifying *influenced*
   B. adverb modifying *biologist*
   C. adverb modifying *Carson*
   D. adverb modifying *people*

2. A. adjective telling what kind
   B. adjective telling which one
   C. adjective telling how many
   D. adjective telling how much

3. A. adverb
   B. possessive pronoun
   C. pronoun used as adjective
   D. noun used as adjective

4. A. adverb modifying *poisoned*
   B. adverb modifying *food*
   C. adverb modifying *also*
   D. adverb modifying *killed*

5. A. demonstrative pronoun
   B. possessive pronoun
   C. possessive noun
   D. noun used as adjective

6. A. adjective modifying *book*
   B. adjective modifying *people*
   C. adverb modifying *woke*
   D. predicate adjective

7. A. proper adjective
   B. adverb
   C. predicate adjective
   D. article

8. A. proper adjective
   B. adverb
   C. noun used as adjective
   D. article

9. A. proper adjective
   B. comparative adverb
   C. predicate adjective
   D. article

10. A. comparative adverb
    B. superlative adverb
    C. comparative adjective
    D. superlative adjective

Student Help Desk

Adjectives and Adverbs at a Glance

Adjectives modify nouns and pronouns.

The wildlife walk was terrific. It was long, too.

Adverbs modify verbs, adjectives, and other adverbs.

The usually quiet tour guide chattered very excitedly.

Modifiers in Comparisons

	Comparative	Superlative
steep	steeper	steepest
leafy	leafier	leafiest
valuable	more valuable	most valuable
rugged	more rugged	most rugged
bravely	more bravely	most bravely
good	better	best
bad	worse	worst

Zoom Lens

Double Forms   Double Take

Double Negative	Fix
we can't hardly	we can hardly we can't
we don't never	we never we don't ever

Double Comparison	Fix
more better	better
most likeliest	most likely, likeliest

Field Guide

Modifier Problems

Good and Well

That's a good book.
↑ ADJECTIVE

I feel good about that.
↑ PREDICATE ADJECTIVE

Did you perform well?
ADVERB ↑

Does she look well?
PREDICATE ADJECTIVE ↑

Real and Really

That's a real problem.
↑ ADJECTIVE

He's really tired.
ADVERB ↗

Bad and Badly

What bad luck!
↑ ADJECTIVE

Do you feel bad?
↑ PREDICATE ADJECTIVE

I sing badly.
ADVERB ↗

ADJ. & ADV.

The Bottom Line

Checklist for Adjectives and Adverbs

Have I remembered to . . .

____ use adjectives to add detail to my nouns?

____ capitalize proper adjectives?

____ use adverbs to describe actions clearly?

____ use the correct comparative and superlative forms?

____ avoid using adjectives as adverbs?

____ avoid double negatives?

Adjectives and Adverbs **145**

Prepositions, Conjunctions, Interjections

Theme: Dragons
The Tale of a Dragon

"Oh-Oh" is right. The man in the photo might follow this interjection with a warning to his neighbors. He'll need plenty of prepositions to describe where the dragon is and some conjunctions to join his thoughts. In this chapter, you will learn how to use prepositions, conjunctions, and interjections. Let's hope you don't have to use them to warn your neighbors about any dragons.

Write Away: If Dragons Could Talk
If dragons could talk, this one might be saying, "I want you in my belly!" What might the man reply? Write a few sentences answering the dragon's threat. Tell the dragon what you will do or where you will hide. Express your fear or your bravery! Save the response in your 📁 **Working Portfolio.**

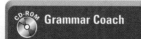 **Grammar Coach**

Choose the letter of the term that correctly identifies each underlined item.

A dragon is a monster of legends. Most dragons have the claws of a lion and the tail of a serpent. Their character can be kind
(1)   (2)
and generous or evil and greedy. In Western myths, a fierce fire-
(3)   (4)   (5)
breathing dragon is common, but Asian myths usually portray a
(6)
kindly dragon. Chinese dragons have five toes on each claw.
(7)
Dragons appear with different numbers of legs and with or
without wings. According to legend, you cannot always tell when
(8)
you will meet a dragon. Yikes! Look behind you!
(9)   (10)

1. A. conjunction
   B. preposition
   C. prepositional phrase
   D. interjection

2. A. preposition
   B. object of a preposition
   C. prepositional phrase
   D. conjunction

3. A. conjunction
   B. preposition
   C. prepositional phrase
   D. interjection

4. A. conjunction
   B. preposition
   C. object of a preposition
   D. interjection

5. A. conjunction
   B. preposition
   C. prepositional phrase
   D. interjection

6. A. conjunction
   B. preposition
   C. object of a preposition
   D. interjection

7. A. conjunction
   B. object of a preposition
   C. prepositional phrase
   D. interjection

8. A. conjunction
   B. preposition
   C. prepositional phrase
   D. object of a preposition

9. A. conjunction
   B. preposition
   C. prepositional phrase
   D. interjection

10. A. conjunction
    B. preposition
    C. prepositional phrase
    D. interjection

What Is a Preposition?

❶ Here's the Idea

▶ **A preposition is a word that shows a relationship between a noun or pronoun and some other word in the sentence.**

The knight on the dragon called for help.
             ↟ PREPOSITION

Here, the preposition *on* shows the relationship between *knight* and *dragon*. In the sentences below, notice how each preposition expresses a different relationship between the knight and the dragon.

The knight is under the dragon.

The knight is above the dragon.

The knight is beside the dragon.

The knight is in the dragon.

Common Prepositions				
about	at	despite	like	to
above	before	down	near	toward
across	behind	during	of	under
after	below	except	off	until
against	beneath	for	on	up
along	beside	from	out	with
among	between	in	over	within
around	beyond	inside	past	without
as	by	into	through	

Prepositional Phrases

▶ **A prepositional phrase consists of a preposition, its object, and any modifiers of the object.**
The object of the preposition is the noun or pronoun following the preposition.

PREPOSITIONAL PHRASE
A Chinese New Year dragon is a symbol of strength.
PREPOSITION ⬈ OBJECT ⬈

People drape silk over a bamboo dragon.
PREPOSITION ⬈ MODIFIER OBJECT

Fifty people walk under the enormous dragon.

Use *between* when the object of the preposition refers to two people or things. Use *among* when speaking of three or more.

The dragon weaved *between* two boys.

The dragon weaved *among* the crowd.

Preposition or Adverb?

Sometimes the same word can be used as a preposition or as an adverb. If the word has no object, then it is an adverb.

PREPOSITIONAL PHRASE
The bamboo dragon toppled over a curb.
PREPOSITION ⬈ OBJECT

The bamboo dragon toppled over.
ADVERB

For more on adverbs, see p. 130.

❷ Why It Matters in Writing

Writers often use prepositions to describe where characters and objects are located in relation to one another. Notice how the prepositions in this dialogue tell the location of the character, the doorstep, and the entrance.

> **LITERARY MODEL**
>
> **Bilbo** (*holding script off and reading it*). "...I am now sitting **on** the very doorstep **of** the secret entrance **to** the dragon's cave."
>
> —J. R. R. Tolkien, *The Hobbit*, dramatized by Patricia Gray

❸ Practice and Apply

A. CONCEPT CHECK: What Is a Preposition?

Write the preposition and its object for each sentence.

Dragon Tales

1. Dragons from different cultures have their own characteristics.
2. The Eastern female dragon holds a fan with her tail.
3. The Chinese show most dragons without wings.
4. Swallows are among the Chinese dragons' favorite foods.
5. In Chinese mythology, nine dragons keep the Kowloon waters safe from harm.
6. Japanese dragons have three toes on each claw.
7. Western dragons are usually associated with evil.
8. Many tales pit brave knights against fierce dragons.
9. Two batlike wings lift the dragon above its victim.
10. Some breeds of Western dragons can change their shapes.

➡ **For a SELF-CHECK and more practice, see the EXERCISE BANK, p. 550.**

B. WRITING: Using Prepositions

Think back to the response you wrote to the dragon in your **Write Away** on page 146. Write the dragon's answer to your response using five prepositions from the following list:

at, behind, below, by, for, in, into, off, on, out, to, up, with, without

Using Prepositional Phrases

LESSON 2

❶ Here's the Idea

A prepositional phrase is always related to another word in a sentence. It modifies the word in the same way an adjective or adverb would.

Adjective Phrases

▶ **An adjective phrase is a prepositional phrase that modifies a noun or a pronoun.** Like an adjective, a prepositional phrase can tell which one, how many, or what kind.

WHICH ONE?

The "dragon" in the water is really a lizard.
NOUN   ADJECTIVE PHRASE

WHAT KIND?

The Komodo dragon is a type of monitor lizard.

Adverb Phrases

▶ **An adverb phrase is a prepositional phrase that modifies a verb, an adjective, or an adverb.** Like an adverb, a prepositional phrase can tell where, when, how, why, or to what extent.

WHERE?

Desert lizards lie under the sand.
VERB   ADVERB PHRASE

HOW?

Their body temperatures are lower without sunlight.
ADJECTIVE

HOW?

This cooling method works well for a simple system.
ADVERB

HOT TIP

Several prepositional phrases can work together. Each phrase after the first often modifies the object of the phrase before it.

A flying dragon glides with flaps of skin like wings.

PREPOSITIONS

Placement of Prepositional Phrases

When you write, try to place each prepositional phrase as close as possible to the word it modifies. Otherwise, you may confuse—or unintentionally amuse—your readers.

CONFUSING

With fiery breath, we surprised a dragon.

(Who has fiery breath?)

CLEAR

We surprised a dragon with fiery breath.

(Now the reader knows who has fiery breath.)

❷ Why It Matters in Writing

When you write about science, you can use prepositional phrases to describe *which one* and *what kind*. Notice how the prepositional phrases in the model describe what kind of lizard.

> **PROFESSIONAL MODEL**
>
> The Komodo dragon is a lizard **of the species *Varanus komodoensis*.** It is a prehistoric relic **from an earlier era.**
>
> —Rudy J. Goldstein

What kind of lizard

What kind of relic

❸ Practice and Apply

A. CONCEPT CHECK: Using Prepositional Phrases

Write the prepositional phrase and the word it modifies for each of the following sentences.

The Largest Lizard
1. The Komodo dragon is the largest lizard in the world.
2. Komodos live on a few Indonesian islands.
3. The Komodo's yellow forked tongue, over a foot long, can taste the air.
4. Its saliva has bacteria with no known antidotes.
5. The Komodo's teeth are dangerous to everyone.
6. The Komodo's teeth can shred a large animal in 20 minutes.
7. The Komodo can run 12½ miles an hour, fast for its 300-pound weight.
8. The residents of Komodo Island call this creature the *ora.*
9. Villagers tell tall tales about the ora.
10. The ora does not interest poachers around the island.

➔ **For a SELF-CHECK and more practice, see the EXERCISE BANK, p. 550.**

B. PROOFREADING: What Kind? or Which One?

Choose the prepositional phrase that most likely belongs in the numbered blank in the paragraph below.

a. from an earlier era   **d.** in Indonesia

b. with picture maps   **e.** with iron jaws

c. about huge lizards

Touring Komodo Island
    We took a tour of Komodo Island ___(1)___. On the island, we found a tour guide ___(2)___. The guide told us a story ___(3)___ that live on Komodo Island. The Komodo dragons look like lizards ___(4)___. They are dangerous predators ___(5)___.

Conjunctions

❶ Here's the Idea

▶ **A conjunction is a word used to join words or groups of words.**

Joining Words and Groups of Words

Conjunctions often join words used in the same way. The words joined by a conjunction can be subjects, predicates, or any other kind of sentence parts.

SUBJECTS

Alligators and crocodiles live mainly in the water.

CONJUNCTION

OBJECTS

Crocodiles live in salt water or fresh water.

CONJUNCTION

Common Conjunctions			
and	but	or	nor

Use *and* to connect similar ideas. Use *but* to contrast ideas.

Crocodiles have a long jaw and sharp teeth.

(*And* connects two parts of a crocodile's mouth.)

A young crocodile is small but powerful.

(*But* contrasts this crocodile's small size with its great power.)

Use *or* and *nor* to show choices.

Some crocodiles can live in salt water or fresh water.

(*Or* connects the choices *salt water* and *fresh water*.)

Joining Whole Thoughts

Conjunctions also can join whole thoughts, such as two sentences that are closely related.

Crocodiles are aggressive. Alligators are passive.

Crocodiles are aggressive, and alligators are passive.
↑CONJUNCTION

(*And* joins two sentences about personality.)

The crocodile's snout is narrow. It has biting power.

The crocodile's snout is narrow, but it has biting power.
↑CONJUNCTION

Use a comma before the conjunction when joining two complete sentences. Do not use a comma when joining two subjects or two verbs.

Alligators can live in 65-degrees-Fahrenheit water, but crocodiles drown at that temperature.

In 65-degrees-Fahrenheit water, crocodiles sink and drown.

CONJUNCTIONS

❷ Why It Matters in Writing

When you are writing science material, the right conjunctions can help the reader know how features and habits relate to each other. Notice how the conjunctions in the model show the relationship between the newborn crocodile and its mother.

> **STUDENT MODEL**
>
> Newborn crocodiles float in water with their eyes **and** snouts above the surface. They swim alone, **but** their mother is always nearby. The young crocodiles must stay warm, **or** they will die.

And connects two similar features.

But joins two whole thoughts that contrast.

Or joins two whole thoughts that contrast.

❸ Practice and Apply

A. CONCEPT CHECK: Conjunctions

Write the conjunction in each sentence, along with the words or groups of words that it joins.

Crocodiles and Alligators

1. There are many ways to tell whether an animal is a crocodile or an alligator.
2. A crocodile's snout is pointy, and an alligator's snout is broad.
3. Both the upper and lower teeth show on the crocodile.
4. Crocodiles often lose their teeth, but they grow new ones.
5. Large crocodiles eat antelope and deer.
6. Cold weather may cause deformity or death to baby crocodiles.
7. The snout usually shows differences, but the Indian Mugger crocodile looks much like an alligator.
8. Alligators do not have an enlarged fourth tooth, nor do they need it.
9. Most crocodiles hunt at night, but hungry ones hunt any time.
10. Never go near an alligator, or you may be badly injured.

➡ **For a SELF-CHECK and more practice, see the EXERCISE BANK, p. 551.**

B. REVISING: Changing Conjunctions

Rewrite the conjunctions so that the following paragraph makes sense.

Crocodile Meals

(1) Newly hatched crocodiles feed on bugs like grasshoppers **but** beetles. **(2)** Some adult crocs eat mammals like deer **but** cattle. **(3)** Crocodile teeth are good for holding prey, **or** they are not so good at cutting it. **(4)** A good hunter, the crocodile blends into the background **but** stays completely still. **(5)** Suddenly, it pounces **but** surprises its prey.

LESSON 4 Interjections

❶ Here's the Idea

> **An interjection is a word or a phrase used to express emotion.**

Wow, there's a monitor lizard.

It's so big! **Awesome!**

> It can stand alone or be set off by a comma.

❷ Why It Matters in Writing

THE FAR SIDE by Gary Larson

Writers often use interjections to express strong emotions, such as anger, joy, concern, surprise, terror, and disgust. Read the cartoon, and figure out what emotion the dog is expressing.

> *Whoa* is an interjection.

❸ Practice and Apply

📁 **Working Portfolio:** Find your **Write Away** from page 146 or a sample of your most recent work. Add to your writing three interjections that express emotions. Use the interjections in the Student Help Desk on page 163 for ideas.

Grammar in Social Studies

Using Prepositions to Show Location

When you write about specific places for social studies, you can use prepositions along with maps to indicate direction and location. Study the map below. Then read the accompanying description of some of the famous places in San Francisco's Chinatown. Notice how prepositions and prepositional phrases help you picture what the area looks like and where different sites are located.

The entrance to Chinatown is guarded by a fabulous dragon in the Chinatown Gateway. As you enter from Bush Street, you'll walk under the dragon's coiled body and beautiful, decorated head. From the gateway, you stroll down Grant Street past the shops, restaurants, and gift stores on both sides of the street.

Practice and Apply

A. USING PREPOSITIONS   Answers in column.

Study this map of today's Chinatown. Then write answers to the questions that follow, using prepositions and prepositional phrases in each of your sentences.

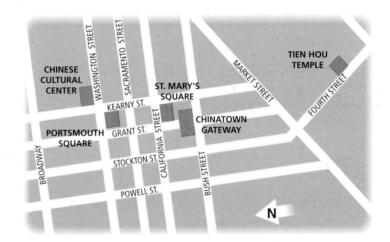

1. What route would you walk to go from the Chinatown Gateway to St. Mary's Square?
2. How would you get from St. Mary's Square to the Tien Hou Temple?
3. What is the best way to get from the Chinese Cultural Center to the Chinatown Gateway?

B. DRAWING A MAP   Answers in column.

Draw a map of a park, a playground, or a gymnasium in your community or school. Then write a brief description, similar to the one on page 158, to accompany your map. Circle the prepositions that you use to explain the location of different landmarks. Finally, share your work with classmates.

Mixed Review

A. **Prepositions, Conjunctions, Interjections** Choose the correct word in parentheses to complete each sentence. Then identify the word as a preposition, a conjunction, or an interjection.

Famous Dragons

1. Dragons are famous (under, around) the world.
2. The Eastern Spiritual Dragon—Shen-Lung—controls the wind (but, and) the rain.
3. The Chinese Yellow Dragon gave the knowledge of writing (to, from) Emperor Fu Hsi.
4. People fear (but, or) respect European dragons.
5. The Vikings put dragon figureheads (to, on) their ships.
6. They believed the dragons would give them keen sight (and, or) skill.
7. Beowulf confronted a dragon in the epic poem *Beowulf*. (Wow! Out!)
8. The dragon has become an official part (by, of) the prince of Wales's armor.
9. Sea serpents are dragons (except, from) the seas.
10. "Nessie," the Loch Ness Monster, is a sea serpent, (or, but) she lives in a lake in Scotland.

B. **Prepositional Phrases** Read the passage and answer the questions below it.

A Komodo Ritual

(1) Dominant male Komodo dragons often compete for a female. (2) This ritual between two male Komodo dragons is typical. (3) The dragons wrestle in upright postures. (4) They use their tails for support. (5) They grab each other with their forelegs. (6) The loser of the battle may lie on the ground or run away.

1. What is the prepositional phrase in sentence 1?
2. What is the prepositional phrase in sentence 2?
3. Why is *between* used instead of *among* in sentence 2?
4. What is the prepositional phrase in sentence 3?
5. What is the object of the preposition in sentence 3?
6. What is the prepositional phrase in sentence 4?
7. What is the object of the preposition in sentence 4?
8. What is the prepositional phrase in sentence 5?
9. What is the object of the preposition in sentence 5?
10. Which prepositional phrase shows location in sentence 6?

Choose the letter of the term that correctly identifies each underlined item.

Eastern dragons have one obvious detail that makes them different <u>from one another</u>. Some Chinese people believe that
(1)
stories about <u>dragons</u> began <u>in China</u>. They say the dragon has
(2)   (3)
always had five toes. A wanderer <u>by</u> nature, the dragon traveled
(4)
the earth. Legend has it that the farther it wandered <u>from</u> China,
(5)
the more toes it lost. By the time it got <u>to Korea</u>, it had only four
(6)
toes, <u>and</u> after it reached Japan it had three. <u>Oh-oh</u>, will it
(7)   (8)
eventually lose all its toes? According to the Japanese, the dragon began <u>in Japan</u>. Their story is the same <u>but</u> reversed. Their dragon
(9)   (10)
grew toes as it traveled.

---

1. A. conjunction
   B. preposition
   C. prepositional phrase
   D. interjection

2. A. object of a preposition
   B. prepositional phrase
   C. preposition
   D. interjection

3. A. conjunction
   B. preposition
   C. prepositional phrase
   D. object of a preposition

4. A. conjunction
   B. preposition
   C. prepositional phrase
   D. interjection

5. A. conjunction
   B. preposition
   C. prepositional phrase
   D. object of a preposition

6. A. conjunction
   B. preposition
   C. prepositional phrase
   D. object of a preposition

7. A. conjunction
   B. preposition
   C. prepositional phrase
   D. interjection

8. A. conjunction
   B. object of a preposition
   C. prepositional phrase
   D. interjection

9. A. conjunction
   B. preposition
   C. prepositional phrase
   D. interjection

10. A. conjunction
    B. preposition
    C. object of a preposition
    D. interjection

PREP. CONJ.

Student Help Desk

Prepositions, Conjunctions, Interjections at a Glance

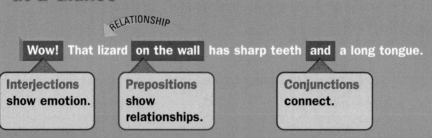

RELATIONSHIP

Wow! That lizard on the wall has sharp teeth and a long tongue.

Interjections show emotion.

Prepositions show relationships.

Conjunctions connect.

Prepositions, Conjunctions, Interjections Summary

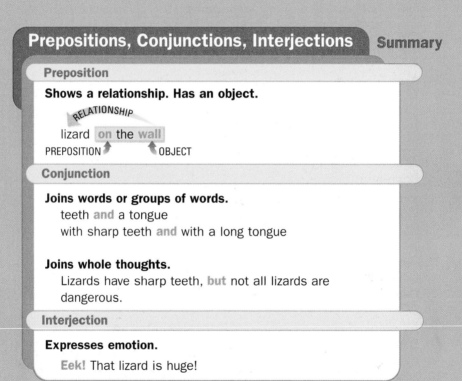

Preposition

Shows a relationship. Has an object.

RELATIONSHIP

lizard on the wall

PREPOSITION   OBJECT

Conjunction

Joins words or groups of words.
teeth **and** a tongue
with sharp teeth **and** with a long tongue

Joins whole thoughts.
Lizards have sharp teeth, **but** not all lizards are dangerous.

Interjection

Expresses emotion.
Eek! That lizard is huge!

Prepositional Phrases — What Do They Do?

Adjective Phrases

Modify a noun or a pronoun.

Tell *which one*	That little lizard **on the wall**
Tell *what kind*	is a member **of the reptile family.**

Adverb Phrases

Modify a verb, an adjective, or another adverb.

Tell *when*	**In April** my little brother
Tell *where*	bought an iguana **at a store.** I was
Tell *why*	happy **for my brother.** This pet works
Tell *how* or to what extent	perfectly **for his age.**

Interjections! — Just a Few Ideas . . .

To express concern	oh-oh, oh no, oops
To express disgust	yuck, ick, gross
To express joy	awesome, hooray, yea
To express surprise	wow, what, whoops
To draw attention to	hey

The Bottom Line

Checklist for Prepositions, Conjunctions, and Interjections

Have I . . .

____ used prepositions to show relationships between two things?

____ placed prepositional phrases close to the words they modify?

____ used conjunctions to connect words or groups of words?

____ used conjunctions to connect whole thoughts?

____ used interjections to express strong emotion?

Subject-Verb Agreement

He fly through the air with the greatest of ease!

Theme: Working Together

What's the Plan?

Timing means everything in a flying trapeze act. The flier and catcher must work carefully together. A mistake may lead to an embarrassing fall or even serious injury.

Agreement errors will not harm people, but they certainly can embarrass the writer. How would you correct the sentence on this photo? This chapter will help you learn to make subjects and verbs work together, or agree.

Write Away: Winning Teams

Think of some people you admire who need to work together to be successful. They can be a musical band, sports team, student organization, or some other group. Describe this group and explain what they are trying to do. Have they accomplished their goal? Save the writing in your ☐ **Working Portfolio.**

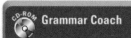

Grammar Coach

Choose the letter of the best revision for each underlined group of words.

What is a team? <u>Most of us immediately thinks</u> of sports. <u>Five</u>
<u>basketball players makes up one kind of team.</u> <u>Orchestras and</u>
<u>rock bands uses</u> teamwork. <u>At an accident scene are paramedics</u>
working as a team to save lives. <u>A team are not</u> just human
beings. <u>Either animals or humans makes</u> up a team. Animal teams
find missing people or assist disabled ones. <u>Many people works</u> as
a team to make a single movie. <u>Doesn't teams all unite</u> for a
common goal?

(1) Most of us immediately thinks
(2) Five basketball players makes up one kind of team.
(3) rock bands uses
(4) At an accident scene are paramedics
(5) A team are not
(6) Either animals or humans makes
(7) Many people works
(8) Doesn't teams all unite

1. A. Most of us immediately
      think
   B. Most of us immediately is
      thinking
   C. Most of us will immediately
      thinks
   D. Correct as is

2. A. Five basketball players is
      making up one kind of team.
   B. Five basketball players
      make up one kind of team.
   C. Five basketball players has
      made up one kind of team.
   D. Correct as is

3. A. Orchestras and rock bands
      has to use
   B. Orchestras and rock bands
      use
   C. Orchestras and rock bands
      used
   D. Correct as is

4. A. At an accident scene is
      paramedics
   B. At an accident scene has
      been paramedics

C. At an accident scene was
   paramedics
D. Correct as is

5. A. A team were not
   B. A team is not
   C. A team cannot
   D. Correct as is

6. A. Either animals or humans
      is making
   B. Either animals or humans
      does make
   C. Either animals or humans
      make
   D. Correct as is

7. A. Many people was working
   B. Many people has worked
   C. Many people work
   D. Correct as is

8. A. Doesn't teams all unites
   B. Don't teams all unite
   C. Don't teams all unites
   D. Correct as is

LESSON 1 — **Agreement in Number**

❶ Here's the Idea

▶ **A verb must agree with its subject in number.**

Number refers to whether a word is singular or plural. When a word refers to one person, place, thing, idea, action, or condition, it is singular. When a word refers to more than one, it is plural.

Singular and Plural Subjects

▶ **Singular subjects take singular verbs.**

AGREE — SINGULAR VERB
Teamwork is important in a jazz band.
SINGULAR SUBJECT

Each musician listens to the others.

▶ **Plural subjects take plural verbs.**

AGREE
The musicians play without sheet music.
PLURAL SUBJECT   PLURAL VERB

They hear changes in each other's sounds.

Most nouns that end in s or es are plural. For example, *musicians* and *sounds* are plural nouns. However, most verbs that end in s are singular. *Listens* and *hears* are both singular verb forms.

Verb Phrases

▶ **In a verb phrase, it is the first helping verb that agrees with the subject.** A verb phrase is made up of a main verb and one or more helping verbs.

AGREE
Miles Davis has led groups in performance.
SINGULAR VERB

AGREE
His music is becoming legendary.

All good groups have become teams.

AGREE

PLURAL VERB

Even the soloists are playing with a musical team.

AGREE

Doesn't and Don't

Two contractions we often use are *doesn't* and *don't*. Use *doesn't* with all singular subjects except *I* and *you*. Use *don't* with all plural subjects and with the pronouns *I* and *you*.

My mom doesn't like our band.
SINGULAR VERB:
does+not=doesn't

My friends don't understand why.
PLURAL VERB: do+not=don't

I don't play alone often.

❷ Why It Matters in Writing

Errors in subject-verb agreement can occur when you revise your work. If you change a subject from singular to plural, or vice versa, make sure that the verb agrees with your revision.

STUDENT MODEL

DRAFT

Our band is always arguing. The guitar **player** wants to break up.

REVISION

Our band is always arguing. The guitar **players** want to break up.

➌ Practice and Apply

A. CONCEPT CHECK: Agreement in Number

For each sentence, write the verb form that agrees with the subject.

Meet the Beatles

1. Rock critics (considers, consider) the Beatles one of the most important groups in rock and roll history.
2. Their musical development (shows, show) constant growth and exploration.
3. In the late 1950s they (was, were) playing other people's songs in clubs.
4. However, their own compositions (was, were) changing popular music.
5. Beatles' songs (attracts, attract) listeners who like great melodies and clever lyrics.
6. By the mid-1960s they (was, were) performing to huge crowds in baseball stadiums.
7. Adults (remembers, remember) mobs of young fans screaming at Beatles' concerts.
8. The Beatles (was, were) considered wild in their day.
9. Such popular groups (affects, affect) clothing and hair styles.
10. Today their music still (plays, play) around the world.

→ For a SELF-CHECK and more practice, see the EXERCISE BANK, p. 551.

B. PROOFREADING: Finding Agreement Errors

Proofread the following paragraph so that the verbs agree with the subjects. There are five errors.

STUDENT MODEL

Do you dislike order and discipline? Then you probably doesn't belong in a marching band. The band members must follow precise directions. A music director plan out every movement. Often the musicians forms words and patterns as they walk. Even their uniforms matches perfectly. Many schools has formed marching bands. The bands play at sporting events and other special occasions.

Compound Subjects

① Here's the Idea

A **compound subject** is made up of two or more subjects joined by a conjunction such as *and, or,* or *nor.*

Subjects Joined by *And*

▶ **A compound subject whose parts are joined by and usually takes a plural verb.**

A firefighter and **a paramedic** help **save lives.**

Subjects Joined by *Or* or *Nor*

▶ **When the parts of a compound subject are joined by *or* or *nor*, the verb should agree with the part closest to it.**

AGREES

A professional or **volunteers** serve **on emergency teams.**

AGREES

Volunteers or **a professional** serves **on emergency teams.**

② Why It Matters in Writing

When you revise your writing, you may decide to change the order of compound subjects to make a sentence sound more natural. If the subjects are joined by *or* or *nor*, make sure that the verb agrees with the new order.

Traffic problems or **bad weather** interferes **with rescue operations.**

Bad weather or **traffic problems** interfere **with rescue operations.**

❸ Practice and Apply

A. CONCEPT CHECK: Compound Subjects

Identify the sentences containing mistakes in subject-verb agreement and rewrite the verb correctly. If a sentence contains no error, write *Correct*.

Searching the Waters

1. Volunteer men and women composes the Larimer County Dive Rescue Team in Colorado.
2. Rescue and critical care are their goal.
3. Desperate calls and dispatches arrives at any hour.
4. Terrible storms and fog often confronts the team.
5. Terrified victims or darkness frustrate their efforts.
6. Ferocious whitewater or dangerous rapids slows them down.
7. These brave men and women often risk their own lives.
8. Donations and fund-raising events supports this important service.
9. Sometimes fatally injured victims or dead bodies is recovered from the rising waters.
10. But these brave men and women has also saved many lives.

→ **For a SELF-CHECK and more practice, see the EXERCISE BANK, p. 552.**

B. REVISING: Making Compound Subjects and Verbs Agree

A member of the Dive Rescue Team wrote these notes quickly, based on a frantic distress call. Rewrite the sentences for your report, making sure the verbs agree with their compound subjects. You may want to reverse the order of some compound subjects to make a sentence sound more natural.

Distress call, Oct. 15, 3:00 P.M.
A man and a woman has fallen into the Big Thompson River. Either two kayaks or one kayak are missing. Susan Brady and Juan Martinez is coordinating the rescue. Heavy rainstorms or fog are expected.

LESSON 3 Phrases Between Subjects and Verbs

① Here's the Idea

Many errors in subject-verb agreement occur when a prepositional phrase falls between the subject and verb.

▶ **The subject of a verb is never found in a prepositional phrase.** Don't be fooled by words that come between the subject and the verb. Mentally block out those words. Then decide whether the subject is singular or plural and match the verb to it.

AGREE

SINGULAR SUBJECT   SINGULAR VERB

A team ~~from several countries~~ was working on the Russian space station Mir.

PLURAL SUBJECT

Members ~~of the Russian and American space programs~~ pose together aboard Mir.

PLURAL VERB

Here's How Choosing the Correct Verb

Astronauts from Russia (has, have) abandoned Mir.

1. Mentally block out a prepositional phrase.
   Astronauts ~~from Russia~~ (has, have) abandoned Mir.
2. Decide if the subject is singular or plural.
   Astronauts = plural subject
3. Choose the verb that agrees with it. (have = plural verb)
   Astronauts from Russia have abandoned Mir.

❷ Why It Matters in Writing

Writers use prepositional phrases to tell more about the subject. When you do the same, make sure your verb goes with the subject, not the object of the preposition.

PROFESSIONAL MODEL

The international **missions** aboard Mir **were** a grand experiment. One **result** of these missions **was** the mutual respect that grew between Russian and U.S. astronauts.

PLURAL SUBJECT, PLURAL VERB

SINGULAR SUBJECT, SINGULAR VERB

—Angel Morales

❸ Practice and Apply

CONCEPT CHECK: Phrases Between Subjects and Verbs

Choose the correct verb for each sentence below.

Teamwork in Space
1. The benefits from a space program (is, are) unpredictable.
2. Tension between the Soviet Union and the United States (was, were) a major reason for Mir's construction.
3. However, the result of this experiment (is, are) greater cooperation among nations.
4. The abandonment of Mir (has, have) become necessary due to mechanical problems.
5. Scientists and engineers from many nations (is, are) building Mir's replacement.
6. Space buffs throughout the world eagerly (awaits, await) its completion.
7. Labs within space stations (provides, provide) great places for science experiments.
8. The astronauts aboard a space station (depends, depend) heavily on their support team back home.
9. A ground crew at the mission control center (oversees, oversee) every mission.
10. Together, government agencies and private companies (makes, make) space flight possible.

➡ **For a SELF-CHECK and more practice, see the EXERCISE BANK, p. 552.**

Indefinite Pronouns as Subjects

LESSON 4

❶ Here's the Idea

Some pronouns do not refer to a definite, or specific, person, place, thing, or idea. These pronouns are called **indefinite pronouns**.

▶ **When used as subjects, some indefinite pronouns are always singular. Some are always plural. Others can be singular or plural depending on how they're used.**

Indefinite Pronouns			
Singular	another	anybody	anyone
	anything	each	either
	everybody	everyone	everything
	neither	nobody	no one
	nothing	one	somebody
	someone	something	
Plural	both few	many several	
Singular or Plural	all any	most none some	

Singular indefinite pronouns take singular verbs.

Everyone knows about camels in desert caravans.

Everything about them seems strange and exotic.

Plural indefinite pronouns take plural verbs.

Few of us realize their importance to desert people.

Many rely on the camel for everyday living.

Both of the camels in this photo are Bactrian camels.

Singular or Plural?

The indefinite pronouns *all, any, most, none,* and *some* can be either singular or plural. When you use one of these words as a subject, think about the noun it refers to. If the noun is singular, use a singular verb. If it is plural, use a plural verb.

REFERS TO

All of the camels carry supplies for humans on their humps.

REFERS TO

Some of the Mongolian desert still has wild Bactrian camels.

Sometimes an indefinite pronoun refers to a noun in a previous sentence.

PLURAL NOUN   INDEFINITE PRONOUN

The camels went eight days without water. All were healthy.   PLURAL VERB

❷ Why It Matters in Writing

When writing about people or animals, you'll often need indefinite pronouns as subjects. Correct subject-verb agreement helps readers know whether you're talking about one individual or several.

> **PROFESSIONAL MODEL**
>
> Sled dogs pull sleds across snow and ice in northern regions. **Many** of the dogs **are** purebred, but **some are** mixed breeds, especially in Alaska. **Each** of the dogs **has** a heavy coat and can sleep outside in temperatures as low as –70 degrees Fahrenheit.
>
> —Lucy Armstrong

❸ Practice and Apply

A. CONCEPT CHECK: Indefinite Pronoun Subjects

Rewrite correctly each sentence in which the verb does not agree with the subject. If a sentence is correct, write *Correct*.

Guiding Lights

1. Everyone have heard of seeing-eye dogs.
2. Few knows the term *hearing dogs*.
3. All of these dogs alerts their owners to sounds of danger.
4. Several of the dog breeds is especially suited for work with visually challenged people.
5. Some of the best dogs includes German shepherds, Labrador retrievers, and golden retrievers.
6. Most of the states guarantees access rights to guide-dog users.
7. No one in these states is allowed to keep people with dog guides from public places.
8. Everyone recognizes a seeing-eye dog by its special harness and U-shaped handle.
9. Many knows that hearing dogs have a bright yellow or orange collar and leash.
10. Both of the canine helpers gives visually challenged and hearing-impaired people more independence.

➡ For a SELF-CHECK and more practice, see the EXERCISE BANK, p. 553.

B. WRITING: Using Indefinite Pronouns Correctly

For each sentence, choose the verb that agrees with the subject.

1. No one (seems, seem) neutral on the subject of dogs as pets.
2. Something about this topic (make, makes) people argue.
3. Many (praises, praise) dogs for their loyalty and obedience.
4. Few of the cat lovers (agrees, agree).
5. Some of them (thinks, think) dogs are just loud and stupid.
6. Somebody (accuses, accuse) a dog of having bad manners.
7. Others (blames, blame) the owner for bad training.
8. Some of the worst fights between neighbors (involves, involve) dogs.
9. Often neither of the sides (want, wants) to compromise.
10. Yet everybody (know, knows) pets are like family members.

Subjects in Unusual Positions

❶ Here's the Idea

In some sentences, the subject comes after the verb or between parts of the verb phrase. For these sentences, you have to find the subject first to make the verb agree.

Sentences that Begin with a Prepositional Phrase

Writers sometimes start a sentence with a prepositional phrase. In some of these sentences, the verb comes after the subject.

From his left hand comes Al's 90-mile-an-hour pitch.
SINGULAR VERB ⬈   SINGULAR SUBJECT ⬈

Sentences that Begin with *Here* or *There*

When a sentence begins with *here* or *there,* the subject often comes after the verb.

Here is a starting pitcher with a serious fastball.
⬆ SINGULAR VERB   ⬆ SINGULAR SUBJECT

There are several games on this field tonight.
⬆ PLURAL VERB   ⬆ PLURAL SUBJECT

Questions

In many questions, the subject follows the verb or comes between parts of the verb.

Does this goofball team ever win?
⬆ SINGULAR HELPING VERB   ⬆ SINGULAR SUBJECT

⬆ PLURAL HELPING VERB
Do both boys play on the team?
⬆ PLURAL SUBJECT

> **Here's How** Choosing the Correct Verb
>
> (**Is, Are**) the starting **pitchers** stronger than the relievers?
>
> **1.** Turn the sentence around, putting the subject before the verb.
> The starting **pitchers** (**is, are**) stronger than the relievers.
>
> **2.** Determine whether the subject is singular or plural.
> **pitchers** (plural)
>
> **3.** Make sure the subject and verb agree.
> The starting **pitchers** are stronger than the relievers.

❷ Why It Matters in Writing

You can vary sentences by beginning with *here* or *there* or by beginning with a prepositional phrase. When you do so, make sure that the subjects and verbs agree.

> **LITERARY MODEL**
>
> Never in all my life **have I seen** such faith and friendship, such loyalty between men. There **are many** among you who call me harsh and cruel. But I cannot kill any man who proves such strong and true friendship for another.
>
> —Fan Kissen, *Damon and Pythias*

❸ Practice and Apply

CONCEPT CHECK: Subjects in Unusual Positions

For each sentence below, first identify the subject and verb. If they agree, write *Correct.* If they don't agree, rewrite them.

World's Favorite Game
1. Does your friends like soccer?
2. There is no sport more popular in the world.
3. In the past, wasn't Americans big soccer fans?
4. Across this country is now thousands of youth soccer leagues.
5. Didn't 20 American soccer players win the Women's World Cup in 1999?
6. There was 12 nations competing in the 32 World Cup matches.
7. In front of their TV sets were one billion fans worldwide.
8. The final American match with China were the U.S.'s best-attended women's sports event.
9. Hasn't the women of Team USA become media favorites?
10. In addition to gymnasts and skaters, here is new heroines for teenaged girls.

➡ For a SELF-CHECK and more practice, see the EXERCISE BANK, p. 554.

Grammar in Literature

Subject-Verb Agreement

When you write, it's important to use correct subject-verb agreement. Like the members of the group of campers in the passage, subjects and verbs need to work together. When sentences are inverted, or when subjects and verbs are written as contractions, it's sometimes harder to choose correct subject-verb agreement. Notice the examples of subject-verb agreement in the inverted sentences in the passage below.

SCOUT'S
from
HONOR
by Avi

When we got off the bridge, we were in a small plaza. To the left was the roadway, full of roaring cars. In front of us, aside from the highway, there was nothing but buildings. Only to the right were there trees.

> In this sentence, the subject is the plural noun *trees.* So the verb, *were,* is also plural.

"North is that way," Max said, pointing toward the trees. We set off.

"How come you're limping?" Horse asked me. My foot *was* killing me. All I said, though, was, "How come you keep rubbing your arm?"

"I'm keeping the blood moving."

> Contraction *you're* is short for *you are.* Contraction *I'm* is short for *I am.* Both verbs agree with their subjects.

"We approached the grove of trees. "Wow," Horse exclaimed. "Country." . . .

"Hey," Max cried, sounding relieved, "this is just like Brooklyn."

Practice and Apply

A. REVISING: Using Correct Subject-Verb Agreement

The following letter was written by a student during a camping trip with her scout troop. Because she dashed off the letter in a hurry, her subjects and verbs don't always agree. Rewrite her letter, correcting all errors in subject-verb agreement

Dear Folks,

What an experience! The rest of the girls and I am having the time of our lives. You wouldn't even recognize your daughter. She, along with the others, get up with the sun about 5:00 AM. Then a team of us meet and decides what activities to do that day. There is swimming, hiking, horseback riding, and bird watching to choose from.

Ceramics are scheduled for tomorrow. I love using the potter's wheel.

My three weeks is almost over, so I may be home even before this message get there.

Love,

Deanna

P.S. Oops, I almost forgot. Several of my new friends is planning to come home and spend the rest of the summer with me.

B. WRITING: Journal

Write a journal entry describing an outdoor experience. Your experience can be real or imaginary. Write your journal entry as if the experience were in the present. Use correct subject-verb agreement. Save your writing in your 🗀 **Working Portfolio.**

A. Agreement in Number Write the verb form that agrees with the subject of each sentence.

1. Emergency Medical Technician-Paramedics (treats, treat) victims when a doctor isn't available.
2. All of the EMTs (is, are) trained medical workers.
3. Many (is, are) first at the scene of an accident or heart attack.
4. Drugs and medical equipment (is, are) carried in their special ambulance.
5. As a first step, paramedics on the scene immediately (contacts, contact) a doctor at a nearby hospital.
6. Any injuries or other important information (is, are) reported to the doctor.
7. A defibrillator (helps, help) correct an irregular heartbeat.
8. Another of the EMT's instruments (reports, report) heart activity.
9. In serious cases, heart attack victims or injured people (is, are) treated on the way to the hospital.
10. These brave men and women (has, have) saved many lives.

B. Additional Agreement Problems Read this report of a movie studio tour. Correct seven errors in subject-verb agreement and write the corrected sentences.

> PROFESSIONAL MODEL

> Are teamwork involved in making a movie? Yes! Here is some strange names for very important jobs. The lights and power distribution are set by the gaffer. Under the director of photography work the key grip. He is the chief builder of the lighting equipment. There is two assistants to the gaffer and the key grip. "Best boy electric" and "best boy grip" is their titles. These titles doesn't always describe the person. One of the best "boys" were about 50, and the other was a woman!

Lighting Technician

Camera Operator

Director

Choose the letter of the best revision for each underlined section.

<u>Search and rescue dogs is trained</u> to find missing persons. <u>There</u>
(1)
<u>are two different types</u> of dogs. <u>Some detects scent particles</u>
(2)   (3)
carried by wind from the missing person's location. Other <u>dogs on</u>
<u>a search team follow</u> the trail of scent particles along the missing
(4)
person's path. The dogs smell the victim's clothing. <u>A garment of</u>
(5)
<u>natural fibers are</u> very helpful. <u>Each of the dogs ignore</u> all scents
(6)
except for the missing person's. <u>Air scent dogs and trailing dogs</u>
(7)
<u>searches</u> for victims in avalanches and in water. <u>Doesn't dog and</u>
(8)
<u>handler teams train</u> for two years for this job?

1. A. Search and rescue dogs are
trained
   B. Search and rescue dogs is
being trained
   C. Search and rescue dogs was
being trained
   D. Correct as is

2. A. There is two different types
   B. There was two different
types
   C. There has been two
different types
   D. Correct as is

3. A. Some detect scent particles
   B. Some has detected scent
particles
   C. Some is detecting scent
particles
   D. Correct as is

4. A. dogs on a search team
follows
   B. dogs on a search team is
following
   C. dogs on a search team is to
follow
   D. Correct as is

5. A. A garment of natural fibers
were
   B. A garment of natural fibers
have been
   C. A garment of natural fibers
is
   D. Correct as is

6. A. Each of the dogs ignores
   B. Each of the dogs was
ignoring
   C. Each of the dogs are ignoring
   D. Correct as is

7. A. Air scent dogs and trailing
dogs searching
   B. Air scent dogs and trailing
dogs was searching
   C. Air scent dogs and trailing
dogs search
   D. Correct as is

8. A. Doesn't dog and handler
teams trains
   B. Don't dog and handler
teams trained
   C. Don't dog and handler
teams train
   D. Correct as is

Student Help Desk

Subject-Verb Agreement at a Glance

A singular subject takes a singular verb.

Our team wins the contest.

A plural subject takes a plural verb.

Many people share in the victory.

Indefinite Pronouns

One for All

If the indefinite pronoun is:	Make the verb:
Always singular everyone, anyone, everything, one, somebody	**Singular** **Everyone is** nervous.
Always plural both, few, many, several	**Plural** **Many come** to play.
Sometimes singular all, any, most, none, some	**Singular** **All** of our preparation **is** over.
Sometimes plural all, any, most, none, some	**Plural** **All** of the players **are** ready.

Compound Subjects

All for One

If the compound subject is:	Make the verb:
Joined by *and*	**Plural** The **winners and losers shake** hands.
Joined by *or* or *nor*	**Match the closest subject** Neither the **winners** nor the **loser looks** tired. Neither the **loser** nor the **winners look** tired.

Tricky Sentences
Make Them get Along

Kind of Sentence	Subject	Verb
Question		
Is the umpire ready?	umpire	is
Sentence Beginning with *Here* **or** *There*		
Here comes the pitch!	pitch	comes
Sentence Beginning with Prepositional Phrase		
Out of the park flies the ball!	ball	flies
Prepositional Phrase Between Subject and Verb		
The batter, in the fans' eyes, looks mighty.	batter	looks
Helping Verb		
Our players are winning.	players	are winning
The runner is scoring!	runner	is scoring

The Bottom Line

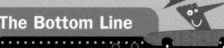

Checklist for Subject-Verb Agreement

Have I . . .

____ used a singular verb with a singular subject?

____ used a plural verb with a plural subject?

____ made the helping verb in a verb phrase agree with the subject?

____ used a plural verb with compound subjects joined by *and*?

____ made the verb agree with the closest part of a compound subject joined by *or* or *nor*?

____ checked whether indefinite pronoun subjects are singular or plural?

____ made verbs agree with subjects in unusual positions?

Chapter 8

Capitalization

Watch out for big bear!
Find the cave at the base
of the mountain and fish
creek. Get the key from
the cave entrance and
follow fish creek
downstream to
shady road.

Theme: What's in a Name?
Follow That Bear!

These explorers carefully followed the directions, but they never found the meeting place. What happened? The person who wrote the directions didn't follow the rules of capitalization. The boys were on the lookout for a big bear instead of Big Bear Mountain. They thought they were supposed to go fishing in the creek instead of finding Fish Creek. They looked for a shady road instead of the road named Shady Road.

Write Away: Can You Get There from Here?
Write directions from where you are now to a particular place, such as your home. Include the names of landmarks, streets, and other places. Put your directions in your 🗂 **Working Portfolio.**

 **Grammar Coach**

For each numbered item, choose the letter of the correct revision.

can you think of any weird place names? Imagine living in a
(1)
place called peculiar, missouri, or in other places like Diamond,
(2)
Zif, or Zig. In the book *Paris, Tightwad, and Peculiar: Missouri
Place Names*, margot ford mcMillen gives a history of place names
(3)
in Missouri. The writer states that Tightwad, Missouri, was
(4)
named after a merchant who cheated a mailman out of his
watermelon. The book covers humorous origins and places that
were named after the way they look, like flat river.
(5)

Another region with unusual place names is Newfoundland.
How would you like to travel to bleak island, dead man's bay, or
(6)
breakheart point? You can find these names in the book *dictionary
of Newfoundland english*. If you are interested in place names, you
(7)
can take a class to learn more about Creative Names worldwide.
(8)

1. A. can You think
   B. Can You think
   C. Can you think
   D. Correct as is

2. A. peculiar, Missouri,
   B. Peculiar, Missouri,
   C. Peculiar, missouri,
   D. Correct as is

3. A. Margot ford McMillen
   B. Margot ford mcMillen
   C. Margot Ford McMillen
   D. Correct as is

4. A. tightwad, missouri,
   B. tightwad, Missouri,
   C. Tightwad, missouri,
   D. Correct as is

5. A. Flat river
   B. Flat River
   C. flat River
   D. Correct as is

6. A. Bleak island, Dead man's
      bay, or Breakheart point
   B. Bleak Island, Dead Man's
      bay, or Breakheart point
   C. Bleak Island, Dead Man's
      Bay, or Breakheart Point
   D. Correct as is

7. A. *Dictionary Of Newfoundland
      English*
   B. *Dictionary of Newfoundland
      English*
   C. *Dictionary of Newfoundland
      english*
   D. Correct as is

8. A. Creative Names Worldwide
   B. creative Names worldwide
   C. creative names worldwide
   D. Correct as is

People and Cultures

❶ Here's the Idea

Names and Initials

▶ **Capitalize people's names and initials.**

Sandra Cisneros   John F. Kennedy

Oprah Winfrey   Natsume Soseki

Personal Titles and Abbreviations

▶ **Capitalize titles and abbreviations of titles that are used before names or in direct address.**

Senator John Bullworth   Professor Henry Higgins

Capt. Kathryn Janeway   Rev. James L. Nash

Is my kitten going to be okay, Doctor?

Capitalize the abbreviations of some titles when they follow a name.

Jamie Crawford, M.D.   Fred Jones, Sr.

Angela Martinez, D.D.S.   George Collins, Ph.D.

▶ **Capitalize titles of heads of state, royalty, or nobility only when they are used before persons' names or in place of persons' names.**

Surgeon General David Satcher

Justice Sandra Day O'Connor

Queen Elizabeth

Czar Ivan IV was also known as Ivan the Terrible.

Do not capitalize titles when they are used without a proper name.

The duchess officially opened the ceremonies.

CHAPTER 8

Family Relationships

▶ **Capitalize words indicating family relationships only when they are used as names or before names.**

Aunt Laura   Cousin David   Uncle Al

Mom helped Aunt Sally choose the name for the new baby.

In general, do **not** capitalize a family relationship word when it follows the person's name or is used without a proper name.

I dreamed my uncle was King Arthur.

The Pronoun *I*

▶ **Always capitalize the pronoun *I*.**

Mother said that I was named after Uncle Henry.

Religious Terms

▶ **Capitalize the names of religions, sacred days, sacred writings, and deities.**

Religious Terms	
Religions	Judaism, Christianity, Islam
Sacred days	Rosh Hashanah, Good Friday
Sacred writings	Torah, Bible, Koran
Deities	God, Yahweh, Allah

Do not capitalize the words *god* and *goddess* when they refer to gods of ancient mythology.

The word *volcano* comes from the name of the Roman god of fire, Vulcan.

Nationalities, Languages, and Races

▶ **Capitalize the names of nationalities, languages, races, and most ethnic groups, and the adjectives formed from these names.**

German	Spanish	Korean
European	Asian American	Jewish

❷ Practice and Apply

CONCEPT CHECK: People and Cultures

Write the words and abbreviations that should be capitalized but are not in the paragraph below. Capitalize each correctly. If a sentence has no errors, write the word *correct*.

Middle Names

(1) Not long ago, i found a book of baby names in the attic that tells about how middle names originated. **(2)** It was written by jonathan p. algernon, jr. **(3)** Mom said it was the book she and Dad used to pick my name. **(4)** The book says that the spanish began using middle names about 1000 A.D. **(5)** Even though the early americans did not give their children middle names, by the mid-1800s german immigrants to the United States had made the practice popular. **(6)** president john quincy adams was the first president to use a middle name. **(7)** The most unusual middle name was chosen by a 13-year-old girl in 1965 who admired the folk song "Don't Ya Weep, Don't Ya Mourn." **(8)** Her name—mary dontyaweepdontyamourn schulz.

➡ **For a SELF-CHECK and more practice, see the EXERCISE BANK, p. 554.**

LESSON 2 — First Words and Titles

❶ Here's the Idea

Sentences and Poetry

▶ **Capitalize the first word of every sentence.**

My pen pal from Japan is named Suzu, which means "little bell."

▶ **In traditional poetry capitalize the first word of every line.**

> **LITERARY MODEL**
>
> All that is gold does not glitter,
> Not all those who wander are lost;
> The old that is strong does not wither,
> Deep roots are not reached by the frost.
>
> —J. R. R. Tolkien, "All That Is Gold"

Modern poets may choose not to begin each line of a poem with a capital letter. If you make this choice in your own writing, make sure the meaning of your work is still clear.

Quotations

▶ **Capitalize the first word of a direct quotation if it is a complete sentence.**

Shakespeare was the first to write, "What's in a name?"

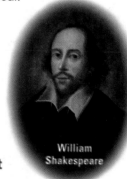

William Shakespeare

▶ **In a divided quotation, do not capitalize the first word of the second part unless it starts a new sentence.**

"I have a name for my new kitten," said Sarah. "It's going to be Kitty!"

"Maybe you should think of another name," Mom said, "since that was the name of your last two cats."

Outlines

▶ **Capitalize the first word of each entry in an outline and the letters that introduce major subsections.**

I. Types of felines
   A. Domesticated cats
      1. Persian
      2. Tabby

Parts of a Letter

▶ **Capitalize the first word in the greeting and in the closing of a letter.**

Dear Mr. Macavity:

Dear Sir:

Sincerely yours,

Titles

▶ **Capitalize the first word, last word, and all important words in a title. Don't capitalize articles, conjunctions, or prepositions of fewer than five letters.**

Type of Media	Examples
Books	*Dogsong, Island of the Blue Dolphins*
Plays and musicals	*Annie, The Sound of Music*
Short stories	"Eleven," "Aaron's Gift"
Poems	"Ode to My Library," "Where the Sidewalk Ends"
Magazines and newspapers	*Highlights, TV Guide, The Washington Post*
Musical compositions	"The Star Spangled Banner"
Movies	*Tarzan, Prince of Egypt*
Television shows	*Seventh Heaven, Touched by an Angel*
Works of art	*Mona Lisa, Sunflowers*
Games	Space Genius, Name Game, Myths and Legends

❷ Practice and Apply

CONCEPT CHECK: First Words and Titles

Write the words that should be capitalized but are not in these sentences. Capitalize each correctly.

Popular Names

1. for centuries, one of the most common boys' names throughout the world has been *John*.

2. The name *John* can be found in many nursery rhymes, such as the following:
   deedle deedle dumpling, my son John
   went to bed with his stockings on.

John F. Kennedy

3. One form of the name *Johnny* is in the title of a famous early rock 'n' roll song by Chuck Berry, "Johnny b. goode."

4. The name *John Henry* might ring a bell, if you've read the legend, where he says, "before I let that steam drill beat me down, I'll die with my hammer in my hand."

5. The singer and composer John Lennon is often remembered for his song "imagine."

Jane Goodall

6. John F. Kennedy's famous words, "and so, my fellow Americans: ask not what your country can do for you; ask what you can do for your country," will endure for generations to come.

7. jane is the feminine form of *John,* and a famous woman with that name is Dr. Jane Goodall.

8. Another example of a famous Jane is the novelist Jane Austen, who wrote *Emma, Sense and sensibility,* and *persuasion.*

9. Jane Fonda, who starred in *Coming home,* has won two Oscars.

10. *John* and *Jane* can be found in a wide variety of forms in different countries and languages, as the following partial outline suggests:
   I. in France
      A. feminine
         1. Jeanne or Jeanette

➔ **For a SELF-CHECK and more practice, see the EXERCISE BANK, p. 555.**

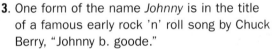

A. Capitalization in Outlining Rewrite the following portion of an outline, correcting the capitalization errors.

I. History of Names
   A. people's names
      1. first names
      2. middle names
      3. last names
   B. geographical names
      1. Land Names
      2. River and Mountain Names
      3. unusual names

B. Proofreading: Parts of a Letter Identify and correct the ten capitalization errors in the following letter.

Mr. John Little
510 N. Addison St.
Chicago, IL 60602

Dear mr. little,

    I am writing about the puppy-naming contest that you advertised in the *Chicago tribune.* Your ad asked for the most creative names we could think of. I personally like Amadeus, after Wolfgang Amadeus Mozart, who composed *the marriage of Figaro.* Now, if you have a female pup, you might want to consider Greek mythology names like Calliope or Calypso, who entertained the Greek hero Odysseus in the long poem *The odyssey.* I recently read in an essay entitled "All about Pet names" that a person should consider the size, breed, and gender of the dog when choosing a name. You wouldn't want to name your male pit bull Muffy unless you have a very strong reason. Other names you might want to consider are Falstaff, Hercules, Lady, Venus, or Pluto.

Sincerely yours,

jemma roberts

CHAPTER 8

Places and Transportation

❶ Here's the Idea

Geographical Names

▶ **In geographical names, capitalize each word except articles and prepositions.**

Geographical Names	
Divisions of the world	Southern Hemisphere, International Date Line
Continents	Antarctica, Europe, South America
Bodies of water	Indian Ocean, Mississippi River, Lake Michigan
Islands	Guam, Prince Edward Island, Easter Island
Mountains	Appalachian Mountains, Himalayas, Adirondacks
Other landforms	Strait of Magellan, Sahara, Cape of Good Hope
Regions	Central America, Eurasia, Great Plains
Nations	Spain, Mexico, England
States	New York, Illinois, Florida
Cities and towns	Dallas, Springfield, Sacramento
Roads and streets	Route 66, Wall Street, Fifth Avenue

Bodies of the Universe

▶ **Capitalize the names of planets and other specific objects in the universe.**

Mercury   Tycho Brahe's Comet

Andromeda   Big Dipper   Ganymede

Saturn, Jupiter, and Mars were each
named after mythical characters.

The planet closest to
the sun is Mercury.

Regions and Sections

▶ **Capitalize the words *north, south, east,* and *west* when they name particular regions of the United States or the world or when they are parts of proper names.**

Some states in the Southeast, such as Virginia, Maryland, and North and South Carolina, were named after British royalty.

Do not capitalize these words when they indicate general directions or locations.

The state of Illinois is west of Indiana and south of Wisconsin.

Buildings, Bridges, and Other Landmarks

▶ **Capitalize the names of specific buildings, bridges, monuments, and other landmarks.**

Empire State Building   Washington Monument

Brooklyn Bridge   Mount Rushmore

The national monument in New Mexico known as the Gila Cliff Dwellings is the site of Pueblo Indian dwellings.

Planes, Trains, and Other Vehicles

▶ **Capitalize the names of specific airplanes, trains, ships, cars, and spacecraft.**

Names	Examples
Airplanes	*Enola Gay, Spruce Goose*
Trains	*City of New Orleans, Cannonball Express*
Ships	USS *Missouri, Titanic,* HMS *Bounty*
Cars	*Volkswagen, Camaro, Jaguar*
Spacecraft	*Discovery, Endeavor, Soyuz*

❷ Practice and Apply

A. CONCEPT CHECK: Places and Transportation

For each sentence, write the words that should be capitalized. Do not write words that are already capitalized.

Naming the Land
1. In the early 1700s, French explorers began to colonize parts of what is now the south.
2. Near the gulf of mexico, the French founded a fort in an area settled by a Native American group called the Maubilian.
3. The French translated that name to mobile.
4. Around a nearby river, the French encountered the Alibamons (for whom the state of alabama is named).
5. Two centuries later, paddle wheel boats with names like the *delta queen* would travel the mississippi river, but in the 1700s French explorers made their way upriver in canoes.
6. Near the great plains, the French encountered a river called *ni* (river) *bthaska* (something flat and spread out).
7. The French called it the *rivière platte*.
8. *Ni bthaska* became the name of the state nebraska.
9. The French marveled at the beauty of the milky way.
10. Today, visitors can appreciate the breathtaking beauty of the land as they drive along interstate 80.

→ **For a SELF-CHECK and more practice, see the EXERCISE BANK, p. 556.**

B. REVISING: Correcting Map Labels

Find and correct the capitalization errors in the map below. Notice that not all labels need to be changed.

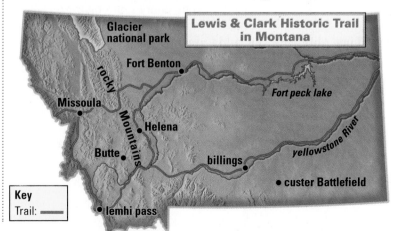

Glacier national park

Lewis & Clark Historic Trail in Montana

Fort Benton

rocky Mountains

Missoula

Fort peck lake

Helena

Butte

billings

yellowstone River

custer Battlefield

Key
Trail: ▬▬▬

lemhi pass

Organizations and Other Subjects

❶ Here's the Idea

Organizations and Institutions

▶ **Capitalize all important words in the names of organizations, institutions, stores, and companies.**

Summerville Middle School   Boston Public Library

Sarah's Beauty Shop   Oxford University

League of Nations   National Honor Society

Do not capitalize words such as *school, company, church, college,* and *hospital* when they are not used as parts of names.

We moved near the hospital.

Historical Events, Periods, and Documents

▶ **Capitalize the names of historical events, periods, and documents.**

Historical Events, Periods, and Documents	
Events	Harlem Renaissance, Revolutionary War
Periods	Space Age, Age of Exploration
Documents	Magna Carta, Constitution of the United States

The Declaration of Independence was adopted more than a year after the Revolutionary War began.

Time Abbreviations and Calendar Items

▶ **Capitalize the abbreviations B.C., A.D., A.M., and P.M.**

The ancient Egyptians developed history's first national government about 3000 B.C.

▶ **Capitalize the names of months, days, and holidays but not the seasons.**

October   Labor Day   fall

St. Valentine's Day   Monday   spring

The Thanksgiving holiday takes place every fall on the fourth Thursday of November.

Special Events, Awards, and Brand Names

▶ **Capitalize the names of special events and awards.**

the World Series   the Country Music Awards

the Stanley Cup   the Caldecott Medal

What runner will win the Boston Marathon this year?

▶ **Capitalize the brand name of a product but not a common noun that follows a brand name.**

Sun Safe sunscreen   Munchies potato chips

❷ Practice and Apply

CONCEPT CHECK: Organizations and Other Subjects

Identify and correct the words that should be capitalized in the following flyer.

Annual roller hockey Tournament

Where: Springdale middle school

When: saturday, October 17, through saturday, october 31. Games begin promptly at 7:00 p.m. each thursday, friday, and saturday of the tournament. The final game will be held on halloween. Come in costume and cheer for your favorite team!

Prizes: Third-place winners receive a case of zap cola and a $10 gift certificate to Jimmy's athletic warehouse. Second-place winners will get a gift certificate for a pair of air lite tennis shoes.

Grand Prize: First-place winners receive $500 and a team trophy, the Springdale silver puck.

Grammar in Math

Capitalization in Tables and Bar Graphs

When you write about statistics for math, you want to make sure your numbers are correct. But what about capitalization? You must pay attention to capitalization too; otherwise, people won't trust your numbers. Notice how proper names and important words are capitalized in the table and graph below.

Most Popular Dog Names	
Name	**Number**
Max	28
Sam	15
Lady	13
Rocky	9
Lucky	6
Missy	4

Capitalize all important words in titles

Capitalize proper names

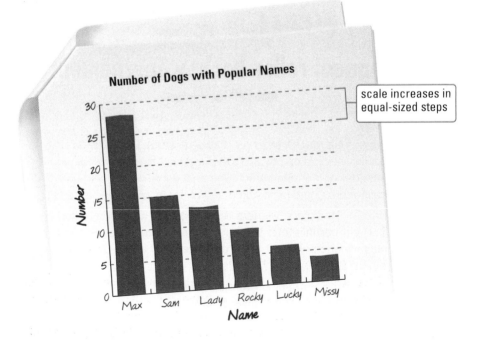

scale increases in equal-sized steps

Practice and Apply

MATH

A. CONCEPT CHECK: Capitalization in Graphs and Tables

A student did some research into popular girls' names in the 1890s and quickly jotted down information. Correct the capitalization in the table. Use the following information to create your own bar graph like the one shown on the opposite page. Don't forget to include a title. Use equal-sized scale numbers that increase in steps of 10 (for example, 10, 20, 30, . . . and so on).

Most popular Names in the 1890s

Girl's Names	Number
Mary	59
anna	55
Elizabeth	46
emma	38
Margaret	32
rose	20

B. WRITING: Summarizing Information

Once you have created a bar graph, summarize the information in a short paragraph. Remember, when you summarize information, you explain the most important points. Be sure to check your capitalization. Save your paragraph in your ⬜ **Working Portfolio.**

A. Proofreading: Capitalization Identify and correct the capitalization errors in the following paragraph.

Imagine having to carry the name Minny vann the rest of your life because uncle Ed or grandma Vann thought it was cute! I admit that I've heard worse, though: Constance Noring, Jim Shortz, and Frank n. Stine, for example. Why do people inflict silly and embarrassing names on their children? My cousin's mother and father, whose last name is Tyme, named my cousin Justin because he was born at 11:59 p.m. on new year's eve. Not all silly names are intentional. When a man named E. Speeking entered the united states army and eventually reached the rank of general, he became general e. Speeking. When Claude Payne reached the rank of major, he became major Payne.

B. Editing and Proofreading Rewrite the business letter below using capitalization rules from this chapter.

U.S. Dept. of interior
National Park service
1849 c street
Washington, D.C. 20240

Dear sir:

I am a student at marietta junior high school in monroe, nebraska, and a member of mr. eric johnson's class Social Studies I. A class assignment is to plan a trip to visit some national monuments and parks. We will be traveling by tour bus and will travel west on interstate 80. We would like information on parks in Colorado and Wyoming, especially yellowstone national park and parks in the Teton mountains. We will probably make the trip in late may or early june of next year.

Please send us brochures about places that we might visit. Also, please send us any other suggestions you may have about our tour of the west.

sincerely,

amanda brady

For each numbered item, choose the letter of the correct revision.

Sometime around <u>4000 b.c. and 3500 B.C.</u>, poets, astronomers,
(1)
and farmers began to create mythological names for constellations.
The names of constellations varied, however, from <u>babylonia, to</u>
(2)
<u>Egypt, to Greece</u>. Most people are familiar with the <u>greek and</u>
(3)
<u>roman</u> names of stars after <u>myths, heroes, or Gods</u>. Take
(4)
<u>orion, the hunter</u>, for example. The story reminds people of a
(5)
great hunter holding his shield. In some cases, constellations were
named after a figure in the sky. For example, a bear has been
associated with the constellation <u>Ursa Major</u> <u>since the ice age</u>. In
(6)   (7)
1930, the <u>International astronomical Union</u> set official boundaries
(8)
that defined the 88 constellations that exist today.

1. A. 4000 b.c. and 3500 b.c.
   B. 4000 B.c. and 3500 B.c.
   C. 4000 B.C. and 3500 B.C.
   D. Correct as is

2. A. babylonia, to egypt, to
      Greece
   B. Babylonia, to Egypt, to
      Greece
   C. babylonia, to egypt, to
      greece
   D. Correct as is

3. A. Greek and roman
   B. greek and Roman
   C. Greek and Roman
   D. Correct as is

4. A. myths, heroes, or gods
   B. Myths, Heroes, or Gods
   C. Myths, Heroes, or gods
   D. Correct as is

5. A. Orion, The Hunter
   B. orion, the Hunter
   C. Orion, the Hunter
   D. Correct as is

6. A. ursa major
   B. Ursa major
   C. ursa Major
   D. Correct as is

7. A. since the Ice age
   B. since the Ice Age
   C. Since the Ice Age
   D. Correct as is

8. A. international astronomical
      Union
   B. International Astronomical
      union
   C. International Astronomical
      Union
   D. Correct as is

Student Help Desk

Capitalization at a Glance

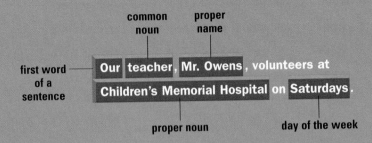

common noun

proper name

first word of a sentence ——

Our teacher, Mr. Owens, volunteers at

Children's Memorial Hospital on Saturdays.

proper noun

day of the week

Do Capitalize Upper Case Ursula

Proper nouns that name people, places, and things:
Traditionally in **M**exico a firstborn daughter is named **M**aria.

Family words used as a name or part of a name:
Billy is **U**ncle William's nickname.

The first word of a sentence:
Do you know the origin of your name?

The first word in every line of traditional poetry:
The winter owl banked just in time to pass
And save herself from breaking window glass.
—Robert Frost, "Questioning Faces"

The first word, last word, and all important words in titles:
Across **F**ive **A**prils

Proper nouns that name a particular date, holiday, event, or award:
On **M**arch 17, **S**t. **P**atrick's **D**ay, people by the name of Pat, Patrick, or Patricia can celebrate their saint's name.

Don't Capitalize   Lower Case Larry

Words after the first word of a closing of a letter:
Sincerely **y**ours,   Yours **t**ruly,

Family words used as ordinary nouns:
I was named after my **m**om.

Calendar items if they name a season:
My name is Summer, but my favorite season is **f**all.

The common nouns that stand for people, places, or things:
My **c**ousin enjoys riding her **b**ike to **s**chool because she can stop at the **s**tore for some **s**nacks.

Compass direction when indicating a general location:
I like to watch flocks of geese flying in formation, migrating **s**outh for the winter.

The Bottom Line

Checklist for Capitalization

Have I capitalized . . .

____ people's names and initials?

____ personal titles preceding names?

____ names of races, languages, and nationalities?

____ names of religions and religious terms?

____ names of bodies of the universe and other geographical terms?

____ names of monuments, bridges, and other landmarks?

____ names of particular planes, trains, and other vehicles?

____ names of organizations, institutions, and businesses?

____ names of historical events, eras, and documents?

____ names of special events, awards, and brand names?

Punctuation

- Mayor demands explanation, pg. A3.
- Power Company blames weather, pg. A5.
- Cost of disaster assessed, pg. B1.
- Propane sales skyrocket, pg. B9.

Volume 36, issue 2,742

The Daily Tribune

Tuesday, March 20, 2000

Emergency Power Lost in City

Theme: Great Mistakes and Disasters

Headline Headache

What event is the headline describing? It's hard to know without proper end marks in place. Is it "Emergency Power Lost in City!" in which the city has lost emergency backup power? Or is it "Emergency! Power Lost in City!" in which the city has lost all power? Punctuation helps make even simple messages easier to understand.

Write Away: Oops! News That's Unfit to Print
Write a headline describing a time you slipped up. It might describe when you forgot to study for a test, tripped over a neighbor's dog, or missed a bus. Be sure to punctuate your headline correctly. Save your work in your  **Working Portfolio.**

Grammar Coach

For each numbered item, choose the letter of the best revision.

Some mistakes are <u>tragic</u> Other mistakes have milder
(1)

<u>consequences</u>; in fact, <u>theyre</u> just plain goofy. Take, for example,
(2)   (3)

the story <u>Cinderella.</u> Did you ever wonder why someone lucky
(4)

enough to have a fairy godmother ended up with <u>glass shoes</u>! An
(5)

older version of the story says that <u>Cinderellas'</u> slippers were
(6)

made of *vair*, a type of fur. Charles <u>Perrault the writer</u>, mistakenly
(7)

assumed that the word *vair* should have been <u>*verre*</u>. (*Verre* means
(8)

"glass.") <u>Oh well</u>? Can you imagine a fancy prince exclaiming that
(9)

he would <u>"marry the owner of a fur slipper?"</u>
(10)

---

1. A. tragic.
   B. tragic,
   C. tragic —
   D. Correct as is

2. A. consequences.
   B. consequences,
   C. consequences?
   D. Correct as is

3. A. their
   B. they're
   C. theyr'e
   D. Correct as is

4. A. "Cinderella."
   B. *Cinderella.*
   C. CINDERELLA.
   D. Correct as is

5. A. glass shoes;
   B. glass shoes?
   C. glass shoes,
   D. Correct as is

6. A. Cinderella's
   B. Cinderellas
   C. Cinderella
   D. Correct as is

7. A. Perrault, the writer,
   B. Perrault the writer
   C. Perrault, the writer
   D. Correct as is

8. A. *verre*
   B. *verre,*
   C. *verre:*
   D. Correct as is

9. A. Oh well;
   B. Oh well,
   C. Oh well!
   D. Correct as is

10. A. he would marry the owner
       of a fur slipper?
    B. he would "marry the owner
       of a fur slipper.
    C. he would marry the owner
       of a "fur slipper."
    D. Correct as is

Periods and Other End Marks

❶ Here's the Idea

Periods, question marks, and exclamation points are known as **end marks** because they indicate the end of a sentence. Periods have other uses as well.

Periods

▶ **Use a period at the end of a declarative sentence.** A declarative sentence makes a statement.

Not all blunders have bad results.

Some important discoveries have happened by accident.

▶ **Use a period at the end of almost every imperative sentence.** An imperative sentence gives a command. When these sentences express excitement or emotion, they end with exclamation points.

Tell us more about these great mistakes.

Don't stop! These stories are really interesting.

▶ **Use a period at the end of an indirect question.** An indirect question reports what a person asked without using the person's exact words.

DIRECT   Tracy asked, "Is this article about x-rays true?"

INDIRECT   Tracy asked whether the article about x-rays is true.

Question Marks

▶ **Use a question mark at the end of an interrogative sentence.** An interrogative sentence asks a question.

How were x-rays discovered?

Who first recognized them?

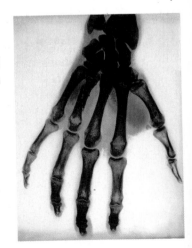

Exclamation Points

▶ **Use an exclamation point to end an exclamatory sentence.** An exclamatory sentence expresses strong feeling.

I can't believe it**!** That's an amazing bit of luck**!**

▶ **Use an exclamation point after an interjection or any other exclamatory expression.**

Hey**!** I bet the scientist who first saw them was surprised.

Wow**!** Strange things do happen in laboratories.

Other Uses for Periods

▶ **Use a period at the end of most abbreviations or after an initial.**

Common Abbreviations and Initials

Abbreviations

sec. second	**Dr.** Doctor	**Sr.** Senior	**tsp.** teaspoon
min. minute	**Nov.** November	**E.** East	**in.** inch
hr. hour	**Tues.** Tuesday	**St.** Street	**Prof.** Professor

Initials

R.R. railroad	**M.T.P.** Maria Theresa Parsons
P.O. post office	**P.M.** *post meridiem* (after noon)
M.D. doctor of medicine	**D.C.** District of Columbia

Abbreviations Without Periods

CD compact disc	**MVP** Most Valuable Player
UN United Nations	**mph** miles per hour
NY New York	**cm** centimeters

▶ **Use a period after each number or letter in an outline or a list.**

Outline

Uses for X-rays
I**.** Medical
   A**.** Pictures of bones and teeth
   B**.** Cancer treatments
II**.** Industrial
   A**.** Security devices
   B**.** Pest control

List

Parts of an X-Ray Machine
1**.** Glass tube
2**.** Negative electrode
3**.** Positive electrode
4**.** Electric current
5**.** Tube housing
6**.** Film compartment

❷ Practice and Apply

A. CONCEPT CHECK: Periods and Other End Marks

Write the words from the following paragraph that should be followed by periods, question marks, or exclamation points. Include these end marks in your answers.

X-rays Exposed

Did you know that x-rays were discovered by accident No kidding In 1895, Prof Wilhelm Roentgen, a German scientist, conducted a new experiment. He worked in a darkened room with a special vacuum tube. The tube used a bright electric current When Roentgen placed a sheet of black paper around the tube, he was surprised by the results Instead of seeing complete darkness, Roentgen noticed an eerie glow coming from a nearby screen How strange Roentgen soon realized that this glow was caused by mysterious invisible rays coming from the tube Can you guess why he called his discovery x-rays In science, the letter x means something unknown

➜ **For a SELF-CHECK and more practice, see the EXERCISE BANK, p. 557.**

B. WRITING: Punctuating Abbreviations

Rewrite the announcement below, adding periods where they are needed.

Don't miss this year's
SCIENCE FAIR!

Date: Sat, Nov 13, 2004
Time: 10:00 AM—3:00 PM
Place: Girls' Gymnasium
        Thomas A Edison Jr High
        School
        1120 N Red Robin Ln
        Mt Vernon, OH

If you would like to participate,
please see Ms Walker.

Commas in Sentences

❶ Here's the Idea

Commas can be used to separate parts of a sentence.

Commas with Items in a Series

▶ **Use a comma after every item in a series except the last one.** A series consists of three or more items.

The story of Daedalus and his son Icarus teaches us about **cleverness, stubbornness,** and **foolishness.**

Each man used **wax, feathers,** and a **harness** to make a pair of wings.

Icarus and Daedalus **put on their wings, ran along the beach, and flew toward the open sea.**

▶ **Use commas between two or more adjectives of equal rank that modify the same noun.**

Both father and son made a **quick, daring** escape.

Here's How **Adding Commas Between Adjectives**

To decide whether to use a comma between two adjectives modifying the same noun, try the following test.

Daedalus used large stiff feathers.

1. Place the word *and* between the adjectives.

Daedalus used large and stiff feathers.

2. If the sentence still makes sense, replace *and* with a comma.

Daedalus used large, stiff feathers.

Do not use a comma between adjectives that together express a single idea.

Each pair of wings had many light feathers.

Commas with Introductory Words and Phrases

▶ **Use a comma after an introductory word or phrase to separate it from the rest of the sentence.**

Recklessly, Icarus flew too close to the sun.

According to Greek myth, Icarus fell when his wings melted.

Commas with Interrupters

▶ **Use commas to set off words or phrases that interrupt, or break, the flow of thought in a sentence.**

Daedalus, however, did fly to freedom.

This myth has been told, I am certain, by many authors.

Commas with Nouns of Direct Address

▶ **Use commas to set off nouns of direct address.** A noun of direct address names the person or group being spoken to.

Devon, explain why Daedalus warned Icarus about the sun.

Don't forget, class, that Icarus didn't listen to his father.

Commas with Appositives

An **appositive** is a word or phrase that identifies or renames a noun or pronoun that comes right before it. Use commas when the appositive adds extra information; do not use commas when the appositive is needed to make the meaning clear.

Olivia E. Coolidge, an English author, wrote about Greek myths. (The phrase *an English author* adds extra information.)

The English author Olivia E. Coolidge wrote about Greek myths. (The phrase *Olivia E. Coolidge* is needed information.)

Commas to Avoid Confusion

▶ **Use a comma whenever the reader might otherwise be confused.**

UNCLEAR   Soon after Icarus left Daedalus followed.

CLEAR   Soon after Icarus left, Daedalus followed.

❷ Practice and Apply

A. CONCEPT CHECK: Commas in Sentences

Write the words from the following passage that should be followed by commas.

Oil Takes Its Toll

In 1989, an oil tanker, the *Exxon Valdez,* went aground off the coast of Alaska. Eleven million gallons of smelly sticky oil spilled out of the tanker. Spread by the ocean current the oil slick soon coated 1,300 miles of Alaska's shoreline. The magnificent, sparkling beaches of Alaska turned oily and black. The spill killed approximately 2,800 otters 300 seals 250 bald eagles and 250,000 other birds.

Ten years later there were signs of recovery. A council was established after the spill to help restore wildlife. Molly McCammon its director indicated that things were looking better. The numbers of bald eagles and pink salmon were strong. She added however that more work needed to be done to improve the numbers of seals, herring, and ducks.

➡ **For a SELF-CHECK and more practice, see the EXERCISE BANK, p. 557.**

B. MIXED REVIEW: Using Punctuation Correctly

Write the words from the following passage that should be followed by end marks or commas. Include these punctuation marks in your answers.

The Great Caterpillar Catastrophe

In 1869, Leopold Trouvelot a French scientist imported caterpillars to Massachusetts. Why did he import them He hoped to crossbreed the adult form of these caterpillars, known as gypsy moths with the moths of silkworms He thought perhaps foolishly, that he could create a new American caterpillar, one that made valuable silk Unfortunately Trouvelot's experiment had a terrible outcome

One day a gust of wind knocked over a caterpillar cage in his house What a mess Crawling out an open window, the caterpillars escaped. Soon they grew into adult moths and migrated Over many years the moths spread to Virginia Maryland and New York Now they are pests that destroy healthy trees Who would believe that so much trouble could come from one mishap with caterpillars It's amazing

Commas: Dates, Addresses, and Letters

CHAPTER 9

❶ Here's the Idea

See these rules in action in the letter below.

Commas in Dates, Addresses, and Letters	
Commas in dates	In dates, use a comma between the day and the year. (Use a comma after the year if the sentence continues.)
Commas in addresses	Use a comma between the city or town and the state or country. (Use a comma after the state or country if the sentence continues.)
Commas in letters	Use a comma after the greeting of a casual letter and after the closing of a casual or business letter.

1   422 Fairfax Road

2   Milton , MA 02186

3   April 13 , 2000

> **Line 2:** comma between city and state

> **Line 3:** comma between day and year

4 Dear Jeri ,

5   Do you remember how we laughed

6 when we saw a picture of the Leaning

7 Tower of Pisa? Well, my grandma told me

8 that the tower tilts because of a terrible

9 mistake. Long ago, in Pisa , Italy , architects

10 planned to make a bell tower for the

11 town's cathedral. Everything went well in

12 the beginning. But during construction,

13 the tower started to lean. The builders

14 realized that the ground underneath the

15 tower was too soft. Unfortunately, the

16 tower leans a little bit more every year.

17   I'm planning to see the tower on

18 March 21 , 2001 , when I visit my grandma

19 in Italy. It will be her 90th birthday. I

20 hope the tower is still standing by then.

> **Line 4:** comma after greeting

> **Line 9:** commas after city and country

> **Line 18:** commas after day and year

> **Line 21:** comma after closing

21   Your friend ,

22   Christa

WATCH OUT

Do not use a comma between the state and the ZIP code.

❷ Practice and Apply

A. CONCEPT CHECK: Commas: Dates, Addresses, and Letters

The letter below is a field trip proposal that a student has been asked to write for class. Write the words and numbers from the letter that should be followed by commas.

175 Green Street
Englewood CO 80110
May 6 2000

Dear Mr. Clayton
    I think that our social studies class should visit the history museum on October 12 2000 our field trip day. We'd have fun seeing exhibits on the things we've studied. So far, we've learned about ancient people of Mesopotamia, Egypt, and China. I especially liked reading stories about the Great Pyramid in Giza Egypt and the Ch'in tomb near Sian China. Of course, if we go, we'll have to stop by my favorite place, the mummy room! It would be a mistake to miss it!
    I hope that you will accept my proposal.

Sincerely

Malcolm

➡ For a SELF-CHECK and more practice, see the EXERCISE BANK, p. 558.

B. WRITING: Dear Friend

Put a letter together using these parts. Don't forget to add commas where they belong.

1300 Dearborn St.

As ever

I enjoyed your letter, especially the sandcastle story. My family is going to a party in Milwaukee Wisconsin next Saturday. Would you like to join us?

Dear Matt

June 25, 2000

Chicago IL 60610

Sarah

PUNCTUATION

Punctuating Quotations

❶ Here's the Idea

To punctuate quotations, you need to know where to put quotation marks, commas, and end marks.

Direct Quotations

A direct quotation is the exact words of a writer or a speaker.

▶ **Use quotation marks at the beginning and the end of a direct quotation.**

"All passengers assemble on deck," said the captain.

▶ **Use commas to set off explanatory words used with direct quotations (whether they occur at the beginning, in the middle, or at the ends of sentences).**

The captain said, "All passengers assemble on deck."

"All passengers," said the captain, "assemble on deck."

"All passengers assemble on deck," said the captain.

▶ **If a quotation is a question or an exclamation, place the question mark or exclamation point inside the closing quotation marks.**

"Have we hit an iceberg?" a crewman asked.

▶ **If quoted words are part of a quotation or exclamation of your own, place the question mark or exclamation point outside the closing quotation marks.**

Did I hear him say, "I believe we're sinking"?

HOT TIP Commas and periods always go inside closing quotation marks. They're too little to stay outside.

Indirect Quotations

▶ **Do not use quotation marks to set off an indirect quotation.**

An indirect quotation tells, in different words, what someone said. An indirect quotation is often introduced by the word *that*. It does not require a comma.

DIRECT   Captain Smith shouted to the radio operators, "You can do no more. Abandon your cabin."

INDIRECT   Finally, Captain Smith told the radio operators that they should abandon their cabin.

Divided Quotations

A divided quotation is a direct quotation that is separated into two parts. Explanatory words such as *he said* or *she said* come between the parts.

▶ **Use quotation marks to enclose both parts of a divided quotation.**

"The ship," the owner said, "is unsinkable."

▶ **Do not capitalize the first word of the second part of a divided quotation unless it begins a new sentence.**

"The ship is unsinkable," he said, "because of its double-bottomed hull."

"The ship is unsinkable," he said. "It has extra protection because of its double-bottomed hull."

▶ **Use commas to set off the explanatory words used with a divided quotation.**

"This ship," he explained, "has extra safety features."

Quotation Marks in Dialogue

▶ **In dialogue, a new paragraph and a new set of quotation marks signal a change in speakers.**

A dialogue is a conversation between two or more speakers.

LITERARY MODEL

" Ready? "
" Ready. "
" Now? "
" Soon. "
" Do the scientists really know? Will it happen today, will it? "
" Look, look; see for yourself! "

The children pressed to each other like so many roses, so many weeds, intermixed, peering out for a look at the hidden sun.

—Ray Bradbury, "All Summer in a Day"

Using Quotation Marks

Use this model to review the punctuation in this lesson.

PROFESSIONAL MODEL

"Did you know that the *Titanic* was not the only large ship to be lost at sea?" Amanda asked.

"What other ship was lost?" replied Linda. — Questions

"In 1840, the largest ship was the *President*," explained Amanda. "On its third trip across the Atlantic, it left New York and was never heard from again." — Divided quotation

"If that's true," Linda questioned, "then why hasn't anyone made a movie about the *President?* Who knows about it?" — Divided quotation

"Well, we do!" exclaimed Amanda. — Exclamations

"Right!" shouted Linda. "Hey, let's use this idea for our social studies project."

❷ Practice and Apply

A. CONCEPT CHECK: Punctuating Quotations

Rewrite each sentence, adding quotation marks and other punctuation where needed. If a sentence is correct, write *Correct*.

A Bug in the Works!

"Why is the word *bug* used to describe a computer problem asked Steve.

Well, began Jessie. "In 1945, a computer scientist named Grace Murray Hopper was working in a computer lab."

"So far, this isn't a very exciting story, commented Steve.

"Let me continue shouted Jessie. "While trying to finish a project, Hopper noticed that the computer continued to have problems."

What happened next questioned Steve.

Jessie explained, "When Hopper looked closer at the inside of the computer, she found a moth messing up everything."

"You're making this up exclaimed Steve

"No, it's true, stated Jessie. "She glued the dead moth to the log book with a note explaining the accident." Jessie added, Ever since then, computer problems have been called bugs."

➡ For a SELF-CHECK and more practice, see the EXERCISE BANK, p. 559.

B. WRITING: He Said; She Said

Choose one frame from this cartoon and write it as a short dialogue. Add explanatory words such as *Calvin bragged* or *Susie explained* to make your work clearer. Be sure to punctuate your dialogue correctly.

Calvin and Hobbes by Bill Watterson

Semicolons and Colons

LESSON 5

❶ Here's the Idea

A **semicolon** separates parts in a sentence. It is stronger than a comma but not as strong as a period. A **colon** shows that a list follows. Colons are also used after greetings in business letters and in expressions of time.

Semicolons in Compound Sentences

▶ **Use a semicolon to join parts of a compound sentence without a coordinating conjunction.**

The mistake was simple; the result was disastrous.

Semicolons with Items in a Series

▶ **When there are commas within parts of a series, use semicolons to separate the parts.**

Bodies within the solar system include the nine planets; about 50 satellites, such as Earth's moon; more than 1,000 comets, such as Halley's comet; and thousands of asteroids.

Colons

▶ **Use a colon to introduce a list of items.**

Planets revolve around the sun in this order: Mercury, Venus, Earth, Mars, Jupiter, Saturn, Uranus, Neptune, and Pluto.

Mars has these earthlike features: ice-covered poles, an atmosphere, and changing seasons.

Do not use a colon directly after a verb or a preposition.

INCORRECT Through the telescope he saw: Mars, the Red Planet.

▶ **Use a colon after the formal greeting in a business letter or letter of complaint.**

BUSINESS   Dear Principal Jones: Dear Ms. Mark:
For a model, see the business letter in the Model Bank.

▶ **Use a colon between hours and minutes in expressions of time.**

The lecture starts at 7:30 P.M. A reception follows at 9:00 P.M.

CHAPTER 9

❷ Practice and Apply

A. CONCEPT CHECK: Semicolons and Colons

Write the words from the following passage that should be followed by semicolons or colons. Include these punctuation marks in your answers.

A "Simple" Mistake

In December of 1998, NASA successfully launched the Mars Climate Orbiter. It was designed to get detailed information about Mars and its weather conditions. According to plan, it would record the following data atmospheric temperatures, dust levels, water vapor levels, and cloud cover.

On September 23, 1999, the Climate Orbiter was ready to go into orbit around Mars. At about 500 A.M. Eastern time, rocket firings began, and radio contact was lost. Contact was expected to be restored about 530 A.M. But instead the worst of sounds came from scientists' computers silence, silence, and more silence.

Hours later, NASA scientists were grim the mission had failed. One team of scientists had used *metric* measurements another team had used *English* measurements. This mix-up put the spacecraft off course by about 60 miles! Of course, NASA lost the orbiter and all of its contents an infrared temperature meter, a device for measuring moisture, communications instruments, and other specialized equipment. A $125-million craft had been lost due to a simple metric conversion mistake.

➜ For a SELF-CHECK and more practice, see the EXERCISE BANK, p. 559.

B. WRITING: Lost in Deep Space

It's easy to lose things, especially in the deep darkness of a closet or locker! Write about a time you misplaced something important, such as your lunch, your uniform, a CD, or a homework assignment. Include information about all the places you looked and the things you picked up while searching. Make sure to include semicolons and colons in your description.

Hyphens, Dashes, and Parentheses

❶ Here's the Idea

Hyphens, dashes, and parentheses help make your writing clear by separating or setting off words or parts of words.

Hyphens

▶ **Use a hyphen if part of a word must be carried over from one line to the next.**

1. Separate the word between syllables.
   RIGHT: let-ter   WRONG: lette-r

2. The word must have at least two syllables to be broken.
   RIGHT: num-ber   WRONG: ea-rth

3. You must leave at least two letters on each line.
   RIGHT: twen-ty   WRONG: a-round

▶ **Use hyphens in certain compound words.**

self-confident   brother-in-law

▶ **Use hyphens in compound numbers from twenty-one through ninety-nine.**

twenty-three   seventy-two

▶ **Use hyphens in spelled-out fractions.**

one-half   three-fourths

Dashes

▶ **Use dashes to show an abrupt break in thought.**

Sojourner Truth—whose birth name was Isabella Baumfree—spent many years of her life speaking out against slavery.

Parentheses

▶ **Use parentheses to set off material that is loosely related to the rest of the sentence.**

Sojourner Truth met Harriet Tubman (a conductor of the Underground Railroad) during the Civil War.

❷ Practice and Apply

A. CONCEPT CHECK: Hyphens, Dashes, and Parentheses

Rewrite each sentence, adding hyphens, dashes, and parentheses where needed. If a sentence is correct, write *Correct*.

Breaking a Promise to the Wrong Woman

1. Isabella Baumfree was born into slavery in the late 1790s the exact date is unknown.
2. John Dumont, Baumfree's owner, promised to give her freedom if she worked extra hard.
3. However, Dumont scoundrel that he was refused to honor his word.
4. In a bold move, Baumfree walked off Dumont's farm in search of freedom.
5. She found safety in the home of neighbors they were peaceful Quakers who bought out the remainder of her time as a slave.
6. At the age of about forty six, Baumfree renamed herself Sojourner Truth and began to speak publicly about her suffering.
7. Truth was an eloquent preacher, although she couldn't read or write she never had a formal education.
8. She traveled all over the country even to the White House speaking about abolishing slavery.
9. Truth was an extremely tall woman over six feet tall which helped her get an audience's attention quite easily.
10. Her quick wit and self confidence helped Sojourner Truth become one of the nation's most popular public figures.

Sojourner Truth

➡ For a SELF-CHECK and more practice, see the EXERCISE BANK, p. 560.

B. REVISING: Using Hyphens

Rewrite the following phrases, adding hyphens where needed. If a phrase is correct, write *Correct*.

1. seventy five days
2. thirty minutes
3. your sister in law
4. one fifth of a year
5. two thirds of an hour
6. your sister's law firm

Apostrophes

LESSON 7

① Here's the Idea

Apostrophes are used in possessive nouns, contractions, and some plurals.

Apostrophes in Possessives

▶ **Use an apostrophe to form the possessive of any noun, whether singular or plural.**

For a singular noun, add 's even if the word ends in s.

   Sam**'s** baseball   Francis**'s** cap

For plural nouns that end in s, add only an apostrophe.

   the spectator**s'** cheers   the player**s'** uniforms

For plural nouns that do not end in s, add 's.

   women**'s** team   family**'s** plan

Apostrophes in Contractions

▶ **Use apostrophes in contractions.**

In a contraction, words are joined and letters are left out. An apostrophe replaces the letter or letters that are missing.

Commonly Used Contractions		
I am → I'm	you are → you're	you will → you'll
she is → she's	they have → they've	it is → it's
cannot → can't	they are → they're	was not → wasn't

Don't confuse contractions with possessive pronouns, which do not contain apostrophes.

Contractions Versus Possessive Pronouns	
Contraction	**Possessive Pronoun**
it's (*it is* or *it has*)	its (belonging to it – *its wing*)
who's (*who is*)	whose (belonging to whom – *whose glove*)
you're (*you are*)	your (belonging to you – *your arm*)
they're (*they are*)	their (belonging to them – *their yard*)

CHAPTER 9

Apostrophes in Plurals

▶ **Use an apostrophe and s to form the plural of a letter, a numeral, or a word referred to as a word.**

Your *i*'s look like *e*'s.   How many 6's are in her uniform number?

The sportscaster's report was filled with *too bad*'s and *next time*'s.

❷ Practice and Apply

A. CONCEPT CHECK: Apostrophes

Find and correct the errors in the use of apostrophes.

Mistakes Turn to Triumph

A series of mistakes came just before the 1996 Olympic Games most memorable moment. It was July 23, the last night of team competition in womens gymnastics. Dominique Moceanu fell on both of her vaults. The U.S. teams chances for a gold medal looked bad. Kerri Strug's turn came next. Kerri fell too—badly. She thought maybe shed broken her ankle. She didnt know if she should take her second vault. Kerris coach, Bela Karolyi, left the decision up to her. Kerri didn't think her team would win if she didn't try again—so she did. Everyones gaze was fixed on her as she sprinted down the runway, vaulted—and landed perfectly. Seconds later, after gently lifting her aching foot, shed crumpled to the mat. Her courage lifted a nations heart. And the womens team won gold!

➡ **For a SELF-CHECK and more practice, see the EXERCISE BANK, p. 560.**

B. WRITING: Using Possessives and Contractions

Write the correct form from the choices in the parentheses.

(Whose/Who's) side are you on for tonight's game? I'm going to cheer for the Wolverines. (Their/They're) offense is incredible! I can't wait to see (Tess'/Tess's) amazing moves. Believe me, (your/you're) going to regret it if you don't support them. (Its/It's) going to be one terrific victory!

Punctuating Titles

❶ Here's the Idea

Use quotation marks and italics correctly in titles to show what kind of work or selection you are writing about.

Quotation Marks

▶ **Use quotation marks to set off the titles of short works.**

Quotation Marks for Titles	
Book chapter	"The Dream" from *Dogsong*
Short story	"Flowers and Freckle Cream"
Essay	"Bringing Home the Prairie"
Article	"Home on an Icy Planet"
Song	"The Star-Spangled Banner"
Poem	"Analysis of Baseball"

Italics and Underlining

▶ **Use italics for titles of longer works and for the names of ships, trains, spacecraft, and airplanes (but not the type of plane).** In handwriting, you show that something should be in italic type by **underlining** it.

Italics or Underlines for Titles			
Book	*The Lost Garden*	**Epic poem**	*The Odyssey*
Play	*The Hobbit*	**Painting**	*Mona Lisa*
Magazine	*World*	**Ship**	*Titanic*
Movie	*The Lion King*	**Train**	*City of New Orleans*
TV series	*Cosby*	**Spacecraft**	*Viking I*
Long musical work	*The Barber of Seville*	**Airplane**	*Air Force One*

❷ Practice and Apply

A. CONCEPT CHECK: Punctuating Titles

Correctly punctuate the titles in each sentence, using either quotation marks or underlining as appropriate.

Mistakes in the Media

1. You can read about real mistakes—big and small—in news magazines such as Newsweek.

2. In the classic film The Wizard of Oz, Dorothy makes the mistake of taking her home for granted until she loses it.

3. Mistakes That Worked is the title of a book that describes mistakes that have helped people.

4. Everyone can relate to the common human mistakes that family members make in the TV series Cosby.

5. In Homer's epic poem the Odyssey, the blinded Cyclops can't see Odysseus and his men escape under the bodies of sheep.

6. Many popular songs, such as You're Gonna Miss Me When I'm Gone, are about mistakes in love.

7. The short story Scout's Honor describes many funny mistakes made by a group of boy scouts on a camping trip.

8. In the poem Casey at the Bat, poor Casey strikes out.

9. The best-selling children's book of all time, The Tale of Peter Rabbit, has a main character who always gets into trouble.

10. Did you read the newspaper article with the blooper headline—Red Tape Holds Up New Bridge?

➜ For a SELF-CHECK and more practice, see the EXERCISE BANK on p. 561.

B. WRITING: Be the Judge

Write down the title of your favorite book, poem, movie, TV show, and song. Exchange your titles with a partner. Review your partner's list and check each title for underlining or quotation marks.

Grammar in Literature

Using Punctuation in Poetry

When you write poetry, punctuation is very important. The first word of each line of poetry is often capitalized even if it doesn't begin a sentence. Furthermore, sentences may not end when a line does. Notice how the punctuation in the following poem helps you understand its meaning.

The Quarrel
by Eleanor Farjeon

Two Birds, One Worm (1989), © William Wegman. Watercolor on paper, 11" x 14".

I quarreled with my brother,
I don't know what about,
One thing led to another
And somehow we fell out.
The start of it was slight,
The end of it was strong,
He said he was right,
I knew he was wrong!
We hated one another.
The afternoon turned black.
Then suddenly my brother
Thumped me on the back,
And said, "Oh, come along!
We can't go on all night—
I was in the wrong."
So he was in the right.

An apostrophe marks a contraction. This tells readers the language of the poem is informal.

Commas indicate that the sentence continues onto the next line.

An exclamation mark ends a strong emotional statement.

Quotation marks enclose the brother's exact words.

Practice and Apply

A. REVISING: Adding Punctuation to Poetry

A student wrote the following poem about an embarrassing moment he experienced. He got so caught up in describing what happened that he completely forgot to use punctuation. Rewrite the poem, adding necessary punctuation marks.

It started just like any day
I quickly dressed I grabbed my books
I got my bike and rode away

When I rode up to the school
An empty playground met my eyes
Which made me think Uh oh not cool
Whats the deal What a strange surprise

I saw my teacher walking by
Her goofy dog walked at her side
It seemed so strange I asked her why
She wasn't getting set inside

She smiled and then she said to me
Todays the day I take it slow
Because its Saturday you see
But I guess you didnt know

B. WRITING: Learning by Mistakes

Many people believe that making mistakes is the best way to learn. Write a poem about a mistake you made and the lesson you learned from it. Be sure to punctuate your poem correctly. Save your writing in your 🗀 **Working Portfolio.**

A. Commas, Semicolons, and Colons Write the words and numbers from the following passage that should be followed by commas, semicolons, or colons. Include these punctuation marks in your answers.

Kudzu—Love It or Hate It!

What's kudzu? It's a thick sturdy vine found in the southeastern United States. The plant was first brought to this country in 1876 for the Centennial Exposition in Philadelphia Pennsylvania. Many Southerners liked its large fragrant blooms. They began to use it in their gardens. For many years kudzu was grown to create shade in hot dry areas.

By the 1950s however people began to see that they made a big mistake when they planted kudzu. Its vines became uncontrollable. They overtook trees poles and abandoned buildings. Kudzu vines destroyed many gardens and forests they blocked out the sunlight.

Today, kudzu continues to be a nuisance to many Southerners. Yet some have tried to make the best of this bad situation by creating the following items from kudzu jellies, syrups, candy and baskets. In fact there are several kudzu recipe books they give instructions for those interested in cooking up the curious creeper. Though they may either love or hate kudzu, most Southerners agree that it's here to stay!

B. End Marks and Other Punctuation Put the letter together using these parts. Add the missing punctuation marks where they belong.

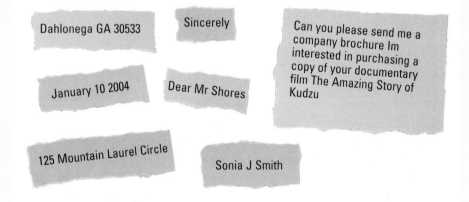

Dahlonega GA 30533

Sincerely

Can you please send me a company brochure Im interested in purchasing a copy of your documentary film The Amazing Story of Kudzu

January 10 2004

Dear Mr Shores

125 Mountain Laurel Circle

Sonia J Smith

For each numbered item, choose the letter of the best revision.

Would you believe me if I told you the sky was <u>falling</u> More than
(1)
likely, <u>youll</u> say no. <u>However—</u>if a highly respected scientist were to
(2)   (3)
tell you that the most glorious comet was going to fly across the sky,
you'd probably believe him or her. Perhaps this story will change
your mind. <u>In January 1974</u> Harvard astronomer Fred Whipple
(4)
predicted that the comet Kohoutek would give the most spectacular
show of the century. Other <u>astronomers</u> declared that Kohoutek had
(5)
a tail 50 million miles long. They said it would stretch <u>one sixth</u> of
(6)
the way across the sky. Hundreds of people began buying <u>telescopes</u>
(7)
<u>binoculars,</u> and even Kohoutek T-shirts as they waited for the
comet. Finally, on the day of the show, the comet fizzled in <u>it's</u>
(8)
display. <u>Time</u> magazine described Kohoutek as <u>a disappointing dud.</u>
(9)   (10)

1. A. falling.
   B. falling!
   C. falling?
   D. Correct as is

2. A. youll'
   B. you'll
   C. you-ll
   D. Correct as is

3. A. However,
   B. However
   C. However;
   D. Correct as is

4. A. In January, 1974,
   B. In January, 1974
   C. In January 1974,
   D. Correct as is

5. A. astronomer's
   B. astronomers'
   C. astronomers-
   D. Correct as is

6. A. one sixth-
   B. one-sixth
   C. one—sixth
   D. Correct as is

7. A. telescopes, binoculars,
   B. telescopes' binoculars,
   C. telescopes—binoculars,
   D. Correct as is

8. A. its'
   B. its
   C. it(s)
   D. Correct as is

9. A. "Time"
   B. *Time*
   C. Time,
   D. Correct as is

10. A. "a disappointing dud,"
    B. "a disappointing dud".
    C. "a disappointing dud."
    D. Correct as is

Student Help Desk

Punctuation at a Glance

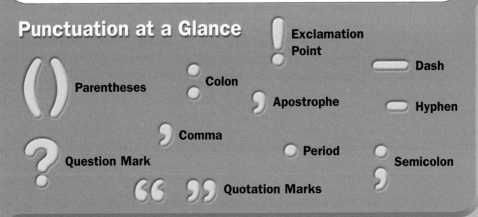

( ) **Parentheses**

Colon

! **Exclamation Point**

Apostrophe

Dash

Hyphen

Comma

? **Question Mark**

Period

Semicolon

" " **Quotation Marks**

Punctuating Titles — Long or Short

Italics (longer works)

Books, Movies, Magazines, Spacecraft, Airplanes,
Plays, Ships, Trains, TV series, Paintings,
Long musical works, Epic poems

Quotation Marks (shorter works)

Stories, Essays, Songs, Poems, Book chapters,
Episodes in a TV series, Magazine articles

Punctuation with Commas — Separating Ideas

	Use commas . . .	Examples
Items in a series	to separate a series of words	I want to find gold, silver, or jewels.
Adjectives	to separate adjectives	Let's look for old, deserted ships.
Introductory words	to separate introductory words	For centuries, grand ships crossed oceans.
Interrupters	to set off interrupters	Many, believe me, held riches.
Nouns of direct address	to set off nouns of direct address	Where should we hunt, Evan?

Punctuation with Quotation Marks — In or Out

Always Inside no matter what

Periods	Rob said, "Hey, let's go to the movies."
Commas	"That's a good idea," replied Ann.

Sometimes Inside if they punctuate the part within the quotation marks

Question marks	"Should we see a disaster movie?" asked Rob.
Exclamation points	"I love disaster movies!" exclaimed Ann.

Sometimes Outside if they punctuate the overall sentence, not just the quote

Question marks	Did you enjoy reading the story "Shipwrecked"?
Exclamation points	No, but I liked "Castaway"! I think it's been made into a movie. Let's see if it's playing!

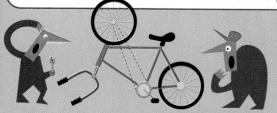

The Bottom Line

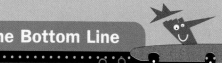

Checklist for Punctuation

Have I . . .

____ ended every sentence with the appropriate end mark?

____ used commas to separate items in a series?

____ used commas correctly in dates, addresses, and letters?

____ used quotation marks before and after a speaker's words?

____ used apostrophes to form contractions and possessives?

____ used italics and quotation marks correctly for titles?

Diagramming: Sentence Parts

Here's the Idea

Diagramming is a way of showing the structure of a sentence. Drawing a diagram can help you see how the parts of a sentence work together to form a complete thought.

Watch me for diagramming tips!

Simple Subjects and Verbs

Write the simple subject and verb on one line. Separate them with a vertical line that crosses the main line.

Tigers growl.

Tigers	growl

Compound Subjects and Verbs

For a compound subject or verb, split the main line. Put the conjunction on a dotted line connecting the compound parts.

Compound Subject

Tigers and lions growl.

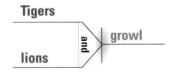

Because there are two subjects, the left side of the main line is split into two parts.

Compound Verb

Tigers growl and roar.

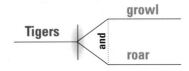

Compound Subject and Compound Verb

Tigers and lions growl and roar.

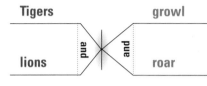

Because there are two subjects and two verbs, both sides of the main line are split into two parts.

A. CONCEPT CHECK: Subjects and Verbs

Diagram these sentences, using what you have learned.

1. Trainers shout.

2. Leopards pace and snarl.

3. Horses and riders circle and bow.

Adjectives and Adverbs

Write adjectives and adverbs on slanted lines below the words they modify.

Marvelous acrobats step quite nimbly overhead.

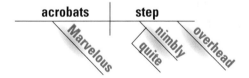

B. MIXED REVIEW: Diagramming

Diagram the following sentences.

1. Tiny Lucinda climbs carefully.

2. The strong young acrobat leaps skillfully.

3. She swings gracefully overhead.

4. Her powerful partner jumps and misses.

5. He plunges sharply downward.

6. The wide net waits below.

7. Lucinda and the other acrobats gasp.

8. The anxious audience fidgets and waits.

9. The lucky acrobat lands and smiles.

10. The audience claps wildly.

DIAGRAMMING

Diagramming: Complements

Subject Complements

- Write a predicate noun or a predicate adjective on the main line after the verb.
- Separate the subject complement from the verb with a slanted line that does not cross the main line.

Predicate Noun

Clowns are skillful performers.

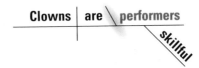

Predicate Adjective

Clowns quite often seem sad.

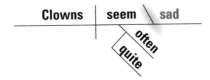

C. CONCEPT CHECK: Subject Complements

Diagram these sentences using what you have learned.

1. The smallest clown appears very serious.
2. His face is a sad mask.

Direct Objects

A direct object follows the verb on the main line.

One clown drives a tiny car.

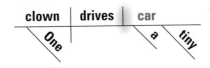

The vertical line between a verb and its direct object does not cross the main line.

Write compound direct objects on parallel lines that branch from the main line.

The driver wears a floppy hat and giant shoes.

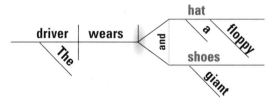

Indirect Objects

Write an indirect object below the verb, on a horizontal line connected to the verb by a slanted line.

The driver gives seven other clowns a ride.

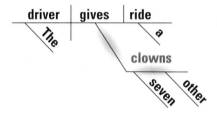

D. MIXED REVIEW: Diagramming

Diagram the following sentences.

1. The Zolanda Circus is very popular.
2. Muscular workers pitch the gigantic tent.
3. Flexible acrobats practice courageous leaps.
4. The lion tamer gives his giant beasts a large meal.
5. An elegant elephant eyes some delicious hay.
6. People gradually fill the empty bleachers.
7. They give the ringmaster their complete attention.
8. The ringmaster creates a hush.
9. The arena becomes a silent stage.
10. Six white horses carry six beautiful dancers.

Diagramming: Prepositional Phrases

Prepositional Phrases

- Write the preposition on a slanted line below the word the prepositional phrase modifies.
- Write the object of the preposition on a horizontal line after the preposition.
- Write any modifier of the object on a slanted line below the object.

Actors in plays need strength and coordination.

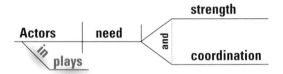

They sometimes leap over scenery on the stage.

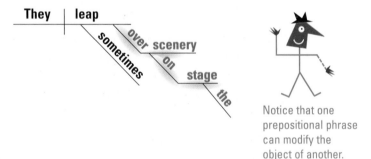

Notice that one prepositional phrase can modify the object of another.

E. CONCEPT CHECK: Prepositional Phrases

Diagram these sentences, using what you have learned.

1. The actor climbed to the top of the ladder.
2. The hat on her head swayed in the breeze.
3. She held tightly to the rungs of the ladder.
4. A gust of wind blew the hat off her head.
5. It fell through the air to the ground.

Diagramming: Compound Sentences

Compound Sentences

- Diagram the independent clauses on parallel horizontal lines.
- Connect the verbs in the two clauses by a dotted line with a solid step in it.
- Write the coordinating conjunction on the step.

  The playwright writes the script, and the director chooses the actors.

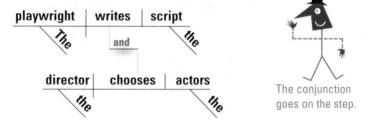

The conjunction goes on the step.

DIAGRAMMING

F. CONCEPT CHECK: Compound Sentences

Diagram these sentences using what you have learned.

1. The actors have come to the first rehearsal, but the writer is still making changes.
2. The actors study their parts, or they walk around nervously.
3. The director is ready, and the rehearsals can now begin.

G. MIXED REVIEW: Diagramming

Diagram the following sentences.

1. Rehearsals of the new play will start today.
2. The director is eager and the cast is ready.
3. Designers are making models of the stage sets.
4. Carpenters will construct the sets in the scene shop.
5. They will paint the scenery, but the stage crew will move it into place.
6. The role of the thief will be played by a well-known actor.
7. An unknown actor from a nearby town will play the detective.
8. The detective does not solve the case of the lost piano, but the audience does.
9. Everyone recognizes the thief by the end of the play.
10. The play will be a big hit with the audience.

Quick-Fix Editing Machine

You've worked hard on your assignment. Don't let misplaced commas, sentence fragments, and missing details lower your grade. Use this Quick-Fix Editing Guide to help you detect grammatical errors and make your writing more precise.

Fixing Errors

1. Sentence Fragments 240
2. Run-On Sentences 241
3. Subject-Verb Agreement 242
4. Pronoun Reference Problems 244
5. Incorrect Pronoun Case 245
6. *Who* and *Whom* 246
7. Confusing Comparisons 247
8. Verb Forms and Tenses 248
9. Missing or Misplaced Commas 249

Improving Style

10. Improving Weak Sentences 250
11. Avoiding Wordiness 251
12. Varying Sentence Structure 252
13. Varying Sentence Length 253
14. Adding Supporting Details 254
15. Avoiding Clichés and Slang 255
16. Using Precise Words 256
17. Using Figurative Language 257
18. Paragraphing 258

QUICK FIX

1 Sentence Fragments

What's the problem? Part of a sentence has been left out.

Why does it matter? A fragment can be confusing because it does not express a complete thought.

What should you do about it? Find out what is missing and add it.

What's the Problem?

Quick Fix

What's the Problem?	Quick Fix
A. A subject is missing. Tripped and broke his glasses.	Add a subject. **My dad** tripped and broke his glasses.
B. A predicate is missing. My skateboard in his way.	Add a predicate. My skateboard **was** in his way.
C. Both a subject and a predicate are missing. In real trouble now.	Add a subject and a predicate to make a complete sentence. **I am** in real trouble now.

For more help, see Chapter 1, pp. 25–27.

② Run-On Sentences

What's the problem? Two or more sentences have been written as though they were a single sentence.

Why does it matter? A run-on sentence doesn't show where one idea ends and another begins.

What should you do about it? Find the best way to separate the ideas or to show the proper relationship between them.

What's the Problem?

Quick Fix

A. **The end mark separating two complete sentences is missing.**

Someone wrote a book about cats who painted with their paws people took it seriously.

Add an end mark to divide the run-on sentence into two sentences.

Someone wrote a book about cats who painted with their paws. People took it seriously.

B. **Two complete thoughts are separated only by a comma.**

Pictures showed the cats "painting," they were just clawing the canvas.

Add a conjunction.

Pictures showed the cats "painting," **but** they were just clawing the canvas.

OR

Replace the comma with an end mark and start a new sentence.

Pictures showed the cats "painting." **They** were just clawing the canvas.

For more help, see Chapter 1, pp. 25–27.

3 Subject-Verb Agreement

What's the problem? A verb does not agree with its subject in number.

Why does it matter? Readers may think your work is careless.

What should you do about it? Identify the subject and use a verb that matches it in number.

What's the Problem?

Quick Fix

A. The first helping verb in a verb phrase does not agree with the subject.

Some **friends has** been working on a class project.

Decide whether the subject is singular or plural, and make the helping verb agree with it.

Some **friends have** been working on a class project.

B. The contraction doesn't agree with its subject.

They doesn't agree on everything.

Use a contraction that agrees with the subject.

They don't agree on everything.

C. A singular verb is used with a compound subject that contains *and*.

The actors and the director wants the film to be good.

Use a plural verb.

The actors and the director want the film to be good.

D. A verb doesn't agree with the nearer part of a compound subject containing *or* or *nor*.

Either the twins or **Elena are** going to star in the film.

Make the verb agree with the nearer part.

Either the twins or **Elena is** going to star in the film.

For more help, see Chapter 7, pp. 166–177.

QUICK FIX

What's the Problem?

E. A verb doesn't agree with an indefinite-pronoun subject.	
Everybody have an opinion about the subject of the film.	
F. A verb agrees with the object of a preposition rather than with the subject.	
The five students on the **team votes** on the final topic.	
G. A verb doesn't agree with the true subject of a sentence beginning with *here* or *there*.	
Here is some old costumes.	

Quick Fix

Decide whether the pronoun is singular or plural, and make the verb agree with it.

Everybody has an opinion about the subject of the film.

Mentally block out the prepositional phrase, and make the verb agree with the subject.

The five **students** on the team **vote** on the final topic.

Mentally turn the sentence around so that the subject comes first, and make the verb agree with it.

(Some old **costumes are** here.)

Here **are** some old **costumes.**

For more help, see Chapter 7, pp. 166–177.

Pronoun Reference Problems

What's the problem? A pronoun does not agree in number, person, or gender with its antecedent, or an antecedent is unclear.

What does it matter? Lack of agreement or unclear antecedents can confuse your readers.

What should you do about it? Find the antecedent and make the pronoun agree with it, or rewrite the sentence to make the antecedent clear.

QUICK FIX

What's the Problem?

Quick Fix

What's the Problem?	Quick Fix
A. A pronoun doesn't agree with its antecedent in number and gender. The **veterinarian** is coming to class with **their** animal "patients."	Find the antecedent and make the pronoun agree in number and gender. The **veterinarian** is coming to class with **her** animal "patients."
B. A pronoun doesn't agree with its antecedent in person or number. **Pet owners** can learn a lot if **you** listen to a vet.	Change the pronoun to agree with the antecedent. **Pet owners** can learn a lot if **they** listen to a vet.
C. A pronoun doesn't agree with an indefinite-pronoun antecedent. **Everyone** argued about **their** favorite pets.	Decide whether the indefinite pronoun antecedent is singular or plural, and make the pronoun agree with it. **Everyone** argued about **his or her** favorite pets.
D. A pronoun could refer to more than one noun. **Kay** and **Arnetta** love dogs, and **she** wants to work at a shelter.	Substitute a noun for the pronoun to make the reference specific. **Kay** and **Arnetta** love dogs, and **Arnetta** wants to work at a shelter.
E. A pronoun agrees with a noun in a phrase rather than with its antecedent. A German shepherd, along with the other **dogs,** did **their** tricks for us.	Mentally block out the phrase and make the pronoun agree with its antecedent. A **German shepherd,** ~~along with the other dogs,~~ did **his** tricks for us.

For more help, see Chapter 3, pp. 69–79.

⑤ Incorrect Pronoun Case

What's the problem? A pronoun is in the wrong case.

Why does it matter? Readers may think your work is sloppy and careless, especially if your writing is for a school assignment.

What should you do about it? Identify how the pronoun is being used, and replace it with the correct form.

What's the Problem?	Quick Fix
A. A pronoun following a linking verb is in the wrong case. The owner of the turtle **was him.**	**Always use the subject case after a linking verb.** The owner of the turtle **was he.**
B. A pronoun used as a direct object is in the wrong case. Mom **told Ben and I** to keep the turtle in our room.	**Always use an object pronoun as a direct object.** Mom **told Ben and me** to keep the turtle in our room.
C. *Who* or *whom* is used incorrectly. **Whom** let the turtle out of its box? **Who** did you see playing with it last?	**Use *who* if the pronoun is a subject and *whom* if it is an object.** **Who** let the turtle out of its box? **Whom** did you see playing with it last?
D. A pronoun in a compound subject is in the wrong case. **Ben and me** looked everywhere for that turtle.	**Always use the subject case for a pronoun used as part of a compound subject.** **Ben and I** looked everywhere for that turtle.
E. A pronoun followed by an identifying noun is in the wrong case. **Us boys** found it in the bathroom before Mom came in!	**Mentally block out the identifying noun to test for the correct case.** **We ~~boys~~** found it in the bathroom before Mom came in!

For more help, see Chapter 3, pp. 57–79.

6 *Who* and *Whom*

What's the problem? The pronoun *who* or *whom* is used incorrectly.

Why does it matter? When writers use *who* and *whom* correctly, readers are more likely to take their ideas seriously.

What should you do about it? Decide how the pronoun functions in the sentence, and then use the correct form.

QUICK FIX

What's the Problem?

Quick Fix

A. *Whom* is incorrectly used as the subject pronoun.

Use *who* as the subject pronoun.

Whom is going to choose the holiday decorations this year?

Who is going to choose the holiday decorations this year?

B. *Who* is incorrectly used as the object of a preposition.

Use *whom* as the object of a preposition.

You're going **with who** to the mall?

You're going **with whom** to the mall?

C. *Who* is incorrectly used as a direct object.

Use *whom* as a direct object.

Who do you **trust** to get inexpensive ones?

Whom do you **trust** to get inexpensive ones?

D. *Who's* is incorrectly used as the possessive pronoun *whose*.

Use *whose* to show possession.

These beautiful decorations are **who's**?

These beautiful decorations are **whose**?

For more help, see Chapter 3, pp. 66–68.

7 Confusing Comparisons

What's the problem? The wrong form of an adjective or adverb is used in making a comparison.

Why does it matter? Comparisons that are not worded correctly can be confusing.

What should you do about it? Use a form that makes the comparison clear.

What's the Problem?

Quick Fix

What's the Problem?	Quick Fix
A. Both *-er* and *more* or *-est* and *most* are used in making a comparison. There is nothing **more grosser** than stale pizza. Yesterday we had the **most stalest** pizza I have ever tasted.	Delete one of the two forms from the sentence. There is nothing ~~more~~ **grosser** than stale pizza. Yesterday we had the ~~most~~ **stalest** pizza I have ever tasted.
B. A superlative form is used where a comparative form is needed. I think it was **worst** than the lunch I had two days ago.	When comparing two things, always use the comparative form. I think it was **worse** than the lunch I had two days ago.
C. A comparative form is used where a superlative form is needed. In any case, it has to be the **more disgusting** lunch I have eaten this month.	When comparing more than two things, always use the superlative form. In any case, it has to be the **most disgusting** lunch I have eaten this month.

For more help, see Chapter 5, pp. 133–135.

8 Verb Forms and Tenses

What's the problem? The wrong form or tense of a verb is used.

Why does it matter? Readers may regard your work as careless or find it confusing.

What should you do about it? Change the verb to the correct form or tense.

What's the Problem?

Quick Fix

A. The wrong form of a verb is used with a helping verb.

Our family **had went** on several sightseeing tours before this one.

Always use a participle form with a helping verb.

Our family **had gone** on several sightseeing tours before this one.

B. A helping verb is missing.

We **been** to every famous place in three states.

Add a helping verb.

We **have been** to every famous place in three states.

C. A past participle is used incorrectly.

I **seen** the United Center, a popular arena, on a previous trip to Chicago.

To write about the past, use the past form of a verb.

I **saw** the United Center, a popular arena, on a previous trip to Chicago.

OR

Change the verb to the past perfect form by adding a helping verb.

I **had seen** the United Center, a popular sports arena, on a previous trip to Chicago.

D. Different tenses are used in the same sentence even though no change in time has occurred.

My dad **drove** for hours, and the road **seems** to go on forever.

Use the same tense throughout the sentence.

My dad **drove** for hours, and the road **seemed** to go on forever.

For more help, see Chapter 4, pp. 96–110.

What's the problem? Commas are missing or are used incorrectly.

Why does it matter? Incorrect use of commas can make sentences difficult to follow.

What should you do about it? Determine where commas are needed, and add them or take them out.

What's the Problem?

A. A comma is missing from a compound sentence. Our town has a skateboard park and we use it nearly every day.	**Add a comma before the conjunction.** Our town has a skateboard park, **and** we use it nearly every day.
B. A comma is missing before the conjunction in a series. The park includes a ramp, a half-pipe and a jumping track.	**Add a comma.** The park includes a ramp, a half-pipe, and a jumping track.
C. A comma is incorrectly placed after a closing quotation mark. "We didn't want kids skateboarding in the streets", the mayor said.	**Always put a comma before a closing quotation mark.** "We didn't want kids skateboarding in the streets," the mayor said.
D. A comma is missing after an introductory word or phrase. After the grand opening all of us skateboarders tried it out.	**Add a comma at the end of the word or phrase.** After the grand opening, all of us skateboarders tried it out.
E. Commas are missing around an appositive that is not essential to the meaning of the sentence. Mom says I live in the skateboard park my second home.	**Add commas to set off the appositive.** Mom says I live in the skateboard park, my second home.

Quick Fix

QUICK FIX

For more help, see Chapter 9, pp. 209–211.

QUICK-FIX EDITING MACHINE

10 Improving Weak Sentences

What's the problem? A sentence repeats ideas or contains too many ideas.

Why does it matter? Sentences that are repetitive or too long can confuse and bore readers.

What should you do about it? Make sure each sentence is complete and contains a clearly focused idea.

QUICK FIX

What's the Problem?

What's the Problem?	Quick Fix
A. A group of words does not express a complete thought.	Add a subject or predicate to make a complete sentence.
The poet Emily Dickinson a very private person.	The poet Emily Dickinson **was** a very private person.
B. A sentence doesn't give any new information or repeats an idea that has already been stated.	Get rid of words and phrases that repeat an idea, and add more details.
Emily Dickinson is my favorite poet. **I really like her a lot.**	Emily Dickinson is my favorite poet, **because her poems tell a lot about everyday life.**
C. A single sentence contains too many loosely connected ideas.	Divide the sentence into two or more sentences. Decide which ideas can be combined and which ideas should be kept separate.
She didn't intend for most of her poetry to be published, and after her death, Emily's sister found many of the poems and she had them published.	She didn't intend for most of her poetry to be published. After Emily's death, her sister found many of the poems and had them published.

For more help, see Chapter 11, pp. 278–279 and Chapter 16, pp. 336–339.

250 Grammar, Usage, and Mechanics

⑪ Avoiding Wordiness

What's the problem? A sentence contains unnecessary words.

Why does it matter? Wordy sentences can confuse and bore readers.

What should you do about it? Use words that are more precise and get rid of any unnecessary words.

What's the Problem?

Quick-Fix

A. An idea is needlessly expressed in two ways.

Emergency room doctors treat everything from broken bones to severe bleeding **and all sorts of cases** at a moment's notice.

Delete words and phrases that repeat an idea.

Emergency room doctors treat everything from broken bones to severe bleeding ~~and all sorts of cases~~ at a moment's notice.

B. A sentence is overloaded with modifiers.

The doctor uses **a small gray battery-operated** computer to take notes.

Substitute a more precise word for a string of modifiers.

The doctor uses a laptop computer to take notes.

For more help, see Chapter 11, pp. 278–279 and Chapter 16, pp. 336–337.

12 Varying Sentence Structure

What's the problem? Too many sentences begin in the same way.

Why does it matter? Lack of variety in sentences makes writing dull and choppy.

What should you do about it? Rearrange the phrases in some of your sentences. Use different types of sentences, such as questions and commands, for more variety and impact.

What's the Problem?

Quick Fix

A. Too many sentences in a paragraph begin the same way.

Have you ever wondered what's inside a baseball? **I took** one apart to find out. **I took** off some pieces of leather in the first layer. They were stitched together with thick red thread. **I then unwrapped** yards and yards of yarn wound very tightly. **I found** two layers of rubber under the wool. **I discovered** a small ball of cork at the center. Now you won't have to destroy your own baseball to see what's inside.

Rearrange the words or phrases in some of the sentences.

Have you ever wondered what's inside a baseball? I took one apart to find out. **The first layer** I took off was made of some pieces of leather. They were stitched together with thick red thread. **Then** I unwrapped yards and yards of yarn wound very tightly. **Under the yarn,** I found two layers of rubber. **At the center,** I discovered a small ball of cork. Now you won't have to destroy your own baseball to see what's inside.

B. Too many declarative sentences are used.

There is a reason why popcorn pops. The corn kernels that are used for popcorn contain a lot of water. When they are heated, the water expands and turns into steam. This causes the kernels to explode into a mass.

Add variety by rewriting one sentence as a command, question, or exclamation.

What makes popcorn pop? The corn kernels that are used for popcorn contain a lot of water. When they are heated, the water expands and turns into steam. This causes the kernels to explode into a mass.

For more help, see Chapter 16, pp. 342–343.

⑬ Varying Sentence Length

What's the problem? A piece of writing contains too many short sentences.

Why does it matter? Choppy sentences without many details can bore readers.

What should you do about it? Combine or reword sentences to create sentences of different lengths.

What's the Problem?

Too many short sentences are used.

My friend Gabriela competed in a race. It was a bicycle race. The race was yesterday. The weather was hard on the racers. The day was hot and humid.

Gabriela easily rode up the mountain trail. It was difficult to steer on the way down. Gabriela won the race. The crowd cheered.

For more help, see Chapter 16, pp. 340–341.

Quick Fix

Get rid of sentences that add only one detail about the subject. Insert those details into other sentences.

Yesterday my friend Gabriela competed in a **bicycle** race. The **hot and humid** weather was hard on the racers.

OR

Use conjunctions such as *or*, *and*, or *but* to combine related ideas or sentences.

Gabriela easily rode up the mountain trail, **but** it was difficult to steer on the way down. Gabriela won the race, **and** the crowd cheered.

QUICK FIX

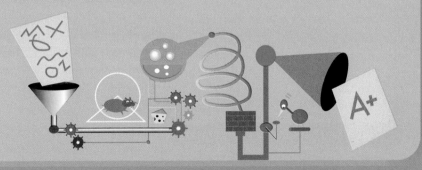

14 Adding Supporting Details

What's the problem? Not enough details are given for readers to fully understand the topic.

Why does it matter? Unanswered questions or unsupported opinions weaken writing.

What should you do about it? Add information and details that will make statements clear.

What's the Problem?

What's the Problem?	Quick Fix
A. Questions are not answered.	**Add details that tell who, what, when, where, why, and how.**
Wolves communicate.	Wolves communicate by using different types of howls.
B. No explanation is given.	**Add definitions and facts to help readers understand the topic.**
Each howl matches a certain situation.	Each howl, or **call,** matches a certain situation. **One kind of howl signals that a wolf wants to "talk." Another warns of danger. When wolves gather to hunt, they howl to greet each other.**
C. No reason is given for an opinion.	**Add a reason.**
My new guitar is great.	My new guitar is great **because it makes me look as cool as my favorite musician.**
D. No details are given.	**Add details describing how the topic looks, sounds, feels, tastes, or smells.**
In fact, everyone is impressed with my guitar.	In fact, everyone is impressed with my guitar. **The wood is as golden as a maple leaf in autumn. There's a fancy design around the sound hole. The nylon strings shine like silvery threads.**

For more help, see Chapter 15, pp. 324–329.

QUICK FIX

15 Avoiding Clichés and Slang

What's the problem? A piece of formal writing contains clichés or slang expressions.

Why does it matter? Clichés have been used so often that they no longer mean anything to readers. Slang is not appropriate in formal writing.

What should you do about it? Reword sentences to replace clichés and slang with clear, fresh expressions.

What's the Problem?

Quick Fix

A. A sentence contains a cliché.

The icicles were **as sharp as needles.**

Replace the cliché with a fresh description or explanation.

The icicles were like crystal daggers.

B. A sentence contains inappropriate slang.

The store owner is unpopular because he will often **dis the kids who hang around** his store.

Replace the slang with more appropriate language.

The store owner is unpopular because he will often yell at the teens who meet in his store.

For more help, see Chapter 17, pp. 348–353.

16 Using Precise Words

What's the problem? Nouns, modifiers, or verbs are not specific.

Why does it matter? Writers who use words that are too general do not give readers a clear picture of their topic.

What should you do about it? Replace general words with precise ones.

What's the Problem?

Quick Fix

A. Nouns are too general.

If you use your **head,** cleaning your room won't be an unpleasant **thing.**

Use specific nouns.

If you use some **creativity,** cleaning your room won't be an unpleasant **task.**

B. Modifiers are too general.

You can **really** whisk away dirt with **some different** objects.

Use vivid adjectives and adverbs.

You can **expertly** whisk away dirt with **three common household** objects.

C. A sentence tells about an action instead of showing it with exact verbs.

First **use** a blow dryer set on high to dust furniture. Next, **get rid of** dirt on the ceiling **using** an old T-shirt and a baseball bat. Then **put** your dirty clothes away.

Use vivid verbs to show action.

First, **blast** away furniture dust with a blow dryer set on high. Then make those nasty cobwebs **vanish** by draping an old T-shirt over the end of a baseball bat and **swiping** it around the ceiling. Make your dirty clothes **disappear** by **stuffing** them into a laundry bag, or **shoving** them under your bed.

For more help, see Chapter 17, pp. 350–351.

QUICK FIX

⑰ Using Figurative Language

What's the problem? A piece of writing is dull or unimaginative.

Why does it matter? Dull writing bores readers because it doesn't help them form mental pictures of what is being described.

What should you do about it? Add figures of speech to make writing lively and to create pictures in readers' minds.

What's the Problem?

A description is dull and lifeless.

The other runner was gaining on me. I heard her breathing as she tried to pass me.

I relaxed for a moment as I ran a few feet ahead. Then I heard her footsteps on the track.

Quick Fix

Add a simile.

The other runner was gaining on me. Her powerful breathing was **like an ocean wave** as she tried to pass me.

OR

Rewrite the sentence, adding a metaphor.

I relaxed for a moment as I ran a few feet ahead. As I rounded the last bend, **her footsteps on the cinder track were pesky mosquitoes.**

For more help, see Chapter 17, pp. 352–353.

QUICK FIX

18 **Paragraphing**

What's the problem? A paragraph contains too many ideas.

Why does it matter? A long paragraph discourages readers from continuing.

What should you do about it? Break the paragraph into shorter paragraphs. Start a new paragraph whenever a new idea is presented or the time, place, or speaker changes.

What's the Problem?

My great-grandfather told me how his family from Poland traveled to the United States. He was only 12 years old at the time. When their ship arrived in New York, his mother was ill. An immigration official put a cross on her jacket with chalk. The official said that anyone with a cross on his or her clothing could not enter the United States. "What did you do?" I asked eagerly. Grandpa smiled as he said, "When nobody was looking, I wiped the chalk mark off my mother's jacket. The family stayed together!" Later as we ate lunch, Grandpa gave me a wink. I knew that he thought I was just as clever as he was.

Quick Fix

My great-grandfather told me how his family from Poland traveled to the United States. He was only 12 years old at the time. When their ship arrived in New York, his mother was ill.

Start a new paragraph to introduce a new idea.

An immigration official put a cross on her jacket with chalk. The official said that anyone with a cross on his or her clothing could not enter the United States.

Start a new paragraph whenever the speaker changes.

"What did you do?" I asked.

Grandpa smiled as he said, "When nobody was looking, I wiped the chalk mark off my mother's jacket. The family stayed together!"

Start a new paragraph to change the time or the place.

Later as we ate lunch, Grandpa gave me a wink. I knew that he thought I was just as clever as he was.

For more help, see Chapter 14, pp. 316–318.

What's the Problem?

An essay is treated as one long paragraph.

In the Old West, mail service was unbelievably slow. Until 1858 California had very irregular mail service. It often took two to three months for a letter to arrive. When the Overland Mail Service began that year, it used stage-coaches to carry mail and passengers as well. Now, imagine a trip to California in 1858. You eagerly board a train in St. Louis, Missouri. After riding nearly 150 miles, you transfer to a stagecoach. Hold on tight, because the ride is really rough. The stage coach speeds wildly downhill at five miles per hour. You and the mail travel almost constantly day and night. Sleep is practically impossible. Don't worry. The coach eventually jolts to a stop in San Francisco. Shaking and exhausted, you climb down. Just think, though, your trip took only 24 days. Now that's service!

For more help, see Chapter 14, pp. 316–318.

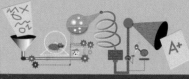

Quick Fix

In the Old West, mail service was unbelievably slow. Until 1858 California had very irregular mail service. It often took two to three months for a letter to arrive. When the Overland Mail Service began that year, it used stagecoaches to carry mail and passengers as well.

Start a new paragraph to introduce another main idea.

Now, imagine a trip to California in 1858. You eagerly board a train in St. Louis, Missouri. After riding nearly 150 miles, you transfer to a stagecoach. Hold on tight, because the ride is really rough. The stagecoach speeds wildly downhill at five miles per hour. You and the mail travel almost constantly day and night. Sleep is practically impossible.

Set the conclusion off in its own paragraph.

Don't worry. The coach eventually jolts to a stop in San Francisco. Shaking and exhausted, you climb down. Just think, though, your trip took only 24 days. Now that's service!

QUICK FIX

Essential Writing
Skills

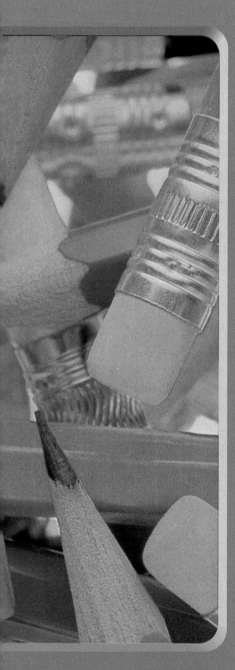

10 Writing Process 263

11 Building Sentences 277

12 Building Paragraphs 289

13 Organizing Paragraphs 301

14 Building Compositions 311

15 Elaboration 323

16 Revising Sentences 335

17 Effective Language 347

The Write Stuff

Whether you use a pencil, a fountain pen, or a high-powered computer, you can express your feelings and opinions through writing. The more you write, the easier it will become for you to find just the right words to use.

Power Words
Vocabulary for Precise Writing

cascade

flow

cautious

careful

We're Not All Sprinters

Here are some useful words to describe being speedy or slow.

Faster than a Speeding Bullet

Are you one of those people who can write as fast as a cheetah can run? When you sit at your desk, do the words **pour** out, **flow** forth, and **stream** smoothly? Do sentences **tumble** and **cascade** onto the page? Do whole paragraphs **race** and **rush** into print? Lucky you!

Slow as Molasses

For the rest of us, writing can be slow going. We may be slow to come up with an idea, but we're not **unwilling, reluctant,** or **loath** to make the attempt; we're not **averse** to trying. We may be slow to commit our words to paper—**hesitant, cautious,** or just plain **careful**—but that's not necessarily a bad way to be!

▷ **Your Turn** Show Your Skill

Think of something that you do well. Perhaps you're a good cook, a superb soccer player, or a video games expert. Work with a partner to create a word web that describes your skill at the activity.

rush

reluctant

HESITAN

Writing Process

On Your Mark! Get Set! Write!

Most runners have a starting line, a set course, and an obvious finish line. But what about writers? Is there a clear starting point? Is there a visible finish line? The answer is yes! Believe it or not, you can use the writing process in ways that keep you on course and lead to your goal—a finished paper— without getting lost along the way. There's only one thing you have to do to get that paper finished. Get started!

Write Away: Write Now
Are you having trouble with a writing assignment that you are working on now? As you work through this chapter, apply the steps of the writing process to your own work. Save your work in your 🗀 **Working Portfolio.**

Prewriting

Have you ever been given a writing assignment and had no idea how to begin? The writing process is a series of steps: prewriting, drafting, revising, editing and proofreading, and publishing and reflecting. You can move through the process one step at a time. You can repeat steps if necessary. No matter how you work, you will probably want to begin with prewriting. During prewriting, you can decide on a topic and then gather information about your topic.

❶ Finding a Topic

Sometimes simply deciding what to write about can be one of the hardest parts of writing. A good place to start is with your own interests. It's easier to write about something that you are interested in or something you are already familiar with.

Interview Yourself

To focus in on some of your main interests, you can give yourself an interview. Try asking yourself some questions.

1. What interesting or unusual thing happened to me this week?
2. What is my favorite way to spend my spare time?
3. What changes would make my community a better place?
4. What person, place, or thing would I like to know more about?

Brainstorm

Get several brains thinking! Work with two or three classmates to see what topic ideas you can come up with.

> **Here's How | Brainstorming to Find a Topic**
>
> • Start with a general topic like movies or sports.
> • Take turns suggesting ideas related to the general topic.
> • Write down every idea without judging or criticizing any. Let each idea trigger a new one.

HOT TIP

You might start a journal to record your thoughts and ideas. It will become a great source of writing topics.

For more on finding ideas, see p. 274.

❷ Focusing a Topic

After you decide on a topic, you might find that it is too big to write about in a single paper. You may need to focus the topic. You can try using a cluster diagram. Or, state the purpose of your paper and decide who your audience will be.

Limiting a Topic

To narrow a large topic, you can draw a cluster diagram. Write the general topic inside a large oval. Then, using smaller ovals, write down some related subjects. Choose one of these subjects as the topic of your paper.

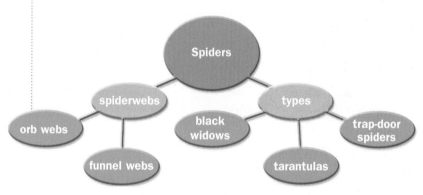

Audience and Purpose

A useful way to determine your audience and purpose is to ask yourself, "*Why* am I writing this paper? *Who* am I writing it for?" Write a sentence stating your audience and purpose.

1. I want to explain to the astronomy club what happens when a star "dies."
2. I want to persuade the community that we need another bike path.
3. I want to describe to my classmates how the trap-door spider builds an underground tunnel.

❸ Finding and Organizing Information

Now that you've decided what to write about, how do you move from idea to draft? One way is to find more information on your topic and organize the information you want to use.

Gathering Information

Even if you already know a little about your topic, you can look for more information in encyclopedias, books, magazines, newspapers, and on the Internet. You may want to take notes on note cards so you can organize information later.

Calvin and Hobbes by Bill Watterson

Organizing Your Notes

After you've gathered information, you can begin to put related facts and ideas together. If you've used note cards, group similar cards together. If you have not used cards, rewrite your notes on paper. This time, put similar ideas together.

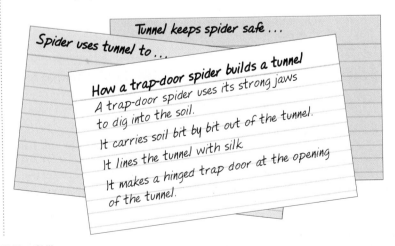

Tunnel keeps spider safe . . .

Spider uses tunnel to . . .

How a trap-door spider builds a tunnel
A trap-door spider uses its strong jaws to dig into the soil.
It carries soil bit by bit out of the tunnel.
It lines the tunnel with silk.
It makes a hinged trap door at the opening of the tunnel.

Drafting

Now you have organized your information, but before you begin your draft, you may want to make a plan for writing. Then you can simply follow your plan as you write your first draft.

❶ Making a Plan

You might base your plan on your groups of organized note cards. Or you could arrange your notes into an informal outline, like the one that follows. Start with the ideas you want to write about. Then add facts that support those ideas. At this stage, you also decide the order in which you will present your ideas.

How a trap-door spider builds a tunnel
Digs with jaws
Lines tunnel with silk
Makes a trap door
How spider uses tunnel
Lays web outside trap door
Waits just under door for bug to come near
Jumps out of door and grabs bug
How tunnel keeps spider safe from enemies
Spider can hold trap door shut
Spider can seal door shut

Remember that you can rethink the order of your plan at any stage. New ideas and better ways of presenting information may occur to you. Don't be afraid to make changes at any time.

Once you start drafting, just keep writing! Get all your ideas down on paper. Don't try for perfection at this stage; you can make improvements and changes at the revising stage.

❷ Using Peer Response

Completing a draft is a major achievement, but even great drafts can be improved. To find out how you might improve your writing, ask your peers or classmates for suggestions. Here are some hints for getting helpful comments.

Reader/Writer Responsibilities

The writer should:
- ask the reader about specific concerns.
- listen politely to the reader's response.
- use only the suggestions that you think are useful.

The reader should:
- first tell the writer what is good about the piece.
- respect the writer's feelings.
- think carefully about the writer's questions and give helpful answers.

Your peer readers' suggestions can help you decide how to revise. For example, if your readers can't follow your draft, you may need to reorganize your ideas. If your readers make a suggestion, don't be afraid to ask them for more details.

What to Ask Peer Readers

You can ask peer readers questions about your draft. Here are some questions you might ask.

- Which parts did you like best?
- Which parts, if any, were confusing?
- What comes across as my main idea?
- What would you like to learn more about?

Revising

No one gets everything exactly right in the first draft. You should look for ways to revise, or change, the draft to make it better organized and more focused. Revising may involve major changes. You might need to omit sentences, rewrite paragraphs, or rearrange the order of information.

1 Six Traits of Good Writing

The chart below shows six traits of good writing. Use these traits to help you improve your draft.

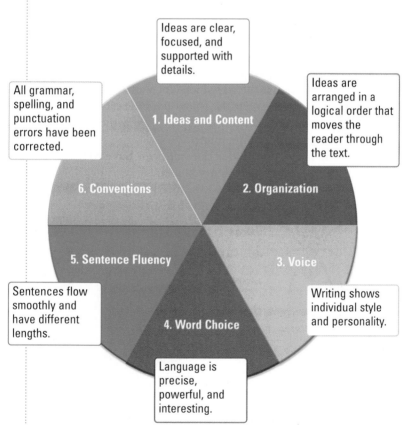

Ideas are clear, focused, and supported with details.

All grammar, spelling, and punctuation errors have been corrected.

Ideas are arranged in a logical order that moves the reader through the text.

1. Ideas and Content

6. Conventions

2. Organization

5. Sentence Fluency

3. Voice

4. Word Choice

Sentences flow smoothly and have different lengths.

Writing shows individual style and personality.

Language is precise, powerful, and interesting.

❷ Traits in Action

The following is part of a student draft. Notice how the six traits appear in this student model.

STUDENT MODEL

Trap-door spiders build themselves underground tunnels to live in. To start building the tunnel, a spider uses its strong jaws to dig into the soil. After it has loosened the dirt, the spider carries it out of the tunnel bit by bit. After a while the tunnel may get to be six inches to a foot deep. The finished tunnel is lined with silk and has a hinged trap door at the top. The trap door fits the tunnel so perfectly that no water can leak in.

Once the tunnel home is finished, the crafty spider rarely travels far from it. At night the spider lays a sheet of web just outside the tunnel. Then it waits inside, just under the trap door. When an unknowing bug steps on the web, the spider feels the vibrations. It flings open the trap door, jumps out, grabs the bug, and then drags it down the tunnel.

The trap-door spider doesn't even have to leave its tunnel when an enemy is near.

> **Ideas and Content:**
> The writer is specific about how the spider builds the tunnel.

> **Word Choice:**
> The writer uses precise words to show what's happening.

> **Sentence Fluency:**
> Sentences flow smoothly and vary in length.

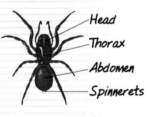

Head
Thorax
Abdomen
Spinnerets

All spiders have the same body features.

A trap-door spider's fangs and claws are very strong. They can hold the door shut if an enemy tries to pry it open. If a lot of enemies—such as a swarm of wasps—are around, the spider might make the tunnel even safer by sealing the trap door shut with silk.

Throughout the draft, notice the following additional traits:

Organization: The writer first explains how the spider builds the tunnel. Then he explains how the spider uses the tunnel.

Voice: The writer expresses ideas in his or her individual style.

Conventions: Grammar, punctuation, and spelling are correct.

Editing and Proofreading

After you've completed your major revisions, it's time to make the smaller—but still very important—corrections. When you edit and proofread, you read through your paper line by line. Look for mistakes in grammar, mechanics, punctuation, and spelling.

HOT TIP You may want to repeat this process several times. You can also ask a friend or family member to proofread your draft. An extra pair of eyes always helps.

For more on proofreading, see p. 275.

Using Proofreading Marks

Use these proofreading marks to show the corrections you need to make in your draft.

Using Proofreading Marks

Symbol	Explanation	Example
⌄	add a comma	Tarantulas are big, hairy, and scary.
∧	add letters or words	Last Friday I saw a guy with ^long green hair playing a saxophone.
#	add a space	Why does this town have only one bike‿path? #
⊙	add a period	I wish I could spend more time playing soccer⊙
≡	capitalize	I'd like to see the monuments in Washington, d.c.≡
⌒	close up	Our crazy rottweiler Sam sleeps on top of his dog ⌒house.
⸍℮	take out letters or words	King cobras have a big wide hood.

WATCH OUT Computer spell checkers don't catch every mistake. The spell checker won't notice that a period is missing or tell you that you typed the word *there* when you meant to type *their*.

Publishing and Reflecting

You've worked hard preparing, writing, and putting the finishing touches on your paper. Now you can choose a way to present your work to others.

1 Ways to Present Your Work

On Paper

- Include a copy of your work in a letter to a friend or family member.
- Submit your work to your school newspaper.
- Get permission to post your work on a school bulletin board.
- Design and distribute a "zine" with original writing and artwork.
- Enter a literary contest through the Internet or a magazine.

In Cyberspace

- E-mail your work to a relative or friend.
- Post your work on an electronic bulletin board.
- Submit your work to your school's Web site.
- Submit your writing to an Internet journal or literary magazine that publishes student writing.

On Stage

- Work with other writers to organize a lunchtime reading of your work. Make posters to advertise the event.
- Give a dramatic reading of your work to friends or family members.
- Make a radio or television "show" by recording your work on audiotape or videotape.

❷ Reflecting on Your Writing

After you've presented your work, take some time to think about how well the writing process worked for you.

Questions for Reflection
- What parts of the process were the easiest? the most difficult?
- How did the writing process help me better understand my subject?
- What would I do differently the next time I write?
- What did I learn that will improve my writing skills?

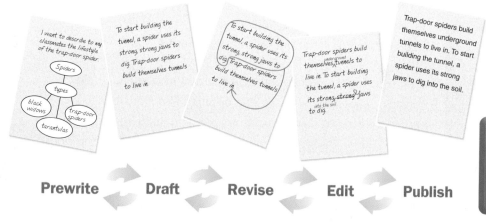

Prewrite → **Draft** → **Revise** → **Edit** → **Publish**

Using Portfolios

You can save all your writing in folders called portfolios.

Working Portfolio

You can put most of your work into your working portfolio— including pieces that are "works in progress" and still need polishing. You can reread the work in your working portfolio every couple of months to track your progress as a writer.

Presentation Portfolio

Put only the pieces that you think are your very best in your presentation portfolio. These are your "masterpieces." You can bring them with you when you enter the next grade as examples of your skills as a writer.

Student Help Desk

Writing Process at a Glance

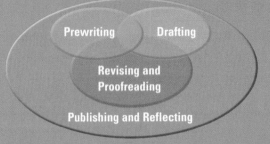

Prewriting Drafting

Revising and Proofreading

Publishing and Reflecting

Finding Ideas Write Until the **Light** Goes On!

- Record your dreams and memories.
- Tape news articles and photos into your journal. Write captions or notes about them.
- Write descriptions of interesting people you have seen.
- Develop conversations you've had or heard into story ideas.
- Keep a log of what happens during a week, a day, or even an hour.
- Solve problems that exist in your school, community, or in the world.
- Discover what you think or feel about controversial issues by freewriting about them.

Tips for Drafting Get the Words Out

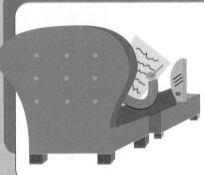

- Find a place where you can write without getting distracted.
- Start writing and follow your plan. If certain sections give you trouble, skip them and come back to them later.
- Don't try to make your first draft perfect. You'll revise later.
- Choose the writing method you like best—print, write in longhand, or type.

Editing Hints | Watch for Word Traps!

If you aren't sure about how to use a word, look it up!

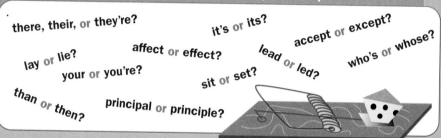

there, their, or they're?

it's or its?

accept or except?

lay or lie?

affect or effect?

lead or led?

who's or whose?

your or you're?

sit or set?

than or then?

principal or principle?

Proofreading Tips | Keep an Eye Out for Errors

One step at a time	Consider each sentence as a single unit. Make sure all sentences begin with a capital letter and end with a period, question mark, or exclamation point.
Listen to yourself	Read your paper aloud. Sometimes it's easier to hear than to see run-on sentences or fragments.
Get help *Help wanted!*	After you've proofread your paper, ask a friend or an adult to proofread it.
Take a fresh look	Proofread your paper once. Then, proofread it again the next day. Most people miss a few errors the first time around.

The Bottom Line

Checklist for Writing

Have I used the six traits of good writing and . . .

____ presented my ideas clearly and supported them with details?

____ organized my ideas logically?

____ made sure my sentences flow smoothly?

____ used precise words?

____ expressed ideas in my own way?

____ fixed all spelling, grammar, and punctuation mistakes?

grow

alter

develop

blossom

spurt of

transmute

transform

CHAPTER 11

growth

A Change for the Better

Use these words to describe transformations.

Changing All the Time

You can **change** your mind, **alter** your clothing, and **vary** your meals. You can **remodel** a house, **convert** a garage, and **renovate** or **refurbish** a kitchen. It seems that you can **transform** almost anything—but you cannot **transmute** lead into gold.

Steady or Startling?

To be alive is to change—to **grow**, **develop**, perhaps even **blossom**. When change is **slow** and **steady**, **gentle** and **gradual**, it often escapes our notice. **Measured**, **incremental** change might not seem like change at all.

On the other hand, a **spurt of growth** can add three inches to your height in just one summer. **Sudden**, **abrupt** changes may seem **instantaneous**, almost like a caterpillar's **metamorphosis** into a butterfly.

▷ **Your Turn** Time for a Change

Working with three or four classmates, brainstorm a list of things that you would like to see changed. You might include issues in your community, environmental problems that you have seen or read about, or rules that your parents set for you. Then choose one item from your list and work together to create a poster about it.

change

metamorphosis

Building Sentences

The caterpillar turned into a butterfly.

Transformations

The magnificent monarch butterfly wasn't born beautiful. It began life as a very ordinary caterpillar. Sentences, too, often begin as ordinary groups of words. This chapter will teach you to turn dull sentences into vivid ones that will hold your readers' interest.

Take a look at the sentence above about the butterfly. What details can you add to make the sentence more vivid? Use the information in the photographs to help you.

Write Away: Time for a Change

Can you remember a time in your life that changed you? Maybe you felt differently about water after you learned to swim. Did math become your favorite subject after someone explained fractions to you so that you *really* understood them?

Write a paragraph describing an accomplishment that helped you to grow. Put this paragraph in your 🗂 **Working Portfolio.**

LESSON 1 Improving Your Sentences

Are your sentences exciting to read? Are they easy to understand? Make sure that your sentences are clear, detailed, and interesting.

① Checking for Completeness

A **complete sentence** is a group of words that expresses a complete thought. Which of the following are not complete sentences?

The boys bathed Nero in a tub.

Splashed water on both boys.

To the dog groomer in the future.

To express a complete thought, a sentence needs both a subject and a predicate. Notice how the addition of a few words fixed the two incomplete sentences from above.

The boys bathed Nero in a tub.
COMPLETE SUBJECT   COMPLETE PREDICATE

That muddy mutt splashed water on both boys.

Nero will go to the dog groomer in the future.

Read over your sentences. If you are missing a subject or a predicate, you have written a **sentence fragment**. Sentence fragments are not complete sentences. They must be fixed to avoid confusing the reader.

For more on fixing sentence fragments, see p. 240.

For more on fixing sentence fragments, see p. 240.

PRACTICE A ▷ Complete the Picture

Rewrite this paragraph so that all its sentences are complete.

Washing a dog is hard work. And pretty messy, too. I tried to wash my dog in the bathtub. That was a bad idea! Water was everywhere. In the tub, on the walls, on the floor. Not much on the dog, though. Next time I will get my sister to help me.

➋ Expanding with Modifiers

Modifiers are words and phrases that tell more about, or modify, the meaning of other words. Modifiers can make a sentence stronger by adding important details. Notice how the modifiers change the following sentences.

I watched the bus leave.

I watched the last bus leave.

Gasping for breath, I watched the last bus leave from the parking lot.

Don't overload your sentences with modifiers. Sometimes it's smarter to substitute more precise words. Instead of writing "Cynthia looked hilarious in her yellow, spotted, long-necked costume," try "Cynthia looked hilarious in her giraffe costume."

PRACTICE B Modifier Magic

Improve the following sentences by adding modifiers. Use the information in the photograph to help you add details.

1. The concert was held outdoors.
2. The audience sat under the stars.
3. Everyone enjoyed the music.
4. Performers signed autographs.
5. People will treasure their souvenirs.

Growing Sentences

As a writer, you will often begin with a simple idea and then help it grow into something more. Notice the differences between these two passages about explorer Matthew Henson.

Three of the sledges broke. Henson was able to repair them.

LITERARY MODEL

Matthew Henson

On the first day, three of the sledges broke, Henson's among them. Fortunately, Henson was able to repair them, despite the fact that it was nearly 50 degrees below zero.

SENTENCE OPENERS

SENTENCE CLOSERS

—Jim Haskins, "Matthew Henson at the Top of the World"

❶ Adding Sentence Openers

The words you use to start a sentence call attention to certain details. Notice how the openers change these sentences.

Terrified, **the coyote dashed under a porch.**

Soon after we called for help, **the city's Animal Control Unit arrived.**

Frightened but unhurt, **the coyote will be released in a wildlife preserve.**

❷ Adding to the Middle

Jazz up the middle of a sentence with a descriptive word or phrase. Place it between the subject and the predicate.

The baby, hearing a siren, **started to shriek.**

The puppies, frightened by all the noise, **began barking.**

Later, after the siren stopped, **we all calmed down.**

③ Sentence Closers

You can also add words or phrases to the end of a sentence, after the predicate. Try putting important details at the end. These sentence closers are perfect for surprise endings—they really save the best for last!

The fox ran into the road, right in front of our bus.

The bus skidded off the road, landing in a huge snowdrift.

Notice how this science writer adds information to the beginning, middle, and end of her sentences.

PROFESSIONAL MODEL

Black holes, **dying stars that are rapidly shrinking,** have enormous gravity fields. They absorb everything in their paths, **even light! Amazingly,** a black hole can shrink from the size of a sun to the size of an eyeball. What happens once something has entered a black hole? That mystery may be solved in the future.

—Patricia Wright

PRACTICE **Make These Sentences Grow**

Use your imagination to add an opener, middle, or closer to each sentence.

1. I spent a lot of time on my science project.
2. My past projects had always been failures.
3. I was determined to succeed.
4. It took me a long time to prepare my materials.
5. I really wanted to win first prize.
6. The day of the science fair arrived.
7. I began my demonstration.
8. My science project exploded.
9. The judges and my teacher were very understanding.
10. I received a special award.

SENTENCES

Combining Complete Sentences

Combining related sentences can make your writing smoother and more readable.

① Combining with *And, But,* and *Or*

You can use a **conjunction,** or connecting word, such as *and, but,* or *or* to join related sentences. When you do this, you create a **compound sentence.**

When to Use *And, But,* and *Or*

Conjunction	Use It To . . .	Example
and	join sentences that have similar ideas	My dog's name is Elmer, **and** my iguana's name is Phoebe.
but	join sentences that have opposite ideas, or ideas that are different but still related	Most of the time they get along well, **but** sometimes Elmer chases Phoebe.
or	join sentences that offer a choice between ideas	We could scold Elmer, **or** we could keep Phoebe in her cage.

When you combine sentences, you make it easier for your reader to understand how your ideas relate to each other. Look at the two sentences below. They describe a young girl's efforts not to discuss her lost brother. Adding the word *but* makes it clear how the two ideas are related.

Each memory brought Hamed's name to Nadia's lips. She stilled the sound.

> **LITERARY MODEL**
>
> Each memory brought Hamed's name to Nadia's lips, **but** she stilled the sound.
>
> —Sue Alexander, "Nadia the Willful"

When you join two complete sentences with a conjunction, be sure to use a comma. Put it before the conjunction, as shown in the example above.

❷ Combining with Other Conjunctions

Sometimes two sentences are dependent on each other to express a complete idea. One of the sentences states the key idea, and the other sentence makes that idea clearer. To combine two such ideas into a **complex sentence,** use the conjunctions *although, because,* or *since,* as in the examples below.

DRAFT

Parrots make great pets. They can be mean.

REVISED

Parrots make great pets, although they can be mean.

DRAFT

Many parrots are able to mimic human speech. They can be taught funny sayings.

REVISED

Because many parrots are able to mimic human speech, they can be taught funny sayings.

Very often, two related ideas joined by *although, because,* or *since* can be presented in either order. You must decide which idea is more important.

I packed my sunglasses, since I was headed for Florida.

Since I was headed for Florida, I packed my sunglasses.

PRACTICE **Function with Conjunctions**

Combine the following pairs of sentences with conjunctions.

1. Rick hates making oral book reports. He doesn't mind written ones.

2. The last book he read was *Island of the Blue Dolphins.* He enjoyed it very much.

3. Book covers can capture his attention. They can turn him off.

4. His reading list is rather short. It contains some exciting books.

5. Rick actually enjoys talking to groups. Perhaps someday he'll be more comfortable with oral reports.

Combining Sentence Parts

If you have two or more sentences that contain very similar ideas, you often can combine them. Combining sentences in this way can make your writing stronger and easier to read.

1 Creating Compound Parts

Sometimes two or more sentences are so closely related that some of the same words or ideas appear in both sentences. You can join the sentences by using *and, but,* or *or* and leaving out the repeated words or ideas. When you combine two or more sentences in this way, the new sentence will have a **compound part.**

> **Dogs** eat meat. **Cats** eat meat, too.
>
> **Dogs and cats** eat meat.
>
> COMPOUND SUBJECT

> **Lizards can eat fruits. They can eat vegetables. They can also eat insects.**
>
> **Lizards can eat fruits, vegetables, or insects.**
>
> COMPOUND OBJECT

 OR **OR**

PRACTICE A Back to the Past!

In your 🗐 **Working Portfolio,** find your **Write Away** paragraph from page 277. Read it again, and then trade papers with a classmate. Discuss what other information you could add to your draft. Are there similar sentences that should be combined?

2 Inserting Words and Phrases

You can combine sentences by taking an important word from one sentence and adding it to another. Leave out the rest of the words. Your new sentence will be smoother and more sophisticated.

This movie is an action film. It is exciting.

This movie is an exciting action film.

You may need to change the form of the words you add. For instance, you might have to add -ly or -ily to the word you move.

Someone was knocking at my door! The knocking was loud and angry.

Someone was knocking at my door, loudly and angrily.

Another way to combine similar sentences is to make one into a phrase and insert it into the other sentence.

I didn't read the entire recipe before baking the cake. I wanted to save time.

To save time, I didn't read the entire recipe before baking the cake.

The result was a soggy mess. It taught me to follow directions.

The result, a soggy mess, taught me to follow directions.

PRACTICE B   **Sentence Shifting**

Combine each pair of sentences by moving an important word or words from one sentence to the other. You may need to change the form of some words.

1. Ramona enjoys books by Judy Blume. She also likes books by Scott O'Dell.
2. Our neighbor speaks French. He also speaks Spanish and Italian.
3. Frederica found a photograph in the attic. The photograph had dust on it.
4. My dad repairs furnaces. He is a skilled mechanic.
5. We went on a whale watch. We saw three whales.

Student Help Desk

Building Sentences at a Glance

Is It Complete?

Plant a complete thought in each sentence.

Is It Colorful?

Modifiers can brighten up your sentences.

Is It Fully Grown?

Try adding openers, middles, and closers.

Finding Fragments   Check for Completeness ✔

Incomplete Thought	Complete Thought
Couldn't believe my eyes.	**I** couldn't believe my eyes.
Biggest squash I had ever seen.	**It was** the biggest squash I had ever seen.
At the state fair. The squash won first prize.	At the state **fair, the** squash won first prize.

Expanding with Modifiers   Add Some COLOR!

Technique	Example
Complete sentence	I planted seeds.
Complete sentence that gives more information	I planted **hundreds of** seeds.
Complete sentence that gives the most information	**I carefully** planted **hundreds of sunflower, marigold, and zinnia** seeds.

CHAPTER 11

Expanding Sentences   Help it GROW!

Technique	Example
Add a sentence opener.	**Almost immediately,** rabbits spread the word about our vegetables.
Add to the middle.	The squirrels, **seeking new thrills,** tackled the corn.
Add a sentence closer.	My pumpkin tipped the scales at a walloping weight, **135 pounds!**

Combining Sentences   Blue-Ribbon Writing

Technique	Example
Use conjunctions to join ideas.	I planted a garden this spring. It was a lot of work. I planted a garden this spring, **but** it was a lot of work.
Add single-word modifiers.	I spent hours in the sun. The sun was blazing. I spent hours in the **blazing** sun.
Add phrases.	I built a robot. The robot takes care of the garden. I built a robot **to take care of the garden.**
Add words that change form.	Now my robot does all the gardening. It is an easy task. Now my robot **easily** does all the gardening.

The Bottom Line

Checklist for Building Sentences

Have I . . .

____ planted a complete thought in each sentence?

____ added detail about my subject?

____ weeded my sentences of repetition by combining similar ideas?

____ added informative words and phrases?

____ combined sentences where needed using words that change form?

Power Words
Vocabulary for Precise Writing

For a Limited Time Only!

The day you got your first allowance, you were ready to become a shopper. Use these words to discuss what kind of shopper you are.

Shopping Styles

When you **purchase** something, do you spend time **browsing** first? Do you buy **impulsively,** without much planning or research? Do you **shop around, bargaining** or **haggling** with the person who is selling? If each of you has something the other wants, you might **trade** or **barter** instead of using money.

Be a Savvy Shopper

It's important to be **reasonable** and **rational** when you are spending money. Smart shoppers are **discriminating** and **discerning.** They know that if something sounds too good to be true, it probably is. Instead of buying something **sight unseen,** they take the time to figure out whether it is a true **bargain.**

CHAPTER 12

▷ **Your Turn** Act Out an Ad

In a small group, talk about commercials and print advertisements that you think are effective. Do effective ads give lots of factual information? How do they appeal to your emotions? After your discussion, work together to write and act out a commercial for an imaginary product.

Building Paragraphs

Bicycles

Bike, BMX, originally $500. Awesome design. 20 inches, hub wheels, handlebars and cranks (4 and 3 pieces). Aluminum frame. Lightweight. Blue. Hydraulic disc brakes. $200 obo. Call (815) 555-7647. Bob.

For Sale

Look at the ad above. It includes all the necessary information, but the writing is choppy and fragmented. The words and phrases in this ad are like the thoughts and ideas in your head before you write. Your job as a writer is to take those fragments and put them together into a paragraph that others can understand. This chapter will show you how.

Write Away! Effective Ads

Think of an item you would like to sell. It can be a piece of sports equipment, an electronic game, or even a childhood toy. Write a classified ad in paragraph form. Save your paragraph in your 🗂 **Working Portfolio.**

Creating Good Paragraphs

A **paragraph** is made up of related sentences that develop one main idea. When you create a well-written paragraph, you make it easier for the reader to follow and understand your ideas.

❶ What Is a Good Paragraph?

All good paragraphs share the same features. First, they all have a strong **topic sentence,** which states the main idea or purpose of the paragraph. Next, good paragraphs have **unity,** which means that all the sentences within the paragraph support the main idea. Finally, the sentences are arranged in a **logical order.**

STUDENT MODEL

> **My favorite place to vacation is Florida because it is so easy to have fun there.** Tourists can go to big amusement parks all over the state. They can **also** swim in sparkling blue pools, body surf in the ocean, and get totally soaked at the water slides. **Another thing** I personally like to do in Florida is chase after those cute little lizards called geckos that dart around everywhere. I haven't caught one yet, but I have a great time!

Topic sentence

Unity: All sentences support the topic sentence by describing ways to have fun in Florida.

Logical order: Transition words *also* and *another thing* connect sentences.

HOT TIP

Make sure that all the sentences in your paragraph help develop the topic sentence. Don't wander off into unrelated ideas.

❷ What Is a Good Topic Sentence?

A topic sentence should present your reader with the main idea of the paragraph. A strong topic sentence also makes the reader want to read further. Look at the chart on the next page to see how the topic sentences can vary in strength.

Identifying Strong Topic Sentences

Example	Strong or Weak?	Why?
A tornado is very loud.	weak	Too general
A tornado sounds like a speeding train.	better	States an interesting fact.
Imagine the rumble of a speeding train—that's what a tornado sounds like.	strong	Makes you want to read more!

Notice how the strong topic sentence uses descriptive words and sets the tone for the paragraph.

STUDENT MODEL

Imagine the earth-shaking rumble of a speeding train—that's what a tornado sounds like. The thundering sound comes from the tornado's powerful winds spinning at more than 300 miles per hour. When a tornado barely missed our town last spring, most people said that the sight of the giant funnel cloud scared them the most. But for me, the scariest thing about that tornado was the sound.

Topic sentence

Information supports main idea.

PARAGRAPHS 1

Here's How Writing a Strong Topic Sentence

1. Write a sentence that clearly states the main idea of your paragraph.
2. Add details to your topic sentence to grab your reader's attention.

PRACTICE Good, Better, Best

Rewrite the following weak topic sentences to be more interesting and informative.

1. Our basketball victory was exciting.
2. Last night I saw a comet.
3. I broke my arm in a bike accident.
4. Halloween is the best holiday.

Focusing Your Paragraphs

You wouldn't add unnecessary pieces to a model you were building. You also wouldn't glue pieces in places where they didn't belong. When you build a paragraph, you have to be just as careful with what you add and where you put it.

❶ Unity: Fitting the Parts into a Whole

When you write a paragraph, aim for unity. **Unity** means that the information in each sentence supports the topic sentence. If a paragraph lacks unity, it lacks focus.

STUDENT MODEL

DRAFT

Most people find their dogs at a pet store or a shelter, but I found mine on the Internet. I love surfing the Web. There are so many interesting sites to explore. One day, I saw a photo of an adorable Tibetan Terrier. It had fluffy hair like a big sheepdog, but it was much smaller. I fell in love. I located a Tibetan Terrier in our town. Quickly I got my mom involved. She's always great at helping me out. Soon we were driving to the Animal Rescue Center to pick up our new puppy.

> **Topic sentence** states main idea.

> **Unrelated information** leads away from the main idea.

REVISION

Most people find their dogs at a pet store, but I found mine on the Internet. One day while I was surfing the Web, I saw a photo of an adorable Tibetan Terrier. It had fluffy hair like a sheepdog, but it was much smaller. I fell in love with it. I located a Tibetan Terrier in our town. Then I got Mom involved. In a few days, we were driving to the Animal Rescue Center to pick up our new puppy.

> **Related information** supports main idea and creates unity.

❷ Logical and Smooth: Making the Parts Connect

You can make sentences flow smoothly in a paragraph by presenting your ideas in a logical order. You can also use transition words, such as *also, but, then, later,* and *because,* to make the order clear.

PROFESSIONAL MODEL

The discovery of the North Pole in 1909 was a life-threatening ordeal for Commander Robert Peary and the explorer Matthew Henson. They had to battle temperatures of 50 degrees below zero, freezing water, thin ice, frostbite, and exhaustion. During the ocean voyage, one member of the expedition fell through the ice and drowned in the frigid water. Later, after leaving the safety of their ship, Peary and Henson traversed the Arctic for weeks battling cold, danger, and hunger with every mile. It was a miracle that they survived the perils of the Arctic long enough to reach the North Pole!

—Trish Tivnan

> Topic sentence

> Transition words help readers follow time sequence.

Robert Peary

For more on transition words, see p. 299.

PRACTICE Making the Necessary Repairs

Of the four sentences below, one does not belong. Join the three related sentences into a unified paragraph using transition words.

1. The possibility of extraterrestrial life has intrigued humans for decades.
2. I would love to see a little green Martian pop out of a spaceship!
3. Fiction and film have portrayed visitors from outer space in many creative ways.
4. Some images look so real that people picture them when they think of spaceships and alien life forms.

PARAGRAPHS 1

Paragraphs: Descriptive and Narrative

There are four main kinds of paragraphs: descriptive, narrative, informative, and persuasive. You will use each kind of paragraph at some point in your writing.

❶ Paragraphs that Describe

Descriptive paragraphs describe a person, place, thing, or experience. They can introduce a character, present a setting, or re-create an event. The paragraph below introduces a little girl.

LITERARY MODEL

Out of the trees on the right side of the house came walking the **blackest, biggest** horse Thomas could remember seeing. Maybe it was not as **huge** as he thought at first, but he was closer to it than he had ever been to a horse. Riding on it was a **tiny** girl, sitting **straight and tall.** She had a **white, frilly** nightcap on her head and she wore **red flannel** shoes on her feet and she sat well forward, her toes clasped in the horse's mane.

—Virginia Hamilton, *The House of Dies Drear*

> Carefully chosen **details** help you picture the girl.

Here's How Writing a Descriptive Paragraph

- List important details about what you're describing. Include sights, sounds, smells, tastes, and textures.
- Think about the order in which you want these details to appear. You might consider top to bottom, front to back, or outside to inside.
- Choose specific nouns, verbs, adjectives, and adverbs.

PRACTICE A Being There

Write a paragraph describing an interesting place you've been. Try to make the description clear enough for readers to "see" a picture in their heads.

❷ Paragraphs that Tell a Story

Narrative paragraphs tell a story. You can use narrative paragraphs to share an experience, introduce an essay, or provide an example when you are making a point.

I was swimming the 100-meter freestyle in an important dual meet. Eight swimmers dove in. **After** four laps, I started to pick up my pace. **As** I touched the side of the pool after my eighth lap, I slumped in exhaustion. My coach walked toward me with a frown on his face. **When** I pulled myself out of the pool, he growled, "You just set a new record for the 200-meter free. Too bad it was the wrong event." **Suddenly,** I realized I had swum four extra laps! It was one victory I never celebrated.

> **Beginning**
>
> **Middle**
> Transition words and phrases help readers follow sequence.
>
> **End**

Here's How Writing a Narrative Paragraph

1. Start by listing events in the order in which they happened.
2. Add details that answer the questions *who, what, when, where, why,* and *how*.
3. Use transition words and phrases to make clear the beginning, middle, and end of the story.

PRACTICE B How Did It Happen?

Write a narrative paragraph about a memorable incident in your life. The incident should be short enough to fit in one paragraph but long enough to have a definite beginning, middle, and end. Write at least six sentences. Here are some ideas for topics:

- meeting your best friend
- a surprise party
- the time you got lost
- carving pumpkins
- a scavenger hunt
- a sports victory or defeat

LESSON 4   Paragraphs: Informative and Persuasive

You will often write paragraphs to explain ideas to others. Sometimes, you just want to inform them. Other times, you want to persuade them.

❶ Paragraphs that Inform

When you want to present facts, explain how something works, give directions, define a term, or explain an idea, you write an **informative** paragraph.

Replica of a woolly mammoth

PROFESSIONAL MODEL

    So you think a woolly mammoth must have been huge? Mammoths in Africa, North American and Eurasia often grew as tall as 14 feet. But when the mammoths took over small islands, they diminished over time. In fact, on Wrangel Island, which is located north of Siberia, the mammoths shrank! They grew to an average of only six feet! Alas, big or small, the last woolly mammoths died out about 3,800 years ago.

                            —Susan Creighton

> **Topic sentence** clearly introduces what is being explained.

> **Related information** gives facts about the topic.

Here's How   **Writing an Informative Paragraph**

- Write a topic sentence to introduce the subject.
- Present the information that is most important for your readers to know.
- Explain your ideas with examples, facts, statistics, and definitions.

PRACTICE A   **Did You Know?**

Choose one of the three terms below. Define and explain the term in an informative paragraph. Use an encyclopedia, dictionary, or the Internet to find information.

Pacific Rim   What is it? Where is it?
bullet train   Where is it? How did it get its name?
endorphins   What are they? What do they do?

❷ Paragraphs that Persuade

When you want your readers to see things your way or to follow your suggestions, you write a **persuasive** paragraph.

STUDENT MODEL

Public schools should be allowed to sell food from popular restaurant chains in school cafeterias. Most students prefer restaurant food over standard cafeteria food. In addition, this food is economical. A hamburger from a restaurant chain costs approximately the same as a burger sold by a cafeteria supplier. Finally, if students are offered the items they really want to eat, they would be more inclined to eat all of the food on their trays, rather than toss half in the garbage, or even worse, around the cafeteria.

Reason 1
Students prefer restaurant food.

Reason 2
Food is economical.

Reason 3
Students will eat food they choose.

Here's How Writing a Persuasive Paragraph

- State your opinion or suggestion in the topic sentence.
- Give clear reasons why your readers should agree with you.
- Use facts, examples, and/or statistics to support your point of view.

Avoid getting too emotional in your persuasive paragraph. Your paragraph will be more convincing if it is based on facts.

PRACTICE B See It My Way

Choose one of the following ideas and write a paragraph that persuades the reader to agree with your point of view.

1. Students should be allowed to choose the foreign language they want to study.
2. It's better to attend a big school with many students than a small school.
3. Every weekend should be a three-day weekend.

PARAGRAPHS 1

Student Help Desk

Building Paragraphs at a Glance

Main Idea

Your topic sentence clearly states the main idea.

Unity

All sentences in a paragraph are related to the topic sentence.

Logic

The sentences flow logically, helped by transition words.

Light the Way

Tips for Terrific Topic Sentences

Strategy	Example
Grab the reader's attention.	Imagine living at the water's edge in a tower that housed an enormous fish-oil lamp!
Speak directly to the reader.	Back in the 1700s, your life as lighthouse keeper would have been peculiar, yet exciting.
Ask an engaging question.	Would you have snuffed out the lighthouse flame on the Massachusetts coast during the Revolutionary War?
Use a real-life situation.	Today, a Coast Guard career will prepare you to operate one of more than 10,000 lighthouses currently in use in the United States.

All for One, and One for All

Test for Paragraph Unity

✓ Check that each sentence relates to the topic sentence.

✓ Revise or remove sentences that distract from the main idea.

✓ Save interesting but unrelated sentences for another paragraph.

Types of Paragraphs   Does It Fit the Part?

Type	Uses
Descriptive	Offers the reader vivid details that enable him or her to imagine what you're describing.
Narrative	Lets the reader follow your story from the beginning, through the middle, to the end.
Informative	Explains something or gives directions.
Persuasive	Shares your point of view and gives reasons for readers to agree with you.

Transition Words   *Make It Flow*

Descriptive	Narrative	Informative	Persuasive
above	first	also	as a result
across	later	instead	because
behind	eventually	as a result	beyond
below	next	similarly	then
inside	suddenly	although	finally
around	after	because	meanwhile
beyond	then	for example	for example
outside	finally	likewise	since
between	meanwhile	for this reason	in conclusion

The Bottom Line

Checklist for Building Paragraphs

Have I . . .

____ decided which type of paragraph to write?

____ identified my main idea?

____ written a topic sentence that will get my reader's attention?

____ revised or removed any unrelated sentences?

____ arranged my sentences in a logical order?

____ used transition words?

Power Words
Vocabulary for Precise Writing

The Main Event

Planning a party takes organizational skill as well as a sense of fun.

The Big Picture

You say you want to throw a party—but what kind of party? Are you thinking of an elegant **soiree** or **fete,** a glittery **gala** or **event,** or a more casual **mixer** or **bash?** The type of party you want to throw affects how you will plan for it.

The Little Details

Planning a party takes work. Make a list that **spells out, itemizes,** or **enumerates** all the tasks you need to complete. **Estimate** how much your party will cost and **determine** how much you have to spend. How will you arrange or order your list? You could **rank** or **prioritize** your "to do" list in order of importance, or you could put the steps in the **sequence** they should occur. If friends are helping you, **divide** or **subdivide** the chores so that everyone gets something to do.

Being organized can make the difference between a **sensational, successful** party and a **disorganized, disastrous** one!

▷ **Your Turn** Life of the Party

If you could throw any kind of party, what kind would you choose? Working with two or three classmates, list where you would hold the party, who would be there, what the entertainment would be, and what you would need to buy.

Organizing Paragraphs

Pizza Recipe

Prepare toppings. Measure flour. Knead dough. Spread dough on a baking pan. Don't forget to wash hands first! Put on topping. Put tomato sauce on before topping. First go shopping for ingredients. Be sure to preheat the oven. Cook for half-hour.

First Things First

You told your friend Mike you want to make a pizza. Mike has given you the instructions shown above. But there are some problems. For example, how can you prepare the toppings before you've even bought the ingredients?

When you are writing, it's important to think about order and organization. First, you need to decide what you want your readers to understand. Next, you should choose a pattern of organization that will help you get your ideas across in a logical and clear way. By doing this, you'll help readers follow your thoughts on paper without getting confused.

Write Away: What Do I Do?

Think of a time someone gave you the wrong instructions for completing a task. What happened when you tried to follow them? In a four- to five-sentence paragraph, write about the experience and what would have made the instructions easier to follow. Save your paragraph in your 🗀 **Working Portfolio.**

Sequential Order

Organizing your writing helps readers follow what you are trying to say. It's important to choose the right way to organize your writing. In this chapter, you'll find out how and when to use different types of organization when writing paragraphs.

Using Time and Sequence

You can use **sequential order** to show how one event follows another in a sequence. Sequential order is often used for explaining a process. One type of sequential order is used to describe how things happen over time. This is called **chronological order.** You might use this order when telling a story or retelling historical events.

In the following model, the writer uses **transitional words and phrases** to introduce events in chronological order. Can you name the three events introduced by each word or phrase?

LITERARY MODEL

A little before five o'clock in the morning, Papa woke everyone up. **A few minutes later,** the yelling and screaming of my little brothers and sisters, for whom the move was a great adventure, broke the silence of dawn. **Shortly,** the barking of the dogs accompanied them.

—Francisco Jiménez, "The Circuit"

> **Transition** to first event
>
> **Transition** to second event
>
> **Transition** to third event

Read the cartoon below and list the four events that Snoopy is thinking about.

Peanuts by Charles Schultz

CHAPTER 13

The model below uses sequential order to describe a process.

To preserve the bodies of rich people who had died, the ancient Egyptians made them into mummies. The **first** step was to cut a slit in the left side of the body and remove the internal organs. **Next,** workers packed the body with a type of salt that would make the body dry up. **After** 35 to 40 days, the workers sewed up the slit in the side. The **last** step was to wrap the body in as many as 80 layers of cloth.

Transition words show how one step in the process follows another.

Here's How Using Sequential Order

1. List the events or steps you want to include in your paragraph.
2. Put the events or steps in order.
3. Add **transition words** like *before, then, when,* or *after* to signal a change from one event or step to the next.

PARAGRAPHS 2

PRACTICE Take the PB&J Challenge!

How easy is it to write a paragraph in sequential order? Try it out with an activity you know well—making a peanut butter and jelly sandwich. You'll need a partner.

• In paragraph form, write instructions for making a peanut butter and jelly sandwich. Include each step in the process.

• Read your instructions out loud to your partner. Your partner should follow the steps *exactly* as they are written, without adding or taking away any steps.

How did the sandwich turn out? If the answer is "not so good," rewrite the paragraph, adding or deleting steps as necessary. Then, try it again.

Reread the cartoon on the previous page. Can you rewrite Snoopy's thoughts in one paragraph? Change wording and add the transition words *first, then,* and *next* where they seem to fit.

Spatial Order

Spatial order describes a space or scene and the objects or people in that space. If your goal is to have your readers "see" a place as you have seen or imagined it, you'll use spatial order to describe your scene.

Organizing Objects and People

There are several ways to describe a scene or space:

- bottom to top
- close up to faraway
- inside to outside
- from one side to the other

In the following example, the writer starts by describing one side of the scene, goes to the other side, and then to the center. He shows exactly how the animals and objects are arranged in the clearing.

> **LITERARY MODEL**
>
> King Gorilla sat **at one end** of the clearing on his throne. Opposite him, **at the other side** of the clearing, all the animals sat in a semicircle. **In the middle, between** King Gorilla and the animals, was a huge mound of what looked like black dust.
>
> —retold by Julius Lester, "Why Monkeys Live in Trees"

> **Directional phrases** help readers know exactly where each animal is.

Here's How Using Spatial Order

1. List the objects and/or people you will describe.
2. Decide where you want to start and end the description, for example, from left to right, or from top to bottom.
3. Choose **direction words and phrases,** such as

next to	*under*	*near*	*behind*
above	*below*	*in front of*	*between*

You can use spatial order to describe places as small as a jacket pocket or as large as the Gobi Desert. If you can visualize it, you can describe it.

Notice how this writer uses direction words.

We opened the door to Jason's room and saw that everything that had once been on the floor was now piled high on his bed. **At the bottom** of the heap were about two weeks' worth of dirty laundry and a bunch of magazines. **In the middle** of the pile, I spotted my fishing rod, which had been missing since last summer! And **at the very top** of the mound, perched on Jason's tuba case, was our cat, Bossman, looking down at us through narrowed eyes.

> This writer describes the scene from bottom to top.

PRACTICE **Can You Write a Picture?**

Using spatial order, describe the photo below. Use directional words to help a reader picture the scene. When you are finished, ask someone who has not seen the photo to read your work. Then, show that person the photo.

Was this what the reader pictured from your paragraph? Even though people "see" things a little differently, your reader should have understood from your description how objects and people are arranged in the photo.

Organizing Paragraphs **305**

PARAGRAPHS 2

Compare-and-Contrast Order

When you **compare** two things, you show how they are alike. When you **contrast** two things, you show how they are different. To both compare and contrast two things, you must be able to show the similarities and differences they share.

Showing Similarities and Differences

The model below compares and contrasts dolphins and sharks. The writer describes ways in which dolphins and sharks are similar and ways in which they are different.

> **PROFESSIONAL MODEL**
>
> Although dolphins (porpoises) are mammals and sharks are fish, the two animals share some traits. Both live in all the seas of the world. Both are superbly adapted for life and speed in water. Both live on fish—but dolphins never eat sharks, while sharks sometimes do eat dolphins.
>
> —*Reader's Digest Book of Facts*

DIFFERENCES

SIMILARITIES

Here's How Using Compare-and-Contrast Order

1. List the objects and/or people you will describe.

2. Make a graphic like the Venn diagram below to organize the similarities and differences of your two subjects.

   Subject A   Similarities   Subject B

3. Use **comparison transition words,** such as *similarly* and *like,* when you want to show similarities. Use **contrast transition words,** such as *but, however,* and *in contrast,* to show when you are switching to a discussion of differences.

Study the following model to see how this writer uses compare-and-contrast order. What two subjects are being compared? Which transition words show similarities and which show differences?

Most American softball teams play slow-pitch softball, **but** a small number of teams play a fast-pitch game. The rules are a bit **different** in each. Fast-pitch teams have nine players, **while** slow-pitch teams have ten players. In fast-pitch softball, batters may bunt and steal bases, **but** neither of these strategies is allowed in a slow-pitch game. **However, both** games use an underhand pitch and last for seven innings.

–Darcy Macdermott

First sentence introduces subjects.

Differences

Similarities

PRACTICE How Do They Compare?

Use the information in the Venn diagram below to write a paragraph that compares and contrasts black bears and polar bears. Use transition words to clearly point out how the two animals are alike and how they are different.

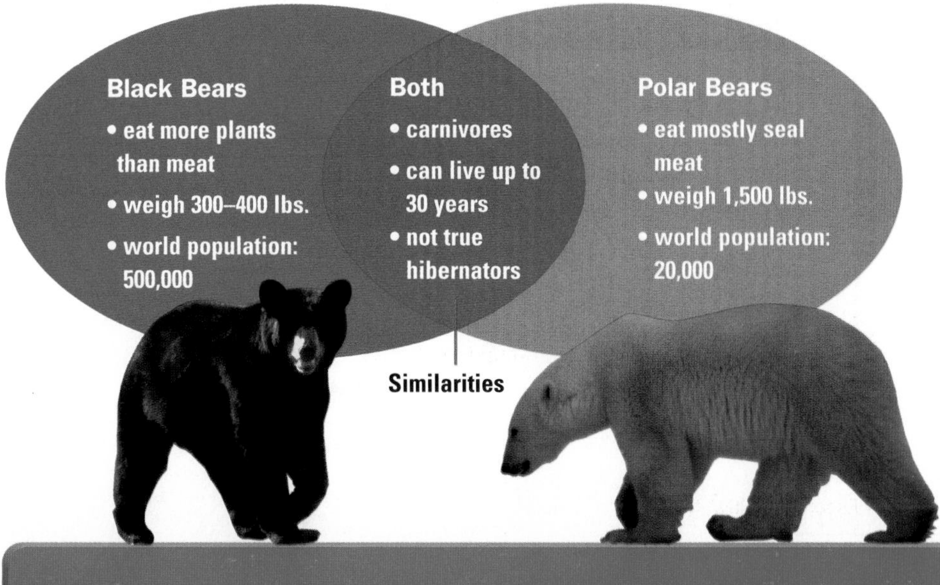

Black Bears
- eat more plants than meat
- weigh 300–400 lbs.
- world population: 500,000

Both
- carnivores
- can live up to 30 years
- not true hibernators

Polar Bears
- eat mostly seal meat
- weigh 1,500 lbs.
- world population: 20,000

Similarities

Student Help Desk

Organizing Paragraphs at a Glance

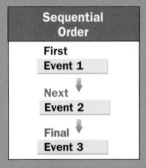

Sequential Order

First
Event 1

Next
Event 2

Final
Event 3

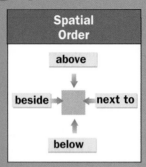

Spatial Order

above

beside → □ ← next to

below

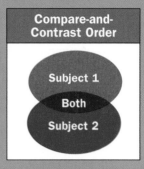

Compare-and-Contrast Order

Subject 1

Both

Subject 2

Paragraph Organization Patterns and Purpose

Sequential Order

What It Does: Describes steps in a process or sequence, or events over time

Used for explaining a science experiment, giving instructions, writing a story, retelling a historical event.

Example: Before you start cooking, be sure to wash your hands. Next, set all the ingredients on the counter. Then, measure the ingredients.

Spatial Order

What It Does: Describes people and objects in a space or scene

Used for setting a scene, introducing a character, describing any subject

Example: Tara sat at the table with a piece of steaming hot pizza on a plate in front of her. Mike set a huge glass of soda next to her plate.

Compare-and-Contrast Order

What It Does: Describes similarities and differences of two things.

Used for scientific writing, book, music, or film reviews, encyclopedias, consumer guides, movie reviews, newspaper and magazine articles

Example: Pepperoni pizza and sausage pizza are both made with cheese, but pepperoni pizza is spicier than most sausage pizzas.

Transition Words and Phrases — Hold Them Together

Transitions can help your sentences stick together.

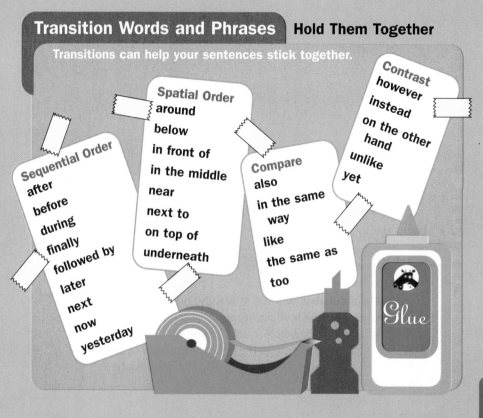

Sequential Order
after
before
during
finally
followed by
later
next
now
yesterday

Spatial Order
around
below
in front of
in the middle
near
next to
on top of
underneath

Compare
also
in the same way
like
the same as
too

Contrast
however
instead
on the other hand
unlike
yet

Glue

The Bottom Line

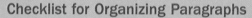

Checklist for Organizing Paragraphs

Have I . . .

____ chosen a pattern of organization that fits my purpose?

____ put my ideas in an order that is easy for readers to follow?

____ used direction or transition words and phrases?

____ included a clear beginning, middle, and end when using sequential order?

____ described the space so that readers can picture it in their minds?

____ described both similarities and differences when comparing and contrasting?

Power Words
Vocabulary for Precise Writing

Building for the Future

If you'd like to be an architect, a construction worker, or a homeowner, here are some words that may come in handy.

A Firm Foundation

Whether you plan to build a cabin, a mansion, or a skyscraper, you will need **blueprints** and **floor plans** that show the **structure** of what you are building. These show the **skeleton** of your construction: the vertical **columns** and the **studs,** the horizontal **beams** and **joists,** the roof's sloping **rafters,** and the **framing-in** of the windows and doors. As you begin construction, be sure to dig down to **bedrock** before laying your **foundation** and building the **substructure.**

Finishing It Off

Once the **framework** is up, the **infrastructure** must be put in place. Various **working drawings** show how the plumbing and wiring must be laid in. Then you can turn your attention to **roofing** and **gutters,** to **insulation,** and to the **façade**—that is, the exterior. If you do your job well, your building will stay standing for generations!

▷ **Your Turn** Your Dream Home

Think about a house that you would like to build. Draw it or describe it in writing. Use some of the terms above in your description or in labels for your drawing.

beam

framework

Building Compositions

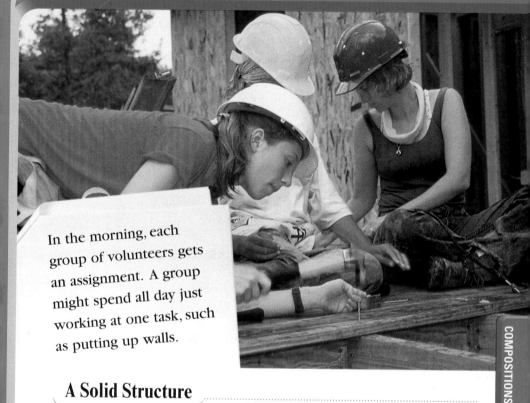

In the morning, each group of volunteers gets an assignment. A group might spend all day just working at one task, such as putting up walls.

A Solid Structure

Imagine being part of a large volunteer project to build a house. What if you were asked to write about it? Do you think you could tell all the important details in two or three sentences? It would probably take several paragraphs just to cover the basics.

Just as the structure of a building is made up of basic parts—floor, walls, roof—a composition is made of some basic parts too—an introduction, body, and conclusion. Once you become familiar with these basic parts, you can build a whole composition on just about any topic.

Write Away: Lending a Hand
Think of a group project you helped with. Write a paragraph describing your favorite part of that project. Save your work in your 📁 **Working Portfolio.**

What Is a Composition?

A **composition** is a piece of writing made up of paragraphs. A composition begins with a **main idea**—what the composition is about. Each paragraph in the composition tells the reader something more about the main idea.

What you already know about writing paragraphs can help you write a composition. This is because paragraphs and compositions share similar features. As the graphic below shows, each begins with a main idea, and each includes more information about the main idea.

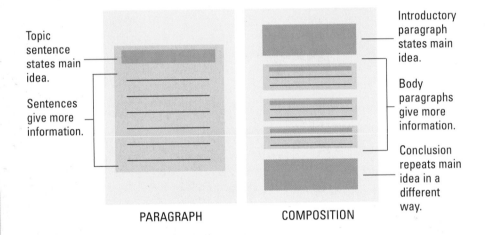

Topic sentence states main idea.

Sentences give more information.

Introductory paragraph states main idea.

Body paragraphs give more information.

Conclusion repeats main idea in a different way.

PARAGRAPH   COMPOSITION

❶ What Does a Composition Look Like?

A composition can be broken down into three parts: an introduction, a body, and a conclusion.

The **introduction** is the first part of the composition. It introduces the topic of the composition and states the main idea of the whole composition.

The **body** comes after the introduction. It usually includes three or more paragraphs that give information about the main idea.

The **conclusion** is the last part of the composition. It states the main idea again, and gives the writer's thoughts on the topic.

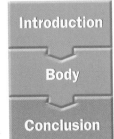

Introduction

Body

Conclusion

At dusk on June 8, 1953, a black twister ripped through Flint, Michigan. It flattened houses, uprooted trees, and overturned cars and trucks. The tornado ruined the town. But Flint's people began rebuilding by planning a two-day event called "Operation Tornado." **Operation Tornado proved that a terrible disaster could not destroy Flint's community spirit.**

Operation Tornado was a volunteer effort. Churches, businesses, and the Flint city government pulled together to organize community members. People of all ages and from all walks of life signed up to help.

The project began early on Saturday, August 29, when 4,000 people came together to help. The volunteers set to work under the blazing sun. Working hard, they laid floors and put up walls and roofs. Amazingly, by nightfall some new homes were almost finished.

Operation Tornado ranks as one of the largest volunteer building projects in U.S. history. It was very successful. By Sunday night, 193 completed and partly completed houses were standing. By the end of the summer many people already had moved into new homes.

The Flint tornado did millions of dollars of damage in a few minutes. Nevertheless, the volunteers repaired much of the damage. In two days they completed what normally would take months. Their efforts show that, although the forces of nature are mighty, they can be matched by the human spirit.

—Anne Hood

The **introduction** presents the **main idea.** Vivid description catches the reader's attention.

Body paragraphs give information about Operation Tornado. Each **topic sentence** tells what the paragraph will be about.

The **conclusion** restates the main idea and gives the writer's opinion.

COMPOSITIONS

Writing an Introduction

The **introduction** is the first paragraph in a composition, where you present your topic. Your introduction should be interesting enough to catch your readers' attention, so they will want to read more.

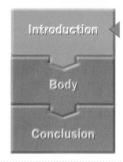

Introduction

Body

Conclusion

❶ Main Idea

At some point in your introduction, you should include a sentence that clearly states the main idea of your composition.

Your Main Idea Statement	
Should	**Should Not**
identify the subject of your composition	be an incomplete sentence: "Weird things about tornadoes."
be able to be supported by facts	be an opinion you can't support: "I think tornadoes are scary."
give your view on the main idea and purpose for writing	be a broad statement of fact: "Tornadoes cause damage."
be stated in an interesting way	be an announcement: "This paper is about tornadoes."

STUDENT MODEL

DRAFT

Tornadoes are dangerous.

(too general and not very interesting)

REVISION

Because tornadoes are so powerful and dangerous, they can turn a familiar place into a scene from a disaster movie.

(more specific and interesting)

② Types of Introductions

It's important to try to "hook" your readers right away. Here are a few ways you can get your reader's attention.

- Mention an unusual fact.
- Tell an anecdote or brief story.
- Ask a question.
- Include lively descriptions.

STUDENT MODEL

In 1840, a person living in Natchez, Mississippi, looked up and thought that chimneys could fly. Chimneys on buildings in the town were shot through the air by the storm's mighty wind. Believe it or not, people have seen tornadoes do even stranger things than sending chimneys through the air.

> Writer mentions an **unusual fact.**

STUDENT MODEL

Have you ever seen it raining frogs outside? A tornado once sucked up an entire pond full of frogs high into the sky. All the frogs eventually fell back to earth in a thick shower. Instead of raining cats and dogs, the sky was raining frogs that day! That's only one of many strange things tornadoes have caused over the years.

> Writer starts with a **question.**

HOT TIP

The main idea does not have to be stated in the first sentence as long as it appears somewhere in the introductory paragraph.

PRACTICE ▸ Tell Me More!

In your 🗀 **Working Portfolio,** find your **Write Away** paragraph from page 311. Write an introduction for that paragraph, using one of the types of introductions discussed above. Trade paragraphs with a partner. Does the introduction make you want to read more?

Writing the Body

The body of a composition is usually at least three paragraphs long. All the body paragraphs should have **unity.** That means each paragraph gives more information about the main idea of the composition. When body paragraphs flow smoothly and are in an order that makes sense, they have coherence.

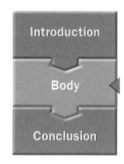

Introduction

Body

Conclusion

❶ Unity in a Composition

Before writing, you can check for unity by writing your paragraph topics in an informal outline. This way, you can take out any topics that do not relate to the main idea of the composition.

Informal Outline: The Strange Ways of a Tornado

Introduction: Main Idea
Because tornadoes are so powerful and dangerous, they can cause strange things to happen and carry objects for miles.

Body:
1st paragraph: lightweight materials carried off by a tornado

2nd paragraph: animals affected by tornados

3rd paragraph: people picked up by a tornado

4th paragraph: heavy objects moved by a tornado

~~5th paragraph: famous tornado scenes in movies~~

Conclusion: Repeat Main Idea a Different Way
Tornadoes are responsible for some funny situations, like featherless chickens and flying cars. However, we should always keep in mind that they are a dangerous force of nature.

Certain facts may be true and interesting to you, but that doesn't mean they belong in the composition you are writing. Be sure to get rid of information that doesn't quite fit.

Paragraphing

Sometimes what seems like a lack of unity is just an overloaded paragraph. **Paragraphing** means breaking one paragraph into two. Begin a new paragraph whenever

- you move on to a new idea
- there is a change in time or place
- a different speaker starts talking

The change marked in the model below gives it more unity.

STUDENT MODEL

It's not hard to imagine that a tornado could carry paper items a long way. A tornado that hit Vernon, Texas, in 1979 is a good example. After the tornado, the Thomas family figured that some of their important business papers were gone for good. Unbelievably, a few weeks later the papers were recovered. They showed up in Woodward, Oklahoma, more than 150 miles away. During many twisters on the open plains, farmers have reported chickens being stripped of their feathers!

> Paragraph topic

¶ Paper, however, is not the only thing tornadoes have carried off.

❷ Coherence in a Composition

A composition with **coherence** flows logically from one paragraph to the next. Use the chart below to help you choose a type of organization.

How to Organize a Composition	
If you need to	**Use**
explain a process or describe a series of events	sequence order
describe how or why something happened	cause-and-effect order
show similarities and differences between subjects	compare-and-contrast order

For more on organization, see pp. 301–309.

COMPOSITIONS

Using Transitions

To help glue your composition together, you can use **transition words and phrases** between paragraphs. You also can use transitions between sentences within paragraphs.

STUDENT MODEL

Once there was a sick woman lying in her bed when a tornado hit. Looking up, she saw her roof cave in. She covered her head and hoped for the best. **When** she took her hands away from her face, she was still lying in her bed, unhurt. **However,** the bed was now 100 yards away in a field.

That same tornado tossed around even larger objects. After the storm a man found that his house trailer had been carried to a town eight miles away.

> These **transition words and phrases** show the sequence (order) of events within the paragraph.

> This sentence creates a transition between paragraphs.

PRACTICE > **Make Some Connections**

The following paragraph about how tornadoes form has neither unity nor coherence. Rewrite it and break it into two paragraphs. Leave out unrelated ideas. Add transition words such as *first, then, next, because, but,* and *however* within and between paragraphs.

Several natural events happen before a storm becomes a tornado. Thunderstorms release huge hailstones. A whirling, funnel-shaped cloud touches down in a cornfield. The black dirt from the corn field gets sucked up by the tornado. The funnel turns black. I found a tornado Web site on the Internet. The black funnel cloud usually moves forward at about 10 to 25 miles per hour. Most tornadoes last less than an hour. Weather forecasters can predict storm conditions, but they can't always tell when a tornado is coming. There is a movie about people who chase tornadoes.

Writing the Conclusion

The **conclusion** of a composition is the ending paragraph. A conclusion should sum up the composition and be interesting to the reader.

Introduction

Body

Conclusion

Summing Up with a Conclusion

To end your composition, you may want to stress your main idea by saying it in another way. You want to leave your reader with something useful to think about. You might make a suggestion or offer your opinion on the subject.

Here's How · Writing the Conclusion

- Think of a different way to state the main idea.
- Mention the main point of each paragraph in a different and interesting way.
- Leave the reader with a suggestion, or with your opinion on the topic of your composition.

STUDENT MODEL

Tornadoes are responsible for some funny situations, like featherless chickens and flying cars. We should always keep in mind that they are a dangerous force of nature. We need to learn more about how they form and how they can affect people, animals, objects, and the land itself. The more we learn, the better we will be able to protect ourselves from their power.

Repeats the main idea in a different way

Ends with a suggestion

WATCH OUT

It's tempting to want to take your topic in a new direction in the conclusion. Stay on track—don't add any new information in the conclusion.

Student Help Desk

Building Compositions at a Glance

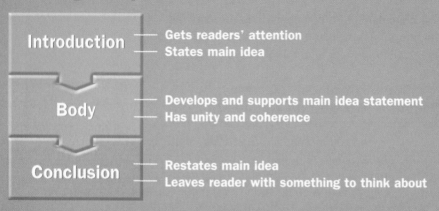

Introduction — Gets readers' attention
— States main idea

Body — Develops and supports main idea statement
— Has unity and coherence

Conclusion — Restates main idea
— Leaves reader with something to think about

The Introduction — Off to a Good Start

Technique	Example
Include lively descriptions.	Imagine the sound of a hundred freight trains roaring by you. Picture a wind so strong that it lifts huge trees out of the ground and spins them through the air.
Ask a question.	Did you know that lightning is always inside a tornado's funnel?
Mention an unusual fact.	Lightning is always flashing on the inside of a tornado's funnel.
Tell an anecdote or brief story.	Kansas farmer Will Keller saw the storm inside a tornado and lived to tell the tale. "There was a screaming hissing sound coming directly from the end of the funnel. I looked up and to my astonishment, I saw right up into the heart of the tornado."

Transition Words — Making Clear Connections

Type of Order	Example
Sequence	first, second, next, finally, while, last, before, after
Cause-and-Effect	so, consequently, for this reason, although, because, resulting from, if . . . then, due to, since
Compare	similarly, like, as, also, likewise, just as, in the same way, in addition
Contrast	however, on the other hand, but, in contrast, unlike, instead, on the contrary, in spite of, although

The Conclusion — Finishing with a Flourish

Technique	Example
State main idea in a different way.	The inside of a tornado is like the worst thunderstorm you've ever seen—times ten!
Summarize main points.	The inside of a funnel cloud usually has three things going on at once. There are swirling clouds, constant lightning flashes, and a screaming, hissing sound.
Make a suggestion.	By the time you hear the roar of a tornado, it may be too late. Get to an underground place at the earliest sign of a tornado.

The Bottom Line

Checklist for Writing

Have I . . .

_____ included a statement of my main idea?

_____ gotten the readers' attention in the introduction?

_____ checked that my paragraphs' topic sentences support my main idea?

_____ made logical paragraph breaks?

_____ chosen a logical method of organization?

_____ used transition words and phrases for coherence?

_____ restated my main idea in the conclusion and left my readers with something to think about?

vague

unhelpful

unspecific

empty

Seven Pairs of Socks?

These words can help you make your meaning clear.

Clear as Mud

In the letter on the opposite page, the camp director's **vague** instruction "everything you will need for a week" is so **general,** so **indefinite,** so **unspecific** as to be nearly **meaningless.** Even when instructions are not as **empty** as the camp director's, they can still be **unclear** or **muddled.** If the instructions are too **imprecise, inexact,** or **ill-defined,** they are pretty **unhelpful** to anyone trying to follow them.

Plain and Simple

It is **apparent, plain,** even **obvious** to some people what you should bring to camp. Still, good instructions should be **definite, exact,** and **specific:** "Bring one sweater, two pairs of shorts," and so on. You need a **straightforward, detailed** list to help you plan.

Whether you are giving directions, instructions, or information, be **precise** and **unambiguous.** Your message should be **unmistakable!**

meaningless

general

▷ **Your Turn** What *Should* I Bring?

Working with three or four classmates, make a list of what a person should bring to camp. Share your list with the class, and discuss whether other groups' lists are vague or specific.

indefinite

unclea

Elaboration

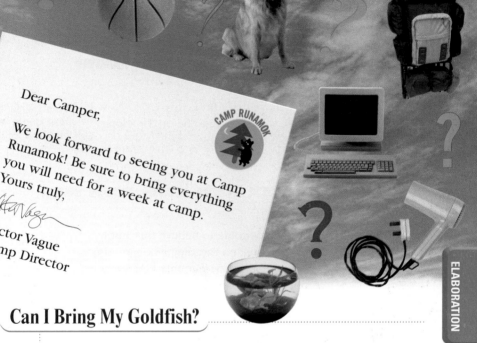

Dear Camper,

We look forward to seeing you at Camp Runamok! Be sure to bring everything you will need for a week at camp.

Yours truly,

Victor Vague

Victor Vague
Camp Director

CAMP RUNAMOK

ELABORATION

Can I Bring My Goldfish?

After reading this letter, would you know what you should bring to camp? The writer of the letter needed to provide more detail.

Adding supporting details and explanations is part of **elaboration.** When you elaborate, you help readers understand your meaning by giving them more information. Elaboration can strengthen the descriptions, arguments, and explanations in your writing.

Write Away: Facing the Unknown
Think of a time when you faced a new situation—maybe while you were playing on a sports team, baby-sitting, or moving to a new neighborhood. What details would have been helpful to know? Write a paragraph that describes the experience and gives advice to someone facing a similar situation. Save your work in your ◻ **Working Portfolio.**

Introducing Elaboration

LESSON 1

❶ What Is Elaboration?

Suppose you received the E-mail below from a friend. Would you be satisfied with the information in the draft version? Chances are that you would want your friend to **elaborate**—to give you more information.

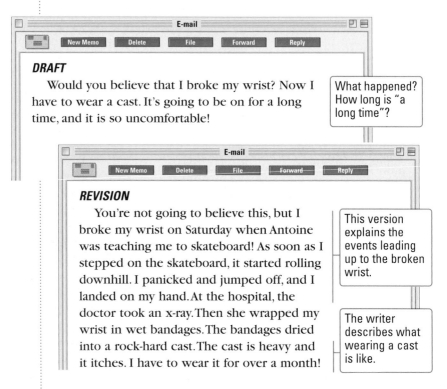

E-mail

New Memo | Delete | File | Forward | Reply

DRAFT

Would you believe that I broke my wrist? Now I have to wear a cast. It's going to be on for a long time, and it is so uncomfortable!

> What happened? How long is "a long time"?

E-mail

New Memo | Delete | File | Forward | Reply

REVISION

You're not going to believe this, but I broke my wrist on Saturday when Antoine was teaching me to skateboard! As soon as I stepped on the skateboard, it started rolling downhill. I panicked and jumped off, and I landed on my hand. At the hospital, the doctor took an x-ray. Then she wrapped my wrist in wet bandages. The bandages dried into a rock-hard cast. The cast is heavy and it itches. I have to wear it for over a month!

> This version explains the events leading up to the broken wrist.

> The writer describes what wearing a cast is like.

In this chapter, you will learn about types of elaboration you can use to improve your writing. Here's a quick preview.

Types of Elaboration	
Sensory details	Tell your reader how something looked, smelled, tasted, felt, or sounded.
Facts	Add proven information to make your point and support your opinions.
Visuals	Use photographs, illustrations, graphs, and charts to help your reader understand your topic.

❷ Methods of Elaboration

You can use elaboration to give more information and to keep your reader from getting bored. Here are different ways you can add details to your writing.

Elaboration Technique	Examples
Answer questions Tell who, what, when, where, why, and how.	I met Antoine at 10:00 on Saturday on the hill by my house. At 10:05, we were on our way to the hospital.
Describe Describe how your topic looks, sounds, tastes, feels, or smells.	The emergency room was quieter than I had expected. I could smell coffee burning at the nurses' station.
Explain Give your reader facts, statistics, or definitions.	The doctor said that I have a multiple fracture, which means the bone broke in more than one place.
Show, don't tell Instead of writing "My friend was scared," show his fear by describing how he looked and acted.	Antoine called home to tell my family what happened. His hands were shaking and he was sweaty. He had to clear his throat before he could talk.
Support opinions Give reasons and facts to support your opinions.	One-third of skateboarding injuries happen to beginners. It's smart to wear a helmet, knee pads, and wrist braces.

PRACTICE   Tell Me All About It

Elaborate on one of the sentences below, using any of the techniques described above.

- You could say that my mother overreacted.
- If I had the skateboarding lesson to do over again, I would act differently.
- Having a broken wrist can make life pretty difficult.

LESSON 2 | Using Sensory Details

❶ Sight, Smell, Taste, Touch, and Sound

Reading about food can be the next best thing to eating it, if the writer includes lots of **sensory details.** You can collect sensory details by using your five senses: sight, smell, taste, touch, and sound. Sensory details help you to show, not tell.

LITERARY MODEL

The men came in their best clothes, their squeaky shoes shined, their hair smelling of camellia hair oil. Papa didn't cook much else, but he was an expert when it came to making sukiyaki, and cooked it right at the table with gas piped in from the kitchen stove. As the men arrived, he would start the fat sizzling in the small iron pan.

— Yoshiko Uchida, "Oh Broom, Get to Work"

SOUND
SIGHT
SMELL

PROFESSIONAL MODEL

Chocolate shouldn't taste burnt or bitter, like old coffee. It shouldn't be gritty like sandpaper. It should be a rich shade of brown, as smooth as satin, and so sweet that a tiny piece can last a long time.

— Vibha Singh

TASTE
TOUCH
SIGHT

WATCH OUT

Sight and sound details are often the first ones to come to mind. Try to include details about touch, taste, and smell in your writing, too.

If you are having trouble thinking of sensory details to add to your writing, you may want to brainstorm by creating a word web like the one on the next page.

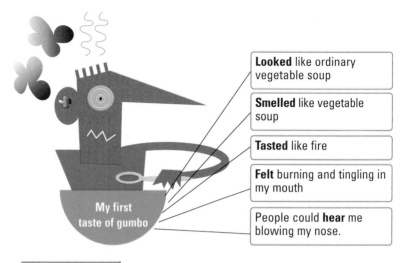

Looked like ordinary vegetable soup

Smelled like vegetable soup

Tasted like fire

Felt burning and tingling in my mouth

People could **hear** me blowing my nose.

My first taste of gumbo

STUDENT MODEL

It looked like vegetable soup. It smelled like vegetable soup. But when I took my first mouthful of gumbo, a spicy Cajun soup, I realized that this was not your average meal. My mouth was full of fire, and my eyes streamed as if they were trying to put it out. I felt as if industrial chemicals were in my nose. I grabbed a tissue, blew my nose with a loud honk, and told the whole world, "This is delicious!"

SIGHT

SMELL

TASTE

TOUCH

SOUND

PRACTICE Summer Senses

In this cartoon, Calvin describes sounds and sensations that remind him of summer. Write a paragraph about a sound, sight, taste, smell, or sensation that reminds you of your favorite season.

Calvin and Hobbes by Bill Watterson

Adding Facts

❶ Facts Help You Make Your Point

What is the largest animal in the world? The answer is the blue whale. The answer is also a **fact,** a statement that can be proved. When you elaborate with facts, you make your ideas and arguments stronger. This writer uses facts to show, not tell, the reader that he is terrified of swimming with dolphins.

> **LITERARY MODEL**
>
> As the streamlined but massive gray creatures cruised around me, I reminded myself they were not sharks. Their eighty-eight white, needlelike teeth, which I could see so clearly, were meant for snagging swift herring on the run, not for ripping out a twenty-pound mouthful of flesh, as a white shark's teeth were. Dolphins were mammals, not fish, and the reason for the up-and-down motion of their tails was to bring them back up to the air.
>
> —Don C. Reed, "My First Dive with the Dolphins"

FACTS ABOUT SHARKS

CONTRASTING FACTS ABOUT DOLPHINS

PRACTICE A ▸ **Just the Facts, Please**

In your 📁 **Working Portfolio,** find your **Write Away** paragraph from page 323. Add facts that make your advice clearer and more useful. For example, if you described your first day at a new school, you might want to tell how many students are in a typical class, or what activities occur after school.

❷ Facts Can Support Your Opinions

Would you be convinced by a person who supported his or her arguments with answers like the ones on the right?

What's missing from these statements are facts and reasons.

I just know.

Everyone knows that.

Because I said so.

To make her argument stronger, the writer of the model shown below added facts and a reason.

STUDENT MODEL

DRAFT

Manatees swim slowly, and sometimes boats hit and kill them. We should protect them, because otherwise they may become extinct.

REVISION

Manatees love Florida's warm waters, but so do boaters. Every year about 300 manatees are killed when speedboats run into them. Fewer than 2,000 manatees are still alive. At the rate manatees are dying, they could be extinct in 30 to 50 years. Manatees are an important part of Florida's natural environment, so they need our protection.

— Facts

— Reason

PRACTICE B Be Reasonable

Choose from the facts and reasons below to write a paragraph that contains one of these topic sentences. Write your own concluding sentence for your paragraph.

Topic Sentence 1: For human safety, the population of wild geese in and around cities must be controlled.

Topic Sentence 2: It isn't right to kill geese just because they inconvenience people.

- More and more geese are nesting in parks and airports.
- The geese can cause plane crashes by flying into airplanes.
- Geese raised in the city often lose their fear of people. They may chase and bite humans who come too close.
- Experts say that geese love to eat well-tended grass.
- Moving the geese usually doesn't work. They fly back to the place where they originally nested.
- Some city governments have killed geese to lower the number of geese in their area.
- Letting lawns grow wild, fencing off nesting areas, and using scarecrows all make geese less likely to nest.

ELABORATION

Creating Visuals

One picture really is worth a thousand words. By adding visuals to your writing, you can quickly show the reader something that might take pages of writing to describe. Visuals can be especially effective when you are writing about science or history. Or use them when you are explaining how something works or how to do something.

① Photographs and Illustrations

You may want to take your own photographs or make your own illustrations using art supplies or computer software. You can also find illustrations in magazines, newspapers, and on the Internet. Be sure to write captions or labels for your visuals to help readers understand what they are looking at.

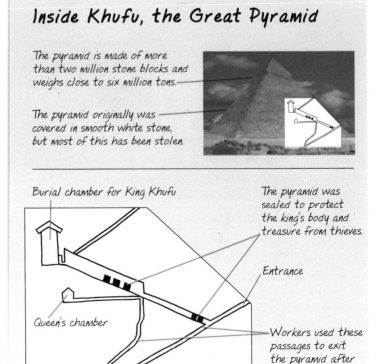

Inside Khufu, the Great Pyramid

The pyramid is made of more than two million stone blocks and weighs close to six million tons.

The pyramid originally was covered in smooth white stone, but most of this has been stolen.

Burial chamber for King Khufu

The pyramid was sealed to protect the king's body and treasure from thieves.

Entrance

Queen's chamber

Workers used these passages to exit the pyramid after it was sealed off.

Sources: *World Book Encyclopedia, Encyclopaedia Britannica Online*

❷ Charts and Graphs

You can use charts and graphs to present facts visually.
Charts use columns and rows to organize information.

The Pyramids of Giza		
Pyramid	**Length of Side**	**Height**
Khufu (the Great Pyramid)	755 ¾ feet	481 ¾ feet
Khafre	707 ¾ feet	471 feet
Menkaure	356 ½ feet	218 feet

Source: *Encyclopaedia Britannica Online*

Graphs can be used to compare numbers. The graph below gives the same information as the chart, but makes it easier to understand how much bigger the Great Pyramid is.

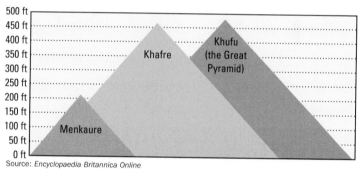

Source: *Encyclopaedia Britannica Online*

When you use visuals that you did not make yourself, include a source line telling readers where the visual came from.

PRACTICE **I See What You Mean!**

Use encyclopedias, newspapers and magazines, or the World Wide Web to research a topic that interests you. Find a photograph or illustration related to your topic. Then write a caption or labels for the visual.

You can choose one of these topics or find one of your own.

- how ancient Egyptians mummified their dead
- what living in a medieval European castle was like
- how rockets work

Student Help Desk

Elaboration at a Glance

What is elaboration?	What kinds are there?	Why should I use it?
Details that give readers more information about your topic	• Sensory details • Facts • Visuals	• To answer questions • To describe • To explain • To show, not tell • To support opinions

Sensory Words Generator Sense-O-Matic

Use the sensory words below to get you started—then think of more sensory details on your own.

triangular	rotten	thump	bitter	cool
cloudy	sweet	boom	mild	slippery
scuffed	moldy	crackle	tangy	scaly
feathered	earthy	crunch	nutty	scratchy

Sentence Doctor Fix It with Facts

Unsupported Statements	Statements Supported by Facts
Carrots are good for you.	Carrots contain vitamin A, which helps your eyes to see better.
Hundreds of years ago, the Incas built lots of roads.	In the 1400s and 1500s, the Incas built 10,000 miles of stone roads in South America.
Beavers have sharp teeth.	Beavers have such sharp teeth that one beaver can cut down a three-inch tree in only 15 minutes.
Alaska can be very cold in winter.	Temperatures in parts of Alaska can drop to minus 65 degrees Fahrenheit.

To show what something looks like, try a **photograph or illustration.**

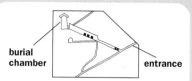

burial
chamber   entrance

To show how something works or what parts it has, try a **diagram.**

California

To show the location of something, try a **map.**

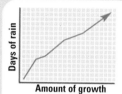

Days of rain

Amount of growth

To show how something changes over time, try a **line graph.**

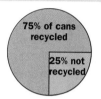

75% of cans recycled

25% not recycled

To show who gets how much of something, try a **pie graph.**

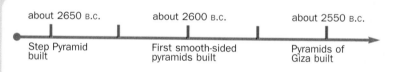

about 2650 B.C.

Step Pyramid built

about 2600 B.C.

First smooth-sided pyramids built

about 2550 B.C.

Pyramids of Giza built

To show the order in which events happen, try a **time line.**

ELABORATION

The Bottom Line

Checklist for Elaboration

Have I . . .

____ told my reader enough about my topic?

____ used sensory details to give my reader a clear picture?

____ included facts to give more information?

____ added visuals to elaborate on written information?

Power Words
Vocabulary for Precise Writing

serpentine

CIRCUITOUS

Highways and Byways

You don't always want to take the most direct route to your destination. Sometimes you may not even have a destination in mind! Here are some words for those laid-back times.

The Scenic Route

You know from math class that the shortest route between two points is a straight line. But who says that's always best? Sometimes you may want to **zigzag** or **meander** along. The most interesting way to get someplace may be **indirect;** you may take a **roundabout** or **circuitous** route down a **winding, serpentine** road.

Taking It Easy

You don't always have to hike **purposefully** to the top of the mountain. Sometimes you may just want to **roam** through the park, **ambling** and **rambling** through meadow and forest. You may want to **saunter** down to the river and stroll along its bank. Instead of using a map, you might **wander** and **drift** aimlessly, enjoying the unknown and unexpected.

saunter

amblir

▷ **Your Turn** Map Your Travels

Draw a map that shows the shortest route from your home to your school. Then show a longer, more interesting route on the same map. Use one or more of the boldfaced words above to help you describe either route. Be ready to explain when you might take one route instead of the other.

zig-zag

winding

Revising Sentences

Eat at Pepperoni Pete's Pizzeria and enjoy our new deep dish pizza or try our thin crust and a salad or our famous garlic bread and spaghetti and ...

Don't Run Out of Gas

Oh, no! Your sentence started out clear and interesting, but it ended up long and boring. You've got a good topic, but the sentence just won't fly. How can this unmanageable sentence be shortened? Just as cars sometime need tune-ups and airplanes might need repairs, your sentences may need to be revised. You may need to rearrange words and phrases or get rid of unnecessary words.

Write Away: Advertise!
Pretend you are advertising the opening of a new video store. On a separate sheet of paper, write an ad that would persuade people to shop at your store. Include plenty of details and descriptions. Save your work in your 📁 **Working Portfolio.**

LESSON 1 · Fixing Empty Sentences

Some sentences don't say anything, or they repeat an idea that you have already stated. Other sentences make statements that are not supported with facts and examples. Empty sentences in your writing will make the reader wonder if you really understand your topic.

Adding Details

You can fix an empty sentence by adding details. This will help make your writing clear and easy to understand. Look at the following model.

STUDENT MODEL

DRAFT

Science fiction films are the best movies to see. I like them a lot. They are my favorite kind of movie. I like the special effects.

> The writer repeats the same idea three times.

REVISION

Science fiction films are my favorite because they are exciting and fun to watch. The special effects in these movies make me feel like I'm flying, or traveling in space, or living on another planet!

> The writer gives specific details to support the opinion.

Here's How Filling Empty Sentences

1. Get rid of words and phrases that repeat an idea.
2. Ask yourself questions about the topic to find useful details.
3. Add the details to your writing.

 HOT TIP Never leave your reader asking why. Add reasons, examples, and facts to support your opinions.

Adding details will help make your writing clear and easier to understand. When writing sentences, ask yourself the six major questions: *who, what, when, where, why,* and *how.* The answers to these questions provide details for your reader and make your writing more interesting.

That cold, windy **March day in 1972** was my first day of work as a professional scuba diver for Marine World, soon to become **Marine World/Africa USA,** an oceanarium-zoo in **northern California.** I didn't let on how strange everything felt. I was only **six months out of deep-sea-diving school** and had almost no idea what to expect.

—Don C. Reed, "My First Dive with the Dolphins"

Reed's use of detail answers the questions *who, what, when, where, why,* and *how.*

PRACTICE **What's the Point?**

Follow the instructions in parentheses to revise these sentences.

1. Fiction is more fun to read than nonfiction. (Why? Give a reason.)
2. The library's book fair had a large variety. There were books for everyone. (Eliminate unnecessary words. Add more information.)
3. She is my favorite author. (Who? Tell why.)
4. My book club reads books. (What kind? When? Add details.)
5. The students volunteered and said that they would help. (Eliminate repeated idea. Add more information.)
6. That novel is the best ever. (Why? Add a reason.)
7. I like villains in stories more than heroes. (Give a reason.)
8. We are going there on our next holiday break. (When? Where?)
9. The author signed books for the people standing in line at the book signing. (Eliminate unnecessary words.)
10. Movies made from novels are not very good. (Why? Add a reason or fact.)

REVISING

Fixing Stringy Sentences

A stringy sentence is long and drawn-out. It uses the word *and* to connect idea after idea. After you write a sentence, stop and count the number of times you used the word *and.* If you used it more than twice, you may have created a stringy sentence!

Creating Separate Ideas

In many cases, dividing your stringy sentence into separate ideas lets you organize your thoughts. However, sometimes it is better to connect closely related ideas and get rid of words you don't need. Find and review a paragraph that you have written. Look at the example below.

Here's How Revising Stringy Sentences

Step #1. Review the paragraph.

Space camp is enjoyable for kids who are interested in learning about space exploration **and** it's fun finding out about astronauts **and** understanding the technology used to build rockets **and** what they use to launch rockets.

Step #2. Break down ideas.

- space camp is enjoyable for kids interested in learning about space exploration
- kids have fun learning about astronauts
- kids learn about the technology used for building rockets
- kids learn about the technology used for launching rockets

Step #3. Decide which ideas to connect or separate.

- Space camp is for kids who are interested in learning about space exploration and astronauts.
- Kids learn about the technology used for building and launching rockets.

Step #4. Revise.

Space camp is enjoyable for kids interested in learning about space exploration and astronauts. Kids learn about the technology used for building and launching rockets.

PRACTICE Keep It Clean!

Rewrite each of the following stringy sentences as several smaller sentences.

Dear Uncle John,
Our family went camping last weekend and we went to a state park in the mountains and I pitched the tent on a little hill and I went in the tent and I got in my sleeping bag and I slid right out of the tent and down the hill.

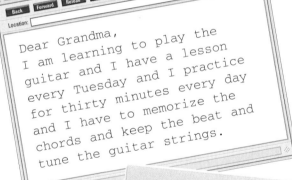

Dear Grandma,
I am learning to play the guitar and I have a lesson every Tuesday and I practice for thirty minutes every day and I have to memorize the chords and keep the beat and tune the guitar strings.

Dear Gaby,
My sister visited Washington, D.C., last weekend and she saw the Lincoln Memorial and took pictures of the White House. She also videotaped the floats at the National Independence Day Parade and took a tour of the Smithsonian.

Varying Sentence Length

Would you enjoy listening to a song that never changed its tune or rhythm? You would probably lose interest by the second verse! The same holds true in writing. If what you write doesn't have some variety, even the best ideas won't hold your reader's attention.

❶ Adding Sentence Variety

One way to keep your reader interested is by mixing long and short sentences. Notice how the writer made some ideas more exciting just by changing the sentence length, and by not beginning every sentence with *I*.

STUDENT MODEL

DRAFT

   I was a finalist in this year's spelling bee. I had easily beaten everyone in my class but this time was different. I was nervous during the competition and began to sweat. I held my breath and closed my eyes. I began to spell the word and the room became very quiet. I reached the last letter and suddenly, the crowd began to cheer. It was then I knew that I had won the competition.

Too many long sentences become boring.

REVISION

   I was a finalist in this year's spelling bee. I had easily beaten everyone in my class before. This time, I was nervous. I swallowed. I began to sweat. I held my breath. Finally, I closed my eyes and began to spell the word. The room became very quiet. Suddenly, as I reached the last letter, the crowd cheered. I had won!

This version combines long and short sentences that help keep the reader interested.

PRACTICE A ▸ **Make It Interesting**

Rewrite the following paragraph. Vary the length and rhythm of the sentences. Add details to make the paragraph interesting.

   My friend and I went roller skating. We wore helmets and elbow pads. We raced down the hill. The hill was steep. We held hands to keep from falling.

❷ Combining Choppy Sentences

Choppy sentences are a series of short sentences that don't contain a lot of details. Choppy sentences are often boring to read. You can revise choppy sentences by combining them and adding conjunctions and connecting phrases.

STUDENT MODEL

DRAFT

    I have a Teen Living class. I am learning to sew. I made an apron last week. I picked out fabric that had chili peppers on it. I pinned the pattern to the fabric. I cut out the pattern pieces. I sewed them together. I tried on the apron. It fit.

> Too many short and boring sentences.

REVISION

    I'm learning to sew in my Teen Living class. **Last week** I made an apron. **First,** I picked out a print fabric with chili peppers on it. **Next,** I pinned the pattern to the fabric and cut out the pieces. **After that** I sewed them together. My new apron fit just right **when** I tried it on.

> This version combines related ideas and uses **connecting words,** and **conjunctions.**

REVISING

Here's How Smoothing Choppy Sentences

- Use conjunctions such as *also, but, and, or,* and *so* to combine sentences.
- If you are writing about a process or telling a story, use sequence words like *first, next, last, after,* and *soon.*
- Use connecting words and phrases such as *then, finally, for example,* and *in addition.*

PRACTICE B Straighten It Out!

Rewrite this choppy paragraph. Add conjunctions.

> We went to the amusement park. The new roller coaster was scary. The line to get on it was long. We all waited. It started off slowly. It went through five loops. We screamed.

Varying Sentence Structure

LESSON 4

Just as rearranging furniture in your bedroom gives the room a new look, rearranging phrases in your sentences adds zip to your writing.

❶ Rearranging Phrases

There are no hard and fast rules about where to place the most important words in a sentence. You could start with something interesting to get the reader's attention. However, saving the best for last also leaves a great impression.

Patti's dog Jack barked loudly and licked her face, making her laugh.

Licking her face and barking loudly, Patti's dog Jack made her laugh.

Patti laughed as her dog Jack licked her face and barked loudly.

PRACTICE A Add Some Spice!

Look at the video frames below. Write a sentence with three phrases. Then rewrite the sentence two different ways.

CHAPTER 16

❷ Varying Sentence Types

Do you remember the four kinds of sentences? Then don't forget to use them when you write! Although statements are the most common, an occasional question, command, or exclamation can wake your readers up. Use the following chart to remind yourself of the choices you have.

Type of Sentence	Definition	Example
Declarative	Gives information	• Our drama club performed *The Miracle Worker.* • We rehearsed every day for four weeks.
Interrogative	Asks a question	• Have you ever been to a play? • How do you think the actors remember all their lines?
Imperative	Tells or requests someone to do something	• Be quiet when the curtain goes up. • Give your ticket to the usher.
Exclamatory	Shows a strong feeling	• What an exciting chase! • That line was really funny!

Try not to overuse any one kind of sentence. Too many exclamations can make your writing seem overexcited. Too many commands can make you seem bossy. If you ask a lot of questions but don't answer them, your reader may get annoyed.

PRACTICE B Revise. Revise? Revise!

In your 🗒 **Working Portfolio,** find your **Write Away** paragraph from page 335. Revise your paragraph so that it includes at least one question, exclamation, or command.

Student Help Desk

Revising Sentences at a Glance

Add important details to empty sentences so that they say something worthwhile.

Reorganize stringy sentences to make your ideas clearer.

Vary the length and kind of sentences to keep your reader interested.

Filling Empty Sentences   Ask Questions ?

Problem	Sentence repeats information needlessly: **My new CD was inexpensive and didn't cost very much.**
Ask	Am I including words that aren't necessary?
Solution	Take out repeated ideas: **My new CD was inexpensive.**
Problem	Sentence is so vague that it says nothing: **We are going tomorrow if it doesn't rain.**
Ask	Does this sentence contain all the important information?
Solution	Add more information: We are going **to the Museum of Science and Industry** tomorrow if it doesn't rain.
Problem	Sentence contains unsupported statements: **Cats are easier to care for than dogs.**
Ask	Did I supply any reasons?
Solution	Add examples, information, and facts: Cats are easier to care for than dogs **because you don't have to walk them.**

We are learning how to use computers and now I can use the mouse and paste in clip art and type a two page report and correct mistakes and . . .

Smoothing Choppy Sentences

> I bought a new jacket | but | it didn't fit right | so | I took it back.

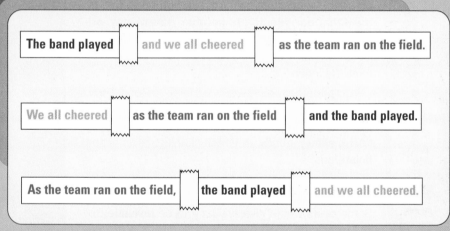

Rearranging Phrases

> The band played | and we all cheered | as the team ran on the field.

> We all cheered | as the team ran on the field | and the band played.

> As the team ran on the field, | the band played | and we all cheered.

The Bottom Line

Checklist for Revising Sentences

Can I improve my sentences by . . .

_____ adding details to empty sentences?

_____ dividing stringy sentences into separate ideas?

_____ making my sentences different lengths?

_____ combining short, choppy sentences?

_____ rearranging phrases in my sentences?

_____ using different types of sentences?

Power Words
Vocabulary for Precise Writing

Hey, Look at Me!

These words can help you describe someone who stands out—or doesn't stand out.

Outstanding or Standing Out?

Most of us enjoy being noticed for our very special personal wonderfulness. We'd like other people to think that our talents are **notable, noteworthy,** or even **unparalleled;** that our looks are **striking;** that our personality is **memorable,** perhaps even **unforgettable.**

On the other hand, it's possible to go too far to get attention. Nobody likes to be thought of as being **peculiar, preposterous,** or **outlandish;** as wearing **flashy, showy, gaudy,** or **garish** clothing; or as acting **boisterous.**

Avoiding the Spotlight

Some of us would give anything to be **invisible,** to go **unnoticed.** People who want to blend in are **shy** and **modest;** their personalities are **subdued, unassuming,** and very **low-key.**

 Your Turn Like Nobody Else

Working in a small group, think of a movie star, an athlete, or someone else who stands out from the pack. Write a one-paragraph description of that person, using at least one of the boldfaced words above.

striking peculiar memorable

noteworthy

gaudy

garish

unforgettable

notable

Effective Language

Fight For Your Rights!

If I were you I'd keep my eyes on the road instead of reading other people's bumper stickers.

Mummelsee

FERNANDEZ FOR CITY TREASURER

MAGNOLIA GARDENS

When your phone doesn't ring, it's me!

SOUTH BORDER

VIRGINIA

SHENANDOAH NAT'L PARK

SAVE THE DOLPHINS!

TEXAS HAS IT ALL

wild & wonderful

NEW ORLEANS

Smile—it will make people wonder what you're up to.

YORKTOWN, VIRGINIA
A REVOLUTIONARY EXPERIENCE · 1781

TEUF & TEUF

Ask me if I care.

SAVE THE WILDERNESS
HUDSON BAY

MARYLAND
DP 1512

People who think they know it all really annoy those of us who do.

EFFECTIVE LANG.

Sticking to the Point

Check out the slogans on these bumper stickers. Some are short and sweet. Others are long and rambling. Which ones are more effective?

Bumper stickers, posters, and buttons are all designed to attract attention. How do they do it? They use effective language, of course! By choosing just the right words and expressing yourself creatively, you too can get your point across in the most effective way.

Write Away: Auto-Biography

Write three bumper stickers that show your interests, opinions, or personality. Use your imagination and try to make your words precise. Save your bumper stickers in your **Working Portfolio.**

Levels of Language

LESSON 1

Formal or Informal?

Luann by Greg Evans

This dad is trying his best to speak the language of his kids, even if he *is* a few decades off! It's important to realize that different kinds of language are appropriate to different audiences and occasions.

Formal language often includes an advanced vocabulary and long sentences. **Informal language** contains everyday words and expressions and generally has a simpler sentence structure. It often uses more contractions than formal language. Compare the example below to the one on the next page. One is an informal E-mail to a friend, and the other is a more formal review for a magazine.

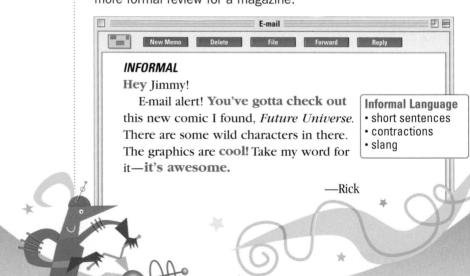

E-mail

New Memo | Delete | File | Forward | Reply

INFORMAL

Hey Jimmy!

E-mail alert! **You've gotta check out** this new comic I found, *Future Universe*. There are some wild characters in there. The graphics are **cool!** Take my word for it—**it's awesome.**

—Rick

Informal Language
• short sentences
• contractions
• slang

FORMAL

Future Universe is an exciting find for comic-book fans. The main character is an **intergalactic** police officer. She chases criminals and writes tickets for spaceships that are illegally parked. The writing is **humorous,** and the illustrations are **imaginative.**

—Rory Michaels

> **Formal Language**
> • longer sentences
> • advanced vocabulary
> • no slang

Do you know when to use informal language and when to use formal? This chart can help you decide.

Choosing Formal or Informal Language		
	Formal	**Informal**
Audience	Someone in authority; a group to whom you are presenting	Friends or family members
Occasion	A formal presentation, essay, report, or speech	Friendly letters and E-mails, casual conversation
Example	That is a superb idea.	That's a great idea!

Words and phrases such as "ain't" and "don't know nothing" are considered **nonstandard English.** Avoid using these expressions in formal school situations—use Standard English instead.

PRACTICE ▸ **Watch Your Words!**

Revise this letter to make its language more formal.

Hey Mr. Principal,

I'm totally steamed about this plan of yours to make the school year longer. What's up with that? I think the idea stinks, and my friends will back me on that! I know you're the principal and all, but what about us students? You shoulda asked us what we thought first!

Nancy

Using Exact Language

LESSON 2

❶ Just the Right Words

When you use precise words, your reader gets a much clearer idea of what you mean. To see what a difference precise language can make, take a look at the chart below.

Making Your Writing More Specific

Noun	**General:** a *thing* **Specific:** a **monster**
Adjective	**General:** *large* monster **Specific:** **towering** monster
Verb	**General:** *walked* past us **Specific:** **stomped** past us
Complete sentence	**General:** A large thing walked past us. **Specific:** A towering monster stomped past us.

Using exact words improves all kinds of writing. This student's article for her school newspaper was much more interesting when she wrote precisely.

STUDENT MODEL

DRAFT

The game was pretty close at the end. Danielle Mills passed the ball to Ellie Hertzoff. That was great, because Ellie was able to take a shot and it went in. People were very excited. Our team worked really hard to win the title.

REVISION

Tuesday night's basketball game **against Braintree Middle School** was **tied with three seconds left.** Danielle Mills made a **lightning-quick** pass to Ellie Hertzoff. Ellie was able to make a **game-winning hook shot. More than 80 cheering, shouting fans leaped to their feet. Chester Middle School** definitely earned its **championship title!**

❷ Kinds of Meaning

A word's **denotation** is its dictionary definition. A word's **connotation** involves the feelings and emotions that the word may bring to a person's mind. Words with the same denotation can have different connotations, so think carefully about the kinds of words you use.

Positive Connotation: This jacket is **inexpensive.** (a good value for the money)

Negative Connotation: This jacket is **cheap.** (poorly made)

Positive Connotation: Someone wearing this jacket would look **casual.** (relaxed, informal)

Negative Connotation: Someone wearing this jacket would look **sloppy.** (untidy, careless)

PRACTICE Say What You Mean

One phrase in each pair below has a positive connotation. The other has a negative connotation. Write a sentence for each phrase that shows its connotation. Use a dictionary if you are uncertain of a word's meaning.

Example: **a timid swimmer; a cautious swimmer**

Negative: The **timid** swimmer was scared to go in water more than two feet deep.

Positive: The **cautious** swimmer made sure the water was deep enough before diving in.

1. rowdy children; playful children
2. my determined little sister; my mule-headed little sister
3. answered confidently; answered arrogantly
4. glared at me; gazed at me
5. a smile on his face; a smirk on his face

The sentence "We sat on the grass" doesn't do much to help a reader imagine a scene. However, the sentence "We sat on a cool, green carpet of grass" presents a much stronger picture. The second sentence uses **imagery**—words that bring a clear picture to a reader's mind.

One way that writers create images is by using figures of speech. A **figure of speech** is an expression that may not be literally true. You can use figures of speech when you want to go beyond a dictionary definition and express something imaginatively. The boy in the cartoon below definitely has the right idea.

Miss Peach by Mell

❶ Say It with Similes

A **simile** is a figure of speech that compares one thing with another using the word *like* or *as*. Notice how these writers use similes effectively.

> **LITERARY MODEL**
>
> My mother laughed her honey laugh. She had **little emerald eyes that warmed me like the sun.**
>
> —Norma Fox Mazer, "Tuesday of the Other June"
>
> That night **the moon was round and white as my Sunday hat.**
>
> —Lynn Joseph, "The Bamboo Beads"

❷ Metaphors Make It Marvelous

A **metaphor** is an expression that compares two things without using *like* or *as*. Can you see the differences between the following expressions?

SIMILE

> **The moon shone like a lantern in the sky.**

METAPHOR

> **The moon was a lantern in the sky.**

SIMILE

> **Sara sings like a nightingale in the school choir.**

METAPHOR

> **Sara is a nightingale in the school choir.**

Avoid figures of speech that have become **clichés**, or overused expressions. We've all heard phrases like "quiet as a mouse" or "pretty as a picture." How about saying "still as a snow-covered forest" or "lovely as a sunflower"? Make up your own phrases to express what you feel!

PRACTICE A Exercise Your Imagination

Rewrite each of the following sentences, adding a simile or a metaphor. Remember, don't use clichés!

1. The dog growled fiercely.
2. This house is cold.
3. She felt tired.
4. He pitched the ball.
5. The rain fell.

PRACTICE B Jazz It Up!

In your 🗀 **Working Portfolio,** find your **Write Away** paragraph from page 347. Rewrite one of your bumper stickers so that it includes a simile and another so it contains a metaphor. If you prefer, you may write two new bumper stickers that have a simile and a metaphor.

EFFECTIVE LANG.

Student Help Desk

Effective Language at a Glance

Choose Your Level
Select formal or informal language based on audience and purpose.

Watch Your Words
Be careful with your connotations.

Be Precise
Say exactly what you mean.

Get Creative
Use metaphors, similes, and imagery.

Formal Language	Informal Language
The language of school and business	The language of everyday conversation
I am extremely unhappy.	I'm feeling down.
Please calm down.	Take it easy!
This film is dull.	This movie is the pits.
I am quite pleased.	That is so cool!

Precise Words — What Do You Mean By That?

Use exact words to get your message across!

Look out for that thing!

What thing?

That thing over there!

Huh?

There's a huge red truck heading straight for us!

Oh. Well, why didn't you say so?

Figurative Language — Paint Some Word Pictures

Imagery brings pictures to a reader's mind.
> **Ray gobbled enough food to feed an entire football team.**

A **simile** compares two things using *like* or *as*.
> **Ray ate like a starving wolf.**

A **metaphor** compares two things without using *like* or *as*.
> **Ray was a starving wolf in the cafeteria.**

Connotations — Words with Strong Feelings

Some words bring emotions to a reader's mind.

When You Write . . .	Your Reader May Think . . .
Marcie is **thrifty.**	Marcie is careful about how she spends her money.
Marcie is **cheap.**	Marcie hates to part with her money, even for a good reason.
That plan is **daring.**	The plan is risky but bold.
That plan is **reckless.**	The plan is too dangerous. It is sure to fail.

The Bottom Line

Checklist for Effective Language

Have I . . .

____ used formal or informal language as appropriate?

____ made my writing clear and effective?

____ checked the connotations of my words?

____ used figures of speech creatively?

____ avoided clichés?

Writing Workshops

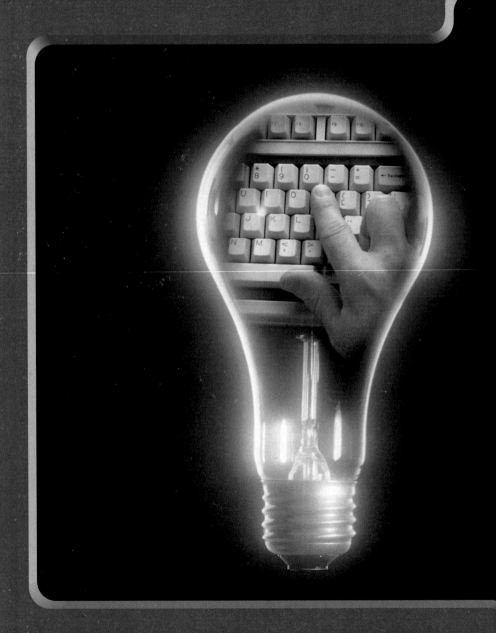

18 Personal Experience Essay   358

19 Describing a Place   366

20 Response to Literature   374

21 Process Description   382

22 Problem-Solution Essay   390

23 Opinion Statement   398

24 Short Story and Poem   406

25 Research Report   418

I Can't Put My Finger On It

Have you ever had a great idea, only to have trouble putting it into words? As you gain writing skill, the right words become easier to find. Whether you are persuading others, sharing information, or explaining your feelings, you will be able to express yourself more clearly.

Personal Experience Essay

Learn What It Is

"You'll never guess what I saw yesterday!" "I thought I'd never get out of that situation." "That was something I'll never forget." Have you ever made one of these statements? If so, you were probably relating a **personal experience**—something that happened to you or that you observed. Writing about an experience is a way to explore what it meant to you.

Basics in a Box

PERSONAL EXPERIENCE ESSAY AT A GLANCE

Beginning

- grabs the reader's attention
- introduces the experience, including the people and places involved

Middle

- describes the experience with sensory details and dialogue
- shows the importance of the incident

End

- tells the outcome or results of the experience
- presents the writer's feelings about the experience

RUBRIC

Standards for Writing

A successful personal experience essay should

- focus on one experience and why it is important to the writer
- grab the reader's attention at the beginning
- provide background information as needed
- make the order of events clear
- have a strong conclusion that summarizes the importance of the incident
- give a sense of time, place, and character through sensory details, precise descriptions, and dialogue

See How It's Done: *Personal Experience Essay*

Student Model
Heidi Wiedenheft
Glasgow Middle School

RUBRIC
IN ACTION

Theater

Do you like theater? Well I do, and I also love to perform.

I come to the theater early to get into my costume. I put on my makeup and do my hair.

Now that I am ready, I have to sit backstage and wait for the audience to come in. As the first person comes in, my stomach starts to rise, and now I think I have little baby butterflies. The crowd starts to grow, my insides begin to flow as the butterflies get bigger and bigger.

I take a deep breath and try to remember my lines. As the crowd grows, it gets very hard to concentrate. It's like there are millions of different kinds of birds all trying to communicate, but they all seem to have a different language. The room fills with the aroma of sweet and sour lollipops and the smell of buttery popcorn.

Finally, they are all settled and the show can begin. The lights start to dim. I'm sitting there, in the dark, all by myself. All of a sudden, my heart begins to pound loudly in my chest. I hope no one else can hear it. I go over my lines once more, and I pray that I don't make a mistake. Then the stage lights come on and the music begins.

I go out on the stage and I can't believe my eyes. The whole place is packed with people of all sizes and ages. I start to say my part and do the best I can, and I pray that it pays off in the end.

❶ This writer begins with a question that focuses on the experience.
Another option: Begin with a question or statement that makes clear the importance of the experience.

❷ Opens with an image that makes the reader want to know more

❸ Uses details that appeal to the senses of sound and smell to describe the setting

❹ Uses transition words and phrases that clearly show the order of events

PERS. EXPERIENCE

The other actors start to come on stage. The stage that was once peaceful is now filled with many voices from booming to soft, from mellow to shrill. After I relax a bit, the show begins to flow. What was to take hours has now turned into minutes. Before I know it, I have gone off the stage and am ready to go back on, to bid the crowd good-bye.

As I grab the hands of the others and run out on stage, the crowd stands up and applauds like thunder.

I go backstage and take off my costume and makeup. As I leave, the aromas of sweet and sour lollipops and buttered popcorn still linger in the air.

❺ Ends with a strong conclusion that reminds reader of details mentioned earlier

Do It Yourself

❶ Prewriting

Think of ideas. List as many ways as you can think of to complete this statement: "An interesting thing that happened to me is ____ ."

For more topic ideas, see the Idea Bank, p. 364.

Pick one idea to explore. Choose one idea from your list, and then make a chart like the one below. The details you list on the chart will help you plan how to tell your experience.

When it happened	Last summer
How it made me feel	Scared, embarrassed
Smells, sounds, sights I remember	Damp wood, crickets, owls, the full moon
Things that were said	"We're never going to get out of here!" "I think we're lost."
Why it was important	Learned there's no reason to be afraid of the dark

❷ Drafting

Cook up your story. Write your essay as if you were telling it to a friend. You can check for spelling and grammar errors later.

Add spice. Start with an image or idea that will make the reader want to know more: "It was the worst day of my life." Use descriptive details and dialogue to make the experience come alive for your readers. "You have to take your sister with you or you can't go," my mother told me.

Add the ingredients in the right order. Make sure that the order of events will be clear to your readers.

For information about getting feedback from your peers, see p. 365.

PERS. EXPERIENCE

❸ Revising

TARGET SKILL ▶**Using Sensory Details** What do you remember most about your experience? Use words that appeal to the senses to bring your memories to life for your readers. For more help with revising, review the rubric on page 358.

> The room ~~is crowded with noisy people eating snacks.~~
> ∧
> _fills with the aroma of sweet and sour lollipops and the smell of buttery popcorn._

❹ Editing and Proofreading

TARGET SKILL ▶**Correcting Fragments** A sentence fragment is a part of sentence that is punctuated as though it were a complete thought. Fragments are confusing because readers may not understand what you mean. Reread your essay carefully and add the missing sentence parts to any fragments you find.

> _I have gone_   _am_
> Before I know it, ∧off the stage and ∧ready to go back on, to
> bid the crowd good-bye.

For more on sentence fragments, see pp. 25–27.

❺ Sharing and Reflecting

Share your essay with a group of classmates by reading it aloud. Use different facial expressions and voice tones to add interest to your presentation. Ask for feedback on the content and delivery of your presentation.

For Your Working Portfolio As you **reflect** on your writing process, ask yourself what you learned. How would you change the process next time? Write down your responses and save them with your finished essay. Keep your work in your
📁 **Working Portfolio.**

Speak for Yourself: *Monologue*

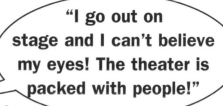

"I go out on stage and I can't believe my eyes! The theater is packed with people!"

It is quite easy to turn your **personal experience essay** into a monologue, a presentation by one speaker. After all, you were simply writing about something that happened to you. Now you can share the same story with an audience. Imagine you see a group of your friends. You say, "You'll never guess what happened to me!" and your story begins.

Here's How Creating a Monologue

- Pick the part of your essay that has the most action or the most interesting characters.

- Change your written language to sound more like a conversation.

- Take on the role of storyteller. You want your audience to see, hear, and feel everything you experienced. Did things smell "dry and musty, like the inside of an old shoe box"? Were the lights "dazzling, almost blinding"?

- Rehearse your monologue in front of a mirror until you have it mostly memorized.

- Act out the different parts if there is more than one person in your essay. Use different voices and actions for each character. Use gestures and facial expressions to build up your performance.

For more information on speaking skills, see pp. 489–491.

PERS. EXPERIENCE

Student Help Desk

Personal Experience Essay at a Glance

Middle
- describes the experience with sensory details and dialogue
- shows the importance of the incident

Beginning
- grabs the reader's attention
- introduces the experience, including the people and place involved

End
- tells the outcome or results of the experience
- presents the writer's feelings about the experience

Idea Bank

Try some memory joggers to find a topic.

Talk with a neighbor about something you both witnessed that happened in the neighborhood.

Think about moments when you did something for the first time.

Look at photographs to help you recall events.

Read literature such as "The Jacket" by Gary Soto (*The Language of Literature*, Grade 6) to see how other writers relate their personal experiences.

Detail Generator   Little Things Count

- **Use metaphors and similes.** Was the experience as boring as cake dough? As noisy as indoor firecrackers? Was the dog's tail a whirligig?

- **Appeal to all the senses.** How did they sound? Look? Feel? How would they taste? Smell?

- **Add descriptive words.** Tell how things felt or looked, or tell how they happened. Was the riverbank soggy? Did the teacher scowl? Were the children rocketing out from the end of the water slide?

Friendly Feedback

Questions for Your Peer Reader

- How could I make the beginning of my essay more interesting?
- Why do you think this experience was important to me?
- What parts of my essay are confusing?
- How could I improve the ending?
- What was your favorite part? Why?

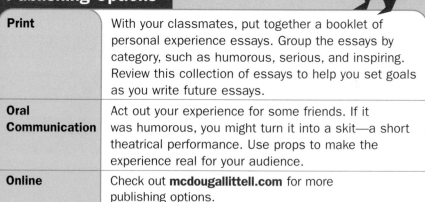

Publishing Options

Print	With your classmates, put together a booklet of personal experience essays. Group the essays by category, such as humorous, serious, and inspiring. Review this collection of essays to help you set goals as you write future essays.
Oral Communication	Act out your experience for some friends. If it was humorous, you might turn it into a skit—a short theatrical performance. Use props to make the experience real for your audience.
Online	Check out **mcdougallittell.com** for more publishing options.

The Bottom Line

Checklist for Personal Experience Essay

Have I . . .

___ concentrated on one well-defined experience?

___ begun in a way that made readers want to know more?

___ made the importance of the event clear?

___ shown clearly the order of events?

___ used sensory words?

___ used dialogue in an effective way?

___ written a strong ending?

Describing a Place

Learn What It Is

When you read about an amusement park, can you smell the cotton candy? When you read about a summer camp, can you feel the cool water? An effective **description of a place** can help your readers feel they are entering the experience you are describing.

Basics in a Box

DESCRIBING A PLACE AT A GLANCE

sensory details

physical description

figurative language

Main Impression of Place

writer's feelings about the place

dialogue

other people's reactions to the place

RUBRIC

Standards for Writing

A successful description of a place should

- focus on a single place
- convey a clear sense of purpose
- include sensory details and precise words to create a vivid picture, establish a mood, or express an emotion
- include figurative language or dialogue when appropriate
- follow a consistent method of organization

See How It's Done: *Describing a Place*

RUBRIC
IN ACTION

My Place

I have a place, my place. I go there when I feel sad. It is surrounded by flowers. There are big, fragrant lilac bushes circling this place. In late spring there are delicate columbine plants with different shades of pinks, purples, reds, yellows, blues, and whites. As the season passes, flowers emerge from plants that had been only leafy foliage. Wild irises cluster around a small, bubbling stream. Beyond the lilacs I find a beautiful meadow of daisies with their yellow heads and dainty white petals. As spring fades, the meadow becomes a field lush with clover.

Summer brings along with it a dimming of spring's newness. The trees become dark as they spread their leaves above me. It becomes hot, and the coolness of the stream trickling past my feet is refreshing.

Fall comes with a cooling of the temperatures. The grove of sugar maples nearby seems to explode with yellows, reds, oranges, and crimsons. Squirrels scamper about, gathering acorns to eat over the long winter.

Too soon, winter settles its white blanket over the land. Everything is tranquil and quiet. The bubbling stream is covered by a thin and delicate sheet of ice.

To get to my place, you must walk down a small, pebbly path. On either side of the walk are towering pine trees that make one feel small and mute. You cross a bridge over a rushing stream. Then you reach the meadow of daisies and clover. From here you can see the lilacs. This is the only real entrance to my place. It is not very visible from

❶ Focuses on one place

❷ Uses sensory details and precise words to create a vivid picture

❸ Uses chronological order to show the place over a period of time

DESCRIPTION

the outside. I believe I am the only person here who knows of this place. At least, I hope I am. This place holds memories for me, especially the small tree house about ten feet up in a tall willow.

I once had a best friend. She lived next door to me. We wanted to share a garden where we could plant flowers of endless variety. We dreamed of finding a secret place that only we knew about. My friend was always wanting to explore. One day in late April I suggested we take the Pine Trail, for I had always been fond of the meadow at its end. I had brought a picnic lunch for us to share. We decided to eat in the shade of the willow tree that we could see over a large hedge of lilac bushes. We circled the bushes until we found the small gap in the bushes. I entered first and saw the large, knobby trunk of the willow with its long and graceful branches. Falling in love with the place instantly, we decided to eat lunch.

Soon we had started constructing the tree house. It was perfect. Well, almost perfect. Before the school year was over, we had finished. We had planted some of our own flowers, but most grew naturally. Then that horrible day came when she told me she was moving.

My place is not really my place, but our place.

❹ This writer tells directly how she and her best friend found the special place.
Another option: Show the discovery through dialogue.

❺ Uses spatial order

❻ Shows why the place is special

Do It Yourself

Writing Prompt Write a description of a place you know well.

Purpose To entertain with a vivid picture that draws your reader into the place

Audience Friends, classmates, and family members

① Prewriting

Pick a place. Recall a place you have visited—possibly a beautiful place, a lonely place, or a place where something exciting happened. Make some notes about how the place looked and how it made you feel. Try to think of some adjectives or adverbs that will make your writing more vivid.

For more topic ideas, see the Idea Bank, p. 372.

Gather details. You might actually go to the place, or you can look at pictures and souvenirs. Try to see the place with your senses.

② Drafting

Decide on the big idea. Think about why the place is special to you. Work on creating one impression of it. As you write, try to make one main idea come through.

Organize the details. Choose one way of organizing the description. Here are some ways to organize.

Patterns of Organization	
Sequential order	Use the order in which events occur to describe your subject.
Order of importance	Use details that progress from most important to least important or from least important to most important.
Spatial order	Give details from left to right, from near to far or far to near, from bottom to top or top to bottom.

Get started. After choosing a way to organize, start writing. If the first organization doesn't work, try another one. The important thing is to start writing. You can revise later.

For information about getting feedback from your peers, see p. 373.

DESCRIPTION

③ Revising

TARGET SKILL ▶**Strong Conclusions** The conclusion will be your readers' final impression of the place, so you want it to show what the place means to you. For more help with revising, review the rubric on page 366.

> *that horrible   came when*
> Then ~~one~~ day/she told me she was moving.
>
> My place is not ~~the same anymore.~~
>   *really my place, but our place.*

④ Editing and Proofreading

TARGET SKILL ▶**Fixing Comma Errors** Remember to put a comma between items in a series, including the last two items. If it is needed to make your meaning clear, place a comma after a phrase or clause that introduces a sentence. Using commas correctly makes your sentences flow more naturally for the reader.

> In late spring there are delicate columbine plants with
> different shades of pinks, purples, reds, yellows, blues, and
> whites. As the season passes, flowers emerge from plants
> that had been only leafy foliage.

For more on commas, see pp. 209–211.

⑤ Sharing and Reflecting

Find an opportunity to **share** your description with friends or family who know about the place or would be interested in it.

For Your Working Portfolio As you **reflect** on the reactions of your readers, make notes on any comments that helped you. What did you learn about how you feel about the place? Save your notes about what you learned, along with your finished description, in your 🗂 **Working Portfolio.**

Speak for Yourself: *Guided Tour*

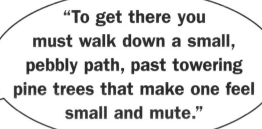

"To get there you must walk down a small, pebbly path, past towering pine trees that make one feel small and mute."

You can use maps, pictures, and specific, descriptive language to introduce people to a place they've never seen. Turn your **description of a place** into a talk with pictures.

Here's How) Creating a Guided Tour

- If you can, go to the place you described. Pretend you are guiding a person who has never seen this place. Take notes or speak into a tape recorder as you walk through it. Make the same trip by memory if you cannot actually visit.

- Keep the order of things logical. What do you see first as you walk into your place? Where are things in relation to each other?

- Find or draw a map of your place. Label some important features and landmarks.

- Use all the senses. Describe how things smell in your place. What sounds can you hear?

- Tell your audience what the place means to you. What stories are connected to this place? How did you first find it?

- As you present your tour in class, bring in pictures of your place to refer to. Arrange the pictures and maps in sequence. Point to them as you tell about each stop on the tour.

For more information on speaking skills, see p. 489–491.

DESCRIPTION

Student Help Desk

Describing a Place at a Glance

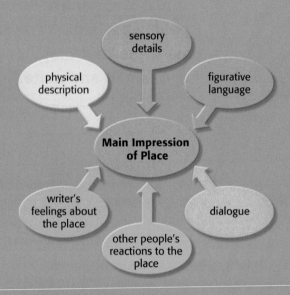

sensory details

physical description

figurative language

Main Impression of Place

writer's feelings about the place

other people's reactions to the place

dialogue

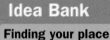

Idea Bank

Finding your place

Your favorite place Where would you most like to be right now?

A place from the past Interview an older relative or friend about how a place you both know has changed over the years.

A place from a trip Look through postcards, picture albums, or souvenirs from a place you have been.

An everyday place Describe a place you see every day to someone who has never been there.

Read literature Descriptions are essential parts of many literary works. Read "Bringing the Prairie Home" by Patricia MacLachlan (*The Language of Literature,* Grade 6) to see the meaning of a place for her.

Friendly Feedback

Questions for Your Peer Reader

- How do you think I feel about the place I described?
- Which details best help you see the place for yourself?
- What else would you like to know about the place?
- How would you feel about visiting the place?

Publishing Options

Print	Ask a friend who likes to draw to illustrate your description. Make a booklet to share with classmates.
Oral Communication	Read your description aloud to classmates and ask whether they would like to see the place you described.
Online	Check out **mcdougallittell.com** for more publishing options.

The Bottom Line

Checklist for Describing a Place

Have I . . .

_____ focused on one place?

_____ been clear about the purpose for describing this place?

_____ used sensory details and precise words?

_____ included figurative language or dialogue where appropriate?

_____ used a consistent method of organization?

Response to Literature

Learn What It Is

Did a story ever make you cry or laugh out loud? The tears or laughter were a part of your **response to literature.** When you write a response to literature, it helps you understand why you felt the way you did. It also helps others to know more about both the literature and you.

Basics in a Box

RESPONSE TO LITERATURE AT A GLANCE

Introduction
Introduces the title, author, and a clear statement of your response

Body
Supports the response with evidence from the work

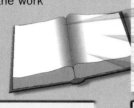

Evidence
examples from the story

quotations

specific reactions

Conclusion
Summarizes the response

RUBRIC

Standards for Writing

A successful response to literature should

- name the literary work in the introduction and clearly state your response to it
- tell enough about the work so that readers unfamiliar with it can understand your response
- contain clearly described, specific reactions and responses to the literary work
- support your statements with quotations and details
- summarize your response in the conclusion

See How It's Done: *Response to Literature*

Student Model
Alec McMullen
Holmes Junior High

RUBRIC
IN ACTION

"All Summer in a Day"

"All Summer in a Day" by Ray Bradbury is a story about a colony of humans who live on the planet Venus where it rains all the time except for one hour every seven years. This story is especially meaningful to me because of the way it relates to my personal experience.

In the story a girl named Margot is the only one in her class who remembers the sun. This makes her different from the other children, and they constantly pick on her. As the children are waiting for the rain to stop, a mean boy named William says that the sun coming out is all a joke. The kids think Margot is lying about remembering the sun, so they lock her up in a closet before the teacher comes. Soon the sun comes out and the children go outside and play. When they come back in after the rain starts again, one of the girls remembers Margot. Very sadly, they go and let her out.

I can relate to the characters in "All Summer in a Day" because I have asthma and allergies. They sometimes make me feel I'm locked up because I can't always just go outside when I want to. One summer I couldn't go outside at all because there was something wrong with my eye. I was very uncomfortable and I had to keep a patch on it all summer long. I was very angry and frustrated because I could not play with my friends. But unlike Margot, I was lucky to find a friend who understood my situation and who liked to play indoors with me. That made me very happy.

❶ Names the literary work and states his overall response to it in the introduction

❷ Tells enough about the work so that readers who are unfamiliar with it can understand his response

❸ Gives clearly described, specific reactions and responses to the story

RESPONSE TO LIT.

After reading this story, I felt sad that Margot did not get to see the sun. She missed it so much that her features had faded along with her happiness. The sun was so important to her that "only when they sang about the sun and the summer did her lips move. . . ." She was too depressed in her new home even to play. I felt sorry that she was so unhappy.

I also think that the way the other children treated Margot wasn't fair. When she read her poem about the sun to the class, William teased her and said he didn't believe she wrote it. No one believed her when she described her memories of what the sun looks and feels like. The children thought that Margot was different. To them ". . . the biggest crime of all was that . . . she remembered the sun. . . ." But just because she was different doesn't mean that she was any less special or important. I was angry at William when he gave the class the idea to lock her in a closet. He reminded me of the few people in my class who treat others unfairly.

I think that in writing "All Summer in a Day," Ray Bradbury was trying to say you shouldn't hate or make fun of someone because they are different from you. It made me more aware of the importance of being nice to everyone, even if they are different, because if you don't, then they will feel bad and soon you will feel guilty that you left them out. This story taught a good lesson about the importance of respecting the feelings of others.

④ Supports his statements with quotations and details

⑤ Summarizes his response in the conclusion

Do It Yourself

Writing Prompt Write a personal response to a short story.

Purpose To explain your feelings about the story

Audience People who might be interested in the story

❶ Prewriting

Choose a story. You might make a list of stories you have read in class, stories that you especially liked, or stories that provoked strong feelings whether you liked them or not.

For more topic ideas, see the Idea Bank, p. 380.

After you have chosen your story, **reread** it carefully. As you read,

- **Look for connections.** Look for material that relates to your own life in some way. What touched you the most? Why? Did the story as a whole have a message for you?

- **Freewrite about feelings.** Jot down whatever thoughts pop into your head about the story. Don't worry about whether your ideas are good or bad, just get them down.

- **Consider your audience.** Imagine that you are talking to an audience that does not know the story. What will they need to know in order to understand your essay? Also, will they need to know certain things about you in order to understand your responses?

❷ Drafting

Get your ideas down. As you write, remember that your response to the story doesn't have to agree with the responses of other people. Express your own ideas.

Organize. Make sure you have these key parts in order:

Response to Literature	
Introduction	Name the story and give your response to it.
Body	Give specific information to support your response including quotations and details.
Conclusion	Summarize your response.

For information about getting feedback from your peers, see p. 381.

RESPONSE TO LIT.

❸ Revising

TARGET SKILL ▶ Effective Introductions Your introduction has to do two important jobs. It has to identify the work you are talking about and it has to tell how you respond to the work. Try to find a balance between the two in the beginning. For more help with revising, review the rubric on page 374.

> "All Summer in a Day," by Ray Bradbury, is about a colony of humans who live on the planet Venus where it rains all the time except for one hour every seven years. A girl named Margot is the only one in her class who remembers the sun.
>
> *The story is especially meaningful to me because of the way it relates to my personal experience. In the story,*

❹ Editing and Proofreading

TARGET SKILL ▶ Subject-Verb Agreement Make the subjects and verbs in your sentences agree in number. When a subject and a verb are both singular or both plural, they agree.

> The kids thinks Margot is lying about remembering the sun so they locks her up in a closet before the teacher come.

For more on subject-verb agreement, see pp. 166-168.

❺ Sharing and Reflecting

You might **share** your response with others who read the same story. Discuss your various reactions. Did your classmates agree or disagree with your interpretation?

For Your Working Portfolio After you have shared your essay, **reflect** on what you learned from writing your response. What did you learn about your own feelings? Did your response change as you wrote about the story? Write your answers and save them along with your response in your ▱ **Working Portfolio**.

Speak for Yourself: *Readers Theater*

Readers Theater is a very simple, straightforward way of presenting a written story. Unlike a drama or skit, there are no costumes or props involved. The action and description all come from the readers' voices. Present the story from your **response to literature** as a piece of readers theater to convey to the audience the meaning the story has for you.

I think the sun is a flower, *(Margot—quiet, small voice, slow)*
That blooms for just one hour.

That was Margot's poem, read in a quiet voice in the still classroom while the rain was falling outside. *(narrator)*

"Aw, you didn't write that!" *(fast, angry)* protested one of the boys.

"I did," said Margot. "I did." *(protesting)*

"William!" said the teacher. *(sharp)*

Here's How **Creating Readers Theater**

- Read over the story and find a brief section to perform. Find a part that is important to the story and has several characters interacting.

- Assign your friends to read each character. You can be the narrator. Give a copy of the story to each person.

- Each reader holds the copy and reads aloud. As narrator, read all the text from the story that is not dialogue. Your friends will read the dialogue for their parts.

- Use your voice instead of your body to convey the emotion of the story. Mark your copy for pace (fast, slow), mood (sad, funny, happy). Get your friends to do the same.

- Don't move around as you would in a drama. The narrator's part will describe the action.

- Practice before your presentation. It may take several rehearsals before you are comfortable that the reading is communicating your response to the story.

For more information on speaking skills, see pp. 492-493.

"I think the sun is a flower, That blooms for just one hour."

RESPONSE TO LIT.

Student Help Desk

Response to Literature at a Glance

Introduction
Introduces the title, author, and a clear statement of your response

Body
Supports the response with evidence from the work

Evidence examples from the story

quotations

specific reactions

Conclusion
Summarizes the response

Idea Bank

It's raining ideas!

Check anthologies. Browse through an anthology for a story you would like to discuss.

Remember favorite authors. Make a list of your favorite authors, then think of stories of theirs that you particularly like.

Think about types of stories. Make a list of the kind of stories you like, such as science fiction or detective stories, then think of your favorite stories in these categories.

Recall special characters. Make a list of fictional characters that you remember. Later you can decide if the characters were interesting enough to make you want to write about them.

Including Quotations   A Shower of Quotes

Tips for using quotations

- **Choose** relevant quotations to support the point you are making about the story.

- **Find** special quotes to add spice and variety to what you are saying.

- **Don't overuse quotes.** Your words are the main ingredient. The quotes are to add flavor to your ideas, not to carry the entire response.

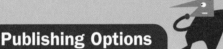

Friendly Feedback

Questions for Your Peer Reader

- What is the main point of my response?
- How do my details and quotations support my point?
- How does my response affect your feelings about the story?
- What part of my response is confusing?
- What part of my response is unneeded?

Publishing Options

Print	Make a class bulletin board display in which you group related responses together.
Oral Communication	Work with a partner to create a tape-recorded response. One of you acts as a commentator, introducing the story and commenting on it at intervals, then finally making concluding remarks. The other partner reads the story.
Online	Check out **mcdougallittell.com** for more publishing options.

The Bottom Line

Checklist for Response to Literature

Have I . . .

_____ included an introduction that names the story and gives my response to it?

_____ told enough about the story so that a person who doesn't know it can understand my responses?

_____ given clear, specific responses to the story?

_____ supported my statements with quotations and details?

_____ summarized my response in the conclusion?

Process Description

Learn What It Is

How would you explain to a new student how to use the school library? You might tell the student, or you might write out directions. Either way, your explanation would be a **process description.** There would be step-by-step directions, and each step would be perfectly clear. You want the new student to do it exactly right.

Basics in a Box

PROCESS DESCRIPTION AT A GLANCE

PART 1

- presents purpose and topic
- provides background information
- lists necessary equipment or materials

PART 2

- describes steps in logical order, using transitional words and phrases
- devotes a separate paragraph to each step

PART 3

- summarizes the process
- describes the outcome or final product

RUBRIC

Standards for Writing

A successful process description should

- focus on a single activity
- begin with a clear statement of the topic and your purpose
- explain to readers how to do something or how something works
- present the steps of the process in a logical order
- give the meaning of terms that may be unfamiliar to readers and provide necessary background information
- use paragraphs and transitional words to signal the start of each new step

See How It's Done: *Process Description*

Student Model
Ryan Powell
Foster Middle School

RUBRIC
IN ACTION

How to Make Yourself a Suit of Armor

Let's say you're attending a costume party and you don't have a costume. I think the perfect costume would be a suit of armor. Here is how you go about making one.

First, you will need the right tools to make your noble armor. You will need wire, twenty yards of the smallest chain, clippers to cut the chain, plastic jewels, a short piece of wood, a large piece of cardboard, nails, screws, a foam ball, rubber cement, scissors, a hammer, a foot of large plastic chain, silver and black spray paint, an old set of clothes that you don't mind ruining, and a lot of aluminum cans. This is all you will need!

When you begin making your armor, start with the most important piece, the breastplate. <u>First</u>, take your old shirt and lay it flat on the ground. <u>Then</u>, take one end of the twenty yards of chain and lay it across the top of the shirt. Cut it at the end of the shirt, so that the chain is just as long as the shirt. Keep laying the chain across the shirt like this, working down row by row, until the shirt is covered. <u>Now</u> take the wire and lace it across each row through the chain and shirt. Be careful not to lace the wire through the back of the shirt also. Cut the wire at the ends, leaving about an inch of wire at both ends of each row. <u>When this is done</u>, flip the shirt over and do the same thing to the back, laying row after row of chain until the back is covered. Tie the ends of the front wires to the ends of the back wires and you have your breastplate!

❶ Begins with a clear statement of the topic and the purpose

❷ Focuses on a single activity

❸ Gives a complete list of the materials needed

❹ Presents each step in a logical order using transitional words to signal the steps

PROCESS

The second part you need to make is your pants. First, lay your pants flat on the ground. Get the aluminum cans and flatten them by stomping on them with your shoe and then use a hammer. After the cans are flattened, use the rubber cement to glue the cans to your pants. Remember to leave space at the knees so you can bend your legs. When the pants are covered with the cans, paint them with the silver spray paint. You could just spray the cans before gluing them to the pants. Now you have a pair of pants for your suit of armor.

Every knight has to have a weapon and shield. Here's how to make a mace to swing for a weapon. Take the short piece of wood and screw the large plastic chain into one end of it. Then screw the other end of the chain into the foam ball. Now paint the ball and the wood handle of the mace with the black spray paint.

Finally, to make the shield you must get the piece of cardboard and draw on it what your shield will look like. Then cut out the shield with the scissors. Spray paint the shield silver and use the rubber cement to cover it with the plastic jewels.

Now you have the perfect costume! All this work will be worth it because everyone at the party will think your costume is the best.

❺ This writer explains *mace,* a word that might be unfamiliar, by describing its purpose and how to make it.

Another option: Give a definition of the word.

Do It Yourself

Writing Prompt   Write a process description that shows how to do something or how something works.

Purpose To explain and inform

Audience Friends who are interested in the subject

❶ Prewriting

Choose a topic you know well. You probably do things every day that show your understanding of a process. Maybe it's rollerblading or playing the trumpet. Maybe it's knowing how the Internet can make connections around the world.

For more topic ideas, see the Idea Bank, p. 388.

Who might learn from your description? Having your audience in mind will help you decide what unfamiliar terms need to be defined and how detailed your explanation needs to be.

What are the steps? Make a list of every step involved in sequential order before beginning your draft. Making a flow chart of the steps can help you.

Step 1 ➡ Step 2 ➡ Step 3 ➡ Step 4

❷ Drafting

Write the purpose and the steps. For now, you can just state what the process is for and start describing the steps. Later you can add details and an interesting introduction.

List any necessary materials. If you are going to tell the readers to use some glue, make sure you've already told them they'll need it.

Use transition words. Words like *first, next, after,* and *now* will help keep the order of steps clear.

Double-check the order. Try to follow the steps as you wrote them to see if everything makes sense. Are the steps in the right order? Is anything left out?

Picture it. Use drawings, photographs, or other visuals to help your readers follow the steps.

For information about getting feedback from your peers, see p. 389

PROCESS

❸ Revising

TARGET SKILL ▶Making the Sequence Clear When you explain how to do something, make sure your readers can tell the correct sequence of the steps. Use transition words to help keep the order easy to follow. For more help with revising, review the rubric on page 382.

> The second part ~~is~~ First,
> ^You need to make~your pants.~~L~~ay your pants flat on the
> Get ✗ and flatten them
> ground. ~~Flatten~~ the aluminum cans~by stomping on them
> then After the cans are flattened,
> with your shoe and~use a hammer.~~U~~se rubber cement to
>
> glue the cans to your pants.

❹ Editing and Proofreading

TARGET SKILL ▶Correcting Run-Ons It will confuse your readers if you write two or more sentences as one long sentence. Rewrite any run-ons by making them into two sentences.

> When you begin making your armor, start with the most
>
> important piece, the breastplate first^take your old shirt and
>
> lay it flat on the ground.

For more on run-on sentences, see pp. 25–27.

❺ Sharing and Reflecting

You might **share** your description by reading it aloud to someone who already understands the process and to someone who doesn't. Ask each listener to imagine how the steps would work. Ask if your description clearly tells what to do.

For Your Working Portfolio Your readers' comments and reactions will help you **reflect** on your description. Could you have included more steps, rearranged parts, or taken out some unnecessary pieces? Keep your answers with your finished work. Save your process essay in your 🗁 **Working Portfolio.**

Speak for Yourself: *Demonstration*

"Here's how to make the perfect suit of armor. . . ."

The many cooking shows on television are perfect examples of a demonstration. The host goes through the process of cooking something interesting while describing it and telling the audience how to do it. You can make your **process description** into a demonstration by showing your audience exactly how to do what you described.

Here's How Creating a Demonstration

- If your process is fairly simple, bring in all the pieces you will need and demonstrate the entire process.
- If your process would take too long to demonstrate in class, bring in examples of the process as it would appear in stages.
- Tell your audience everything that is involved in the process. Show them the materials you are using as you introduce them.
- Talk to your audience as you perform your demonstration. Tell them exactly what you're doing and make sure they can see it.
- Practice your demonstration and memorize the explanations you will give.

For more information on speaking skills, see p. 489–491.

PROCESS

Student Help Desk

Process Description at a Glance

PART 1
- presents purpose and topic
- provides background information
- lists necessary equipment or materials

PART 2
- describes steps in logical order, using transitional words and phrases
- devotes a separate paragraph to each step

PART 3
- summarizes the process
- describes the outcome or final product

Idea Bank

Tips for finding an idea

Remember how you taught a pet to obey a command.

Recall how you first learned to use a computer.

Tell how to play your favorite sport.

Explain why there is night and day.

Tell how a batter is able to hit a home run.

Describe how to do something at home that only you know how to do.

What's Next Logic Checklist

✔ **Are materials needed?** If so, did you list them first?

✔ **Do your steps work backward?** Look at the last step and the next-to-last step. Is anything missing in between? Follow this procedure through to the first step.

✔ **Are there two steps where either one could be done first?** If so, have you told your readers?

✔ **Do any steps require other people?** If so, have you made that clear?

Friendly Feedback

Questions for Your Peer Reader

- What did you like best about my description?
- How easy would it be for you to follow the process?
- How could I explain the process more clearly?
- What words should I have defined?
- What could I have left out?

Publishing Options

Print	Give copies of your process description to people who might want to use it.
Oral Communication	Read the description aloud to someone who doesn't already know about the process. Ask them to try the process as you watch.
Online	Check out **mcdougallittell.com** for more publishing options.

PROCESS

The Bottom Line

Checklist for Process Description

Have I . . .

___ focused on a single activity?

___ started by naming what the process is and why I am describing it?

___ explained how to do something or how something works?

___ presented all the steps that were needed?

___ used a logical order?

___ provided definitions where they were needed?

Problem-Solution Essay

Learn What It Is

Every day, you probably hear people talking about problems. Some people see problems everywhere. Some see solutions. Writing a **problem-solution essay** is a way to suggest a logical solution to a problem and convince others that your solution is a good one.

Basics in a Box

PROBLEM-SOLUTION ESSAY AT A GLANCE

Introduction	Body	Conclusion
presents and describes the problem	presents and explains possible solutions	restates the problem and the benefits of the solution

RUBRIC

Standards for Writing

A successful problem-solution essay should

- have an introduction that catches readers' attention
- give a clear picture of the problem
- explore all aspects of the problem
- offer a reasonable solution and explain how to put it into effect

- use facts, statistics, examples, opinions, or other details to support the solution
- use logical reasoning to convince the reader
- have a strong conclusion

CHAPTER 22

See How It's Done: *Problem-Solution Essay*

Student Model
Trilly Bagwell
Nichols Middle School

RUBRIC
IN ACTION

How Racism Affects Children

Young children always watch and listen to what grownups are doing, and then they imitate it. However, sometimes adults can set a bad example, such as being racist. Even though parents may not know they are passing racism on to their kids, children will pick it up and think acting in a racist way is okay because adults do it.

❶ This writer begins by stating the problem.
Another option: Give a quotation or example to get readers' attention

Racism means discriminating against other people because they are of a different race. It could mean not hiring someone just because they are not like you or leaving someone out because they do not have the same racial background as you. People can be racist and not know it, but it can come out in little ways like the tone of voice they speak in or how they behave around others. For example, a group of children on a school playground might automatically separate themselves from a group of other kids who are of a different race. They don't actually think, *I shouldn't play with them; they aren't like me.* It's more likely to be a reflex, something they've picked up from their parents.

❷ Gives a clear description of the problem

Children also look to the kids around them for clues on how to behave. If some kids at school have picked up racism from their parents, other kids can easily pick it up from them as an acceptable way to act.

❸ Begins exploration of all aspects of the problem

It seems like a continuing chain of people learning racism and passing it on to others, but the situation is not hopeless. There is a solution. Although parents who have racist attitudes can pass their racism on to their children, it is also true that parents who are not racist can pass that attitude on to their kids. Parents can examine their feelings and

PROB.-SOLUTION

actions and work on improving them. It's not enough for parents to tell their kids that racism is bad or that they should treat everyone fairly.

Parents need to pay attention to the way they act in front of their kids. If a parent tells a child that racism is wrong but then the child sees the parent laugh at a racist joke, the child will follow the example more than the words. The body language parents use and the way they say things is important, too, because children are sharp. Even the smallest things such as not making eye contact when talking to someone, using a more severe tone of voice, or crossing one's arms can all say, "I don't respect you because you're different." So, parents who improve their actions toward others can help their children learn to treat other people fairly.

> **4** Presents one part of the solution

> **5** Uses examples to show how the solution can work

Children can be part of the solution, too. Children should notice racism around them and realize that they don't have to follow the poor examples of some parents, teachers, and friends. They can decide against racism. They should try to set an example for other kids. When they see kids being discriminated against, they can go over and make friends. Also, when they see their friends being racist, they can try to talk to them and explain what racism is and how bad it is. There's a chance the child didn't know he or she was being racist in the first place.

> **6** Uses examples to further support the solution

Many people think racism is too big an issue for people to fight on their own, but in a sense that isn't really true. If everyone works against racism, we're all fighting together. That is exactly what needs to happen. Kids are our future. It will only be a good one if they don't grow up racist.

> **7** Uses logical reasoning to convince the reader

> **8** Has a strong conclusion

Do It Yourself

Writing Prompt Write an essay that identifies a problem and proposes a solution.

Purpose To inform and persuade

Audience Anyone concerned with the problem you are writing about

❶ Prewriting

Look around for a topic. Pay attention to every problem you hear about today. Start thinking about possible solutions. Then decide on one of the problems that interests you and for which you may have a solution.

For more topic ideas, see the Idea Bank, p. 396.

Collect information. Find out all you can about the problem.

• Listen to people talk about the problem.

• Read newspaper articles and Internet sites about it.

Work out your own solution. Work out your own ideas for a solution. Make notes about different solutions you come up with. Then choose one idea to develop.

❷ Drafting

Define the problem. Try to phrase the problem in one clear statement. Put the statement in the opening paragraph.

Organize. As you begin writing, think about how your information will fit in the three main sections of your essay.

Pattern of Organization	
Introduction	Identify the problem. Tell why it is significant.
Body	Explain the causes and effects of the problem. State your solution. How will it work?
Conclusion	Summarize the problem and the benefits of your solution.

Be clear. Be simple. Work with your draft until you have presented both the problem and the solution clearly and simply.

For information about getting feedback from your peers, see p. 397.

PROB.-SOLUTION

③ Revising

TARGET SKILL ▶**Considering Audience** Keep your audience in mind as you write. Don't leave them struggling to understand. Give them plenty of clear definitions and examples so they can follow your ideas. For more help with revising, review the rubric on page 390.

> *such as not making eye contact when talking to someone, using a*
> Even the smallest things ~~can make the point that the~~
> *more severe tone of voice, or crossing one's arms can all say, "I*
> ~~person is discriminating against other people.~~
> *don't respect you because you're different."*

④ Editing and Proofreading

TARGET SKILL ▶**Avoiding Confusing Comparisons** Be careful about how you use comparative forms. Don't use *most* and *–est* together or *more* with *–er*. Sometimes you don't need a comparative form to get your ideas across.

> Even the ~~most~~ smallest things . . . can all say, "I don't
> respect you because you're ~~more~~ different~~er than me.~~"

For more on comparisons, see pp. 133–135.

⑤ Sharing and Reflecting

Find friends, classmates, or others who are concerned about the problem you've written about and **share** your essay with them. Ask their opinion about your solution.

For Your Working Portfolio As you **reflect** on writing your essay, make notes about what you learned during the process. Did you learn more about the problem? What was easy to write? What was hard? Save your notes along with the finished essay in your ▢ **Working Portfolio.**

Speak for Yourself: *Persuasive Speech*

Solution to the Problem of Rac...

Parents
- treat everyone ...
- don't te.. ...acist jok...
- ...ake eye contact

Chil...ren
- ...lp friends avoid ...ist behavior
- ...ke friends with ...yone

"**The problem of racism may seem hopeless, but there is a solution.**"

When people give a persuasive speech they make every effort to convince others that their ideas are good ones. Present the ideas in your **problem-solution essay** as a persuasive speech. You will be able to clearly outline your ideas for a solution to a problem and convince your audience.

Here's How) Creating a Persuasive Speech

- Build your speech around the most important parts of your essay. Highlight those parts, but don't plan to read your whole essay aloud.

- Write out your speech in outline form. Use the same organization as your essay. Describe the problem, then explain your solution point-by-point.

- Make a flip chart showing an outline of your solution. Refer to this as you give your speech to help the audience follow the logic of your ideas.

- Practice your gestures, tone of voice, and pacing (how quickly or slowly you speak) before you present the speech.

- End your speech by taking questions from the audience.

For more information on speaking skills, see pp. 489–491.

Student Help Desk

Problem-Solution Essay at a Glance

Introduction

presents and describes the problem

Body

presents and explains possible solutions

Conclusion

restates the problem and the benefits of the solution

Idea Bank

Don't exclude good ideas because they're different!

Watch television news. What problems in the world interest you?

Talk to family members. What concerns them about young people? About the environment?

Think about your school. Consider where traffic is worst around school. Think of how the school building could look better.

Examine your environment and your daily life for problems you can try to solve.

Ask yourself. If there were one thing you could change in the world, what would it be and how would you change it?

Read literature. Get ideas from what others have said about problems and solutions. You might read the excerpt from *All I Really Need to Know I Learned in Kindergarten* to see Robert Fulghum's solution to how to live one's life (*The Language of Literature*, Grade 6)

Friendly Feedback

Questions for Your Peer Reader

- What is the problem I presented?
- What are the main points of the solution I propose?
- What are the most convincing parts of my essay?
- Where do I need to strengthen my position?

Publishing Options

Print	Collect all the problem-solution essays in a class notebook. Attach blank pieces of paper and encourage comments on the problems and solutions proposed by members of your class.
Oral Communication	Make an oral presentation describing the problem and your proposed solution. Lead a discussion among your classmates about the pros and cons of your solution.
Online	Check out **mcdougallittell.com** for more publishing options.

The Bottom Line

Checklist for Problem-Solution Essay

Have I . . .

_____ written an introduction that catches the reader's attention?

_____ given a clear picture of the problem?

_____ explored all aspects of the problem?

_____ offered a reasonable solution?

_____ explained how to put my solution into effect?

_____ used facts, statistics, examples, opinions, or other details?

_____ used logical reasoning?

_____ given a strong conclusion?

Opinion Statement

Learn What It Is

You're probably used to giving your opinion on everything from how much homework is fair to whether your soccer team has a chance to win the next game. To persuade others to respect your opinion, you need to back it up with clear reasons. Writing an **opinion statement** can help you think through your ideas.

Basics in a Box

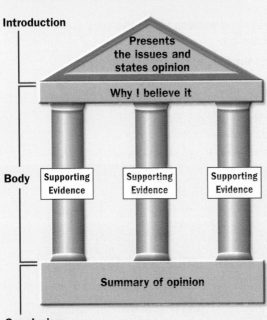

OPINION STATEMENT AT A GLANCE

Introduction

Presents the issues and states opinion

Why I believe it

Body

| Supporting Evidence | Supporting Evidence | Supporting Evidence |

Summary of opinion

Conclusion

RUBRIC

Standards for Writing

A successful opinion statement should

- clearly state the issue and your position on it
- use language and details appropriate for your audience
- support your opinion with examples, facts, and statistics
- show clear reasoning
- sum up your opinion in the conclusion

CHAPTER 23

See How It's Done: *Opinion Statement*

Student Model
Luke Pendry
Churchill Junior High

RUBRIC
IN ACTION

School Schedule

My summer was going great. I had just made the baseball all-star team, and I was making lots of cash mowing lawns. I was sitting down to relax when I turned on the television just in time to hear the 12:00 news say my school was going to be open year-round!

Immediately my mind started racing. What about baseball? When do we get vacation time? Will we really have to go to school on 100-degree days? I started to sweat just thinking about it. And my little sister—would I have to baby-sit her every vacation? In my opinion, this new schedule can't work. My life seems ruined.

For one thing, my summer sports will be upset because of the new vacation times. If school goes on in the summer, we simply cannot have baseball. A one-month baseball season during a school vacation would be too short to determine the best teams. I love baseball and would hate to have the season shortened or eliminated.

As for other school sports, the new schedule may result in shorter seasons to coincide with the breaks. But if my school changes the times of its sports seasons and other schools do not, then we might not have as many teams to play and competition could deteriorate.

Next, I thought about sweltering hot days in the middle of July and August, when I will be in school. If school is in session year-round, then the school will definitely need air conditioning. This will cut deeply into the school budget. The school will need more money, which will mean an increase in taxes.

❶ This writer states his opinion after setting the scene in the first paragraph.

Another option: Begin the introduction with the opinion.

❷ Supports opinion with reasons

❸ Shows clear cause-and-effect reasoning

OPINION

❹ Uses facts to support his opinion

Also, my family will be affected. It seems to me that child care will be a major problem. I am old enough to be on my own, but my little sister needs child care. I do not think my parents would expect me to watch her full time during my school vacations. We have a college student who comes on her summer vacation to watch my sister daily, but it will be difficult to find someone to come three times a year for just one month each time. It may also be difficult for other parents to get vacation time from work at odd times of the year if the family wants to get away.

And how will the school vacations work? If school runs year-round, students will be in session for three months and then have a one-month vacation. Some people think that three shorter, separate breaks might not be so bad. Maybe I wouldn't get as bored as I do over the three-month drag we have now. Also, with shorter breaks, there is not much time to forget the material already learned, so we shouldn't have to take time to review.

With my mind still racing, I decided going to school year-round might have some interesting possibilities. Learning more and having air conditioning actually sounds good. Still, the new schedule will greatly change my life, my parents' lives, and my friends' lives. My routine will never be the same again. It just won't be worth all the hassle and change it will cause. For right now, I'm going to enjoy the rest of my summer to the fullest.

❺ Uses a transition word to introduce another reason

❻ Gives and answers possible objections to stated opinion

❼ This writer concludes with the action he will take—enjoy *this* summer.
Other options:
• Summarize the opinion.
• Call for an action.

Do It Yourself

Writing Prompt Write an opinion statement about an issue you are interested in.

Purpose To persuade others to see the worth of your opinion

Audience Those who also have an interest in the subject

❶ Prewriting

Pick a topic you care about. You might choose to write about something that really bothers you or something you think other people ought to care more about.

For more topic ideas, see the Idea Bank, p. 404.

Support your opinion. Make a list of the reasons you have this opinion. Gather facts and statistics that support your position.

Consider your audience. Who will read your statement? What do they think about the issue? What do they need to know?

❷ Drafting

Get started. Your opinion statement should have three parts: an introduction, a body, and a conclusion.

- **Introduction** Begin with a clear statement of your opinion. You may also include a question or some dialogue to get your readers' attention.

- **Body** Support your opinion with reasons, examples, facts, and other evidence to prove your point.

- **Conclusion** Summarize your opinion and perhaps include a call for action. Do you want your readers to make phone calls? To vote a certain way? You need to say so.

Watch your language. Beware of using language that is unfair or biased or that cannot be fully supported by evidence.

- **Name calling** Be careful to avoid labeling things or people without strong evidence to back up your opinion. Words like *stupid, senseless, evil, greedy,* and *ridiculous* are often used unfairly.

- **Vague words** Avoid using words like *all, never,* and *totally* unless you can back them up with evidence that your statement is always true.

For information about getting feedback from your peers, see p. 405.

OPINION

❸ Revising

TARGET SKILL ▶Supporting an Opinion with Reasons In presenting your opinion, it isn't enough to show you have a strong feeling. You need reasons to back up your opinion. For more help with revising, review the rubric on page 398.

> If school goes on in the summer, we simply cannot have baseball. ~~I love baseball and would hate to have the season shortened or eliminated.~~ *A one-month baseball season during a school vacation would be too short to determine the best teams.*

❹ Editing and Proofreading

TARGET SKILL ▶Shifting Verb Tense Shifting verb tenses can confuse readers. Within a sentence or between sentences keep to the same verb tense unless the meaning calls for a change.

> We ~~had~~ *have* a college student who comes on her summer vacation ~~watching~~ *to watch* my sister daily, but it ~~is~~ *will be* difficult to find someone to come three times a year for just one month each time.

For more on verb tenses, see pp. 101–110.

❺ Sharing and Reflecting

When you have completed your opinion statement, **share** it with friends or classmates who also have an interest in the topic. Talk about how your opinions agree or differ.

For Your Working Portfolio Consider the ideas of your friends and classmates as you reflect on your opinion statement. Have you changed your opinion because of points others made? Did you think of other points you could have made? Put your responses with your finished work, and save your opinion statement in your 🗀 **Working Portfolio.**

Speak for Yourself: *Discussion*

Many TV shows use the format of a panel discussion to discuss the ideas and opinions of a group of people. You can use this same format to present the ideas in your **opinion statement** in a lively and engaging way.

Here's How Setting Up a Panel Discussion

- Find two or three friends who are interested in your topic and ask them to be on your panel. Make sure they are all informed about the topic before you begin.

- As moderator of the panel, introduce the topic to the class. Include some of your own opinions on the subject.

- Turn the topic over to the panel. Ask each person on the panel to briefly state his or her opinion on the topic and to support it with reasons and examples. Ask questions to clarify each position.

- If there is time after each person has had a turn, have the panel ask each other questions about their different opinions.

- Briefly sum up your own ideas and those of the panel at the end.

For more information on speaking skills, see p. 487–491.

"School on a year around basis would be a huge change for all of us!"

OPINION

403

Student Help Desk

Opinion Statement at a Glance

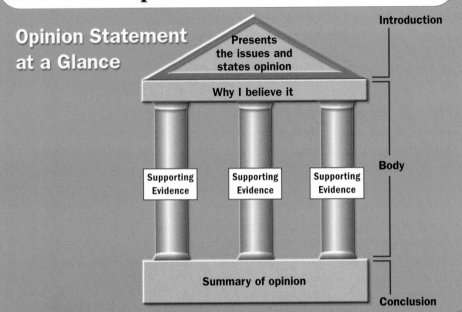

Introduction — Presents the issues and states opinion

Why I believe it

Body — Supporting Evidence · Supporting Evidence · Supporting Evidence

Conclusion — Summary of opinion

Idea Bank

Where do I start?

Read editorials and letters to the editor in the newspaper. In these columns, people commonly express their opinions on a wide variety of subjects.

Listen to the lunchtime conversation around you. What subjects do your classmates seem to have strong ideas about?

Make a list of things that have really upset you lately and another list of things that are working really well in your life.

Remember an ongoing debate or argument that you have with someone. How can you persuade your reader to take your side of the issue?

Charting Your Ideas

Make a for-and-against chart to help you think clearly.

For	Against
• variety of vacation times	• child care problems for families
• air conditioning	• expense of air conditioning

Friendly Feedback

Questions for Your Peer Reader

- How did I show that this topic is important to me?
- Which of my points was most convincing?
- What other reasons could I have added?
- Which part was not convincing?
- What new idea did my statement give you?

Publishing Options

Print	Post all the opinion statements around the classroom and invite comments. To make your paper visually appealing, consider using desktop publishing software for various formats.
Oral Communication	Find others who have an opinion about the same topic. Read your statements aloud and then discuss how you agree and disagree. Ask your classmates to evaluate your persuasiveness.
Online	Check out **mcdougallittell.com** for more publishing options.

The Bottom Line

Checklist for Opinion Statement

Have I . . .

____ stated my position on the topic clearly in the introduction?

____ written in a style that is appropriate for my audience?

____ supported my opinion with facts, statistics, and reasons?

____ answered possible objections to my position?

____ shown clear reasoning?

____ concluded with a summary or a call to action?

OPINION

Short Story and Poem

Learn What It Is: *Short Story*

When something funny or fascinating or moving happens to you, you may want to express the experience in writing. In this workshop, you will have the opportunity to capture your experience in a story or a poem.

You might write a **short story** about a real or imagined event. Whether your short story is based on something real or imaginary (or on a combination of the two), you can create an entertaining narrative with vivid descriptions and lively characters.

Basics in a Box

SHORT STORY AT A GLANCE

Introduction

Sets the stage by
- introducing the **characters**
- describing the **setting**

Body

Develops the plot by
- introducing the conflict
- telling a sequence of **events**
- developing **characters** through words and actions
- building toward a **climax**

Conclusion

Finishes the story by
- resolving the **conflict**
- telling the **last event**

RUBRIC

Standards for Writing

A successful short story should
- have a strong beginning and ending
- use the elements of character, setting, and plot to create a convincing world
- use techniques such as vivid sensory language, concrete details, and dialogue to create believable characters and setting
- have a central conflict
- present a clear sequence of events
- maintain a consistent point of view

CHAPTER 24

See How It's Done: *Short Story*

Student Model
Lydia Eickstaedt
Arizona School for the
Arts

RUBRIC
IN ACTION

Lion and the Peculiar Purple Peach

One day Lion was out for a walk in the bushy mountain land. Lion was a trickster. He was walking along, thinking of things to do, when all of a sudden he stopped. He had seen something purple. He walked up to it and saw it was a peach. But, as you know, purple peaches are rare, so he said, "Hmm. What a peculiar purple peach." PLOP! Down went Lion.

When he woke up, his head was spinning. "Oh!" he said. "What happened? Let's see. The last thing I did was I said, 'Hmm. What a peculiar purple peach.'" PLOP! Down he went again. This time when Lion woke up, he knew what he didn't want to say.

"Hmm," he thought. "Maybe I can use that peach in a plot." So he walked off to Panther's house because he knew Panther had blackberries.

"Oh, Panther," he said, "I am so hot. Would you like to take a mountain walk with me?"

"Why, yes, Lion," said Panther, for she was very hot. "That would be nice."

So they went along the P.P.P. trail. When they came to the peach, Lion said, "Do you see what I see?"

"My, what a peculiar purple peach." PLOP! Down went Panther. Lion went to Panther's house to take the blackberries. When Panther woke, she had a headache. She went home and found out nothing, besides that, she was out of blackberries.

Then Lion went to Giraffe because he had seen her hauling bananas into her house.

"Oh, Giraffe," said Lion, "I've found a beautiful path."

❶ Identifies the setting, the main character, and the beginning of the plot in the introduction

❷ Uses dialogue to create believable characters

SHORT STORY

"I would love to go down it," said Giraffe.

So they were walking along, when Lion and Giraffe stopped.

"Do you see that?" said Lion.

"What a peculiar purple peach!" PLOP! Down went Giraffe. Off went Lion to collect his prize.

Well, Lion did this all afternoon. He robbed Monkey of coconuts, Fox of strawberries, Crocodile of granny apples, Cardinal of cherries, and Ostrich of pears. While all this was happening, Tigress sat behind a tree nearby. Well, she wasn't going to let Lion do this and get away with it. So, she went off and got some oranges. She carried them to her house, making sure to carry them past Lion's house. But Lion waited a little bit. Then he went to Tigress' house.

"Hey, Tigress," said Lion. "Want to see a neat waterfall?"

"Sure!" said Tigress, and they were on their way. Lion and Tigress suddenly stopped.

"Look at that!" said Lion.

"What a weird peach!" said Tigress.

"Say it right!" Lion growled.

"It is right!" said Tigress.

"No!" said Lion. "I want you to say what a peculiar purple peach!" PLOP! Down went Lion. Tigress ran off and gave the others back their fruit. Lion went home and found the fruit gone. He groaned and went to sleep.

But Tigress thought while eating an orange, "Well, this plot was just peachy."

❸ Presents a clear sequence of events

❹ Resolves a central conflict

❺ This writer maintains a consistent third-person *(he, she)* point of view.

Another option: Have Lion tell the story using the first-person *(I)*.

Do It Yourself

❶ Prewriting

Daydream a little. Let your mind roam freely on any fantastic idea you might have. Note words or phrases about your thoughts. Then play with the notes to see if you can join any of them to come up with an idea for a story.

For more topic ideas, see the Idea Bank, p. 416.

Who? When? Where? What? You might make a chart to help you decide on your subject by thinking of characters, the setting, and the plot.

Story Elements		
Characters	**Setting**	**Plot**
Name _____	Time _____	Background _____
Looks _____	Place _____	Conflict _____
Actions _____		Resolution _____

❷ Drafting

Begin writing. Use your chart to help you fill in details about the plot, setting, and characters. Then begin writing. Try to keep going without stopping. You can go back later to revise.

Be sense-ible. Show how things look, smell, feel, sound, or taste. Use all the senses in your descriptions.

Show, don't tell. Be specific. Tell *how* big, *what kind* of difficulty, *who* the character is afraid of. You can add these details as you fine-tune your draft.

For information about getting feedback from your peers, see p. 417.

SHORT STORY

❸ Revising

TARGET SKILL ▸**Using Dialogue** When your characters speak in their own words, they become real to the reader. Maybe one character speaks in slang. Maybe another always uses big words. Use quotation marks to show a speaker's exact words. Start a new paragraph for each new speaker. For more help with revising, review the rubric on page 406.

"Oh, Giraffe," said "I've found a beautiful path."
Lion told Giraffe that he had found a beautiful path.
"I
Giraffe said she would love to go down it," said Giraffe.

❹ Editing and Proofreading

TARGET SKILL ▸**Punctuating Dialogue** Put the words your characters say in quotation marks. Remember to put end punctuation inside the quotation marks. Start a new paragraph and new quotation marks when another character begins speaking.

"Oh, Panther, he said. I am so hot. Would you like to take a mountain walk with me?"

"Why, yes, Lion, said Panther, for she was very hot. "That would be nice."

❺ Sharing and Reflecting

Find a way to **share** your short story with an audience. You might provide a copy for your classmates to read or read your story aloud to younger students in another class. If necessary, adapt the language to fit your audience.

For Your Working Portfolio As you **reflect** on the process of writing your short story, make notes about your readers' reactions. Is there anything you would change if you were to rewrite the story? Save your responses along with your finished story in your 🗀 **Working Portfolio.**

Learn What It Is: *Poem*

Poems express emotions. Although poems can take many forms, they have some characteristics in common. The language of poetry is careful and sometimes playful. It often rhymes. Writing an original **poem** gives you a chance to create a picture in words and to share a personal feeling.

Basics in a Box

POETRY AT A GLANCE

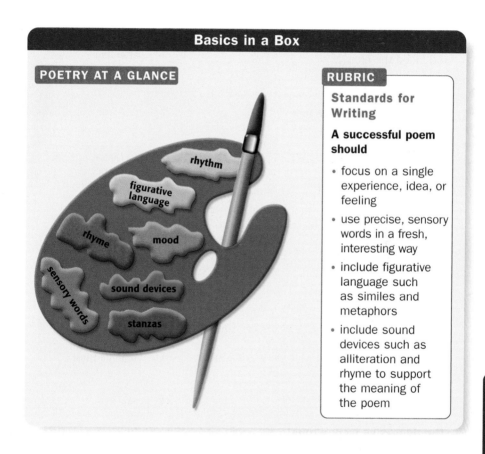

- rhythm
- figurative language
- rhyme
- mood
- sensory words
- sound devices
- stanzas

RUBRIC

Standards for Writing

A successful poem should

- focus on a single experience, idea, or feeling
- use precise, sensory words in a fresh, interesting way
- include figurative language such as similes and metaphors
- include sound devices such as alliteration and rhyme to support the meaning of the poem

POEM

See How It's Done: *Poem*

Student Model
Lynette Michelle Fisher
Monforton School

RUBRIC
IN ACTION

Who

Who fought for freedom
of slaves and blacks
and stood up for rights
and faced the facts?

The speeches he gave
influenced us all,
though some didn't like him,
he stood proud and tall.

Who said those words,
"I have a dream"
and lived out the meaning
"Let freedom ring!"

Who spoke to the Nation,
delivered a clue
and told us that finally
freedom was due.

Who said let us be judged
by what is within,
by content of character
not color of skin?

Who wanted us only
to love one another,
to walk together
as sister and brother?

The things that were wrong
he did try to mend,
but as it turned out
he fell in the end.

Whose murder sparked mourning
across the land.
United in spirit,
we all took a stand.

Martin Luther King Jr.,
although he is gone
now he is free
and his name will live on.

1 Begins with a question and catches readers' attention

2 Makes specific reference to a famous speech

3 This writer uses rhyme at the ends of the second and fourth lines of each stanza.
Another option Write a poem without rhyme.

4 Uses alliteration (repeated *m* sound) for emphasis

5 Ends by answering the question in the first stanza

CHAPTER 24

Do It Yourself

Writing Prompt Write a poem about anything that matters to you.

Purpose To write expressively

Audience Friends, classmates, and family members

❶ Prewriting

Choose an idea. Your poem can be about anything you like. Think about feelings you have for special people or places. Perhaps you can start with a day at the beach you especially remember or a playful new pet.

For more topic ideas, see the Idea Bank, p. 416.

Freewrite. Take one of your ideas and write as much about it as you can for five minutes without stopping. If you get stuck, just write "I'm stuck" again and again until you think of something to write. Now look over your freewriting and circle words and phrases that might work in a poem.

Make an observation chart. Make a chart listing the five senses. Write down details about your topic under each one.

Observation Chart	
Sight	bright sun, sand castles
Sound	waves, children shouting
Touch	wet sand, cool water
Taste	sweet popsicles
Smell	suntan lotion, peanut butter sandwiches

POEM

❷ Drafting

Put your ideas on paper. Take images and details from your observation chart and start putting them into a poem.

Play with your poem. Rearrange the lines. See whether they sound better another way and how changing their order affects the meaning. Decide if you want your poem to rhyme. Take out every word you don't absolutely need.

For information about getting feedback from your peers, see p. 417.

➌ Revising

TARGET SKILL ▶**Choosing Precise Words** Because every single word in a poem counts, choose only the most precise words. Even when your poem rhymes, be sure you are choosing words for their meanings, not only for their rhyme. For more help with revising, review the rubric on page 411.

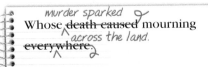

murder sparked
Whose ~~death caused~~ mourning
      across the land.
~~everywhere.~~

➍ Editing and Proofreading

TARGET SKILL ▶**Avoiding Forced Rhyme** Don't force your poem to rhyme. If you must change the natural order of words or use a vague word to create a rhyme, your reader will be distracted from your meaning.

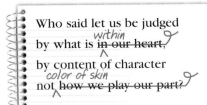

Who said let us be judged
        within
by what is ~~in our heart,~~
by content of character
        color of skin
not ~~how we play our part?~~

➎ Sharing and Reflecting

Read your poem aloud to **share** it with friends or classmates. Ask them to respond to the meaning of your poem.

For Your Working Portfolio As you **reflect** on writing your poem, make some notes about which parts of the writing went well and which parts were difficult. How did your audience's response help you? Save your notes along with your poem in your 🗀 **Working Portfolio.**

Speak for Yourself: *Skit*

Have you ever read a story and tried to picture in your mind how it would look as a movie or a play? You can turn your **short story** into a skit and act it out for your class. That way, they can see the story in action.

Student Model
Lydia Eickstaedt
Arizona School for the
Arts

"My, what a peculiar purple peach." PLOP! Down went Panther. Lion went to Panther's house to take the blackberries.

PANTHER: My, what a peculiar purple peach!

Panther falls right to the ground. Lion rubs his hands together craftily.

LION: It worked! Now I can go steal all her blackberries!

Here's How) Creating a Skit

- Break your story into two parts: lines that describe what is happening, and lines that are spoken by characters.
- Write out the spoken lines for each character. Assign parts to your friends. Create the lines for a narrator to describe what is happening.
- Assemble costumes and props. A costume can be as simple as a hat or a scarf or can be more elaborate.
- During the skit, you can be the narrator. You will need to tell the audience what is happening. For example, you might say, "So, Lion and Panther walked along the path until they came to the purple peach."
- Rehearse your skit with your friends until everyone knows all their lines and the actions of each character.

For more information on speaking skills, see pp. 487–493.

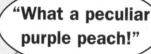

"What a peculiar purple peach!"

SHORT STORY

Student Help Desk

Short Story and Poem at a Glance

SHORT STORY

POEM

Introduction
Sets the stage by
- introducing the **characters**
- describing the **setting**

Body
Develops the plot by
- introducing the conflict
- telling a sequence of **events**
- developing **characters** through words and actions
- building toward a **climax**

Conclusion
Finishes the story by
- resolving the **conflict**
- telling the **last event**

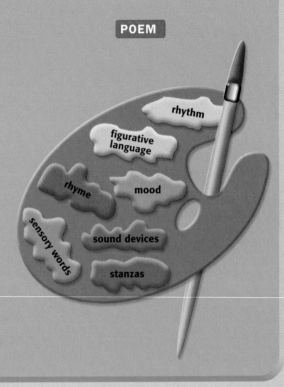

rhythm

figurative language

rhyme   mood

sensory words

sound devices

stanzas

Idea Bank

Finding a topic for a short story or poem

- **Write** another episode for a favorite novel.
- **Develop** the story behind a song you know.
- **Imagine** a school day in the year 2100.
- **Look** around you. What sounds, sights, and smells do you experience?
- **Make** a list of the people who matter most to you.
- **Examine** how you feel. What makes you happy? Sad? Angry?

Friendly Feedback

Questions for Your Peer Reader

- Did the beginning of my story or poem grab your attention?
- How do you think I feel about the main character of my story?
- What is the main feeling in my poem?
- What was the best part of my story or poem?
- What was confusing about my story or poem?

Publishing Options

Print	Submit your story or poem to your school's literary magazine.
Oral Communication	Read your story or poem aloud to a small group or turn it into a dramatic reading. Ask friends to take part in the reading.
Online	Check out **mcdougallittell.com** for more publishing options.

The Bottom Line

Checklist for Short Story

Have I . . .

____ provided a strong beginning and ending?

____ used character, setting, and plot effectively?

____ used techniques such as vivid sensory language, concrete details, and dialogue?

____ developed a central conflict?

____ presented events in a clear order?

____ maintained a consistent point of view?

Checklist for Poem

Have I . . .

____ focused on a single idea, experience, or feeling?

____ used precise, sensory words?

____ included figurative language whenever possible?

____ used sound devices to support the meaning?

Research Report

Learn What It Is

What do you do when you want to know more about a subject?
Do you ask someone? Do you go to the library or search the
Internet? As you search for answers, you are doing research.
A **research report** is a report that gives the results of such a
search. Here is how to write a research report.

Basics in a Box

RESEARCH REPORT AT A GLANCE

Introduction → Body → Thesis → Conclusion → Works Cited

Research

RUBRIC

Standards for Writing

A successful research report should

- include a strong introduction
  with a clear thesis statement
- use evidence from sources to
  develop and support ideas
- credit the sources of information
- follow a logical pattern of
  organization, using transitions
  between ideas

- use information from more than
  one source
- summarize ideas in the
  conclusion
- include a correctly formatted
  Works Cited list at the end of
  the report

See How It's Done: *Research Report*

Juana Martinez
Mr. Levy
English
20 May 2000

Greek and Roman Gods

People in ancient Greece and ancient Rome believed in a number of gods who were responsible for everything that went on in the world. Civilization in Rome developed later than it did in Greece, and the Romans adopted many of the Greek gods. Although the names of the Greek and Roman gods were different, what the gods did and what they were like were very similar. In stories about the gods, there are clear similarities between the Greek gods Zeus, Hera, Hermes, and Poseidon and the parallel Roman gods, Jupiter, Juno, Mercury, and Neptune (Long).

❶ Includes a clear thesis statement

The Greeks told of lively gods who had complicated lives of their own. On the other hand, the Romans told of gods who mainly protected or punished humans (Guirand 216). What the gods controlled and what they used to control it, though, were about the same in both ancient Greece and ancient Rome.

❷ Uses evidence from writings about myths to develop and support ideas

Zeus and Hera were the rulers of the Greek gods, and Jupiter and Juno were the rulers of the Roman gods. Hermes, a son of Zeus, was the messenger of the gods. The Roman messenger god was Mercury, a son of Jupiter. These three Greek and

REPORT

three Roman gods were similar in their work and in their positions as great gods. There is a difference, though, between Poseidon and Neptune. Poseidon, the sea god, was very powerful in Greek mythology. The Roman sea god, Neptune, was a minor god for many years. He wasn't as important to the Romans as Poseidon was to the Greeks ("Neptune").

The most powerful god in Greek stories was Zeus. In Roman stories, the most powerful was Jupiter. Each was god of the sky and ruler of the earth. The Encyclopedia Mythica explains that "Jupiter is completely identical with the Greek Zeus" ("Jupiter"). Zeus's power was often connected to thunderstorms. As Charles Freeman says, when it rained, people would say that Zeus was raining (22).

❸ This writer compares each Greek god with his or her Roman parallel, using a clear pattern of organization.

Another option: Discuss all the Greek gods, then all the Roman ones.

❹ Credits all sources of information

Works Cited

Freeman, Charles. The Ancient Greeks. New York: Oxford UP, 1996.

Guirand, Felix, and A.-V. Pierre. "Roman Mythology." Larousse Encyclopedia of Mythology. New York: Prometheus, 1963. 213-33.

"Jupiter." Encyclopedia Mythica. Ed. Micha F. Lindemans. 20 Apr. 2000 <http://www.pantheon.org/mythica/articles/j/jupiter.html>.

Long, Charles H. "Mythology (II)." Grolier Multimedia Encyclopedia. CD-ROM. Deluxe ed. Danbury: Grolier, 1999.

"Neptune." Grolier Multimedia Encyclopedia. CD-ROM. Deluxe ed. Danbury: Grolier, 1999.

Works Cited
- Identifies sources credited in the report
- Presents entries in alphabetical order
- Gives complete publication information
- Contains correct punctuation in entries
- Is double-spaced throughout
- Follows a preferred style, such as the MLA guidelines

CHAPTER 25

Do It Yourself

Writing Prompt   Find a topic you are interested in and write a research report about it.

Purpose   To inform

Audience   Your teacher, classmates, anyone interested in your topic

❶ Developing a Research Plan

The first topic you think of will probably be too broad to cover in the limited number of pages you will write. If it is, gather information on the broad topic in order to help you find a part of it that will be the right size.

Narrowing Your Topic

Learn more about your broad topic, using several sources. Try to find a part that interests you and can be covered in the length of your report. Here are some ideas for sources:

- Question people who know something about the topic.
- Find and skim books on your broad topic. The chapter titles might give you some ideas for breaking down the topic into smaller parts.
- Browse the Internet.
- Write down in a chart or graphic organizer anything you already know about your topic.

Developing Research Questions

Think of some good questions to guide your research. For example, the writer of the report on Greek and Roman gods thought of these questions:

- Who were the main Greek gods?
- Who were the main Roman gods?
- How were they alike?
- How were they different?
- When were the myths developed?

As you learn more during your research, you may want to change your approach to the topic. That is OK.

REPORT

❷ Finding Information

For a research report, you must use several sources. Each source will give you a deeper understanding of your subject. Here are some of the sources you might use.

> **Information Resources**
>
> | | | |
> |---|---|---|
> | • Magazines | • Dictionaries | • On-line databases |
> | • Encyclopedias | • Almanacs | • Internet sites |
> | • Books | • Atlases | • CD-ROM encyclopedias |
> | • Newspapers | | |

For more help in finding and using sources, see Finding Information, pp. 437–449.

Evaluating Sources

The better your sources, the better your report will be. Therefore, you want to make sure you can trust your sources. Ask questions such as these:

• Is the material on my topic up to date?

• Is the author an expert on the topic?

• Is the author fair?

For more on evaluating sources, see p. 447.

Making Source Cards

When you find a good source, don't let it get away. Write down the publication information on an index card. This becomes your **source card.** Write the information for each source on a separate card, as shown on the next page. Give each source card a number. The source cards will help you in two ways:

• When you take notes, you can refer to the source by number instead of having to write the title and author again and again.

• You will use the source cards to make your Works Cited list. (You will learn more about how to make a Works Cited list on page 429).

- **Book** Write the author's name, the title, the city where it was published, the publisher's name, the copyright date, and the library call number.

- **Magazine or newspaper article** Write the author's name (if one is given), the title of the article, the name and date of the publication, and the page numbers of the article.

- **Encyclopedia article** Write the author's name (if one is given), the article title, and the name and copyright date of the encyclopedia.

- **Internet** Write the author's name (if one is given), the title of the document, publication information for any print version, the date you accessed the document, and the document's network address (in angle brackets).

Source Cards

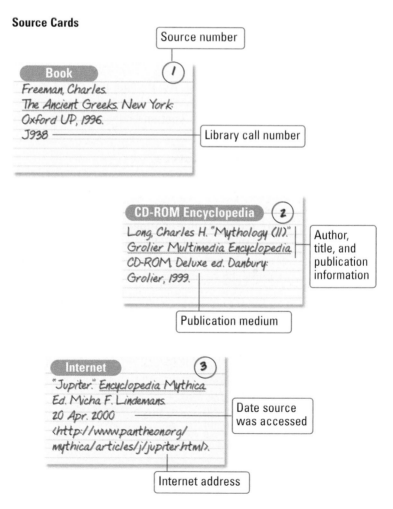

Source number

Book *1*

Freeman, Charles.
The Ancient Greeks. New York:
Oxford UP, 1996.
J938

Library call number

CD-ROM Encyclopedia *2*

Long, Charles H. "Mythology (II)."
Grolier Multimedia Encyclopedia.
CD-ROM Deluxe ed. Danbury:
Grolier, 1999.

Author, title, and publication information

Publication medium

Internet *3*

"Jupiter." Encyclopedia Mythica.
Ed. Micha F. Lindemans.
20 Apr. 2000
<http://www.pantheon.org/
mythica/articles/j/jupiter.html>.

Date source was accessed

Internet address

REPORT

❸ Taking Notes

When you read something that might be useful for your paper, make a note of it. Write every note on a separate index card.

> **Here's How** **Making Note Cards**
>
> - **Use a separate index card** for each batch of information.
> - **Give each card a heading** to show the subject of the note.
> - **Write the source-card number** on each note card.
> - **Write the page number** where you found the information in the source.
> - **Put quotation marks around anything** you copy word for word from the source.

For more on taking notes, see pp. 456–458.

Paraphrasing

When you take notes, you **paraphrase,** or put in your own words, what the sources say. Here is part of a paragraph from an encyclopedia article. The note card paraphrases the passage.

> **PROFESSIONAL MODEL**
>
> In Roman mythology, Jupiter was the king of the gods and the lord of life and death. He was also called Jove. Jupiter was the son of Saturn and Rhea, the husband of Juno, and the father of Minerva. The Romans identified him with the Greek god Zeus, but he retained to some degree his own distinctive character. Unlike Zeus, for example, he never came to visit humankind on earth.
>
> —*Grolier Multimedia Encyclopedia*

Note Card

> **Paraphrase** ② ── Source number
>
> Jupiter (Zeus) ──
> Jupiter is the Roman god for Zeus, ── Heading shows subject.
> the king of the gods. He is different
> from Zeus. Jupiter never came to
> earth, but Zeus did.

Quoting

Always use quotation marks when you copy an author's exact words. However, only use a quotation when you really need it. Here are two good reasons for using a quotation.

- The author's point is so important that you need to make sure it is stated exactly.
- The author said something so well that you want to use his or her words.

Avoiding Plagiarism

Using an author's words or ideas without giving the author credit is **plagiarism.** You are passing off someone else's words or ideas as your own. Even if you don't use the author's exact words, it is easy to slip into plagiarism when you are paraphrasing.

ORIGINAL

Zeus was the father of the gods and the most powerful. His throne was on Mount Olympus. He was god of the sky and storms, and when it rained people would say "Zeus is raining."

—Charles Freeman,
The Ancient Greeks

PLAGIARIZED VERSION

Powerful Zeus, father of the gods, was god of the sky and storms, and when it rained people would say "Zeus is raining."

The writer left out the sentence about the throne and rearranged the first sentence, but that is not enough. The source has been plagiarized. Here is a version that credits the source and avoids plagiarism.

STUDENT MODEL

Zeus's power was often connected to thunderstorms. As Charles Freeman says, when it rained, people would say that Zeus was raining (22).

Source is credited.

④ Organizing and Outlining

Planning Your Report

Every research report has these three parts: **introduction, body,** and **conclusion.** Each part has a specific job to do.

Introduction The introduction should
- be lively
- tell what your paper will be about
- include a statement of your thesis, or main idea. Your **thesis statement** should tell what your report is about and be supported by facts in the body of your paper.

Body Here is where you give the information that supports your thesis statement. Paragraphs in the body should
- be logically organized so that one idea flows smoothly to the next idea
- contain topic sentences that support the thesis statement

Conclusion This is the end of your report. Here you should
- sum up your ideas
- restate your thesis, using different words

Making an Outline

To be sure that your paper is well organized, make an outline. Here is a good way to make an outline.
- Group your note cards according to key ideas.
- Put the cards in logical order, moving from one idea to the next.

Here is part of an outline for the report on Greek and Roman gods.

Greek and Roman Gods
Thesis statement: Although the names of the Greek and Roman gods were different, what the gods did and what they were like were very similar.

I. Introduction
II. Overall likenesses and differences
III. Likenesses and differences of specific gods

For more about creating outlines, see p. 459.

⑤ Drafting

You do not have to begin your draft at the beginning and go step by step to the end. You can start by writing the parts you know best. You can put the paragraphs in order later. As you work, follow these guidelines:

Support your thesis. Everything in your paper should back up your main idea.

Follow your outline. For every major part of your outline, you will need to write one or more paragraphs. What if you don't have enough information to write a good paragraph? Either do more research or revise your plan.

Check your paragraph order. Once you have all of your paragraphs written, make sure they are in the right order.

Using Your Notes to Write Your Paper

You will probably have a lot of notes. When it is time to write your paper, you will want to group those notes into sections. Here is how the writer of the report on Greek and Roman gods grouped two notes about Poseidon and Neptune.

> **Poseidon**   ②
> Poseidon was the brother of Zeus and god of the sea and of earthquakes. He was violent and powerful. The Mycenaeans worshiped him as their main god.

> **Neptune**   ②
> Neptune was the main Roman god of the sea. Not important at first. When the Romans began going to sea, he became more important and more like Poseidon.

STUDENT MODEL

The Roman sea god, Neptune, was a minor god for many years. He wasn't as important to the Romans as Poseidon was to the Greeks ("Neptune").

⑥ Documenting Information

When you are giving information that most people know, you do not have to supply a source reference, or **documentation,** for that information. However, when you give any information that is not widely known, you need to tell where you got the information.

In a research paper, you do this with **parenthetical documentation.** (You put a reference to your source in parentheses in the body of your research report.) The reference tells your readers where to look in the Works Cited list at the end of your report. The Works Cited list gives the publication information for all the sources in your report.

Include parenthetical documentation for every quotation or paraphrase that you use. Here's how to do parenthetical documentation.

Here's How **Guidelines for Parenthetical Documentation**

- **One Author** If you mention the author's name in the sentence, include only the page number in parentheses.

  > As Charles Freeman says, when it rained, people would say that Zeus was raining (22).

  If the writer had not mentioned the author's name, the documentation would look like this:

  > When it rained, people would say that Zeus was raining (Freeman 22).

- **No Author Given** Include the title and the page number if the source is a book or a magazine. You will not have a page number for an electronic source.

  > The Roman sea god, Neptune, was a minor god for many years. He wasn't as important to the Romans as Poseidon was to the Greeks ("Neptune").

- **Electronic Source** Include the author's last name. If no author is given, use the title.

  > The Encyclopedia Mythica explains that "Jupiter is completely identical with the Greek Zeus" ("Jupiter").

Preparing a Works Cited List

- First, gather up your source cards.
- Next, read through your report.
- If you used a source, put a check mark by the reference in the report and keep the card handy.
- If you didn't use a certain source, put that card aside. Your Works Cited list should include entries only for the sources that you actually used in your paper.
- Arrange the source cards in alphabetical order, according to the authors' last names. If a source has more than one author, use the first author's name. If no author is given, use the first word of the title. (Don't count *A, An,* or *The*.) The proper format for a Works Cited list is shown below.

Martinez 4

Center the title, "Works Cited."

Works Cited

Freeman, Charles. The Ancient Greeks. New York: Oxford UP, 1996.

Guirand, Felix, and A.-V. Pierre. "Roman Mythology." Larousse Encyclopedia of Mythology. New York: Prometheus, 1963. 213–33.

"Jupiter." Encyclopedia Mythica. Ed. Micha F. Lindemans. 20 Apr. 2000 <http://www.pantheon.org/mythica/articles/j/jupiter.html>.

Long, Charles H. "Mythology (II)." Grolier Multimedia Encyclopedia. CD-ROM. Deluxe ed. Danbury: Grolier, 1999.

"Neptune." Grolier Multimedia Encyclopedia. CD-ROM. Deluxe ed. Danbury: Grolier, 1999.

Indent the second line and additional lines of each entry 1/2 inch or five spaces.

Double-space the whole list.

For more about documenting sources, see **MLA Citation Guidelines, pp. 582–589.**

REPORT

⑦ Revising

TARGET SKILL ▶**Varying Sentence Beginnings** Your writing will be more interesting if you vary the way you begin sentences. Try to avoid starting every sentence with "The." For more help with revising, review the rubric on page 418.

> ~~The~~ civilization in Rome developed later than it did in
> ∧and,
> Greece. ̶T̶he Romans adopted many of the Greek gods. *Although* ̶T̶he
> names of the Greek and Roman gods were different, ~~but~~ the
> gods' duties and characteristics were very similar.

⑧ Editing and Proofreading

TARGET SKILL ▶**Avoiding Shifts in Verb Tense** Be sure to use the same verb tense for all actions that occur at the same time.

> *used*
> What the gods controlled and what they ~~use~~ to control it,
> *were*
> though, ~~are~~ about the same in both ancient Greece and
> ancient Rome.

For more help with verb tenses, see pp. 101–110.

⑨ Sharing and Reflecting

Find several people who are interested in your topic and **share** your report with them. Using the rubric, or standards, for a successful research report, ask them to help you find ways to improve your report.

For Your Working Portfolio After you have had a chance to discuss your report, **reflect** on what you have learned. Are there parts of your topic that you would have handled differently? Make notes about your reflections. Save your notes, along with your report, in your ⬜ **Working Portfolio.**

Speak for Yourself: *Oral Report*

"The Greek and Roman gods had different names, but what they did and what they were like were very similar."

Greek and Roman Gods

Zeus → Jupiter

Hera → Juno

Hermes → Mercury

Poseidon → Neptune

Reports often have a lot of information. When you present your **report** orally, you need to help your audience follow it. Use simple language. Use charts, graphs, and other visuals to show the audience what you mean.

Here's How Creating an Oral Report

- Decide which points from your written report you will use. You won't be able to use everything, so choose important and interesting parts.

- Use a separate note card for each main point you will include. Make notes to yourself about when you will point to the visuals you have prepared.

- You might use a flip chart to present your main points. You may also use photographs, maps, and charts to add to your report.

- If a video exists related to your topic, try to show a portion of it.

- Make sure your visuals can be seen from the back of the room. Practice your oral report including how you will handle the visuals.

For more information on speaking skills, **see p. 489–491.**

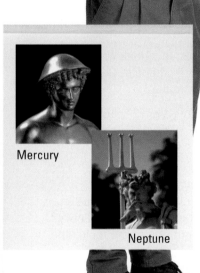

Mercury

Neptune

REPORT

Student Help Desk

Research Report at a Glance

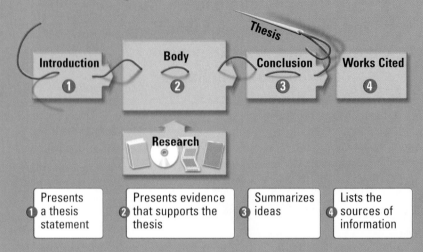

Thesis

Introduction ❶ → **Body** ❷ → **Conclusion** ❸ → **Works Cited** ❹

Research

❶ Presents a thesis statement
❷ Presents evidence that supports the thesis
❸ Summarizes ideas
❹ Lists the sources of information

Idea Bank

Tips for Finding a Topic

Go to a store. Look at the items on display. Think about the steps that went into creating one of the products. Could you write a report on how the product was made?

Think about changes. For example, what devices do you use for listening to music today? What did your parents use when they were your age?

Browse the newspaper. Look for topics you would like to know more about.

Read literature. What more would you like to know about an author you've been reading, such as Gary Soto or Lois Lowry? What more would you like to know about one of the topics the author writes about?

Friendly Feedback

Questions for Your Peer Reader

- What did you learn from my report?
- What part did you find most interesting?
- What should have been left out?
- What should have been added?

Publishing Options

Print	Add pictures, charts, diagrams, or other visual material to your report. Then present it in booklet form to a lower-level class. Use a computer graphic program to create any charts or diagrams.
Oral Communication	Read your report to a class that is studying the topic your report covers.
Online	Check out **mcdougallittell.com** for more publishing options.

The Bottom Line

Checklist for Research Report

Have I . . .

____ written an interesting introduction?

____ included a clear thesis statement in the introduction?

____ used evidence from sources to develop and support ideas?

____ credited the sources of information?

____ used a logical pattern of organization?

____ used transitions between ideas?

____ summarized ideas in the conclusion?

____ used information from more than one source?

____ included a Works Cited list at the end of the report?

REPORT

Communicating in the
Information Age

26 Finding Information   437

27 Study and Test-Taking Skills   451

28 Thinking Clearly   467

29 Listening and Speaking Skills   481

30 Examining Media   497

31 Building Your Vocabulary   511

Techno-Color

Whoever said information was dull? You can
liven up the way you think and see the world by
using information in a skillful way. Enter here to
explore the world of knowledge that awaits you.

Power Words
Vocabulary for Precise Writing

persist

scale

scramble

scuttle

summit

PERSEVERE

SCAMPER

scramble

Facing the Mountain

Meeting a challenge can be like climbing a mountain. Here are some words to help you put things in perspective.

Scaling the Heights

You must climb this mountain, whether you **scramble** or **clamber** up using your hands as well as your feet; whether you **scuttle** and **scrabble** up like a spider, crab, or squirrel; whether you **scamper** rapidly like a monkey or **inch** slowly like a caterpillar. However you do it, you must **ascend** the mountain; you must **scale** the heights.

Is there another way you could reach the top? You might try **digging in** instead. **Bore** and **tunnel** your way in. Then **drill** your way through and **excavate** a path for yourself.

You Can Do It!

If you are **determined, resolute,** and **steadfast,** if you **persist** and **persevere,** if you **plug away, keep at it,** and **hang in there,** you will reach the top, the **peak,** the **pinnacle**—the **summit!**

▷ **Your Turn** Climb Every Mountain

Working with two or three classmates, create a poster or brochure for a mountaineering expedition. Describe what the mountain looks like and what it is like to climb it. If you like, include sketches of what the mountain looks like from the bottom and from the top.

clamber

inch

determined

STEADFAS

Finding Information

A Mountain of Information

There's a mountain of information in the world today. At times, you might feel you're about to be buried under an avalanche of books, magazines, newspapers, Web sites, and other information sources. Hang on—don't give up! There is a way to climb this mountain and find the information you're looking for. The chapter you're about to read will give you everything you'll need for the climb—a map, important research skills, and information about search tools. Have a great trip!

Write Away: A Question of Curiosity
Do you ever wonder how the dinosaurs died or where lightning comes from? Write a paragraph about a topic you'd like to know more about. Explain why you're curious about the topic. Place your paragraph in your 📁 **Working Portfolio.**

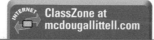
ClassZone at
mcdougallittell.com

Finding Information **437**

The Library and Media Center

The library and media center is the best place to go when you need information. Here you will find many different information sources as well as information experts who can help you with your research.

❶ Library Collection

The library collection is made up of all the items that a library owns. In addition to books, a library has newspapers, magazines, videotapes, audiotapes, CDs, computers, and CD-ROMs. This floor plan shows the sections of a typical library. How many of these sections have you used?

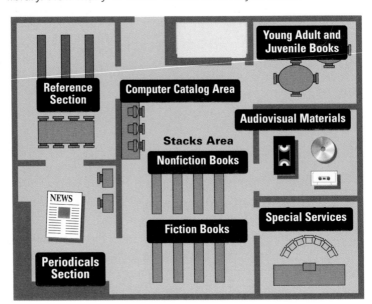

❷ Special Services

Public libraries often have special collections that include old photographs, journals and scrapbooks, manuscripts, rare books, and family histories. Ask the librarian about special collections at your library. Librarians are information experts. They can help you find and use all kinds of information sources.

❸ Fiction and Nonfiction

Most library books are found in the stacks area—an area filled with many bookshelves. Library books are divided into two main types: fiction and nonfiction. These two types of books are shelved separately and organized using different systems.

Fiction Books Made-up stories, such as novels and short stories, are fiction. Fiction books are arranged on the shelves alphabetically by the author's last name.

Every fiction book has the author's last name, or the first few letters of the last name, on its spine.

FIC
Aiken

Nonfiction Books Nonfiction books are sorted into subject areas, such as science and history. Most school and public libraries use a numbering system called the **Dewey Decimal system** to help them organize nonfiction books. In this system, each subject area is assigned a number. Each

Every nonfiction book has a call number on its spine.

591.5
Paten.D

book is given a special code called a **call number.** The call number is like a street address. It tells you the location of the book in the stacks.

To find a particular nonfiction book, you need to find out its call number, or address. The next lesson will show you how to do this.

For more information on the Dewey Decimal system, see p. 448.

FINDING INFO.

Using Library Catalogs

A library catalog lists every item in the library. It also gives you the information you need to find these items.

❶ The Computer Catalog

Today, many libraries use computer catalogs to store information about library items. Each library item has its own record, or screen, in the computer catalog. A record for a nonfiction book is shown below.

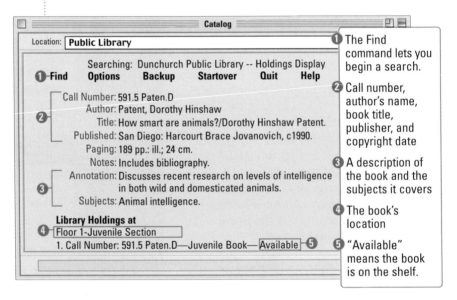

Catalog

Location: **Public Library**

Searching: Dunchurch Public Library -- Holdings Display
❶ Find   **Options**   **Backup**   **Startover**   **Quit**   **Help**

Call Number: 591.5 Paten.D
Author: Patent, Dorothy Hinshaw
Title: How smart are animals?/Dorothy Hinshaw Patent.
Published: San Diego: Harcourt Brace Jovanovich, c1990.
Paging: 189 pp.: ill.; 24 cm.
Notes: Includes bibliography.
Annotation: Discusses recent research on levels of intelligence in both wild and domesticated animals.
Subjects: Animal intelligence.

Library Holdings at
Floor 1-Juvenile Section
1. Call Number: 591.5 Paten.D—Juvenile Book— Available

❶ The Find command lets you begin a search.

❷ Call number, author's name, book title, publisher, and copyright date

❸ A description of the book and the subjects it covers

❹ The book's location

❺ "Available" means the book is on the shelf.

Searching the Catalog

You can search the computer catalog using an author's name, a title, or a subject. Searching by subject is often the easiest way to find sources that tell about your topic. Sometimes you can find more sources by searching with keywords. **Keywords** are words, phrases, and synonyms that describe your subject. Here are some keywords you might use to find books about dogs that help people: *guide dogs, seeing-eye dogs, hearing dogs.*

If you don't know a lot about your topic, read an encyclopedia article first to help you come up with keywords.

❷ The Card Catalog

Some libraries still use the traditional card catalog. This kind of catalog holds cards in alphabetical order that give basic information about library items. There are at least three kinds of cards for each book—an author card, a title card, and a subject card. A subject card is shown below.

❶ JUV ❷ ANIMAL INTELLIGENCE

❸ 591.5 ❹ Patent, Dorothy Hinshaw.
   ❺ How smart are animals?/Dorothy Hinshaw Patent.
   Paten.D San Diego: Harcourt Brace Jovanovich, 1990.
   189 p.: ill.; 24 cm. ❻
   ❼
   Includes bibliography.

❽ Discusses recent research on levels of intelligence in both wild and domestic animals.

❾ I. Title   II. Author

❶ Section of the library
❷ Subject
❸ Call number
❹ Author
❺ Title
❻ Copyright date
❼ Number of pages; illustrated
❽ Description
❾ Other entries in the card catalog for this book

Combine what you know about sections of a library, call numbers, and the library catalog to locate books and other library items. When you're researching a topic, you'll often be looking for nonfiction books.

> **Here's How** **Finding a Nonfiction Book**
>
> 1. From the library catalog, copy down the title, author, call number, and location of the book you want to find.
> 2. Go to the section of the library where the book is located.
> 3. Look for labels on the bookshelves that show which call numbers are kept on the shelves. Find the shelf that holds the call number you want.
> 4. Search the call numbers on the book spines until you find your book. If you can't find the book, ask the librarian for help.

Some call numbers are very long—longer than you might expect. When you copy information from the library catalog, make sure you write down the full call number.

Finding Magazine Articles

Current magazine articles are good sources of up-to-date information. Older magazine articles can give you details and opinions about events from the past. Libraries keep both current and older issues of many different magazines.

Using a Magazine Index

The best way to get magazine articles on the topic you're researching is to use a magazine index. This kind of index lists magazine articles and the information you need to find them.

Readers' Guide

You can find an index called the *Readers' Guide to Periodical Literature* in most libraries. This index is a monthly list of articles that have appeared in well-known magazines. The articles are sorted by subject and author. At the end of the year, the monthly indexes for the entire year are combined into one book. Below is a sample subject listing from the *Readers' Guide*.

❶ **ANIMAL INTELLIGENCE**
   See also
❷   Animal communication
      Guide dogs
❸ How smart is your dog? [condensed from the dog IQ test] M. Miller il *Reader's Digest*
   ❹   ❺   ❻
   ❼   ❽   ❾
   v154 no923 p93-5 Mr 1999

❶ Subject heading
❷ Cross-references to other subject headings
❸ Article title
❹ Author
❺ Illustrated
❻ Magazine title
❼ Volume and issue numbers
❽ Page numbers
❾ Date of publication

If you want to find current articles on your subject, look in the most recent volume of the index. If you want to find articles about an event that happened in the past, look in the volume from that period of time. For example, to find out about an event that happened in 1942, you would look in the 1942 volume.

Computer Indexes

Many libraries have computer indexes, such as *Electric Library* and *Infotrac,* that help you find information quickly and easily. You can search them using an author's name, a title, a subject, or a keyword. The *Readers' Guide* is also available on computer.

After using a periodical index to get titles of articles on your topic, follow the steps below to find the articles.

> **Here's How** **Finding a Magazine Article**
>
> 1. From the index, copy down the article title ("How Smart Is Your Dog?"), the magazine title (*Reader's Digest*), the date of publication (March 1999), the volume number (154), and the page numbers (93–95).
> 2. If the article is in the latest issue, look for the issue in the area where current magazines are displayed.
> 3. If the article is in an older issue, fill out a form that shows the name, date, and volume of the magazine. The library clerk in charge of magazines will find the magazine for you.
> 4. When you get the magazine, look for the article using the page numbers you wrote down. You may want to photocopy the article.

Most libraries keep a list of all the magazines they receive. If the magazine you want is not on the list, a librarian may be able to get a copy of the article for you from another library.

Magazine articles often include photographs, artwork, maps, and graphs. You may be able to use these to illustrate your report. Give credit to the person who created the visual by copying his or her name next to the visual.

Using Reference Materials

You will find encyclopedias, dictionaries, and many other reference materials in the library's reference section. Use these materials to find facts, background information on a topic, and suggestions for other sources of information. The reference section is a good place to begin researching a topic.

❶ Reference Books

Most reference books are reliable sources because the information within them has been written and checked by experts. The most popular kinds of reference books are shown in the chart below.

Library References		
Type of Reference	**Kind of Information**	**Examples**
Encyclopedia	General information articles on a variety of topics	• *World Book Encyclopedia* • *Compton's Encyclopedia*
Dictionary	Spellings and definitions of words	• *American Heritage Dictionary* • *Webster's Elementary Dictionary*
Atlas	Maps and geographical information	• *World Atlas* • *Atlas of World History* • *Cultural Atlas of Africa*
Almanac	Facts and statistics	• *Information Please Almanac* • *The World Almanac*
Thesaurus	Synonyms for commonly used words	• *Roget's Thesaurus* • *Webster's New World Thesaurus*

The information in reference books is usually organized in one of the following ways: by alphabetical order, by subject, by date, or by geographic region. Take some time to figure out how a book is organized before you use it. If you need help, ask the reference librarian.

Using Parts of a Book

Listed below are three important parts of reference books and nonfiction books. Use these parts to decide whether a book will be helpful to you in your research.

The copyright date is the year a book was published. Use this date to figure out whether a book has current information.

The table of contents lists chapter titles and page numbers. Use this section to find out whether a book has information about the topic you are researching.

The index lists the important topics and details covered in a book. Use this section to quickly find specific details about a topic. If your topic is not in the index, use a different book.

❷ Electronic Reference Sources

Electronic reference sources include CD-ROM encyclopedias and Web sites.

Electronic Encyclopedias

Just like print encyclopedias, CD-ROM and online encyclopedias contain articles on a variety of topics. Electronic encyclopedias also have special features that print books don't have, such as video clips (very short movies), sound effects, and links to Web sites. You can find information by looking at a list of topics or by searching with keywords.

Web Sites

Web sites created by libraries, museums, government agencies, universities, and educational organizations may contain useful information. Many Web sites include a site map that lists the different sections of the site. Read the next lesson to find out how to conduct a Web search.

The World Wide Web

If you plan to do research on the Web, you need to know how to search for information and how to judge the information you find.

❶ Smart Searching

Directories and search engines are two tools you can use to search for information on the Web.

- A **directory** is a collection of Web sites organized into categories, such as art and history. Click on a category to look through the Web sites it contains.

- A **search engine,** such as *Alta Vista* or *Infoseek,* lets you look for information using a keyword. After you type in a keyword, the search engine finds Web sites that contain that keyword.

Use these tips to understand the results of a keyword search.

L-Net

Back   Forward   Reload   Home   Images   Print   Security   Stop

Location:

Search Results

❶ "assistance dogs"   Search Agai

Select words to add to your search. . .
☐ guide dog   ☐ seeing-eye dog
☐ hearing dog   ☐ guard dog

842 pages found; best matches first   About Your Results

Display: ● Full Descriptions ○ No Descriptions ○ Web Site Only   Change Disp

❷ **100% Loving Paws Home Page**
Loving Paws is a nonprofit organization that trains dogs to assist children who are disabled. http://www.lovingpaws.com
More Like This

❸ **68% Canine Companions for Independence**
A nonprofit organization that provides highly trained assistance dogs to people with disabilities and to professional caregivers providing pet assisted therapy. http://www.caninecompanions.org
More Like This

❶ **Type in a Keyword**
Use different keywords to get the results you need. Make sure you spell your keywords correctly.

❷ **Start at the Top**
Search results are often scored to show how closely each site matches your keyword. The most closely matched sites are at the top.

❸ **Read Descriptions** Search results include a short description of each Web site. Read these to figure out whether a site will be helpful to you.

HOT TIP

Different search engines scan different sites. Use more than one search engine to get a variety of results.

❷ Judging Search Results

Unlike reference books, most Web sites are not reviewed by experts to make sure the information they contain is correct. Use the questions below to decide whether a Web site, book, magazine article, or other source contains correct information.

1. Is the author an expert on the subject?
An expert has indepth knowledge on the subject. Experts include:
• a teacher or professor who teaches about the subject
• an individual who works in a field connected to the subject

Someone who has a personal interest in the subject but no professional experience connected to it is NOT an expert.

> **NET NOTE**
>
> **Web sites are often created by groups instead of individuals. Expert groups include government agencies (NASA), educational institutions (Harvard University, the Smithsonian Institution), and libraries (New York Public Library).**

2. Does the source give a balanced point of view?
A well-balanced source gives all points of view on a topic. This lets you decide for yourself what to think. Watch out for sites that promote their own products or services. They usually include only the information that makes their products or ideas sound great.

3. Is the material current for the subject?
Use the most current source available when you're researching a subject that changes all the time, such as computer technology. Using current material isn't as important if you're researching a subject that doesn't change, such as the causes of World War II.

Here's the golden rule for conducting research:

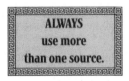

ALWAYS use more than one source.

Try to find at least three sources that agree on the information you use.

Student Help Desk

Finding Information at a Glance

Use a variety of information sources.
- Books
- Magazine articles
- Reference sources
- Web sites

Use a variety of search strategies.
- Subject
- Keyword
- Author's name
- Title

Use a variety of search tools.
- Library catalogs
- Periodical indexes
- Search engines
- Web directories

Dewey Decimal System — Dewey Leads the Way!

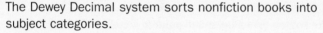

The Dewey Decimal system sorts nonfiction books into subject categories.

Numbers	Subject Areas	Examples
000-099	General Works	Encyclopedias, bibliographies
100-199	Philosophy	Psychology, ethics, logic
200-299	Religion	Mythology, theology
300-399	Social Sciences	Education, law, economics
400-499	Language	Dictionaries, grammar books
500-599	Science	Earth science, mathematics
600-699	Technology	Engineering, medicine
700-799	The Arts	Music, theater, recreation
800-899	Literature	Poetry, essays, novels
900-999	History	Biography, geography, travel

The Web Traps and Truths

Traps	Truths	What You Should Do
"I can trust the information on a Web site."	Anybody can create a Web site, so there's no guarantee that the information is correct.	Use sites created by libraries, museums, government agencies, and educational institutions.
"A Web site gives all sides of an issue."	Web sites may tell you only what their creators want you to know.	Use encyclopedias, magazine articles, and other sources to make sure you get a balanced point of view.
"The Web is so new that the information on it must be up-to-date."	Actually, the Web has been around for longer than you think. Some Web sites contain out-of-date information.	Check the date a Web site was last revised. If the site has not been updated recently, look for a more up-to-date site.

The Bottom Line

Checklist for Finding Information

Have I . . .

____ looked up books on my topic in the library catalog?

____ looked up articles on my topic in a periodical index?

____ used a directory or a search engine to locate sources on the Web?

____ used different keywords to search for my topic?

____ used reference sources to find basic information on my topic and to check facts?

____ evaluated the reliability of my sources?

____ used three or more sources of information?

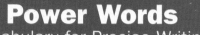

Power Words
Vocabulary for Precise Writing

The Game of Life

The qualities you develop by playing sports or games can help you face real-life challenges.

The Will to Win

Whether you are competing in a swim meet or playing a board game, you can **improve** your skills, **enhance** your performance, and **make the most of** your abilities. With enough **determination** and **persistence, perseverance** and **tenacity,** you can succeed.

Any skill you want to develop requires **practice** and **rehearsal.** With enough **drill** and **repetition,** enough **exercise** and **training,** something that was once difficult will become second nature.

Your Personal Best

"Personal best" means trying to be the best you can be. Unlike many competitions, you are not trying to **surpass, outdo,** or **beat out** anyone else. You are in a contest with yourself, working to **excel,** and if you keep improving your skills, you will **prevail.**

▷ **Your Turn** Create a Comic Strip

In a small group, talk about people who have achieved their goals through hard work and perseverance. These can be people you know, famous athletes or historical figures, or characters in books. Choose one person and draw a comic strip illustrating his or her achievements.

CHAPTER 27

Study and Test-Taking Skills

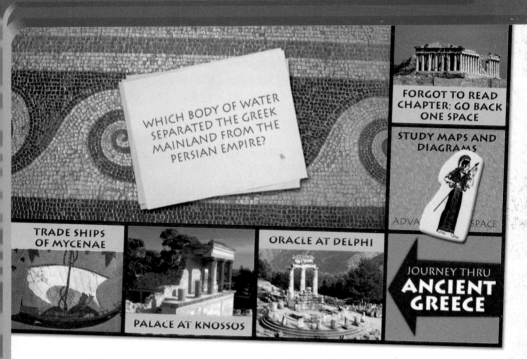

WHICH BODY OF WATER SEPARATED THE GREEK MAINLAND FROM THE PERSIAN EMPIRE?

FORGOT TO READ CHAPTER; GO BACK ONE SPACE

STUDY MAPS AND DIAGRAMS

ADVA   SPACE

TRADE SHIPS OF MYCENAE

PALACE AT KNOSSOS

ORACLE AT DELPHI

JOURNEY THRU **ANCIENT GREECE**

Strategies for Winning

You probably wouldn't want to play a game without knowing at least some of the rules. In fact, you'd probably like to know a few of the secrets and strategies that winners have learned.

Preparing to take classroom or standardized tests is not that different from preparing to play a game of skill. To perform well, you need to know the basic rules and some strategies for handling tough situations—like questions you don't quite know how to answer. Winning strategies can help you defeat invading barbarians and safeguard the empire in a game. They just might help you pass some tests, too.

Write Away: Games of Skill
Make a list of your favorite games. Describe the skills required for each one. Save your paragraph in your 🗂 **Working Portfolio.**

STUDY SKILLS

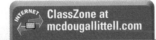
ClassZone at mcdougallittell.com

Reading for Information

Using Aids to Reading

When you're studying or doing research, you need to know what to look for. In textbooks, certain features help guide you through information. Titles, subtitles, and graphics point out key information and help you find what you need.

Preview

- Skim the pages

- Read the chapter title, introduction, and conclusion for an overview.

- Note any subheads, key words and phrases, pronunciation guides, and margin information.

- Read the questions at the end of the chapter to give you an idea of the information you'll need to learn.

- Note the maps, diagrams, and other graphics.

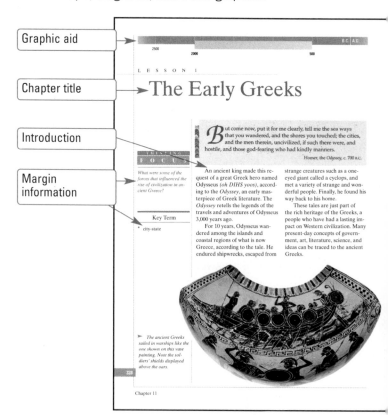

Graphic aid

Chapter title

Introduction

Margin information

2500 2000 500 B.C. A.D.

LESSON 1

The Early Greeks

*B*ut come now, put it for me clearly, tell me the sea ways that you wandered, and the shores you touched; the cities, and the men therein, uncivilized, if such there were, and hostile, and those god-fearing who had kindly manners.

Homer, the *Odyssey*, c. 700 B.C.

THINKING FOCUS

What were some of the forces that influenced the rise of civilization in ancient Greece?

Key Term

- city-state

An ancient king made this request of a great Greek hero named Odysseus (oh DIHS yoos), according to the *Odyssey*, an early masterpiece of Greek literature. The *Odyssey* retells the legends of the travels and adventures of Odysseus 3,000 years ago.

For 10 years, Odysseus wandered among the islands and coastal regions of what is now Greece, according to the tale. He endured shipwrecks, escaped from strange creatures such as a one-eyed giant called a cyclops, and met a variety of strange and wonderful people. Finally, he found his way back to his home.

These tales are just part of the rich heritage of the Greeks, a people who have had a lasting impact on Western civilization. Many present-day concepts of government, art, literature, science, and ideas can be traced to the ancient Greeks.

► *The ancient Greeks sailed in warships like the one shown on this vase painting. Note the soldiers' shields displayed above the oars.*

329

Chapter 11

CHAPTER 27

Read actively
- Read the text thoroughly.
- Read the first sentence of every paragraph for main ideas.
- Examine and answer all questions posed by the text.

Interpret maps and graphics
- Read the labels, captions, and explanations of graphics.
- Look through the text for references to graphic aids.
- Compare text information with the graphic aids.

Review and take notes
- Reread difficult sections.
- Jot down important words, phrases, and facts.

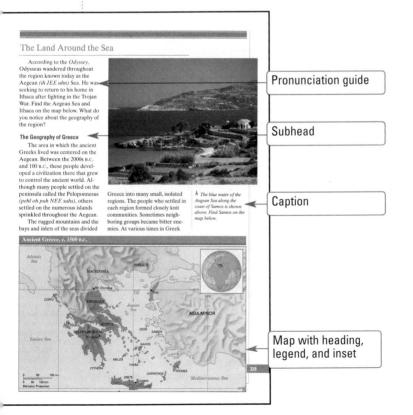

The Land Around the Sea

According to the *Odyssey*, Odysseus wandered throughout the region known today as the Aegean *(ih JEE uhn)* Sea. He was seeking to return to his home in Ithaca after fighting in the Trojan War. Find the Aegean Sea and Ithaca on the map below. What do you notice about the geography of the region?

The Geography of Greece

The area in which the ancient Greeks lived was centered on the Aegean. Between the 2000s B.C. and 100 B.C., these people developed a civilization there that grew to control the ancient world. Although many people settled on the peninsula called the Peloponnesus *(pehl oh puh NEE suhs)*, others settled on the numerous islands sprinkled throughout the Aegean.

The rugged mountains and the bays and inlets of the seas divided Greece into many small, isolated regions. The people who settled in each region formed closely knit communities. Sometimes neighboring groups became bitter enemies. At various times in Greek

The blue water of the Aegean Sea along the coast of Samos is shown above. Find Samos on the map below.

Ancient Greece, c. 1500 B.C.

Pronunciation guide

Subhead

Caption

Map with heading, legend, and inset

STUDY SKILLS

Understanding Visuals

Types of Graphic Aids

Information is often easier to understand when it is presented in a graphic, or visual, way. Textbooks include graphics to help readers understand a passage. Diagrams, maps, and time lines are types of graphics that show difficult concepts in easy-to-read ways.

Diagrams

Diagrams are simple drawings that explain how things work. Some diagrams show how parts connect to form a whole.

Read the caption, which explains the graphic.

Study the picture and use the key to learn the meanings of colors and symbols.

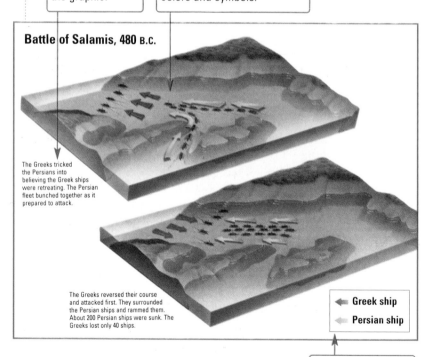

Battle of Salamis, 480 B.C.

The Greeks tricked the Persians into believing the Greek ships were retreating. The Persian fleet bunched together as it prepared to attack.

The Greeks reversed their course and attacked first. They surrounded the Persian ships and rammed them. About 200 Persian ships were sunk. The Greeks lost only 40 ships.

◀ Greek ship
◀ Persian ship

Refer to the key for an explanation of colors and symbols.

Maps

Maps visually represent a physical area. Use the key or legend to help you understand the symbols and colors in the map.

Read the title for an overview.

Note that different styles of type are used to designate place names (italics for names of seas, capital letters for names of empires).

Refer to the legend for an explanation of colors and symbols.

Time Lines

Time lines show events that occurred over time. They are usually horizontal, with dates and captions marked along them. Time lines help you understand the order of events.

Read the title

Read all the text, and note the dates of events.

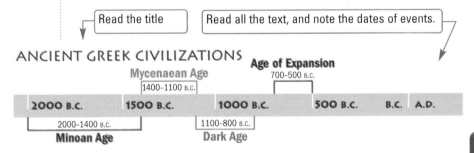

PRACTICE Drawing Conclusions

Use the diagram, map, and time line to answer the questions.

1. Look at the diagram. The yellow arrows represent the direction of ships from which empire?
2. Look at the map. Name at least one major city-state.
3. Look at the time line. What ages occurred before 1000 B.C.?

Taking Notes

Taking notes is a way to record important information. Usually you take notes for one of two reasons. Sometimes you take notes to remember what you read and hear in class. At other times, you take notes as part of doing research for a report.

❶ Taking Notes for Studying

When you take notes, write down only the most important information. How do you know what's important? Titles, subtitles, and topic sentences can signal the main ideas. Terms in boldface type, dates, and statistics often point to the details that support these main ideas. Here is an example.

PROFESSIONAL MODEL

1 The subhead gives an overview of the content.

2 The topic sentence tells the main idea of each paragraph.

1 The Geography of Greece
2 The area in which the ancient Greeks lived was centered on the Aegean. Between the **3** 2000s B.C. and 100 B.C., these people developed a civilization there that grew to control the ancient world. Although many people settled on the peninsula called the **4** Peloponnesus (*pehl oh puh* NEE *suhs*), others settled on the numerous islands sprinkled throughout the Aegean.

—Beverly J. Armento, et al.,
A Message of Ancient Days

3 Note dates and statistics.

4 Note specific names and items.

Once you've identified the important information, put it in your notes in modified outline form.

Ancient Greek Civilization
- Between 2000 and 100 BC, a powerful civilization developed around the Aegean Sea.
- Most people lived on the Peloponnesus.
- Others lived on Aegean islands.

The notes list the main idea and the most important details from the passage.

❷ Taking Notes for Research

When you take notes for a report or research paper, jot down main ideas, important details, examples, and quotations related to your topic. It is best to write each piece of information and quotation on a separate index card. Follow these guidelines when writing note cards.

The heading shows the subject.

Author, source, and page number

Development of Ancient Greece

- "Between the 2000s B.C. and 100 B.C., these people developed a civilization there that grew to control the ancient world."

- Armento, Beverly J., et al., *A Message of Ancient Days*, page 329

Quotation marks show that this is the exact wording from the source.

As you take notes, you should paraphrase the information you're reading. When you **paraphrase,** you rewrite the text in your own words. Be sure to change the wording completely to avoid plagiarism. **Plagiarism** is the use of someone else's words and phrases without giving that person credit. Compare the two versions of the student model below, each written from the following example.

Although many people settled on the peninsula called the Peloponnesus (*pehl oh puh NEE suhs*), others settled on the numerous islands sprinkled throughout the Aegean.

STUDENT MODEL

PLAGIARIZED

Many people settled on the Peloponnesus, while others settled on islands throughout the Aegean.

PARAPHRASED

The early people of Greece lived mainly on the Peloponnesus peninsula and Aegean islands.

If you use the author's exact words, be sure to put them in quotation marks and to provide the name of the source.

STUDY SKILLS

❸ Organizing Note Cards

As you prepare to write your report, you will need to organize your note cards into groups of related, or similar, ideas. This will help you to create an outline for your report later. These cards are sorted into two groups: one for Athens and one for Corinth.

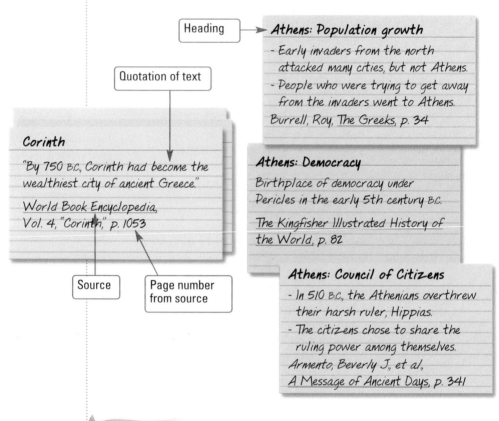

Heading →

Athens: Population growth
- Early invaders from the north attacked many cities, but not Athens.
- People who were trying to get away from the invaders went to Athens.
Burrell, Roy, *The Greeks*, p. 34

Quotation of text

Corinth

"By 750 B.C., Corinth had become the wealthiest city of ancient Greece."

World Book Encyclopedia,
Vol. 4, "Corinth," p. 1053

Athens: Democracy

Birthplace of democracy under Pericles in the early 5th century B.C.

The Kingfisher Illustrated History of the World, p. 82

Source

Page number from source

Athens: Council of Citizens
- In 510 B.C., the Athenians overthrew their harsh ruler, Hippias.
- The citizens chose to share the ruling power among themselves.
Armento, Beverly J., et al,
A Message of Ancient Days, p. 341

⭐ Tips for Success

1. Read through your note cards.
2. Separate the cards into piles according to topic.
3. Read through the cards in each pile. Each pile should include only those cards that relate to the same topic.
4. Set aside any cards that don't fit into your topics, but do not discard them.
5. Arrange the piles in the order you will use them in your report. Reorder the piles as often as necessary to create a logical order.

To avoid writing source information on every note card, create a source card. For more on source cards, see page 422.

Creating an Outline

Creating a Formal Outline

Outlines help you organize information. An **informal outline** is used for taking notes in class and planning writing-test answers. A **formal outline** helps you arrange the information you will include in a report or an essay. Below is an example of a formal outline for an essay.

STUDENT MODEL

Achievements of the First City-States
I. Athens
   A. Largest city-state
      1. Geography
      2. Population growth
   B. Birthplace of democracy
      1. Council of citizens
      2. Written laws
II. Corinth
   A. Wealthiest city-state
      1. Geography
      2. Population growth
   B. Trade center
      1. Types of trade
      2. Transportation

I. TOPIC
Use Roman numerals for main topic headings.

A. SUBTOPIC
Indent and use capital letters for subtopics.

1. DETAIL
Indent and use numbers for details.

When outlining, remember to keep all items of the same rank in parallel form. If subtopic *A* is expressed as a noun, then *B* and *C* also should be expressed as nouns. Also remember that when subtopics follow a topic or when details follow a subtopic, there must be two or more of each level: for every *I*, there must be a *II*; for every *A*, a *B*; and for every *1*, a *2*.

PRACTICE ▷ Outlining a Plan

From your 🗂 **Working Portfolio,** take out your **Write Away** exercise from page 451. Write an outline for a paper describing the games you like to play. How would you organize the paper? Would you organize it according to the skills needed to play the games? Or would you organize it by types of games, such as computer games, board games, and so on?

Taking Objective Tests

Objective tests are designed to test your ability to remember and understand important facts and details. Usually each question in these tests has only one correct answer. To know what is required for an answer, you need to understand the directions and the various test formats.

Common Formats

Objective tests usually include several types of questions, or formats. The most common are **true-false, matching, multiple-choice,** and **short-answer** questions.

True-False Questions

A true-false question asks you to decide whether a statement is accurate. If any word or phrase in the statement makes it inaccurate, the statement is false.

Directions: Mark each statement as true or false.

1. The written language of the ancient Greeks was based on the Phoenician alphabet.
   ☐ TRUE ☐ FALSE

Answer: This statement is true.

2. When the tyrant Hippias was driven out of Athens in 510 B.C., the citizens of Athens decided to share the decision-making power among themselves in a form of government called a dictatorship.
   ☐ TRUE ☐ FALSE

Answer: This statement is false. Although Hippias was driven out of Athens in 510 B.C., the new form of government was a democracy, not a dictatorship.

⭐ **Tips for Success**
- All parts of a statement must be accurate for the statement to be true. If any part is inaccurate, the statement is false.
- Beware of statements that include words such as *all, none, always, never, every,* and *only.* If there is one exception, the entire statement is false.

Matching Questions

Matching questions ask you to connect items in one column to items in another column. Connected items must be related in a specific way.

Directions: Match each item on the left with its description on the right.

    ___ **1.** oligarchy   **a.** rule of a group by a king

    ___ **2.** monarchy   **b.** government by the people

    ___ **3.** aristocracy   **c.** a few people holding power over a large group

    ___ **4.** democracy   **d.** a government ruled by wealthy nobles

Answers: **1-c; 2-a; 3-d; 4-b**

Tips for Success

- Match those items you are sure of first.
- Cross out each answer after you use it.
- Check to see whether you have used an answer more than once or not at all.

Multiple-Choice Questions

Multiple-choice questions give you several answers from which to choose. Be sure to read the directions carefully. Some tests give directions that require only one correct answer per question. On other tests, the directions may ask you to mark all the correct answers.

Directions: For each item, choose the best answer.

What percentage of Athenian society was made up of slaves?

a. 1%

b. 25%

c. 10%

d. 50%

Answer: **b**

Tips for Success

- Read the question carefully.
- Try to answer the question before looking at the choices.
- Cross out answer choices you know are wrong.
- Watch for words such as *always, never,* and *only*. They often signal incorrect answers.
- Read all the choices. Don't pick just any answer. Pick the *best* answer.

Short-Answer Questions

In short-answer questions, you will have to provide the answer yourself. You may be asked to fill in the blank with a word or phrase, or you may have to write a sentence or two to answer the question.

> **Directions:** Answer the following questions with a word, a phrase, or a short sentence, as needed.
>
> **1.** Until the 500s B.C., Athenians did most of their trading through _____.
>
> **2.** Around 570 B.C., the government began to make gold and silver _____.
>
> **3.** Wealthy citizens were expected to contribute large amounts of money to _____.

Answers: **1.** barter; **2.** coins; **3.** government projects

Tips for Success

- Make sure you understand what the question is asking.
- If the question asks for two separate answers, be sure you include both.
- Make sure your answer grammatically fits into the sentence.
- When you are asked to reply in a sentence, make sure to avoid sentence fragments. Also include phrases from the question in your answer.

HOT TIP Answer the easier questions first. Save the harder ones for last.

Writing for Tests

In some tests, you will be asked to respond to a writing prompt. For these questions, you must write an answer based on what you've learned about a topic. Writing questions test your ability to organize your thoughts and express them clearly with appropriate facts and language.

❶ Understanding the Question

When you read the question, be sure to identify the topic and how you should write about it.

Directions: In an essay, describe three important aspects of the Olympic Games to the ancient Greeks.

- Asks for an **essay**
- Asks you to **describe,** or look at a topic from all sides
- Asks for **three aspects**

❷ Writing the Response

Before you begin to write your answer, decide on your main ideas and write them down in a statement. Then draft a brief informal outline to guide you in arranging your main ideas and their supporting details. Here is an example.

> **STUDENT MODEL**
>
> Importance of the Olympic Games
>   - Begun in 776 B.C. as a footrace
>   - Nothing, not even war, could interrupt the games
>   - Used to honor the Greek gods

⭐ Tips for Success

- Jot down key ideas and supporting details you want to use.
- Draft a quick outline.
- Choose words and phrases that say what you mean.
- Include examples and details.
- Avoid unnecessary or irrelevant information.
- Proofread your writing when you are finished.

Student Help Desk

Study Skills at a Glance

Read for Information	Use Graphic Aids and Visuals	Take Good Notes	Make an Outline

Study Tips

- Be sure to complete all your reading assignments.
- Take notes while you're reading or listening to a speaker.
- List key words, phrases, names, and dates.
- Define or describe terms that are new or unfamiliar to you.
- Review your notes.
- Study with a friend and quiz each other on your knowledge.

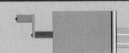

Preparing for a Test

- Find out what the test will cover, what question formats may be used, and whether you may use books and notes for the test.
- Give yourself plenty of time to study all the material several times.
- Review your notes.
- Memorize the most important facts. You'll need to know them.
- Practice by answering the chapter review questions in your textbook.
- Several days before the test, ask the teacher to explain any topic that is still unclear to you.

Types of Essay Questions You May Need to Answer

If the question asks you to . . .	you should . . .
compare/contrast	show similarities and differences between two or more topics
describe	explain the most important aspects of a topic
define	tell the meaning of a term
discuss	tell about the topic from many viewpoints
explain	tell how and why something happened or how something works
analyze	examine the parts of a whole
evaluate	examine and judge the topic
summarize/outline	write a brief overview of the topic

The Bottom Line

Checklist for Study and Test-Taking Skills

Have I . . .

____ found the main ideas in a chapter or lesson?

____ learned the key words and phrases that I must know?

____ looked thoroughly at all the visual aids and tried to understand them?

____ taken notes to help me remember?

____ made an outline showing important facts and ideas?

____ read the test directions carefully?

____ answered every question to the best of my ability?

foolish

questionable

ingenious

nonsensical

Whose Idea Was That?

Use these words to describe good and not-so-good ideas.

Back to the Drawing Board

The ten-pound camping hat on the opposite page wasn't the great idea that you had hoped it would be. You might even call it a **blunder,** an **error in judgment,** or a **miscalculation.**

The hat may have led to **embarrassment,** but it didn't lead to national **calamity,** worldwide **catastrophe,** or terrible **tragedy.** This minor **mishap** did not lead to **misfortune** and **misery;** it did not turn into a dreadful **disaster.**

Let There Be Light

Don't we all wish that we never fell for the **foolish** or **nonsensical** idea, the **impractical** or **ineffectual** notion, or the **unsound** plan? Sometimes an idea that seems **questionable** at first glance turns out to be **inventive** and **ingenious, brilliant** and **profound.** If we could have a **revelation** or **epiphany** of **astute** ideas whenever we wanted, that would be true **inspiration!**

unsoun

brillian

▷ **Your Turn** Impractical Inventions

In a small group, come up with an idea for an invention as silly as the camping hat. The invention should seem to solve a problem, but should not actually do so. Be ready to describe your invention to the class.

inventive

impractical

blunder

calamity

Thinking Clearly

What was I thinking?

Not Such a Bright Idea

That camping hat seemed like a good idea when the salesperson was talking to you. After all, how can you beat having all your camping equipment in one handy place? But what about the camp counselor who said to pack light? If you'd listened to her, you wouldn't be carrying ten pounds on your head!

These days, everyone has a bright idea to share. But whom should you believe, and why? This chapter shows how to use your thinking skills to make the most of information.

Write Away: Pretty Please?
Write a paragraph about a time when someone tried to persuade you to do something you didn't want to do. What reasons did the person give? Were the reasons effective? Keep your paragraph in your 📁 **Working Portfolio**.

THINKING SKILLS

LESSON 1 · How Ideas Are Related

The first step toward clear thinking is understanding how ideas are related. Three common relationships are main idea and supporting details, cause and effect, and similarities and differences.

❶ Main Idea and Supporting Details

When you hear or read something, look for the **main idea**—the most important point. This chart can help you.

> **Here's How** Identifying the Main Idea
>
> **To find the main idea,** look for ideas that
> • appear in the topic sentence or first paragraph
> • appear as headlines, titles, or subheads
> • follow statements such as "The point is" or "Most importantly"
> • are repeated several times
> • are *italicized,* **boldfaced,** or underlined in print
> • are spoken with emphasis or forceful gestures

Once you find the main idea, look for the facts and details that support it.

PROFESSIONAL MODEL

Some scientists say that animals may have emotions and thoughts like those of humans. Has your cat ever cuddled with you while you were sick in bed? If so, was it concerned and trying to make you feel better, did it want company . . . or was it just looking for a cozy spot?

—"Animals to the Rescue"

Main idea

Supporting details

PRACTICE What's the Big Idea?

In your 🗂 **Working Portfolio,** find your **Write Away** paragraph from page 467. Identify the main idea of the persuasive message and any supporting details.

❷ Cause and Effect

One way that ideas are connected is by cause and effect. This model shows how one specific event **(cause)** can directly result in another event **(effect).**

> **LITERARY MODEL**
>
> There once was a Wolf who got very little to eat because the Dogs of the village were so wide awake and watchful. He was really nothing but skin and bones, and it made him very downhearted to think of it.
>
> —Aesop, "The Wolf and the House Dog"

Cause—dogs are watchful
Effect—wolf gets little to eat

Just because one event happened after another doesn't mean that the first caused the second. Decide whether it is a coincidence or a real connection.

❸ Similarities and Differences

Another way ideas are connected is by **similarities and differences,** as in the model below.

> **PROFESSIONAL MODEL**
>
> Frogs and toads both lay eggs and have webbed feet. However, frogs generally have smooth, slimy skin and prefer moist environments, while toads usually have dry, warty skin and prefer drier environments.
>
> —Michael Polycarpe

Ways frogs and toads are the same

Ways they are different

For more on related ideas, see p. 478.

THINKING SKILLS

Separating Facts from Opinions

LESSON 2

Another part of clear thinking is understanding the difference between facts and opinions. Both facts and opinions have their place in speaking and writing. However, you must know how to tell the difference between them so you can judge how useful they are.

By Frank Modell

"Just because the painting doesn't happen to appeal to Marvin doesn't necessarily mean it stinks."

Copyright ©The New Yorker Collection 1972 Frank Modell from cartoonbank.com

❶ Identifying Facts

A **fact** is a statement that can be proved. Remember: just because you agree with a statement doesn't mean it's a fact!

Here's How Proving or Disproving a Statement

Make a personal observation or test the statement yourself.
Your friend says that new jacket you want is out of stock.
To prove: Go to the store to see for yourself.

Check with a source you can trust.
Your brother tells you the whale is the largest mammal.
To prove: Look up the information in an encyclopedia.

Ask an expert or authority (a real, live person).
An advertisement says drinking milk will help you grow.
To prove: Ask your doctor or school nutritionist.

❷ Identifying Opinions

An **opinion** is a statement of personal belief that cannot be proved. Pay attention to words or phrases that signal opinions.

Words that Signal Opinions

believe	best	feel	excellent
doubt	worst	think	useless
don't see why	disagree	would argue	agree

CHAPTER 28

Opinions can sometimes be as valuable as facts. If they are supported by facts or come from people who are experienced in that subject, opinions may help you make choices.

The new Rachel Rimsa book is her best effort yet.

The new Rachel Rimsa book is a good choice for young adults.

The new Rachel Rimsa book is excellent!

Book Reviewer

Reliable Opinion?
Yes. She has read all of Rimsa's books and many others of the same type.

Librarian

Reliable Opinion?
Yes. He has read the book and knows about young adults' tastes in reading.

Your Friend

Reliable Opinion?
Maybe. But you'd have to check his reasons. He may simply like short books!

PRACTICE Is That a Fact?

For each sentence, write *F* for fact or *O* for opinion. Be ready to explain your answers.

1. The Paralympic Games are a part of the Olympics.
2. The Paralympic Games are exciting to watch.
3. Athletes in the Paralympics should be proud to participate.
4. Athletes in the Paralympics have disabilities that prevent them from taking part in Olympic competition.
5. "Paralympics" means "next to" or "parallel to" the Olympics.
6. They ought to get just as much attention as the Olympics.
7. They are held right after the Olympics, in the same city.
8. I think that they should be held at the same time.
9. The 1996 Paralympics in Atlanta were the best.
10. The first Paralympics were held in Rome in 1960.

LESSON 3 Going Beyond the Facts

Sometimes you can gain new understanding by combining new information with what you already know. Two ways to do this are by making inferences and by drawing conclusions.

❶ Making Inferences

An **inference** is a logical guess you make when you "read between the lines" of information. You do this when you combine what you already know with new information.

You make inferences all the time. For example, suppose you walk into your classroom and see an unfamiliar adult sitting at your teacher's desk. You might infer that that person is your substitute teacher.

New Information + **Prior Knowledge** = **Inference**

Colorful tents spotted in town

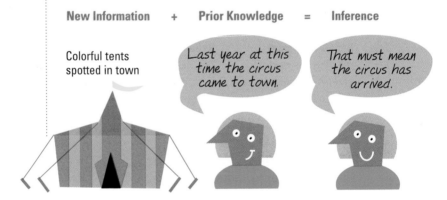

Last year at this time the circus came to town.

That must mean the circus has arrived.

❷ Drawing Conclusions

A **conclusion** is a belief or judgment you make when you go "beyond the lines" of what you hear or read. A conclusion carries more weight than a guess or an inference. To draw a conclusion, you should consider

• the information you already have
• any new information that relates to the topic
• any inferences you have made based on that information

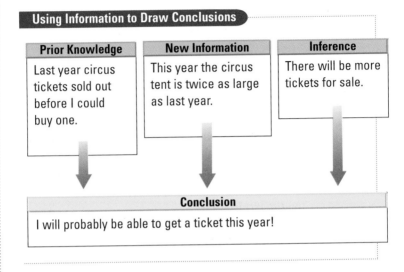

Prior Knowledge	New Information	Inference
Last year circus tickets sold out before I could buy one.	This year the circus tent is twice as large as last year.	There will be more tickets for sale.

Conclusion
I will probably be able to get a ticket this year!

PRACTICE Look Before You Leap

List the inferences you can make and the conclusions you can draw about the characters in this cartoon. Think about these questions:

- What is the boy doing?
- What do you think his mother is yelling?
- What conclusions can you draw about his behavior?

Calvin and Hobbes by Bill Watterson

THINKING SKILLS

Avoiding Errors in Reasoning

LESSON 4

Some writers or speakers use **faulty reasoning** to persuade you to feel a certain way or to do something. Use thinking skills to find the errors!

❶ Overgeneralization

Watch out for **overgeneralizations**—statements that are so broad that they can't possibly be true. "Everyone loves cats" and "Everybody should own a cat" are overgeneralizations. After all, some people are allergic to cats, or aren't able to care for them, or simply don't like them.

Overgeneralization

All students who play video games do badly in school.

> That's not true. It's all right to play video games, as long as you don't overdo it.

True Statement

Some students who spend too much time playing video games do badly in school.

Safe generalizations allow for exceptions by using words such as *some, many, few, almost,* and *sometimes.*

❷ Circular Reasoning

A writer or speaker who uses **circular reasoning** just repeats an idea in different words rather than giving reasons to support it. "Running is exhausting because it makes you tired" is an example of circular reasoning. "Is exhausting" and "makes you tired" are different ways of saying the same thing.

Circular Reasoning

Snow leopards are endangered because they are dying out.

> "Endangered" and "dying out" have the same meaning.

Clear Reasoning

Snow leopards are endangered because so many have been killed for their fur.

❸ Either/Or Thinking

Either/or statements suggest that there are only two choices available in a situation. "Either I get a new computer or I fail math!" is an either/or statement.

When you read or hear an either/or statement, ask yourself whether there are other possibilities. In the example above, the person might be able to use a computer at school or the library. He or she might also be able to get math tutoring.

Either/Or Thinking

> **Either I get a private coach or I'll never make the team.**

Clear Thinking

> **If I want to make the team, I need to practice more and maybe take some private lessons.**

PRACTICE   **Spot the Errors**

For each sentence below, identify the error in reasoning. Then rewrite the statement to correct the error.

1. Either you enjoy the Rock and Roll Hall of Fame, or you don't like music.
2. Everybody wants to be famous.
3. The football stadium was crowded because a lot of people were there.
4. Ms. Allen is wealthy because she has so much money.
5. Nobody watches black-and-white movies anymore.
6. School board members should either have solar panels installed in all schools or admit that they don't care about saving energy.
7. I'll either win first prize or fail miserably.
8. Stan is popular because so many people like him.
9. Acid rain will always be the most important environmental issue in this country.
10. A week in Florida is a perfect vacation for anyone.

Recognizing Emotional Appeals

When a writer or speaker wants to persuade you, he or she may use **emotional appeals**—statements directed at your feelings—instead of facts. If you know how to recognize when someone is using an emotional appeal, you won't be misled. Here are some common types of emotional appeals.

❶ Loaded Language

Loaded language is language that stirs up either very positive or very negative feelings in people. Writers or speakers who want to sway your opinion on a subject often present their arguments with loaded language.

Examples of Loaded Language

Positive language: The state legislature should pass the Bear Protection Act because bears are **noble, brave** animals.

Negative language: The state legislature should not pass the Bear Protection Act because bears are **savage, vicious** animals.

Ask yourself: What are the facts? What would the act do?

For more on positive and negative language, see p. 351.

❷ Name-Calling

Name-calling means to attack a person's character or personality instead of focusing on his or her ideas. This type of emotional appeal sometimes occurs in campaigns and debates.

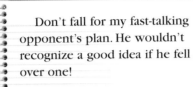

Don't fall for my fast-talking opponent's plan. He wouldn't recognize a good idea if he fell over one!

Criticizes opponent but says nothing about the issue being debated

❸ Bandwagon and Snob Appeal

Bandwagon statements appeal to a person's desire to be like everyone else. **Snob appeal**, on the other hand, targets people who want to stand out from the crowd.

Examples of Bandwagon Appeal
• Everyone wants to ride the Corkscrew Coaster of Doom!
• Don't be left behind. Order your Dynamax snowboard today!

Examples of Snob Appeal
• This jacket will make your friends drool with envy!
• Adventure Mountaineering—for daredevils only.

When you read or hear something, think about how you are feeling. If you find yourself becoming angry, sad, or afraid in response, emotional appeals may be the reason.

PRACTICE Don't Be Fooled!

Find the different types of emotional appeals used in this advertisement.

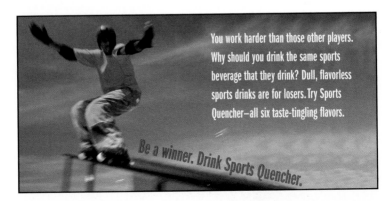

You work harder than those other players. Why should you drink the same sports beverage that they drink? Dull, flavorless sports drinks are for losers. Try Sports Quencher—all six taste-tingling flavors.

Be a winner. Drink Sports Quencher.

THINKING SKILLS

Student Help Desk

Thinking Clearly at a Glance

DO

- find main ideas and look for details to support them.
- think about how ideas are related.
- gather enough information to make inferences and draw conclusions.

DON'T

- confuse facts with opinions.
- fall for faulty reasoning.
- be taken in by emotional appeals.

Related Ideas · Similarities and Differences

These words often show how ideas are related.

SIMILARITIES	DIFFERENCES
Also	Unlike
In comparison	In contrast
Similarly	On the other hand
As well	Instead
Likewise	

Fact or Opinion · Where's the Proof?

A **fact** is a statement that can be proved.

"There are two kinds of diving competitions—springboard and platform."

An **opinion** is a statement of personal belief. It can't be proved.

"Diving is the best sport there is."

When you hear or read a fact or opinion, ask yourself:

Can I make a personal observation?
Can I check a source that I can trust?
Can I consult an expert?

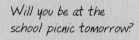

Will you be at the school picnic tomorrow?

I don't think so. Nobody ever goes to those things!

Hey, that's a bit of an overgeneralization, isn't it?

I don't want to go because I just don't feel like it.

Stop using circular reasoning!

I mean, only losers go to the school picnic!

I'm not going to listen to this name-calling.

OK, fine. I'd go, but I have to baby-sit my brother.

Oh, well, that's reasonable. But is that true? Is that a fact?

The Bottom Line

Checklist for Thinking Clearly

Have I . . .

____ found main ideas and supporting evidence?

____ separated facts from opinions?

____ made sure that my inferences and conclusions are logical?

____ recognized and avoided errors in reasoning?

____ recognized and avoided emotional appeals?

THINKING SKILLS

Power Words
Vocabulary for Precise Writing

It Takes Two

Here are some words about good and bad listeners.

Listening for the Essentials

"I love talking with Luis. He's such a good listener!" What do you mean when you say this? You probably mean that Luis **concentrates** on what you say, **pays attention** to you, and **stays focused.** He is **interested** in you and **responds appropriately** to your comments.

Luis doesn't just nod and say, "Yeah, uh-huh," while you do all the talking. He **asks questions** about details. Sometimes he **challenges** your logic or **disagrees** with you. When you talk with Luis, you know you're having a real conversation!

Listening with the Ears Shut

Some people seem to have invisible fingers in their ears. They don't hear a word you say. Are they usually **inattentive** and **indifferent?** Are they **preoccupied** with or **distracted** by some problem of their own? Are they **daydreaming** or **lost in thought?** Why are they so **oblivious?** Whatever the reason, they sure are lousy listeners!

▷ **Your Turn** Listen Up!

In a small group, talk about a time when you were frustrated because someone didn't seem to be listening to you. Discuss ways to improve your listening skills and eliminate some of the barriers to listening effectively.

Listening and Speaking Skills

PEANUTS reprinted by permission of United Feature Syndicate, Inc.

Are You Listening?

Have you ever talked to someone who wasn't really listening? Like many people, Charlie Brown's friend Lucy mistakenly believes that the only person communicating in a conversation is the speaker. The truth is that without a listener, you might as well be talking to yourself! This chapter will help you develop your skills both as a speaker and as a listener.

Write Away: Communication Schedule
Make a list of all your classes and activities in a typical day. Put a check next to each class or activity that involves communicating. Then write whether you communicate mainly by listening or by speaking in each activity or class. Compare your list with a classmate's. Do you speak and listen at the same times? Save your list in your ▱ **Writing Portfolio.**

LISTEN/SPEAK

Listening Actively

Listening isn't as easy as you may think. The fact that you hear sounds and words doesn't mean that you're really listening. In order to be a good listener, you must keep your mouth closed and your ears and mind open.

❶ Listening with a Purpose

Good listeners know what they are listening for, and they pay attention to what a speaker is saying. There are many reasons for listening to a speaker. Some common reasons are listed below.

Reasons for Listening

Situation	Reasons for Listening	How to Listen
Your brother tells you a funny story.	**For enjoyment;** to be an audience for your brother	Look the speaker in the eye. Nod to show you understand what the speaker is saying. Make comments when appropriate.
A classmate gives an oral report on the history of your town.	**For information;** to learn something new	Think about what you already know about the subject. Listen for ideas that interest you or add to your own knowledge.
A friend explains why she would rather go rollerblading than go to see a movie.	**For an explanation;** to understand your friend's point of view	Listen carefully to what is being said. Respond positively to the good points the speaker makes. Listen for chances to share your reasons.
You and your sister plan a surprise birthday party for your mother.	**For problem-solving;** to come up with ideas	Identify goals and possible problems. Listen closely to each other's ideas and build on them.

❷ Strategies for Active Listening

As a student, your purpose for listening is usually to learn new information. Some of this information is hard to understand. You may be tempted to stop listening when you are confused. Instead, try using the tips below to become an active listener.

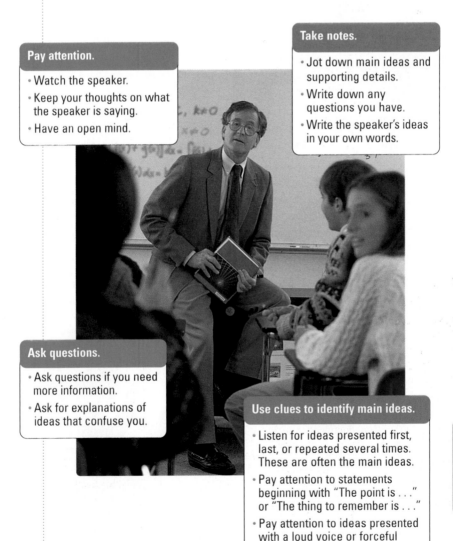

Take notes.

- Jot down main ideas and supporting details.
- Write down any questions you have.
- Write the speaker's ideas in your own words.

Pay attention.

- Watch the speaker.
- Keep your thoughts on what the speaker is saying.
- Have an open mind.

Ask questions.

- Ask questions if you need more information.
- Ask for explanations of ideas that confuse you.

Use clues to identify main ideas.

- Listen for ideas presented first, last, or repeated several times. These are often the main ideas.
- Pay attention to statements beginning with "The point is . . ." or "The thing to remember is . . ."
- Pay attention to ideas presented with a loud voice or forceful gestures.

❸ Judging What You Hear

Once you understand a speaker's message, you're ready to think about whether the message makes sense. Use the questions below to judge the **content,** or information, in a speaker's message.

Judging Content

- Does the information make sense? Can you understand what the speaker means?

- Does the information agree with what you know is true?

- Does the speaker achieve his or her purpose for speaking?

- Are the speaker's points supported with facts and examples?

- Are the speaker's ideas presented in an order that makes sense?

If you answer no to any of these questions, you should think carefully about the information. You may decide not to believe the information or to find another source for the information you need.

Words are not the only way speakers present information to listeners. Speakers also use facial expressions and body movement. The way a speaker presents information is called the **delivery.** Use these questions to judge a speaker's delivery.

Judging Delivery

Does the speaker . . .

- speak clearly and understandably?

- seem confident about his or her knowledge of the topic?

- use voice and body movement to get points across?

- make eye contact with the audience?

- stand up straight and avoid fidgeting?

LESSON 2 Interviewing

You will need to use all your listening skills when you conduct an interview. An interview is a formal conversation in which you ask questions of a person with special knowledge. Interviewing is a good way to gather firsthand information for reports and oral histories.

❶ Planning an Interview

Plan your interview by **(1)** finding a person to interview, **(2)** setting up the interview, and **(3)** preparing yourself.

Finding a Person to Interview

Finding people who know about your subject area is not as difficult as you may think. Here are some people to consider.

People You Can Interview	
People you know	A neighbor, a family member, a friend's parent
People in your community	A town leader, a police officer or firefighter, a teacher, a doctor
People in business	A person who works in an industry related to your topic

Find the names of two or three people you would like to interview. Then research each person's background to make sure he or she has the kind of knowledge you need.

Setting Up an Interview

Telephone, write, or e-mail one of the people you researched to ask for an interview. Be sure to cover these points:

- Introduce yourself and explain why you want an interview.
- Ask the person for a convenient time and place you can meet.
- Find out whether the person will let you audiotape or videotape the interview.
- Let the person know how you can be contacted in case plans need to be changed.

LISTEN/SPEAK

Preparing for an Interview

Follow these steps to prepare for the interview.

Do research. Do more background research about the person. This will help you figure out what questions you want to ask.

Write questions. To get as much information as possible, ask open-ended questions. Open-ended questions can't be answered with just yes or no. These questions often begin with words like *what, why, how, explain,* and *describe.*

Yes or No Question	Open-ended Question
Were you nervous when you flew an airplane for the first time?	How did you feel when you flew an airplane for the first time?

Confirm. A day or two before the interview date, call the person to remind him or her of your appointment.

❷ Conducting and Following Up on an Interview

Follow the tips below to get the information you need from the person you interview. Make sure you are on time and have all the supplies you need.

Here's How Interviewing

During the Interview

- Ask your questions clearly and listen carefully. Give the person enough time to answer and don't interrupt.
- Ask follow-up questions if something interests you or confuses you.
- Take notes, even if you're recording the interview. Jot down the main ideas or interesting statements that can be used as quotes.
- Thank the person for the interview, and offer to send him or her a copy of your final material. Ask if you may call with any follow-up questions.

After the Interview

- Review your notes while the interview is still fresh in your mind. Then write a short summary of the conversation.
- If you recorded the interview, you may want to make a written version for your records.
- Send a thank-you note to the person you interviewed.

Speaking Informally

LESSON 3

Most of the speaking you do is informal. In other words, you don't usually practice what you're going to say.

❶ Everyday Speaking

Informal speaking situations often take place between you and just one other person. Examples include answering a teacher's question or talking on the phone with a friend. Even though you don't prepare to speak informally, you still need to follow some basic rules for clear communication.

Tips for Speaking Informally

Speaking
- Speak clearly and don't mumble.
- Get to the point, and don't ramble.
- Avoid using empty words such as "like" and "you know."

Using Body Language
- Make eye contact with the person you're speaking to.
- Use facial expressions to show your feelings about what you're saying.

Listening
- Let the other person respond without interrupting him or her.
- Listen carefully to what the other person says. Answer any questions and nod to show you understand.

---

❷ Speaking in Groups

Group discussions are another kind of informal speaking. You take part in group discussions both in and out of school. For example, you might work on a school project with other students or talk with your family about where to go on vacation. You can use the tips in the chart above to help you take part in group discussions. In addition, you should remember these points:

Be considerate. Respect other people's feelings and opinions, and let everyone contribute his or her ideas.

Be cooperative. Work with the other members of your group to accomplish the group's goals.

LISTEN/SPEAK

Group Tasks

Group members must decide how they will work together to accomplish their goals. Groups should complete the tasks listed below in order to work effectively.

Define the purpose of the group. The purpose might be to solve a problem, to brainstorm ideas, or to make a decision.

Assign roles to individual members. Roles include note-taker, chairperson, and participant.

Decide on a list of items to discuss. Group members should know what decisions they will have to make.

Evaluate the group's progress often to make sure the group stays on track. The group leader should help group members stay focused on their purpose.

Here's an example of how one student group completed these tasks.

> Group's purpose to plan our class party
> Roles Chairperson—Marla; Note-taker—Devin;
> Participants—Keith, Tanya, Miguel, Ann, Yasmin, David
> Items for discussion
>   1. when to have the party
>   2. what kind of decorations to use
>   3. what kind of food to serve

Discussion Skills

Although group members play different roles, every group member should use the discussion tips below.

Here's How Taking Part in a Discussion

DO	DON'T
• Take turns speaking.	• Interrupt someone who is speaking.
• Listen carefully to each speaker and take notes.	• Think only about what you're going to say next.
• Ask questions or comment on others' ideas.	• Use disrespectful language.
• Speak clearly and confidently.	• Dismiss others' ideas without first thinking about them.

Preparing an Oral Report

A formal speaking situation is one in which you present information to an audience. An oral report is probably the most formal oral presentation you'll make as a student. It involves research, preparation, and practice.

❶ From Writing to Speaking

You can prepare an oral report using material you've already written, but you'll need to revise this material. Remember, readers can reread sections of a written report that are hard to understand. Listeners cannot do this. They have to be able to keep up with you. Use these tips to help your listeners.

> **Here's How Revising Written Reports**
>
> **Timing**
> - Shorten the material so your report runs no longer than 15 minutes.
>
> **Introduction**
> - Create an attention-getting opener.
> - Clearly state your topic in your introduction.
>
> **Main Section and Conclusion**
> - Use short and simple words.
> - Shorten your sentences.
> - State important points more than once.
> - End with a summary.
>
> **Delivery**
> - Use facial expressions and body movement to emphasize ideas.
> - Use audio or visual aids or both.

Changing Different Types of Writing

Some of the changes you make to a written report will depend on the kind of writing you're working with. What was your original purpose for writing the report? Did you want to persuade your readers to believe something? inform them about an idea? entertain them? Make sure your oral report has the same purpose. For more information on turning your writing into an oral presentation, see the Speak for Yourself feature at the end of every Writing Workshop.

Choosing Presentation Aids

When you give an oral report, you can use presentation aids to show your ideas as you talk about them. Here are some presentation aids to choose from.

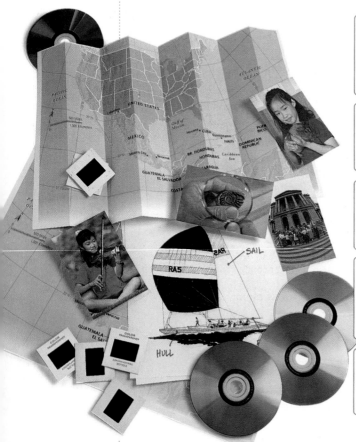

Maps Show locations and geographic information; must be large, simple, and well labeled

Drawings Illustrate ideas or things; must be large, simple, and well labeled

Photos Show people, places, and things; should be passed around to listeners

CDs Provide sound effects and background music; require special equipment

Slides Show real people, places, and things; require special equipment

Create report notes for yourself that summarize the information you will present in your report. Your notes should include reminders of when to use your presentation aids. Before the day of your report, make sure all the equipment you need is available and working.

❷ Presentation Skills

How you present information is as important as what you're presenting. Use voice and movement to make your report a success. Pay attention to the following points.

Tips for Delivery

- Make eye contact with audience members.
- Speak clearly, slowly, and loudly.
- Pause to emphasize ideas.
- Vary your tone of voice.
- Use facial expressions to show emotions.
- Use your hands and body to emphasize ideas.
- Stand up straight but stay relaxed.

Make sure you give yourself enough time to practice your presentation several times.

Dealing with Fear

It's hard not to feel self-conscious when you're standing up in front of a group of people. You'll feel better if you do something about these feelings, rather than try to ignore them.

Here's How Overcoming Stage Fright

- Before you begin your report, breathe deeply and slowly for a few minutes to help your body relax.
- Sip some water before you begin speaking to get rid of dry mouth. Keep a glass of water nearby in case your mouth gets dry again.
- To help a queasy stomach, eat lightly before you give your report. Don't eat chocolate or drink milk—they thicken your voice.
- Try to focus on a friendly face in the audience.

Presenting an Oral Interpretation

When you interpret a piece of writing, you explain its meaning. In an oral interpretation, you show the meaning of a piece of writing by reading it out loud and acting out parts of it.

❶ Choosing a Selection

The selection you choose could be a short poem or a scene from a story, memoir, novel, or play. It could be something written by you, by a friend, or by a professional writer. Try to find a selection that you truly like and that includes one or more of these qualities:

- dramatic action
- interesting rhythm
- interesting characters and settings

Once you've chosen your selection, you can begin to interpret it. Use your imagination as you think about how to show the meaning of your selection.

> **Here's How** **Interpreting a Selection**
>
> 1. **Figure out the mood of your interpretation.** What feeling do you want to show in your interpretation? Anger? Sadness? Joy?
> 2. **Find parts of the text to highlight.** What actions, settings, or words do you want to emphasize?
> 3. **Choose methods of interpretation.** What will you use to interpret your selection? Sound? Movement? Speaking? Costumes? How will you show different characters? By changing your voice or your posture? Choose methods that will show the mood and meaning of the selection.

Jot down notes about which sounds and actions you will use and when you will use them. Practice your interpretation as you create it to make sure your ideas work. You'll probably change it a few times.

② Practicing Your Delivery

Once your interpretation is final, you'll need to create a **reading script.** This kind of script is a neatly typed or handwritten copy of your selection. Mark it with notes and cues to remind you when to express an emotion, pause, move, or emphasize something. The model below shows one student's script.

STUDENT MODEL

The Dream

slowly and quietly ⟶ Even though I'm fast asleep,

call out, excited voice I hear you say, "Let's go down to the river!"

slowly and quietly ⟶ Even though I'm as still as a stone,

regular voice I'm skating with you on a ribbon of ice.

sleepy voice Even though I'm lying under a down comforter,

rub arms and act cold the wind is chilling me to the bone.

slowly and rhythmically Even though I'm breathing like a ticking clock,
I'm twirling fast and losing my breath.

Practice your interpretation, including the gestures, expressions, sounds, and movements that go with it. Do a dress rehearsal for a few friends. Use their comments to improve your interpretation. Make sure you have all the props and equipment you need for this performance.

Student Help Desk

Listening and Speaking Skills at a Glance

- Think about what you're going to say.
- Speak clearly and confidently.
- Consider your listeners.

- Listen actively.
- Judge the information you hear.
- Respect others' opinions.

Tips for Effective Listening   Lend an Ear

Remember your purpose. Think about *why* you are listening.

Pay attention to the speaker. Keep your eyes on the speaker and don't daydream.

Take notes. Jot down main ideas and any questions you have.

Listen for clues. Pay attention to repeated ideas and statements beginning with "The point is" or "The thing to remember is."

Respect other people's feelings, opinions, and ideas. Don't interrupt a speaker or criticize ideas you don't agree with.

Speaking Tips   You Said It!

- Know your purpose for speaking.

- Stand up straight, but stay relaxed.

- Speak clearly, loudly, and confidently.

- Avoid empty words, such as "like" and "you know."

- Make eye contact with people in your audience.

- Use your voice, face, and body movement to emphasize ideas.

Letter for an Interview   Dear Expert

Dear Ms. Delaney:

My name is Tracy Sparks. I am a sixth grade student at Hudson Middle School. I got your name from my uncle, Bruce Goforth, who worked with you at the <u>Lindhurst Record</u>.

> Introduce yourself.

I am writing a career report about journalism, and I would like to interview you to find out about your experiences as a journalist. I only need about an hour of your time. I could meet with you after school or on a weekend. Also, I would like to record the interview on audiotape, unless you object to this.

> Explain why you want an interview.

> Suggest when interview could take place.

> Ask about recording the interview.

My telephone number is listed below. Please call me if you are interested in being interviewed. Thank you for your time.

> Let the person know how you can be contacted.

Sincerely,

Tracy Sparks

(857) 555-6249

> Add your signature and phone number to your letter.

The Bottom Line

Checklist for Listening and Speaking Skills

Have I . . .

____ paid careful attention to the speaker?

____ looked for main ideas and supporting details?

____ identified relationships between ideas?

____ asked questions if necessary?

____ judged the information?

____ waited for my turn to speak in a group?

____ spoken confidently and clearly?

____ used my voice for emphasis?

____ used appropriate gestures and facial expressions?

____ included presentation aids and props when necessary?

Power Words
Vocabulary for Precise Writing

ENTERTAINING

Media Messages

What is it about a TV show, Web site, or other form of media that makes you want to tune in, boot up, or read on? You can use these words to describe media's effects on you.

The Media Get Your Attention

You probably count on media to tell you about topics that are important to you. A radio broadcast can **inform** you about your favorite sports and **update** you on the latest scores. A magazine article can **explain** how the space shuttle takes off. A Web site can **educate** you about undersea life or let you **explore** the decks of the *Titanic*.

Media can also be **persuasive** and **influential.** TV commercials **urge** and **implore,** "Buy this! Act now! This is a limited time offer!" Movie previews are designed to **sway** you, to **convince** you that you have just *got* to see that film.

The Media Take You to New Places

Just about every media product is **entertaining** in some way. The media messages you receive have images to **entice** and **lure** you, music to **captivate** you, spoken or written words to **draw** you in, and special effects to **enthrall** you. At their best, media can be **mesmerizing.**

▷ **Your Turn** You Call the Shots

With a small group, come up with your own media product. First, determine what your purpose is—to inform, persuade, or entertain. Then, choose which form of media to use—video report, magazine or newspaper article, music, etc. When you are finished, have classmates evaluate the overall effect and appeal of your media product.

explain

entice

influential

SWAY

EDUCATE   inform   enthrall

Examining Media

Media Hounds

What do you notice first about these media products? the pictures or the words? Does one interest you while another one doesn't? People who create media products use colors, images, sound, and words in special ways to attract a certain audience. By looking closely at a media product, you can see how the messages are meant to influence the way people think. In turn, you can use this knowledge to create your own media project.

Write Away: Start With What You Know
Think of your favorite movie, TV show, music video, or electronic game. Write a paragraph or two explaining what you specifically like about it. Is it the characters, the music, the images, the humor, the subject, or something else? Save your writing in your ⬜ **Working Portfolio.**

MEDIA

VIDEO **Media Focus**

The Elements of Media

A **medium** is a system of communication—a way for a message to be told to another person or an audience. For instance, a book is a medium for someone who wants to tell a story through printed words. The term **media** refers to more than one medium. Books, newspapers, magazines, TV, radio, electronic games, music CD's, and the World Wide Web are all types of media.

❶ Print Media

Print media include newspapers, magazines, books, posters, billboards, brochures, and flyers. The basic elements of print media are text, photos, and graphics.

Tour de France champion Armstrong credits support from his doctors, family, and friends with sending him on his winning ways.

Photos, images, and **graphics** are used to highlight important stories.

Racing for the cure
How cyclist Lance Armstrong beat cancer and the competition

Titles and subtitles give you an overview of the article.

BY STACEY SCHULTZ AND LINDA KULMAN

Two months before the start of the Tour de France, bicycling's greatest race, Lance Armstrong's coach knew his protégé was going to do well. "We ran some [endurance] tests," says Chris Carmichael, Armstrong's coach for the past decade. "And I could see that he was going to give this race a run for its money." Indeed, Armstrong, 27, endured three weeks of high-speed cycling over 2,290 miles to become the second American in history and the only cancer survivor ever to wear the victor's yellow jersey down the Champs-Élysées.

But his glorious finish last month was not always as apparent as it was to his coach. The professional cycling community had written him off, and he signed a contract for only a fraction of the sponsorship money awarded just a year earlier. Armstrong's promising cycling career came to a halt when he was diagnosed in 1996 at age 25 with advanced testicular cancer. It had spread to his brain, lungs, and abdomen, and his doctors gave him less than a 50 percent chance of survival. Of that terrifying time, he now says, "I just wanted to make it to my 26th birthday." His spectacular comeback has astounded oncologists, sports physicians, and the world. Everyone wants to know: How did he do it? The consensus is that Armstrong had several forces working in his favor. He was in great shape before his diagnosis and received the finest medical care. But he also was a pro

Breaking away

A few months after Armstrong completed his cancer therapy in January 1997, he embarked on the task of rebuilding his body. Armstrong first had to regain his muscle strength and cardiovascular endurance. He then focused on athletic training until he could return to racing. Here's how he did it:

■ **Rebuilding the cardiovascular system.** At first, Armstrong took one-hour bike rides, three to four times a week at a moderate pace. His coach monitored his heart rate and kept track of his weight. After a few months, he was able to complete longer rides.
■ **Weight training.** Twice a week, Armstrong focused on lower-body strength and stretching.
■ **Nutritional needs.** Armstrong was on a low-fat diet high in protein to build muscle and replenish

The **text** tells the story and offers important details.

60   U.S. NEWS & WORLD REPORT, AUGUST 9, 1999

PATRICK SCHMIDT · AFP

❷ Video and Film

Video includes television programming, documentaries, animation, and CD-ROM games. **Film** is used mostly to make movies and some documentaries. The basic elements of video and film are moving pictures, sound, and special effects.

Taped or **live action** gives the details.

Lighting, sound, and **special effects** add drama to the action.

❸ World Wide Web

Sites on the **World Wide Web** offer news, books, e-zines (on-line magazines), documents, reference sources, business and organization information, entertainment, and personal pages. The basic elements of Web pages include text, photos, graphics, and links to other sites. Some pages also have sound, video clips, and interactive opportunities.

Hyperlinks allow you to move quickly from one Web site to another that has related information.

Web sites rely on **text** and use **images** and **graphics** to highlight subjects.

Video and **sound** options give you a multimedia experience.

MEDIA

LESSON 2 · Understanding Media Influence

You are bombarded with media messages every day through TV shows, magazines, and the radio. Yet you probably don't realize how these messages influence your opinions and buying habits. To understand the media's influence, start by looking at why a media message was created, who created the message, and who the intended audience is.

❶ What's the Purpose of the Message?

When a book or TV show is created, it becomes a **media product.** Each media product is created to send a message that serves a purpose.

Purpose in the Media	
Primary Purpose	**Media Product**
To inform: present factual information or analyze an event or issue	News reports and articles, textbooks, documentary films, educational and reference Web sites
To persuade: try to sway the feelings, beliefs, or actions of an audience	Advertisements and commercials, infomercials, editorials, reviews, political cartoons
To entertain: amuse or delight an audience	TV dramas and sitcoms, movies, recorded music, electronic games, cartoons, novels

A media message frequently serves more than one purpose. A documentary, for instance, may be entertaining as well as informative.

❷ Who Sends the Message?

The people who decide what you will see in media include directors, producers, editors, writers, artists, owners of media companies, and advertisers. These decision-makers control the type of information you receive and how it is produced. Their decisions determine what you will see and read, and how you will receive it.

❸ Who Receives the Message?

For any TV show, magazine, or advertised product, the audience is usually targeted, or identified, by the media decision-makers and advertisers. A **target audience** is a specific group of consumers with shared characteristics, which include

- age
- gender
- habits
- income
- interests
- location

For example, teenage girls who are interested in health would be one type of target audience for a fitness magazine.

To aim a message at an audience, media executives and advertisers try to appeal to the needs, desires, and, sometimes, fears of the target audience. The appeals usually come through the language and visuals used. Notice how the following ad uses appeals to target two different audiences.

Directly addresses "kids"

Appeals to kids by showing kids having fun snowboarding

Personal instruction and supervision by trained professionals who put safety first.

The best value and experience in town. Payment plans available.

Appeals to parents by discussing supervision, safety, and cost value

Hey, kids!

Learn to snowboard

with

Powder Hound
Club for Teen Skiers

Join the club at **Snow Dog's Ski Hut** 2500 N. Mercer Rd.

PRACTICE ▸ **Going Behind the Scenes**

From your 📁 **Working Portfolio,** take out your **Write Away** exercise from page 497. For the media product you wrote about, list what you know about the product. Include:

- The artist, writer, singer, or actors of the production
- The director, publisher, producer, or Webmaster
- The company that produced it
- The type of people most likely to enjoy it

If you can't provide information for each category above, how would you find this out?

MEDIA

When you analyze a media message, you think about the purpose and the target audience. You should also notice how the different elements of that message are used to create a specific effect. Examine the design elements—photos, layout, camera angles, lighting, and special effects. These will help you understand how the media product is influencing you.

The following examples are media productions on human space flight. Think about why the creators of these media products made the choices they did. Notice how each media form delivers the message.

❶ Film

Television programs and movies often dramatize history to make a story that is entertaining and sometimes informative. Below is a scene from *Apollo 13,* a film dramatizing the events of the failed *Apollo 13* moon mission. The film's purpose is to entertain a general audience. Think about the choices made in planning this shot.

Lighting is used to show the mood of the scene. What do the shadows and light on the faces tell you about the mood of this scene?

Camera angle is used to focus your attention on an aspect of the scene. Why do you think the director chose this close angle?

In movies, **visual details** provide as much information as dialogue. What can you tell about this scene from the actors' expressions?

Below are the first two pages of an article from *Time* magazine. The purpose of the article is to inform a news-seeking audience about the experience of the entire Apollo Moon Mission program. Think about the choices made in planning the layout of this article.

The style and placement of the **title** attract your attention and give visual clues. What do you think the designer was trying to show with the style of this title?

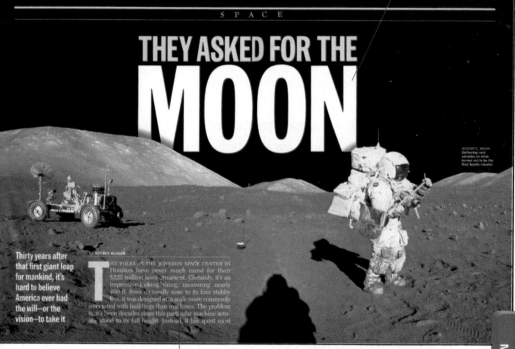

SPACE

THEY ASKED FOR THE MOON

BY JEFFREY KLUGER

Thirty years after that first giant leap for mankind, it's hard to believe America ever had the will—or the vision—to take it

THE FOLKS AT THE JOHNSON SPACE CENTER IN Houston have never much cared for their $225 million lawn ornament. Certainly, it's an impressive-looking thing: measuring nearly 400 ft. from its needly nose to its four stubby fins, it was designed on a scale more commonly associated with buildings than machines. The problem is, it's been decades since this particular machine actually stood to its full height. Instead, it has spent most

The **text** is given very little space on the first page. Why do you think the editor put so little text here?

The **photo** covers the entire two-page spread. Why do you think the editor wanted the photo so large?

MEDIA

❸ World Wide Web Site

Below is the NASA Human Space Flight home page. Its purpose is to provide facts and current information for an audience interested in past, present, and future space flight.

Links are set off in a brightly colored box. How does this reflect the purpose of this site?

This site has **up-to-the-minute information**. How does this serve the purpose of the site?

Photos and graphics are used to organize the page and attract your attention to stories. Where is your attention drawn to first on this page?

PRACTICE **Reading the Media**

Political cartoons are also media with a message. Study the message of this political cartoon, and answer the following questions.

- What do the visual cues in the background of the cartoon tell you?

- What is the message of this cartoon?

- What is the purpose of this cartoon? Is there more than one purpose?

Creating a Class Newspaper

In this chapter, you've read about the techniques that media decision-makers use to get and hold your attention. How would you like to be the one in charge for a change? You can be a media creator too.

❶ Choose Your Medium

There are so many types of media products. Which kind should you create? What message do you want to send? Keep these questions in mind as you decide.

- What is your message? What subjects do you think are interesting, important, or entertaining?
- What is your main purpose? Do you want to inform, persuade, or entertain?
- Who is your audience? What are their interests?

One way to make yourself heard is to get together with your classmates and create a newspaper of your own.

❷ Understanding Newspapers

Look through any daily newspaper, and you'll find many of the features listed below. You'll also notice that a newspaper serves all three purposes of media through its various sections.

Features of a Newspaper

Information	Persuasion	Entertainment
News stories report on current events and issues.	**Columns** describe political issues, provide humor, or give advice.	**Feature stories** often focus on interesting people or on art, fashion, or cooking.
Interviews give extensive information on leaders, policy-makers, and other important people.	**Editorial page** has political cartoons, letters, and essays.	**Sports section** covers national and local sporting events.
Listings for TV and radio, movies, and other local events are included.	**Advertisements** occur throughout the newspaper.	**Comics section** features cartoons and may also feature puzzles, trivia, and word games.
	Reviews cover recent books, movies, TV shows, and music.	

MEDIA

❸ Planning and Creating

You don't have to include *all* the features of a newspaper in your class newspaper. However, you still need to plan carefully before you start writing.

> **Here's How** **Planning a Class Newspaper**
>
> 1. **Identify your purpose and target audience.** Will your newspaper have more than one purpose? Will your audience be other members of your class, students your age, or everyone in the school?
>
> 2. **Brainstorm the features of your newspaper.** Do you want news stories and articles? Are you going to cover sports? What about feature stories and editorials?
>
> 3. **Get your resources together.** You'll probably need a computer and word-processing software, a printer, a scanner, a photocopier, a camera, and a telephone.
>
> 4. **Decide roles and responsibilities.** You may need editors, reporters, photographers, cartoonists, and graphic designers, who organize text and photos on the pages.

Your newspaper doesn't have to be printed on paper. You could produce it electronically and e-mail it to your audience or post it on the Internet.

Here are some tips to keep in mind as you create your newspaper.

- Decide which stories your audience would consider most important. Put those stories on the **front page.**

- For **news stories,** stick to the facts. Tell your readers who, what, when, where, why, and how.

- For **features,** find an interesting new twist to a familiar or not-so-familiar topic.

- For **interviews,** find out information about the person ahead of time and prepare a few questions. Take notes during the interview. At the end, read the notes to the person to be sure you've understood him or her.

- For **essays or editorials,** give reasons to support your point of view. Think about both sides of the issue. If necessary, do research to back up your opinion.

④ One Classroom's Newspaper

Here's the front page of one class's paper. What parts of it do you like best? What would you do differently in your newspaper?

Give the top story the biggest headline.

Include specific details and quotations in articles.

If possible, include photographs or graphics to catch your reader's eye.

Make sure your captions explain the photographs.

Encourage your readers to read more by letting them know what's inside.

FREE

March 15

The Strickland Times

"The news you need to know about Strickland Middle School"

Blackout Dims Afternoon Classes

By Natasha Johnson

Teachers and students got a surprise last Thursday at 1:48 P.M. when the lights went out in their classrooms. The lights stayed off for about an hour, but classes were not stopped, because there was enough daylight coming in through the windows.

Students had to leave the computer lab, though, because there was no electricity for the computers. Those students spent the hour in study hall.

(More on p. 2)

Strickland Student Wins Science Award

By Mike Kim

Eric Lewis

Eric Lewis, a sixth grader in Mr. Clemons's science class, placed third in the engineering category of the science fair held at the Brunswick Convention Center on Feb. 21. Eric's entry was a scale model of an oil well with a battery-powered drill that can dig about six inches into the ground.

"The hardest part was building the clear plastic box to hold the dirt in," he said. "I couldn't find the right kind of glue at first, and the box kept breaking and spilling the dirt all over the place."

Students from all over the state competed in the annual fair. This was the first time anyone from Strickland has won a prize in the fair.

Eric's oil rig and medal will be in the display case near the school office if you want to take a look.

MORE INSIDE

- Reviews of video games, movies, and the latest Harry Potter book.
- Strickland basketball team creams Lincoln.
- New coach for girls' softball.

After your newspaper is published and distributed, ask your readers for feedback to help you improve the next edition. What did your readers like best? What other information could you provide?

MEDIA

Student Help Desk

Examining Media at a Glance

Think about the differences among types of media:
TV
Radio
Newspapers
Magazines
Web sites

Understand media influence by identifying:
Purpose
Decision-Makers
Target audience
Design elements

Media Influence Hitting the Target

Media Decision-Makers

↓

Define Purpose and Audience

↓

Develop the Message to fit the Medium

↓

Use Appeals
Language | Visuals | Sound

↓

Target Audience

Questions for Media Literacy   Asking the Right Questions

- Who created the message and why?
- What techniques are used to attract your attention?
- What lifestyles, values, and viewpoints are represented in the message?
- How might others understand the message differently?
- What do you think is omitted from the message?

Creating a Newspaper

1. **Identify purpose and audience.**	Ask what service the newspaper will provide and who you want to reach with it.
2. **Define content and style.**	Decide on the kind of stories you will print and the type of layout the paper will have.
3. **Locate and secure equipment.**	Basically you will need a computer and word-processing software, a printer, a scanner, a photocopier, a camera, and a telephone.
4. **Establish newspaper staff.**	Staff could include an editor, reporters, photographers, cartoonists, and graphic designers.

The Bottom Line

Checklist for Learning About Media

Have I . . .

- ____ identified the purpose of a media product?
- ____ understood who controls the media?
- ____ recognized a target audience?
- ____ been aware of how media try to influence me?
- ____ analyzed the methods used to communicate a media message?
- ____ understood how to plan and create a class newspaper?

MEDIA

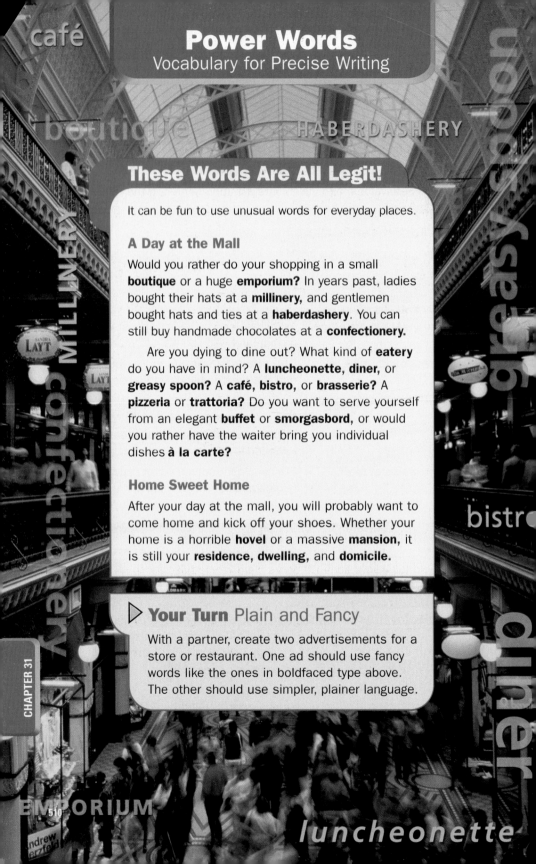

Power Words
Vocabulary for Precise Writing

These Words Are All Legit!

It can be fun to use unusual words for everyday places.

A Day at the Mall

Would you rather do your shopping in a small **boutique** or a huge **emporium?** In years past, ladies bought their hats at a **millinery,** and gentlemen bought hats and ties at a **haberdashery**. You can still buy handmade chocolates at a **confectionery**.

Are you dying to dine out? What kind of **eatery** do you have in mind? A **luncheonette, diner,** or **greasy spoon?** A **café, bistro,** or **brasserie?** A **pizzeria** or **trattoria?** Do you want to serve yourself from an elegant **buffet** or **smorgasbord,** or would you rather have the waiter bring you individual dishes **à la carte?**

Home Sweet Home

After your day at the mall, you will probably want to come home and kick off your shoes. Whether your home is a horrible **hovel** or a massive **mansion,** it is still your **residence, dwelling,** and **domicile.**

▷ **Your Turn** Plain and Fancy

With a partner, create two advertisements for a store or restaurant. One ad should use fancy words like the ones in boldfaced type above. The other should use simpler, plainer language.

Building Your Vocabulary

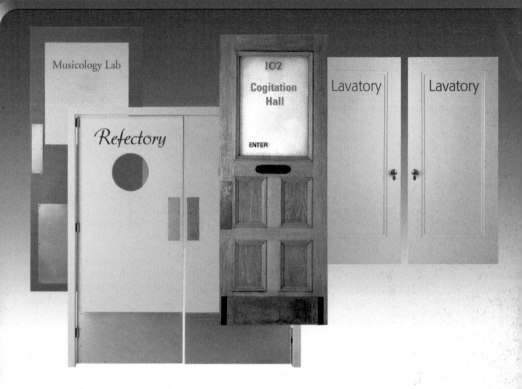

Vocabulary Building: Enter Here

What if your school's doors were labeled like those above? Would you be able to find the study hall? the cafeteria? a bathroom? If so, how?

You might use the strategy of recalling the meanings of similar words that are more familiar—*music,* for example. Or you could ask someone. In this chapter, you'll learn additional ways to determine the meanings of new words.

Write Away: What's the Word?
Write about a time when you got confused by an unfamiliar word. The word may have been on a door or a menu, in a book, or in a conversation. Save your account in your
📁 **Working Portfolio.**

VOCABULARY

LESSON 1 **Using Vocabulary Strategies**

❶ Strategies for Understanding New Words

To learn the meaning of a new word, you can look it up in a dictionary. However, you're already an expert at learning new words without a dictionary. In fact, you probably learned most of the words you know in one of these ways:

- from clues in the word's **context**—that is, the words and sentences surrounding it
- by breaking the word into parts
- by thinking about the meanings of similar words you already know

As you read the following passage, notice how one student figured out the meanings of some unfamiliar words.

PROFESSIONAL MODEL

Suddenly a blur of movement caught my eye. A dolphin was **hurtling** toward me. Although it was closing the distance between us unbelievably fast, I saw it as if it were in slow motion.

The dolphin's lower jaw hooked over its top one: it was Arnie. His head moved up and down violently, and his tail moved so fast that a trail of bubbles formed behind it. As the dolphin charged, I heard a roar of **cavitation** as the very water tore, breaking into hydrogen and oxygen. . . .

Whooosh! I felt rather than heard a wash of water like a great wind. I saw the dolphin's stomach—he had a bellybutton!— then the animal turned like a **veering** jet.

But not to go away. No more than six feet from me, he stopped. I saw his narrow face, saw his jaws move, heard the *klonk* that I knew signaled **aggression**. . . .

—Don C. Reed, "My First Dive with the Dolphins"

> The dolphin was "closing the distance . . . fast." *Hurtling* must mean "moving fast."

> *Cavitation* sounds like *cavity,* which is "a hole." So *cavitation* must have to do with making a hole (or a pocket of air?) in water.

> The dolphin's turn is compared to "a veering jet." So is *veering* a way of turning?

> The dolphin is acting as if he wants to fight. *Aggression* probably has to do with wanting to attack.

➋ Strategies for Remembering New Words

Once you learn a new word, you won't want to forget its meaning. The following strategies can help you remember.

> **Here's How** **Remembering a New Word**
>
> - **List each new word as you learn it.** Keep this list in a journal or small notebook. Later, look up the word in a dictionary and add its definition.
> - **Think of related words.**
> - **Use the word right away at least three times.** Use it in conversations, writing, or both.
> - **Create a device to remember its meaning.** This could be a tongue twister, a rhyme, or a catchy phrase or sentence.
>
>   **sentry** (guard or watcher): Sarah the **sentry** saw Sid the snoop sneak a sip of split-pea soup.
>
>   **hibernate** (to be in a sleepy, inactive state): Don't **hibernate** or you'll be late.

To expand your vocabulary, find a new word in the newspaper every morning. Then look up its meaning, add it to your word list, and try to use it often during the day. To have some fun with this, challenge your friends to do the same thing and see who is the first to guess the other's word of the day.

Zits

VOCABULARY

LESSON 2 · Using Context Clues

You can find clues to a word's meaning in its context, the words and sentences surrounding it. Often these clues can help you to infer, or figure out, the meaning of a word.

❶ Definitions and Restatements

Look again at the second sentence above. You probably guessed the meaning of the word *infer* from the phrase "or figure out." This phrase restates the meaning of the unfamiliar word.

Often the words near an unfamiliar word define the word or restate its meaning. Definitions and restatements may be set off by commas, dashes, parentheses, or a semicolon. They may also be signaled by words such as those in the following chart.

Words that Signal Definition or Restatement			
which	in other words	that is	or
this means	is/are	is/are called	is/are defined as

Can you spot the words that tell you that *condiments* is being defined in this sentence?

> **The sauces and relishes used to flavor foods are called condiments.**

If you picked out the words *are called,* you are correct.

Below, the meaning of *condiments* is made clear in a restatement. What clues help you spot this restatement?

> **The condiments —that is, the sauces and relishes used to flavor foods—are on the side table.**

Here, both dashes and the words *that is* serve as signals.

❷ Examples

Writers sometimes provide examples that reveal a word's meaning. For instance, look at the example of *stringent* here.

> **We have very stringent time limits, including a 14-minute lunch period and three minutes between classes.**

These are all words that often introduce examples.

Not all examples are signaled by clue words, however. Here, the examples of amphibians are introduced by a colon.

We have three amphibians in our science classroom: a toad, a frog, and a salamander.

❸ Comparisons and Contrasts

Sometimes a sentence compares or contrasts a familiar word with a less familiar one. When it compares the words, the unfamiliar word is similar in meaning to the word you know. When it contrasts them, the two words have opposite meanings. The following words often signal comparison and contrast.

Words that Signal Comparison and Contrast

like	as	in contrast to	on the other hand
likewise	similarly	instead of	not
		but	unlike

In the first sentence below, *like* signals the comparison between *shy* and *timid*. In the second sentence, *instead of* points out that *withdrawn* is the opposite of *talkative* and *pushy*.

Like my shy friend, Anna, I am timid in large groups.

With just Anna, I tend to be talkative and pushy instead of withdrawn.

VOCABULARY

❹ General Context

Sometimes the general context provides clues to a word's meaning. Photos, charts, signs, or even a whole paragraph can serve as the general context. Notice how the details in this description help you understand the word *shunned*.

> **LITERARY MODEL**
>
> In third grade, we had a very sweet nun, Sister Bridget, who used to play kickball with us. . . . One time someone kicked a ball so that it rolled foul. Retrieving it, I threw it to Sister; but. . . . I wound up hitting her in the head; and though there was no physical harm, I broke her glasses. Even though my parents paid for replacements, the rest of my class treated me as if I were taboo for striking a nun. I learned what it meant to be **shunned** and to be invisible.
>
> **CLUES**
>
> —Laurence Yep, "Chinatown"

PRACTICE → **Using Context Clues**

Use context clues to define the following underlined words.

1. We live in the <u>hinterlands</u> of Arizona—not in a city.
2. So when I wake up feeling <u>befuddled,</u> or foggy headed, I walk through the desert on my way to the bus.
3. One morning, to avoid stepping on a piece of cactus, I <u>lurched</u>—you know, staggered—to one side and fell.
4. That's when I noticed the snake, lying inches from my face, <u>lolling</u> in the uneven shade of a mesquite tree.
5. This was no <u>puny</u> garter snake but, rather, a big rattler.
6. Now, some people get startled if you drop a pencil, but I consider myself to be pretty <u>unflappable.</u>
7. I <u>gazed</u> at the snake and it, likewise, stared at me.
8. I was afraid to move, but if I remained <u>petrified</u> I would miss the bus.
9. Of course, missing the bus was a much smaller problem than the <u>dilemma</u> of how to get away from the rattler.
10. I decided to move backwards <u>gingerly.</u> I crept carefully until I was far enough away to get up and run.

(LESSON 3) Analyzing Word Parts

Words can be made up of various kinds of parts: base words, word roots, prefixes, and suffixes. You can often figure out the meaning of an unfamiliar word from the meanings of its parts.

❶ Base Words

A **base word** is a complete word that can stand alone. However, other words or word parts may be added to base words to form new words. The examples below show how adding a word part to a base word can form a new word.

fear + less = fearless
art + ist = artist

You can form a **compound word** by connecting two base words. The meaning of the new compound word is often, but not always, related to the meanings of the base words.

BASE + BASE = COMPOUND WORD
skate + board = skateboard

❷ Prefixes and Suffixes

A **prefix** is a word part attached to the beginning of a word or a word part. Prefixes change the meanings of words. As you read the examples below, try to think of other words that use the same prefixes.

Some Common Prefixes		
Prefix	**Meaning**	**Examples**
co-, com-, con-	together	coworker, compromise, contribute
de-	remove, reduce	depart, depopulate
in-, il-	not	incorrect, illogical
mis-	bad, wrong	mistake, misuse
re-	back, again	replace, reorganize
un-	the opposite of	untie, undrinkable

VOCABULARY

A **suffix** is a word part attached to the end of a word or a word part. The suffix usually determines the word's part of speech—that is, whether the word is a noun, verb, adjective, or adverb. For example, by adding different suffixes to the adjective *real* you can make *real**ity*** (noun), *real**ize*** (verb), and *real**ly*** (adverb).

You can create many new words simply by adding different prefixes and/or suffixes to one base word. Try it. How many words can you make from the word parts below?

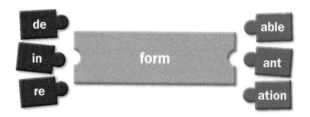

Notice how the base words below take on different meanings as prefixes and suffixes are added to them.

PREFIX +	BASE +	SUFFIX =	NEW WORD
un +	fair +	ness =	unfairness
in +	excuse +	able =	inexcusable
dis +	appear +	ance =	disappearance
re +	mind +	er =	reminder

You may need to change the spelling of some base words when adding suffixes: **excuse + able = excusable.**

For more about spelling changes, see Quick-Fix Spelling Machine, p. 568.

❸ Word Roots

Word roots, like base words, provide the basic meaning of a word. Unlike base words, however, word roots cannot stand alone. A prefix, a suffix, a base word, or another root must be added to a word root to make a word.

Many word roots in English come from ancient Greek or Latin. Becoming familiar with the meanings of common roots can help you figure out the meanings of unfamiliar words.

Common Roots

GREEK	Root	Meaning	Examples
	auto	self, same	automobile, autobiography
	hydr	water	hydrant, dehydrated
	meter, metr	measure	thermometer, metric
	plas	mold, form	plaster, plastic
	zo	animal	zoology, zookeeper

LATIN	Root	Meaning	Examples
	cent	hundred	century, centipede
	circ	ring	circle, circus
	oper	work	operate, cooperate
	pass	step	passage, trespass
	port	carry	portable, support

If you don't know what a word part means, you can look it up. Most dictionaries include entries for word roots, prefixes, and suffixes.

PRACTICE **Figure Them Out!**

Use the charts in this lesson and what you have learned about word parts to figure out the meanings of these words. Check your answers in a dictionary.

1. misdirect
2. unresponsive
3. commission
4. hydropower
5. misinformation
6. confirm
7. deport
8. recirculate
9. reinforce
10. insupportable

VOCABULARY

Understanding Related Words

LESSON 4

❶ Word Families

A **word family** is a group of words that share the same root. This word family shares the Latin root *fin*, from *fīnis*, meaning "end," "limit," or "boundary."

fin al
fin ally
fin alize
fin e
fin ish

fin alist
fin ality
fin ite
in **fin** ite
in **fin** ity

con **fin** e
de **fin** e
de **fin** ite
de **fin** itely
de **fin** ition

You can use the meanings of familiar words from a word family to figure out what their root means. You can also use their meanings to determine the meanings of unfamiliar words that share that root.

Here's How Using Word Families	
1. To figure out the meaning of the word *infinite*, first look for the root.	*fīnis* **or** *fin*
2. Think of other words with the same root.	*final*, *finish*, and *finally*
3. Figure out the meaning they share.	"end"
4. Look for prefixes and suffixes that may affect the meaning of your word.	*in-* ="not" *-ite* = "from"
5. Use all these clues to guess the word's meaning.	*Infinite* means "something that has no end."

CHAPTER 31

❷ Synonyms

Synonyms are different words that have similar meanings. For example, all of the words following the sentence below are synonyms for *ran*. However, since their meanings are slightly different, replacing *ran* with any one of them changes the meaning of the sentence. Try it and see.

I _ran_ **up the beach.**

jogged   hurried   dashed   raced

As you learn new words, pay attention to the slight differences in their meanings. Being aware of these differences can help you choose words more precisely.

Don't assume all synonyms can be used to replace one another. For example, *handsome* and *attractive* are both synonyms for *beautiful*, but most people don't use either to describe the weather.

PRACTICE **Fishing for Synonyms**

Replace the underlined word in each sentence with a synonym.

1. Although I don't <u>like</u> fishing, I do like boats, so I accepted my friend's invitation to join him and his family on a fishing trip.
2. The sea was calm when we <u>got</u> aboard the boat.
3. Despite the <u>calm</u> water, his mother offered ginger candy to anyone who thought he or she might get seasick.
4. Ginger is an old-fashioned <u>remedy</u> for nausea.
5. I wasn't worried about getting <u>seasick</u> because I never get seasick.
6. When we got a few miles offshore, though, the wind started to <u>blow</u> and I began to worry.
7. The water became choppy, making the boat <u>sway.</u>
8. Then I got a <u>fluttering</u> feeling in my belly.
9. "<u>Look</u> at the horizon," my friend's dad said reassuringly, "and don't forget to breathe."
10. I couldn't believe that doing two such simple things would <u>save</u> me, but it did.

VOCABULARY

What do you do if you come across a new word whose meaning you can't figure out from context clues or word parts? You could ask someone what it means—or you could look up the word in a dictionary.

❶ Dictionaries

Dictionaries can tell you more than just what words mean. Look at the following dictionary entries to see some of the many details a dictionary can provide about a word.

curable | currency	**GUIDE WORDS:** First and Last Entry Words on Page
cu·ri·ous (kyŏŏr′ ē əs) *adj.* **1.** Eager to learn more: *curious detectives.* **2.** Arousing interest because of strangeness: *We found a curious shell at the beach.* [First written down about 1340 in Middle English and spelled *curiouse,* from Latin *cūriōsus,* careful, inquisitive, from *cūra,* care.] **–cu′ri·ous·ly** *adv.* **–cu′ri·ous·ness** *n.*	**ENTRY WORD DIVIDED INTO SYLLABLES** · **PRONUNCIATION GUIDE** · **PART OF SPEECH** · **WORD ORIGINS** · **OTHER FORMS OF THE WORD**
Synonyms: curious, inquisitive, snoopy, nosy. **Antonym:** indifferent.	**SYNONYMS** · **ANTONYM**
curl (kûrl) *v.* **curled, curl·ing, curls.** *–tr.* **1.** To twist or form into coils or ringlets: *curl one's hair.* **2.** To make curved or twisted: *I curled the string around a pencil.* *–intr.* **1.** To form ringlets or curls: *Her hair curls when it dries.* **2.** To move in a curve or spiral: *Smoke curled from the chimney.* *–n.* **1.** A coil or ringlet of hair. **2.** Something with a spiral or coiled shape: *a curl of smoke.* **3.** A weightlifting exercise in which a barbell is raised to the chest or shoulder and lowered without moving the upper arms, shoulders, or back. *–idiom.* **curl up.** To sit or lie down with the legs drawn up: *He curled up on the sofa to read.*	**DEFINITION** · **SAMPLE SENTENCE** · **IDIOM**

—adapted from *The American Heritage Student Dictionary*

If a word has more than one meaning, how do you choose the right one?

Here's How Choosing the Right Definition

1. **Rule out definitions that don't make sense**, given what you're reading about. If you're reading about a girl getting ready for a party, for instance, you could rule out the third definition of *curl*.

2. **Try adding words to the sentence** that go with each particular meaning of the word. In "Sasha *has been doing curls* at the gym," you could try *"doing curls [in her hair]"* and *"doing curls [with weights]."*

3. **Pick the definition that best fits the sentence.** In "Sasha wants to wear her hair in curls," the first definition for the noun form works best.

❷ Thesauruses

A **thesaurus** is a dictionary of synonyms. Some thesauruses also include definitions, sample sentences, and **antonyms**— words that have opposite meanings to that of the entry word.

When you need to find a replacement for a word, look up the word in a thesaurus. Entries are often listed in alphabetical order.

curl, *verb*   PART OF SPEECH
   1. To have or cause to have a curved, winding, or wavy   DEFINITION
   form or surface. **syn:** *coil, curve, wave.* **2.** To move along a
   winding course. **syn:** *coil, corkscrew, snake, twist, weave,*   SYNONYMS
   wind. **ant:** *straight, uncurl.*   ANTONYMS

PRACTICE Check Your Definitions

In your 🗐 **Working Portfolio,** find your **Write Away** paragraph from page 511. Use a dictionary to find and include the definition of the word you wrote about. Then use a thesaurus to substitute specific, vivid words for more general ones.

Student Help Desk

Building Your Vocabulary at a Glance

Look for context clues.	Break the word into parts.	Look for similar words.	Use a dictionary.
Alice's singing was always **disruptive.** For example, today it stopped class.	dis rupt ive dis = apart rupt = break ive = inclined to	ab**rupt** **rupt**ure e**rupt**ion inter**rupt**ion bank**rupt**	**dis·rupt'·ive** (dĭs rŭp tĭv) *adj.* Causing disruption, disorder, or confusion

Pull Apart Puzzling Words

nonconformist: someone who refuses to behave and/or believe as most others do, an individual who refuses to try to "fit in" with the mainstream

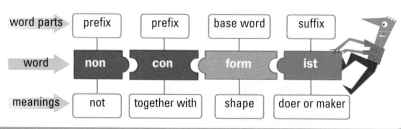

word parts	prefix	prefix	base word	suffix
word	**non**	**con**	**form**	**ist**
meanings	not	together with	shape	doer or maker

Spot Specific Context Clues

Type of Clue	Examples
Definition	You can just begin to see the stars at **dusk**—that time of the evening just before dark.
Restatement	At that time of day, my parents always go for a **brisk stroll**—that is, for a quick, energetic walk.
Example	Their evening walk is part of a whole health **regimen,** which includes drinking eight glasses of water a day and flossing after meals.
Comparison	My mom is now **ardent** about walking, and my dad is similarly passionate about it.
Contrast	They also have a lot more **vitality** since they began walking, unlike before, when they had very little energy for anything.

Interpret Suffix Signals

	Suffix	Meaning	Examples
Nouns	-er, -ist, -or	doer, performer	runner, columnist
	-ation, -ment	action, process	admiration, astonishment
	-ism	idea, theory	patriotism
	-ity, -ness, -ship, -tude	condition, quality, state	fragility, shyness, friendship, gratitude
Verbs	-ate	to act upon	aggravate
	-en	to become, to cause to have	tighten
	-ize	to cause to be, to become	terrorize
Adjectives	-able, -ible	able, inclined to, worthy	reasonable, terrible
	-ant	to act a certain way	important
	-ful	full of, resembling	wonderful
	-ous	full of, having	glorious
Adverbs	-ily, -ly	in the manner of, like	craftily, slowly

The Bottom Line

Checklist for Building Your Vocabulary

Have I . . .

_____ looked at the context of the word to find clues to its meaning?

_____ analyzed the parts of the word?

_____ tried to think of other words in the same family?

_____ looked up the word in the dictionary?

_____ used a thesaurus to find synonyms for the word?

_____ used the word in my conversations and writing?

Student Resources

Exercise Bank   528

Model Bank   562

    Book Review
    Editorial
    Letter of Complaint
    Thank-You Letter
    Comparison-Contrast Essay
    Cause-and-Effect Essay
    Analyzing a Subject

Quick-Fix Spelling Machine   568

    Plurals of Nouns
    Possessives
    Words Ending in Silent *e*
    Words Ending in *y*
    Words Ending in a Consonant
    Adverbs
    Compounds
    Open and Closed Syllables
    Contractions
    Seed Sorter
    ie and *ei* Engines
    Borrowed Words
    Commonly Misspelled Words

Commonly Confused Words   578

MLA Citation Guidelines   582

Glossary for Writers   590

Index   598

Acknowledgments   621

Exercise Bank

Boost your grammar fitness! Use the Exercise Bank to find the answers to the Self-Check items that are circled in yellow ➡ . In addition, you can complete exercises in this section to get extra practice in a skill you've just learned.

1 The Sentence and Its Parts

1. Complete Subjects and Predicates (links to exercise on p. 7)

➡ **1.** CS: People around the world; CP: tell Cinderella stories.
2. CS: The oldest version of all; CP: comes from China.

On a sheet of paper, label one column "Complete Subjects" and a second column "Complete Predicates." Write the complete subject and the complete predicate in each sentence below.

1. "Cinderella" is one of the best-known folktales.
2. Similar stories exist in many cultures.
3. The main characters go by different names.
4. An ancient Egyptian story tells of Rhodopis.
5. The poor young woman is sold into slavery.
6. Her master gives her a pair of slippers.
7. A great falcon carries off one of the slippers.
8. The bird drops it in the Pharaoh's lap.
9. This powerful ruler searches for the slipper's owner.
10. Rhodopis marries the Pharaoh at the end of the story.

2. Simple Subjects (links to exercise A, p. 9)

➡ **1.** tortoise   **2.** rabbit

On a separate sheet of paper, write the simple subject in each sentence.

1. A poor woodcutter lived with his wife in a humble cottage.
2. One day, a fairy granted him three wishes.
3. The excited couple discussed their good fortune at dinner.
4. The hungry husband carelessly wished for a sausage.
5. A huge sausage fell onto the table.
6. The wife complained about his wasteful wish.
7. Her spouse made another wish.
8. Now the sausage hung from the wife's nose.
9. The startled man wished for the disappearance of the sausage.
10. Three wishes brought him nothing but regret!

3. Simple Predicates, or Verbs (links to exercise A, p. 11)

➡ **1.** is **2.** served

On a separate sheet of paper, write the simple predicate, or verb, in each sentence.

1. Diane Wolkstein is a distinguished storyteller, writer, and teacher.
2. After college, this New York City native studied pantomime in Paris.
3. She returned to New York City in 1967.
4. The city's Department of Parks and Recreation offered her a job as a recreational director.
5. In the city's parks, Wolkstein told stories from around the world.
6. She hosted the radio program *Stories from Many Lands with Diane Wolkstein* for 12 years.
7. One writer described her as New York City's official storyteller.
8. Wolkstein travels to many lands in search of folktales.
9. Her seven trips to Haiti provided material for three books.
10. Students eagerly attend Wolkstein's classes and workshops on storytelling.

4. Verb Phrases (links to exercise on p. 13)

➡ **1.** was searching **2.** should be

Write the verb phrase in each sentence. Be sure to include all the helping verbs.

1. Perhaps you have heard some stories by Hans Christian Andersen.
2. People have been enjoying this Danish writer's tales for more than 150 years.
3. A statue of Andersen was built in New York City's Central Park.
4. You may have read Andersen's tale "The Ugly Duckling."
5. The main character is hatched from an unusually large egg.
6. He does experience cruelty and rejection because of his appearance.
7. Of course, a surprise is awaiting him at the end of the story.
8. He has been a swan and not a duckling all along.
9. Andersen's stories probably will be popular for years to come.
10. You might know some of his other tales as well.

5. Compound Sentence Parts (links to exercise A, p. 15)

→ **1.** ant *and* grasshopper   **2.** hopped *and* sang

On a separate sheet of paper, write the compound subject or compound verb in each sentence.

1. Homer composed and recited epic poems in ancient Greece.
2. The *Odyssey* and the *Iliad* are his two great works.
3. Odysseus, the hero of the *Odyssey,* travels home after a war and experiences difficulties along the way.
4. Many different characters and events delay him.
5. Scheming goddesses and horrible monsters set traps for him.
6. Cyclops, a giant one-eyed monster, captures and threatens Odysseus.
7. Odysseus thinks fast and invents a clever trick.
8. He and some of his companions blind the monster.
9. They race to the shore and sail away.
10. The furious Cyclops curses them and vows revenge.

6. Kinds of Sentences (links to exercise A, p. 17)

→ **1.** D   **2.** INT

Identify each of the following sentences as declarative (D), interrogative (INT), exclamatory (E), or imperative (IMP).

1. Have you read the Chinese folktale "A Grain of Rice"?
2. Pong Lo, a poor young man, asks to marry the Emperor's daughter.
3. How dare he make such a request!
4. The Emperor threatens to have Pong Lo beheaded.
5. Instead, Pong Lo works hard for the Emperor and proves his worth.
6. Didn't the Emperor's daughter become sick?
7. Tell me how Pong Lo saves her life.
8. The grateful Emperor offers Pong Lo anything except his daughter's hand in marriage.
9. Pong Lo cleverly asks for one grain of rice, to be doubled each day for 100 days.
10. Explain how Pong Lo grows rich and marries the Emperor's daughter.

7. Subjects in Unusual Order (links to exercise A, p. 20)

➡️ **1.** Subject: *friends;* verb: *are* **2.** Subject: *(You)*; verb: *Tell*

In two columns on a separate sheet of paper, write the simple subject and the verb (or verb phrase) in each sentence.

1. Listen to the tale of Alfred Bulltop Stormalong.
2. Across the ocean sailed this enormous ship's captain.
3. There goes his unbelievably large ship.
4. Did the crew ride across the colossal deck on horses?
5. To the top of an extremely tall mast climbs a young sailor.
6. Here comes the most incredible part!
7. Years later, down climbs the same fellow with a long, gray beard!
8. Do you know any more tall tales?
9. Tell me another.
10. Use plenty of exaggeration.

8. Complements: Subject Complements (links to exercise A, p. 22)

➡️ **1.** legendary PA **4.** storytellers PN

Write the underlined word in each sentence, and identify it as either a predicate noun (PN) or a predicate adjective (PA).

1. John Henry is an American folk <u>hero</u>.
2. Maybe this African-American man was a real <u>person</u>.
3. According to some, he was a <u>worker</u> on a railroad-building project in the 1870s.
4. His life is the <u>subject</u> of a famous ballad.
5. In the ballad, his strength is <u>extraordinary</u>.
6. He is the <u>winner</u> in a contest with a powerful new steam drill.
7. His determination is <u>remarkable</u>, although the strain of winning kills him.
8. The victorious steel-driving man became a <u>legend</u>.
9. The legend grew more <u>famous</u> with each passing year.
10. John Henry is a <u>symbol</u> of the unbeatable human spirit.

9. Complements: Objects of Verbs (links to exercise on p. 24)

➔ **1.** beans (DO)   **4.** Jack (IO), breakfast (DO)

Write each object of a verb, and identify it as a direct object (DO) or an indirect object (IO).

1. Our class is planning a storytelling festival.
2. We called a professional storyteller.
3. She taught us her secrets.
4. We will invite students from other classes to our festival.
5. We can send them flyers a week before the big event.
6. At the library, Ms. Leung showed me several collections of folktales.
7. I must find just the right story.
8. Perhaps my grandmother can give me some advice.
9. The drama department lent our class a video camera.
10. Now we can film our performances.

10. Fragments and Run-Ons (links to exercise A, p. 27)

➔ **1.** CS   **2.** RO

Identify each of the following sentences as a fragment (F), a run-on (RO), or a complete sentence (CS).

1. Are cartoons that tell a story.
2. The boxes containing the scenes are called panels, the spaces containing the dialogue are called speech balloons.
3. Comic strips first appeared in newspapers in the 1890s.
4. Early comic strips featured humorous characters and situations, many people called them "funnies."
5. Some people still use that word to refer to comic strips.
6. Cartoonists of the 1930s.
7. Created dramatic and adventurous comic strips.
8. Today's audiences will recognize several comic-strip characters from the 1920s and 1930s.
9. Include Superman, Dick Tracy, and Little Orphan Annie.
10. Two of these characters have appeared in both movies and television shows, and one has appeared in a play.

2 Nouns

1. What Is a Noun? (links to exercise on p. 37)

➜ **1.** *place:* common   **2.** *Pompeii, Italy:* proper

Write each noun and identify it as common or proper.

1. In 1879, a father and his young daughter, Maria, explored a cave in Spain.
2. The cave was near their castle.
3. Maria held her candle up and saw paintings on the ceiling.
4. Each painting of an animal had been made by an artist more than 12,000 years ago.
5. In 1947, a young boy named Muhammad ed-dhib lost a goat near his village in Palestine.
6. While searching for the goat, Muhammad discovered a cave.
7. Later, Muhammad and a friend went back to the cave and found ancient biblical scrolls more than 2,000 years old.
8. The important writings are called the Dead Sea Scrolls.
9. In about 1871, Heinrich Schliemann found the lost city of Troy in what is now Turkey.
10. He had dreamed of finding the city since his days as a student.

2. Singular and Plural Nouns (links to exercise A, p. 39)

➜ **1.** priests; bodies   **2.** Egyptians

Rewrite the nouns in parentheses in their plural forms.

1. The ancient Egyptians buried precious (object) with their dead rulers.
2. Some ancient (Sumerian) buried other people with their royalty.
3. (Archaeologist) found many tombs in Ur, one of the ancient (city) of the Sumerians.
4. (Search) uncovered as many as 74 skeletons in one tomb.
5. Some skeletons were (man) clutching spears.
6. Others were (woman) wearing fancy gold (headdress).
7. (Photo) of the tombs show gold helmets and jewelry.
8. Also found in the tombs were the (remain) of (donkey) and oxen but no (sheep).
9. The Sumerians apparently believed that some people should take their (journey) to the afterlife with their king.
10. Did they agree to die so that their (life) could continue along with their king?

3. Possessive Nouns (links to exercise A, p. 42)

➡ **1.** England's; singular   **2.** Harbor's; singular

Write the possessive form of each noun in parentheses. Then identify each possessive noun as singular or plural.

1. Until recently, (archaeologists) discoveries were made without the help of technology.
2. Explorers hacking through a jungle stumbled upon a (temple) remains.
3. Farmers opened a huge mound in their fields and found an ancient (peoples) burial site.
4. (Today) aerial photos can reveal unusual sites to explore.
5. Vegetation, for example, grows lush in (Guatemala) deep soil.
6. A bare site may signal that something solid lies underneath the (soil) surface.
7. Satellite photos can show a (ruin) outlines.
8. A (technician) discovery of the faint outlines of forgotten roads has led to the finding of lost cities.
9. (Explorers) use of radar has located objects buried in the earth.
10. Computers have been used to improve a (document) image.

4. Nouns and Their Jobs (links to exercise A, p. 44)

➡ **1.** Inca: subject   **2.** Cuzco: subject; capital: complement

Identify each underlined noun as a subject, a complement, or an object of a preposition.

1. John Lloyd Stephens was an American lawyer.
2. In 1836, he researched ancient ruins in Central America.
3. Stephens was interested in lost civilizations.
4. He planned an expedition to find the ruins.
5. Stephens gave artist Frederick Catherwood a chance to go along on the trip.
6. In 1839, the two men explored a humid jungle in Honduras.
7. As they hacked through the thick vegetation, they came upon a tall stone pillar.
8. They also uncovered buildings overgrown with lush vines.
9. Their discovery was an ancient city.
10. Catherwood's drawings sparked interest in Mayan cities.

3 Pronouns

1. What Is a Pronoun? (links to exercise A, p. 55)

➡ **1.** you   **4.** they

List the personal pronoun(s) in each sentence.

1. Sheila is my best friend, but she makes really bad puns.
2. Once I told her that our family flew to Los Angeles.
3. "Did your arms get tired?" she asked. *Ha, ha,* I thought.
4. Reggie made the mistake of saying he ate a can of soup for his lunch.
5. What did Sheila say? "I hope you got the lead out."
6. My cousin Judith once complained to her, "This pencil needs sharpening."
7. Sheila fired back, "So, what's your point?"
8. We just groan at some of her jokes and how bad they are.
9. One day, I told her, "Don't punish us like this."
10. "Good one!" she said. "I will write it down."

2. Subject Pronouns (links to exercise on p. 58)

➡ **1.** They   **2.** she

Choose the correct pronoun in parentheses to complete each sentence.

1. Who reads books about childhood friends of famous people? That reader is (I, me).
2. (I, Me) read a story about the architect Frank Lloyd Wright.
3. (He, Him) designed many famous buildings in the United States.
4. One day, when Frank was 14, (he, him) noticed a group of bullies across the street.
5. (They, Them) had pulled crutches away from a classmate.
6. Was their victim Robie Lamp, a boy who had had polio? Yes, it was definitely (he, him).
7. Frank stood up to the bullies, and (they, them) backed off.
8. After that, Frank and Robie became good friends. Full of ideas, (they, them) often drew sketches of their inventions.
9. In one article, (I, me) read that they designed fantastic kites.
10. Lifelong friends and creators were (they, them)!

3. Subject and Object Pronouns (links to exercise on p. 60)

→ **1.** us (object)   **3.** He (subject)

Choose the correct pronoun(s) in parentheses. Identify each correct pronoun as a subject or an object.

1. (I, Me) just started going to a new middle school.
2. Rosa gave (I, me) advice about making friends.
3. (She, Her) said to smile and act friendly.
4. Let people know you're interested in (they, them).
5. (They, Them) want to make friends too, you know.
6. Do you like someone's new outfit? Tell (he or she, him or her) that.
7. I told (she, her) that one of the boys looked friendly.
8. She told me, "Ask (he, him) questions to find out if you like some of the same things."
9. I followed her advice, and guess what? (We, Us) both happen to like diving.
10. Between you and (I, me), making new friends is easier than I expected.

4. Possessive Pronouns (links to exercise A, p. 63)

→ **2.** its   **4.** Your

Choose the correct word in parentheses.

1. (Your, You're) not going to believe this story about a loyal friend.
2. (Its, It's) main character is a real dog named Hachi, who lived in Japan years ago.
3. Imagine this: (it's, its) 5:00 P.M. at a railroad station in Tokyo.
4. Every night at this time, Hachi goes to the station to greet his master. (It's, Its) no different this night.
5. City workers are getting off the train. (They're, their) tired after a long day's work.
6. Hachi searches (they're, their) faces. He doesn't see his master.
7. How could the dog know that his master died in the city that day? (You're, Your) probably thinking that's the end of the story, but it isn't.
8. Every evening for the rest of his life, Hachi comes to the station at 5:00 to wait for his master. You could set (your, you're) watch by him.

9. Each night, Hachi returns home alone. (Its, It's) a sad story but true.
10. The Japanese showed (their, they're) respect for Hachi's loyalty. After he died, they erected a statue of him on the spot where he used to wait for his master.

5. Reflexive and Intensive Pronouns (links to exercise on p. 65)

➡ **1.** herself—reflexive   **3.** themselves—reflexive

Write the reflexive or intensive pronoun in each sentence. Then identify it as reflexive or intensive.

1. Have you ever found yourself going a little crazy during a sporting event?
2. I myself went wild when the U.S. women's soccer team won the World Cup in 1999.
3. More than 90,000 fans in the Rose Bowl cheered themselves into a frenzy.
4. President Clinton himself was there to see the thrilling triumph.
5. The game itself was long and grueling: 120 minutes of play without a score.
6. Then both teams—the United States and China—found themselves playing in sudden-death overtime and facing a final shootout.
7. Brandi Chastain herself scored the winning penalty kick.
8. The 1999 event didn't mark the first time that the young women proved themselves champions.
9. The team had set a high standard for itself by winning the World Cup in 1991 and an Olympic gold medal in 1996.
10. Today, more than 7 million girls in the United States challenge themselves by playing on soccer teams.

6. Interrogatives and Demonstratives (links to exercise A, p. 68)

➡ **1.** Who; Int. **4.** who, Int.

Choose the correct word in parentheses to complete each sentence.

1. This Bugs Bunny video is (who's, whose)?
2. Bugs Bunny has starred in 263 short films, 10 long movies, 11 TV movies, and 6 TV series. (That, Those) would be big numbers for a human actor!

3. (Whose, Who's) always saying, "You're disss-picable!"
4. (That, Those) is Daffy Duck, who always loses out to Bugs.
5. (Who, Whom) is the guy called "Doc"?
6. I know to (who, whom) you're referring. It's Elmer Fudd.
7. (Whose, Who's) often grumbling "that rackin' frackin' varmint"?
8. Yosemite Sam—that's (who, whom)!
9. Your favorite character on Bugs Bunny is (who, whom)?
10. (Who, Whom) do you think of first?

7. Pronoun-Antecedent Agreement (links to exercise on p. 71)

➜ **2.** her—Annemarie Johansen   **5.** their—Nazis

Write the pronoun and its antecedent in each sentence or pair of sentences.

1. Chimpanzees raised in captivity cannot survive on their own in the wild.
2. People have donated their time and money to build chimpanzee shelters in Africa.
3. Jane Goodall, a famous wildlife expert, said she would help set up the shelters.
4. In the wild, a baby chimp might nurse from its mother for as long as five years.
5. At the shelters, baby chimps receive their milk from bottles.
6. Each caretaker, as part of his or her job, must teach the chimps new survival skills.
7. One female chimp had lived for years in a cage. She had to learn how to climb trees and pick berries.
8. One orphan had become sick and had lost all his hair.
9. The orphan was named Uruhara. It means "bald" in an African language.
10. In the sanctuary, Uruhara received lots of love and good care. Now he has hair again!

8. Indefinite Pronoun Agreement (links to exercise A, p. 74)

➜ **1.** their   **2.** his

Choose the correct pronoun(s) to complete the sentences.

1. All of the early Pilgrims owed (his or her, their) survival to the Wampanoag Indians.
2. Because nobody knew what to eat, (he or she, they) had to learn from the Wampanoags what foods to plant and harvest.

3. In 1621, many of the Pilgrims asked the Wampanoags to join (them, him or her) in a feast of thanksgiving.
4. At the feast, everyone could eat (his or her, their) fill of venison stew.
5. If someone preferred other food, (he or she, they) could have wild turkey or oysters.
6. All of the oysters were baked in (its, their) shells over an open fire.
7. Pumpkins were baked also. Each simmered in (its, their) maple syrup flavoring.
8. All could fill (his or her, their) wooden plates with sweet corn baked in the husk.
9. At least one of the Wampanoags brought venison as (his, their) contribution to the feast.
10. All of the Wampanoag and Pilgrim leaders ate (his or her, their) meal at a special table.

9. Pronoun Problems (links to exercise A, p. 76)

➡ **2.** us

Write the correct word in parentheses to complete each sentence.

1. (We, Us) tennis players are impressed by the champion sisters Venus and Serena Williams.
2. Our tennis coach gave (we, us) players tickets for the 1999 U.S. Open.
3. Serena Williams stunned (we, us) viewers at the final by defeating No. 1–ranked Martina Hingis.
4. In the semifinals, (we, us) spectators had seen Martina defeat Venus Williams, Serena's older sister.
5. Serena's victory even surprised (we, us) fans since this was her first appearance in a Grand Slam final.
6. (We, Us) sports historians know that she is the first African-American woman to win a major tennis title since 1958.
7. Serena and Martina competed fiercely for the trophy. When the match finally ended, (Serena, she) had won!
8. Both Venus and Serena are coached by their father. (Venus, She) and her sister have played together since childhood.
9. I wonder what that's like for (her, Serena).
10. Serena and Venus practice tennis on their home courts. (Serena, She) always gets a good workout!

10. More Pronoun Problems (links to exercise A, p. 78)

➜ **1.** me **4.** her

Write the correct pronoun to complete each sentence.

1. Natalie and (me, I) surveyed kids who were best friends.
2. Both (she, her) and (me, I) reported the answers in our school newspaper.
3. Between you and (I, me), we thought our questions were pretty good.
4. We interviewed several people. Natalie asked (them, they) all, "Is it okay for friends to fight?"
5. Dominic, unlike most of the kids, wanted (his, their) answers kept private.
6. Richard, who has lots of friends, brought (his, their) oldest friend, Greg, to the interview.
7. We asked (he, him) and Greg, "How much time do you think friends should spend together?"
8. Hillary and Ming-Jie had (their, her) turn next.
9. We asked Hillary and (her, she), "Would you lie to a friend to save her feelings?"
10. Ming-Jie and (she, her) agreed that friends should be honest, even if sometimes the truth hurts!

4 Verbs

1. What Is a Verb? (links to exercise A, p. 90)

➜ **1.** developed **2.** traveled

Write the verb or verb phrase in each of the following sentences.

1. Submarines float easily.
2. They also can dive all the way to the ocean floor.
3. They may stay underwater for months.
4. They operate underwater with the help of double-hull construction.
5. Between the inner and outer hulls are ballast tanks.
6. The sailors flood these tanks with seawater.
7. The seawater increases the ship's weight.
8. Horizontal rudders, or hydroplanes, steer the ship downward.
9. While underwater, the sailors navigate with radar, sonar, and periscopes.
10. The ship rises to the surface with the removal of the seawater from its ballast tanks.

2. Action Verbs and Objects (links to exercise A, p. 93)

→ **1.** us (indirect object); risks (direct object)
2. world (indirect object); automobile (direct object)

Write the 15 complements in these sentences. If the sentence contains no complements, write *None*.

1. Motorcycle-type engines give snowmobiles power.
2. The vehicles' handlebars connect to a pair of skis up front.
3. This connection gives drivers steering ability.
4. Instead of a rear wheel, a continuous rubber track propels them.
5. A throttle lends drivers a means of acceleration.
6. A brake lever enables drivers to stop.
7. Snowmobiles can achieve speeds exceeding 85 miles an hour.
8. They can climb slopes of 65 degrees.
9. Snowmobiles take people groceries in inaccessible areas.
10. They also can give their riders a thrill.

3. Linking Verbs and Predicate Words (links to exercise on p. 95)

→ **1.** was (linking verb); woman (predicate noun)
4. seemed (linking verb); candidate (predicate noun)

Identify each linking verb, predicate noun, and predicate adjective in the sentences below.

1. Bangladesh is a small country between India and Myanmar, on the Bay of Bengal.
2. It has become a very densely populated country.
3. Its capital, Dacca, has grown large.
4. The main mode of transportation in Dacca is the rickshaw.
5. These rickshaws are three-wheeled vehicles powered by humans.
6. They are completely dependent on human power, with no motor of any kind.
7. There must be about 400,000 rickshaws in Dacca.
8. Many people appear dependent on them for transport.
9. Rickshaw transport looks convenient for riders.
10. Yet the job of powering them seems very hard on the drivers.

4. Principal Parts of Verbs (links to exercise on p. 97)

➡ **1**. past participle   **3**. past

Identify the form of each underlined verb as the present, the present participle, the past, or the past participle.

If you **(1)** <u>walked</u> somewhere today, you **(2)** <u>used</u> the most healthful form of transportation. Walking **(3)** <u>gives</u> you a sense of well-being and energy. It **(4)** <u>helps</u> you beat stress. Walking two miles a day **(5)** <u>protects</u> your heart. A person who **(6)** <u>is running</u> down the road is also protecting his or her heart. But running eventually **(7)** <u>causes</u> wear and tear on the body, especially knee joints. However, walking **(8)** <u>benefits</u> your health for a lifetime. And if you **(9)** <u>have gone</u> for a walk in the woods on a beautiful day, you **(10)** <u>have discovered</u> another good reason to walk: it's fun.

5. Irregular Verbs (links to exercise on p. 100)

➡ **1**. began   **2**. ran

Choose the correct form of the verb to complete each sentence.

1. People around the world have always (made, maked) use of rivers and oceans for transportation.
2. In the 19th century, it (costed, cost) a fortune to transport goods to California from the east coast.
3. Ships (goed, went) all the way around South America—nearly 8,000 additional miles—to get there.
4. Sometimes ships (sank, sinked) at sea, which killed passengers and destroyed cargo.
5. Eventually, people (thought, thinked) of a way to shorten the trip.
6. They (digged, dug) a canal across the Isthmus of Panama.
7. They (spent, spended) ten years working on the canal.
8. It (runned, ran) more than 40 miles between the Caribbean Sea and the Pacific Ocean.
9. Many of the canal workers (fell, falled) ill with malaria.
10. The Panama Canal (became, becomed) a much-needed shortcut for cargo ships carrying such important goods as fuel and food.

6. Simple Tenses (links to exercise A, p. 103)

➡ **1**. past   **5**. present

Identify the tense of each underlined verb as present, past, or future.

1. In the middle of the 19th century, the Oregon Trail <u>served</u> as the route to the West for 80,000 to 200,000 pioneers.

2. The 2,000-mile journey <u>attracted</u> gold hunters, fur traders, missionaries, and especially farmers.
3. To this day, their destination, the Pacific Northwest, <u>has</u> some of the most fertile farmland in the world.
4. During much of 1986, pilot and history buff Maurice Brett <u>was retracing</u> the settlers' trip in his airplane.
5. He <u>documented</u> the journey with photographs and movies.
6. In rocky sections of the trail, the ruts from heavy wagons <u>are</u> still three feet deep.
7. In grassy sections, the tracks from the wagon wheels <u>are</u> still <u>showing</u> in the soil.
8. It <u>took</u> the pioneers four to six months to make the journey Brett completed in 12 days by plane.
9. Brett <u>will write</u> a book about the experience.
10. He <u>will enjoy</u> the memory of his experience for many years to come.

7. Perfect Tenses (links to exercise A, p. 106)

➡ **1**. Past. Perf.   **3**. Pres. Perf.

Write the verb in each sentence, and identify its tense as present perfect, past perfect, or future perfect.

1. For centuries, navigation has been a challenge.
2. At the end of their journeys sailors in ancient times often had ended up continents away from their destinations.
3. By the late 1950s, scientists had invented artificial satellites.
4. Satellites have been a huge help to navigation.
5. They have led to the development of the Global Positioning System (GPS).
6. This navigation system has used signals from at least three satellites at any one time.
7. People in trackless wilderness have found their way with portable GPS receivers, accurate to within 10 meters.
8. People also have used GPS successfully from cars, ships, and planes.
9. Perhaps someday, every car will have acquired a GPS receiver.
10. By then, global positioning will have rescued millions of lost travelers.

8. Using Verb Tenses (links to exercise A, p. 110)

➡ **1.** have used   **2.** opened

Choose the correct verb form from the choices in parentheses to complete each sentence.

1. One of the biggest drawbacks of cars always (has been, had been) pollution.
2. Early cars were so few in number that they (have done, did) little damage to the air.
3. The petroleum-based fuels used in automobiles (produce, will have produced) toxic emissions, such as carbon monoxide.
4. Petroleum-based engine oils (stay, had stayed) dangerous to the environment for a long time—they aren't biodegradable.
5. Now, scientists (had developed, are developing) new car fuels and lubricants from plants.
6. One of these new plant sources (is, was) sunflowers.
7. Sunflower oil (will create, creates) fewer particles than petroleum-based oils.
8. Therefore, sunflower oil (can keep, will have kept) a car's exhaust system cleaner than petroleum-based oils.
9. Some scientists predict that plant-based fuels and oils (will replace, have replaced) petroleum in the not-too-distant future.
10. They (reduce, will reduce) air pollution in years to come.

9. Troublesome Verb Pairs (links to exercise A, p. 113)

➡ **1.** lies   **3.** learned

Choose the correct word in parentheses in each of the following sentences.

1. Isle Royale (lies, lays) in the northwest section of Lake Superior.
2. When the state of Michigan was (laid, lay) out, Isle Royale became part of it.
3. This island first (rose, raised) to fame thousands of years ago when Indians mined its copper deposits.
4. Now it (teaches, learns) backpackers to appreciate the beauty of nature.
5. Rock ridges (raise, rise) hundreds of feet along the island's spine.
6. Moose and wolves (lay, lie) hidden in the pine forests.

7. Isle Royale is unspoiled partly because of the barriers nature has (raised, risen) around it.

8. Park rangers (taught, learned) us that the island became Isle Royale National Park in 1931.

9. To get to the island, pilots (sit, set) down seaplanes on the lake regularly.

10. The only other way to get to Isle Royale from the mainland is by (sitting, setting) for hours on a ferryboat.

5 Adjectives and Adverbs

1. What Is an Adjective? (links to exercise on p. 124)

→ 1. American, landmark
  2. dirty, swamp; ugly, shacks; much, garbage

Write each adjective and the noun or pronoun it modifies. Do not include articles.

1. Camping during a cold winter has numerous advantages.

2. Ordinary insects cannot live in the extreme cold.

3. Wild animals can be spotted easily against the white snow.

4. Knowledgeable campers appreciate the natural beauty of the wintry wilderness.

5. Winter camping provides a great opportunity to have the whole campsite to yourself.

6. On the other hand, slippery ice can complicate outdoor activities.

7. The variable temperatures of North American winters can create a variety of dangerous conditions.

8. If you have snowy weather and can't use your stove, you can't just order fast food.

9. Wet woolen sweaters take a long time to dry.

10. Even normal winter temperatures may cause serious discomfort.

2. Predicate Adjectives (links to exercise A, p. 126)

→ **1.** inactive, Mount St. Helens   **2.** dangerous, volcano

Write the predicate adjective in each sentence, along with the noun it modifies.

1. On August 26, 1883, the island of Krakatoa looked frightful.
2. The island's volcano became active.
3. The ground felt shaky.
4. Explosions, which happened every ten minutes, sounded loud.
5. Because of thick smoke, the entire area seemed foggy.
6. As a result of the volcanic activity, waves in the sea grew gigantic.
7. For months after the eruptions, the atmosphere remained dusty.
8. The sky felt dark because thick clouds blocked the sun's light.
9. Following the eruptions, the sun sometimes appeared green.
10. Most of Krakatoa collapsed into the sea; the island was lost forever.

3. Other Words Used as Adjectives (links to exercise A, p. 129)

→ **1.** most, climbers; mountain, formations   **2.** city, buildings

Write each noun or pronoun that is used as an adjective in these sentences, along with the word it modifies.

1. Would you crawl on your belly in a dark cave?
2. That activity appeals to many people known as cavers.
3. A cave adventure is nearly irresistible to them.
4. Cavers crawl through limestone passages, climb over rock bridges, and explore unusual formations.
5. These adventurers wear a helmet lamp, knee pads, warm clothes, and safety boots.
6. A cave guide helps cavers find their way.
7. One South Dakota cave is famous for its length of hundreds of miles.
8. Its temperature is always the same, no matter what the weather situation aboveground.
9. This cave has never been completely explored.
10. In some caves, you can see popcorn formations and soda straws, an unusual cavern feature.

4. What Is an Adverb? (links to exercise A, p. 132)

➡ **1.** *very, curious,* adjective
2. *studied, quite, often,* V, Adv.

Write each adverb and the word it modifies. Then identify the modified word as a verb, an adjective, or an adverb. There may be more than one adverb in a sentence.

1. Sacajawea played a very valuable role in the Lewis and Clark expedition.
2. Initially, Lewis and Clark hired a French-Canadian trader to help them understand the Native Americans they encountered.
3. They realized that the trader's wife was a more suitable interpreter.
4. Sacajawea, a Shoshone Indian, was just barely 17 or 18 when she joined the expedition.
5. She was obviously quite familiar with Native American culture.
6. As the expedition traveled west, her presence helped reassure wary tribes.
7. Patiently, Sacajawea showed the explorers how to find food.
8. She once bravely rescued scientific instruments from a sinking boat.
9. Sacajawea's son, Jean Baptiste, later became a translator himself for western travelers.
10. Today, many monuments honor Sacajawea's extremely important contributions.

5. Making Comparisons (links to exercise A, p. 135)

➡ **1.** largest   **2.** richest

Choose the word in parentheses that correctly completes each sentence.

1. Growing only about 13 feet long, a pygmy sperm whale is the (smaller/smallest) of all sperm whales.
2. A sei whale swims (more rapidly/most rapidly) than a blue whale.
3. The gray whale makes one of the (longest/more longest) migrations of any mammal, a journey of about 12,000 miles per year.
4. Sperm whales are the (better/best) divers of all.
5. A male humpback sings (more distinctively/most distinctively) than a female.
6. Humpbacks produce (more varied/most varied) sounds than gray whales.

7. Humpbacks sing (less/least) frequently than usual when they are feeding.
8. Whales can breathe (more efficiently/most efficiently) than humans because they can store and transport more oxygen.
9. Right whales are (more easily/most easily) hunted than other whales because right whales are slow swimmers.
10. Because they use technology to hunt whales, humans pose the (worse/worst) of all threats to whale populations.

6. Adjective or Adverb? (links to exercise on p. 137)

➜ 1. *well,* adverb 2. *real,* adjective

Choose the correct modifier in parentheses, then identify it as an adjective or an adverb.

1. When John James Audubon was a young adult, his business ventures turned out (bad/badly).
2. Because he could paint (good/well) and had a great love of nature, he eventually became an artist and a naturalist.
3. In the early 1800s, he had roamed the countryside and studied birds (real/really) closely.
4. Usually, he sketched (real/really) specimens of birds.
5. His paintings capture birds very (good/well) in their natural settings.
6. In Pennsylvania, Audubon took a (bad/badly) fall into a frozen creek.
7. While in the South, he felt (bad/badly) after he got yellow fever.
8. Despite such risks, Audubon conducted a (good/well) search for many different species of birds.
9. *The Birds of America* is a (real/really) beautiful collection of his paintings.
10. Audubon made a (real/really) contribution to natural history as well as to art.

7. Avoiding Double Negatives (links to exercise A, p. 139)

➡ **1.** any   **2.** have

Write the word in parentheses that correctly completes each sentence.

1. There hasn't (ever/never) been a higher temperature recorded in the world than 136°F.

2. This temperature couldn't occur (anywhere/nowhere) but in a desert—in this case, the Sahara, in northern Africa.

3. Much of the Sahara isn't (nothing/anything) but empty plateaus and plains.

4. Most plants and animals can't thrive (nowhere/anywhere) but near an oasis.

5. Grasses, shrubs, and trees (can/can't) scarcely get by in some parts of the Sahara.

6. Some short-lived plants there don't (ever/never) live for more than six to eight weeks.

7. Lizards, some gazelles, and foxes that inhabit the Sahara can live for long periods without (no/any) water to drink.

8. Many human residents don't live (nowhere/anywhere) permanently but travel seasonally to find available water.

9. Typically, these nomads don't have (no/any) cars.

10. Because the roads in the Sahara are so poor, these people couldn't go (nowhere/anywhere) without a camel.

6 Prepositions, Conjunctions, and Interjections

1. What Is a Preposition? (links to exercise A, p. 150)

→ **1.** from (preposition); cultures (object)
2. with (preposition); tail (object)

Write the preposition in each sentence, along with its object.

1. The helmeted iguana is a lizard that reminds people of a small dragon.
2. This iguana has a tall crest on the nape of its neck.
3. The crest shortens and tapers at its back.
4. A shorter crest runs the length of the iguana's body.
5. The helmeted iguana has a slender body with long legs.
6. Casque-headed iguanas are green or brown with darker crossbands.
7. Like all iguanas, they are covered with scales.
8. Pet casque-headed iguanas need water but rarely bathe in it.
9. Some pet-store iguanas come from southern Mexico.
10. Generally, they live in areas where leafy plants grow.

2. Using Prepositional Phrases (links to exercise A, p. 153)

→ **1.** in the world (prepositional phrase), lizard (word modified)
2. on a few Indonesian islands (prepositional phrase), live (word modified)

Write the prepositional phrase in each sentence, along with the word or words it modifies.

1. From a distance, salamanders may resemble small lizards.
2. Salamanders are amphibians with long bodies and long tails.
3. Many salamanders have glands in their skin that secrete a slimy substance.
4. When they are under attack, they ooze this slime.
5. Some salamanders live in water.
6. Others live on land.
7. Still others divide their time between land and water.
8. In very hot weather, salamanders find damp places.
9. All salamanders require exposure to water.
10. Without it, they will die.

3. Conjunctions (links to exercise A, p. 156)

➜ **1.** or (conjunction); crocodile, an alligator (words joined)
  2. and (conjunction); A crocodile's snout is pointy, an
    alligator's snout is broad (groups of words joined)

Write the conjunction in each sentence, along with the words or
groups of words that it joins.

  1. Lizards and crocodiles are different types of reptiles.
  2. Most crocodiles spend much of their time in water, but many
    lizards are land lovers.
  3. Lizards come in all shapes and sizes.
  4. Most lizards are found in the tropics or in deserts.
  5. Typically they lay eggs, but some lizards have live young.
  6. Lizards eat small animals or plants.
  7. A few lizards have small legs or none at all.
  8. Usually a lizard has four legs and its body is scaly.
  9. The slow-worm is a lizard, but it doesn't have legs.
  10. Most lizards are harmless, but the Gila monster is poisonous.

7 Subject-Verb Agreement

1. Agreement in Number (links to exercise A, p. 168)

➜ **1.** consider   **2.** shows

Write the form of the verb that agrees with the subject of each
sentence.

  1. A medical worker (is, are) also known as a health care provider.
  2. Nurses (forms, form) an important part of the health care team
    in every hospital.
  3. These health care providers (cooperates, cooperate) closely
    with doctors.
  4. A nurse also (need, needs) to work well with patients and their
    families.
  5. Nurses (completes, complete) one to four years in a
    certification program.
  6. A nurse's responsibilities (includes, include) the observation
    and treatment of patients.
  7. However, a nurse (doesn't, don't) prescribe medication for
    patients.
  8. One type of specially trained nurse (has, have) the title of
    nurse practitioner.

9. Nurse practitioners (performs, perform) some tasks formerly assigned to doctors.
10. Today, more men (is, are) becoming nurses than in the past.

2. Compound Subjects (links to exercise A, p. 170)

➡ **1.** Volunteer men and women compose the Larimer County Dive Rescue Team in Colorado. **5.** Terrified victims or darkness frustrates their efforts.

Proofread these sentences for errors in subject-verb agreement. If a sentence contains an error, rewrite the sentence correctly. If a sentence contains no error, write *Correct*.

1. Humans and dogs works together all over the world to raise sheep.
2. Herding dogs and their puppies move sheep from one pasture to another.
3. The border collie and the Australian kelpie is two popular herding breeds.
4. Neither rain nor snow prevent a good herding dog from doing its job.
5. Whistles or spoken commands are two ways the shepherd communicates with the dog.
6. "Come by" and "That'll do" has special meanings to the shepherding dog.
7. The skill and ability of the dog makes the shepherd's job much easier.
8. A well-trained herding dog or puppy sometimes cost hundreds of dollars!
9. Shepherds and farmers agrees, however, that the cost is worth every penny.
10. The love and affection of a herding dog for its owner are marvelous to see.

3. Phrases Between Subject and Verb (links to exercise on p. 172)

➡ **1.** are   **2.** was

Write the correct verb to complete each sentence. Choose from the verbs in parentheses.

1. The world under the seas (is, are) explored in the films of Jacques Cousteau and his sons, Philippe and Jean-Michel.
2. But the story of their lives (is, are) worth filming also.
3. Many important events in the history of their work (is, are)

good possibilities for scenes, for example, the events below.
4. Jacques Cousteau, with the help of an engineer, (is, are) responsible for the invention of the Aqua-Lung, which allowed humans to breathe underwater.
5. Cousteau, with a crew, (renovate, renovates) a minesweeper which he names the *Calypso,* to use in exploring the ocean.
6. Perhaps Cousteau, in his free time, (write, writes) about sea exploration.
7. Philippe, under his father's guidance, (film, films) ocean life for the Cousteau Society.
8. Jean-Michel, Philippe, and Jacques (build, builds) a miniature submarine, the Diving Saucer.
9. Jacques and Jean-Michel, throughout the world, (publicize, publicizes) the threat of ocean pollution.
10. Their movies, without fail, (make, makes) the public aware of limited water resources.

4. Indefinite Pronoun Subjects (links to exercise A, p. 175)
➡ 1. Everyone has heard of seeing-eye dogs.
2. Few know the term *hearing dogs.*

Proofread these sentences for errors in subject-verb agreement. If a sentence contains an error, rewrite the sentence correctly. If a sentence contains no error, write *Correct.*

1. Almost everyone has seen a rowboat on a lake or river.
2. But not many has seen a shell, the sleek, pencil-thin boat used in rowing races.
3. Both is propelled through the water by pulling on oars, long wooden poles with a blade on one end.
4. Everything on a racing shell has been designed for speed.
5. Each of the eight rowers need to pull the oars in perfect rhythm with the other members of the team.
6. Many admires the strength and stamina of the rowers.
7. Some lifts weights to improve their strength and stamina.
8. None train harder than the members of the U.S. Olympic rowing team.
9. All of the rowers' special skills is needed to make the boat glide straight.
10. One is the ability to follow the orders of the coxswain, or leader of the rowing team.

5. Subjects in Unusual Positions (links to exercise on p. 177)

➡ **1.** subject, friends; verb phrase, does like; Do your friends like soccer?

2. subject, sports; verb, is correct

Identify the subject and the verb in each sentence below. If they agree, write *Correct.* If they don't agree, write the form of the verb that goes with the subject.

1. Would you enjoy an adventure under the surface of the sea?
2. Under the waves are just the place for me.
3. There is no noisy crowds and traffic.
4. Before your eye appears all the wonders of the ocean.
5. Can you imagine the many varieties of colorful fish?
6. Just think of the brilliant corals and shells!
7. There is no more beautiful sights anywhere.
8. Here is another thing to think about.
9. In the oceans swims some of the most intelligent creatures on the planet—dolphins and whales.
10. Give me a job like Jacques Cousteau's anytime!

8 Capitalization

1. People and Cultures (links to exercise A, p. 188)

➡ **1.** I **4.** Spanish

Write the word or initial that should be capitalized in each sentence. If a sentence contains correct capitalization, write *Correct.*

1. When I was born, my parents nicknamed me "hooper."
2. As a kid, i hated the name.
3. My family kept the name because aunt Ellen thought it was cute.
4. In elementary school, my best friend was named Alfred e. Zee.
5. Naturally, he was nicknamed "Easy," and by fourth grade even principal Johnson called him by that name.
6. Most people in the british Isles where I live object to insulting nicknames, like "Stinky."

7. Researchers, headed by professor Rom Harre, found that nicknames were common in all cultures.
8. A nickname can be a shortened form of a person's birth name.
9. For example, princess Diana was nicknamed "Di."
10. Whether you are american, german, or some other nationality, chances are you have a nickname, though you may not like it.

2. First Words and Titles (links to exercise on p. 191)

→ **1.** For   **2.** Deedle, Went

Write the word that should be capitalized in each sentence. (Do not write the words that are already capitalized.)

1. both first and last names have special meanings and origins.
2. When I wrote a letter to the local genealogical society about last names, I did not know the name of the director, so I began my letter, "dear sir or madam."
3. I found out that English last names often are related to occupations, such as miller, a word used in this nursery rhyme:
   there was a jolly miller,
   lived on the river Dee.
4. You may be asking, "what is a miller?" A miller is "someone who grinds grain into flour."
5. According to the *encyclopaedia britannica,* most cultures use names that refer to the occupation of one's father.
6. some names have very specific meanings, such as the Hawaiian name Kanani, which means "the beauty."
7. I asked my mom, "does my name have a special meaning?"
8. Names of characters in books and movies often have particular meanings, such as the name of the character Luke Skywalker in *star wars.*
9. Some writers choose names not for meaning but for the sound, as T. S. Eliot did for his poem "macavity: The Mystery cat."
10. I used the following outline section to research the origin of names:
   I. Names
     A. arabic
       1. occupational
       2. titles

3. Places and Transportation (links to exercise A, p. 195)

➜ **2.** Gulf, Mexico   **3.** Mobile

Write the word or words that should be capitalized in each sentence. (Do not write the words that are already capitalized.)

1. In 1579, the English explorer Sir Francis Drake anchored his ship, the *golden hind,* near the western coast of North America.
2. Drake claimed land we now know as part of the Pacific northwest.
3. Almost exactly 200 years later, another ship from england, piloted by the famous Captain Cook, reached the area.
4. Cook encountered foul weather soon after he reached land, and so he gave the name cape foulweather to the first land he saw.
5. The pacific ocean continued to fascinate explorers; from 1791 to 1794, Captain George Vancouver sailed the northern pacific coast.
6. Vancouver left his name on many landmarks in the region, including Vancouver island.
7. In addition to leaving his own name on landmarks, Vancouver named a mountain in the area mount rainier, after a friend of his.
8. Today, the region explored by these men can be viewed by traveling north on interstate 5.
9. One of the largest cities along the interstate is seattle.
10. The interstate ends at the northern border of washington.

4. Organizations and Other Subjects (links to exercise A, p. 197)

➜ Where: Middle School   Grand Prize: Silver Puck

Write the word or words that should be capitalized in each sentence. (Do not write the words that are already capitalized.)

1. At the fall meeting of the senior class of Stockingdale high school, we decided we would hold a special sports event.
2. We named the event the spring sports festival.
3. It was planned for the month of may, which gave us plenty of time to prepare the games and to get sponsors lined up.
4. Getting sponsors was my job, and the first company I approached was flyrite sporting goods.
5. The company agreed to deliver an assortment of sporting goods on the friday before the games started.
6. When Mr. Hawkins, who teaches world history II, heard about our plans, he suggested that we expand the festival.

7. He thought we should name it after the golden age of greece and that it should include other events, such as debates and art exhibits.

8. We decided to invite representatives from Bradford university and other local colleges.

9. A lot of university representatives came, and even a scout from the nfl showed up at the exhibition football game.

10. The festival was to have ended by 10 p.m. on saturday, but the last group of people left at midnight.

9 Punctuation

1. Periods and Other End Marks (links to exercise A, p. 208)

→ accident?   kidding!

Write the words in the passage that should be followed by periods, question marks, or exclamation points. Include these end marks in your answers.

How many symbols of the United States can you name In addition to the American flag and the Statue of Liberty, you might mention the Liberty Bell But did you know that this famous bell was flawed from its very beginning No kidding Commissioned by the Pennsylvania Provincial Assembly, the bell was completed in 1752 Can you believe that the bell cracked the first time it was tested It's true In fact, the bell was so poorly made that it needed to be recast twice before it was hung in the Pennsylvania statehouse Unfortunately, the bell cracked again, in 1835

In 1846, on the anniversary of George Washington's birthday, the bell cracked so badly that it could not be fixed Today, the Liberty Bell rests in a pavilion close to Independence Hall in Philadelphia, but it cannot be rung. How sad

2. Commas in Sentences (links to exercise A, p. 211)

→ smelly   current

Write the words in the passage that should be followed by commas.

In 1928, Sir Alexander Fleming a British scientist accidentally discovered a solution to a serious medical problem. While working at a London hospital, Fleming had begun to study staphylococci, a strain of bacteria. His research involved preparing bacteria cultures examining any changes in the cultures, and recording any important findings.

One day Fleming noticed something strange while cleaning his laboratory equipment. Inside one dish, a small patch of mold grew. Fleming wondered how this could be. After all, the bacteria were known to harm most living things. He realized almost instantly that this mold held the answer to the great medical problem. In time Fleming and other scientists used the mold to develop penicillin the world's first antibiotic drug. Today, when patients recover from pneumonia, spinal meningitis and other serious infections treated with penicillin, they have Fleming to thank.

3. Commas: Dates, Addresses, and Letters (links to exercise A, p. 213)

➡ Englewood   6

Write the words in the letter that should be followed by commas.

222 Green Street
New York NY 10010
May 3 2000

Dear Harry,

How are you? I'm sure you're looking forward to the big race. I'll be arriving in Phoenix Arizona on May 10 2001 the day before you compete. I can't wait to see you!

Speaking of races, I heard a story you might appreciate about a man named Wim Esajas. In 1960, he was scheduled to run in the 800-meter event at the Summer Olympics in Rome Italy. On the morning of the race, Esajas decided to rest at the Olympic Village. Later that afternoon at the track, he discovered that he had made a terrible mistake. To his horror, Esajas learned that heats for the race had already been held, and that he had been withdrawn from the event! Sadly, he returned to his home in Surinam Dutch Guiana never having competed in the Olympics.

I hope you don't repeat Esajas's mistake! Remember to set your alarm clock. I'll be cheering for you!

Your big sis

Elsie

4. Punctuating Quotations (links to exercise A, p. 217)

➡ **1.** "Why is the word *bug* used to describe a computer problem?" asked Steve.

3. Correct

Rewrite each incorrect sentence, adding quotation marks and other punctuation where needed.

"Did you know that people today are still trying to straighten the Leaning Tower of Pisa?" asked Rosemary.

"No, I didn't," replied Kayla. What have they done so far to fix it

"The tower's foundation was strengthened with concrete in 1934, explained Rosemary, but that didn't seem to help.

Kayla asked, Have they done anything else to straighten it

"Well, steel cables were added to support the tower in 1992," Rosemary stated.

I'm sure it's all fixed by now said Kayla.

"Not yet," sighed Rosemary. "In 1999, engineers began a project to straighten the tower by removing soil under its base." Rosemary added They think this approach will correct the monument's famous tilt and save it from toppling over.

I sure hope it works! exclaimed Kayla.

5. Semicolons and Colons (links to exercise A, p. 219)

➡ data: 5:00

Write the words in the paragraph that should be followed by semicolons and colons. Include these punctuation marks in your answers.

In 1609, Galileo Galilei built his own telescope to study the night sky. Using this device, he made the following observations spots on the sun, crags on the Earth's moon, and moons circling Jupiter. Galileo's discoveries were remarkable they eventually lead to greater advances in astronomy and physics. At the time, however, his work was widely criticized by authorities.

Leaders were particularly upset by Galileo's view of the Earth and its relationship to the sun. They believed that the Earth was the center of the universe. Galileo, however, supported an entirely different opinion it caused him a great deal of trouble. Galileo observed scientifically that the planets, including the Earth, all revolved around the sun. Galileo published his theory in 1632 as a result, he was punished. Galileo experienced many hardships at the hands of his enemies trials, isolation, and house arrest. Through it all, he remained true to his beliefs and to science.

6. Hyphens, Dashes, and Parentheses (links to exercise A, p. 221)

➡ **1**. Isabella Baumfree was born into slavery in the late 1790s (the exact date is unknown).

2. Correct

Read the following passage. Insert hyphens, dashes, and parentheses in the underlined portions where necessary. If the underlined text is correct, write *Correct*.

Have you ever wondered why the **(1)** <u>twenty six</u> letters on a computer keyboard are arranged the way they are? It's because of the invention of the typewriter **(2)** <u>first introduced in 1874</u>. Christopher Latham Sholes, an American printer, had been working on typewriting devices in the 1860s. After reading an article about a typewriting machine **(3)** <u>an article from an issue of *Scientific American*</u>, Sholes made a **(4)** <u>primitive</u> typewriter from **(5)** <u>a telegraph key, piano wire, carbon paper, and glass</u>. Though this machine could type only one letter **(6)** <u>the letter *w*</u> it caught the attention of financial investors. Sholes improved the machine and patented it in 1868.

Sholes found a problem, though, with **(7)** <u>the alphabetical arrangement of letters on the keys</u>. If he typed too quickly, the keys would jam. To solve this problem, Sholes invented QWERTY **(8)** <u>a new way of organizing letters on the keyboard</u>. By keeping the keys of frequently used letters apart from each other, Sholes **(9)** <u>discovered</u> that he could type without jamming the keys. Although another letter arrangement **(10)** <u>one that was faster and more accurate</u> was invented by August Dvorak in the 1930s, we continue to use the QWERTY system invented by Sholes.

7. Apostrophes (links to exercise A, p. 223)

➡ Games' women's

Find and correct the errors in the use of apostrophes.

Have you ever wondered how some places were named? Well, theres an amusing story behind Greenlands' name. Contrary to what you might think, Greenland, the largest island in the world, was not named for it's rich green fields. In fact, only the coasts of Greenland turn green, and this change occurs only during the islands summers. No, the name comes from an ancient trick.

According to historians, the Vikings interest in settling new areas prompted the naming of Greenland. The Vikings are said to have called this frigid place Greenland in order to entice people to move there, far away from their homes. Apparently, the Vikings trick was successful in attracting some families to Greenland.

Today, Greenland is populated almost entirely by Inuit and European people. Though theyr'e able to farm in the countrys southwestern coastal areas, Greenlanders spend more time fishing, hunting, or sheep herding.

8. Punctuating Titles (links to exercise A, p. 225)

→ **1.** *Newsweek*   **3.** *Mistakes That Worked*

Write the 10 titles in this passage, setting them off correctly with either quotation marks or underlining.

The 1977 movie Close Encounters of the Third Kind was first shown in a sneak preview. Business reporter William Flanagan from New York magazine attended. In his review, Flanagan gave the film poor marks and said that it lacked the spark of Star Wars. Eventually, the later movie was appreciated as a groundbreaking science fiction film, but certainly not because of this critic!

Of course, other critics are known to have made mistakes too. Walter Kerr, an esteemed drama critic for the New York Times, attended a performance of the musical West Side Story when it opened on Broadway. Kerr is said to have openly yawned and declared the production a bore. However, the musical, based on William Shakespeare's tragedy Romeo and Juliet, went on to enjoy success on Broadway for many years. Its music was also popular, with chart-topping songs such as Tonight and Maria.

Though it may seem surprising today, many critics did not appreciate the work of John Keats in his day. Author of the classic poems Ode to a Nightingale and Ode on a Grecian Urn, Keats was told by one critic to give up writing and to go back to working in a pharmacy.

Model Bank

Book Review

My favorite book that I read this year was *Island of the Blue Dolphins* by Scott O'Dell. It's about a young girl named Karana who lives on an island in the Pacific with her people. After a battle with people from another island, her group decides to leave the island. White men come to take them away, but Karana and her younger brother are left behind. She has to survive by herself after her little brother is killed by wild dogs. Eventually, she becomes friends with the leader of the dogs. After Karana spends 18 years alone on the island, a hunting boat comes back to the island and takes her to the mainland.

I thought that a book about one girl on an island would get very boring after awhile, but it didn't. First there is the story about the Aleuts who come to hunt otters and the fight that breaks out when they try to leave without paying. This was exciting, but it was also upsetting because so many of Karana's people were killed.

Even after Karana is left alone on the island, the story is still very interesting. Karana is such a strong character and such a survivor that I never wanted to stop reading about her. At first, she's scared and alone on the island, but by the time she is rescued, she has grown to love her home, even if she misses being with people. I especially liked when she saved a wounded otter and became friends with it and its young. After that she decided not to kill any more otters or birds for clothes or feathers. She had too much love and respect for them now.

I was happy to hear that this book was based on a true story. I'm glad that someone like Karana really existed and survived the same difficult trials.

RUBRIC
IN ACTION

❶ Names the book and author in the introduction and gives a brief summary of the story

❷ Clearly explains a personal reaction to the book

❸ Tells why the book was interesting by using details from the story

❹ Concludes by telling why the book was meaningful

Editorial

Recently, the school board has talked about the idea of having a very strict dress code. One of the new rules would be that no T-shirts with any writing on them could be worn to school. The Board is worried that some shirts that kids are wearing now may be offensive to other kids. It's not hard to see where that worry comes from. Some students have been questioned about shirts they were wearing that had racial slurs on them. That is definitely a problem, but trying to solve it by excluding all shirts with writing is unfair.

❶ This writer gives a clear statement of the issue and her opinion on it in the introduction.
Another option: Start with the opinion and give the background later.

Some T-shirt writing can be bad, but not all of it is. Most kids wear shirts that have the names of bands, products, or movies that they like. Wearing these shirts is a way of expressing themselves. Other kids wear shirts telling people to recycle or not to wear fur. These are positive messages that these students are trying to get out, and the school board should support them in that.

❷ Supports her position with examples

There's really no reason why this problem couldn't be dealt with as it comes up. Students should know that if they come to school wearing an offensive shirt they will be sent home to change.

❸ Shows clear reasoning by suggesting a different plan

Of course the school board is trying to make school a safe and comfortable place for kids to learn in. No one wants to go to school surrounded by slogans and pictures that offend them. Wearing clothes with words or slogans on them is a form of expression, though. Banning all expression of this kind would certainly get rid of the negative clothes, but it would silence the good as well as the bad.

❹ Concludes by strongly stating her opinion again

Letter of Complaint

99 Summer Lane
Boulder, CO 56789
March 4, 2001

Atavacron Braingames
1000 Webster Ave
Fort Stockton, NC 77865

Dear Sir or Madam:

    I am writing to you to complain about the World Wide What? electronic quiz game I received for my birthday. I was upset when I saw that the World Wide Writer light pen wasn't included. It says clearly on the box and in the instructions that it should be in there, but it's not. The game cannot be used without this pen, so the gift was a total disappointment.

    I am returning the incomplete set, and I would appreciate your sending me a complete one.

Thank you,

Heather Hazelwood

Heather Hazelwood

1 Sender's address

2 Date

3 Recipient's address

4 Opens with the complaint, giving details of the problem

5 Says what action she requires

6 Signature above typed name

Thank-You Letter

May 14, 2000

Dear Aunt Lucy,

    I'm so excited! You were able to find the last action figure I needed to complete my whole collection! I don't know where you found it, but thank you.

    This whole birthday has been great. Uncle David and Aunt Laura are here. It's too bad you couldn't come over, too, but Mom told me about your business trip. I'm sure I'll see you over the summer, though.

    Thanks again, Aunt Lucy. You made my birthday!

Love,

Pete

1 Date

2 Thanks the reader and explains how special the gift is

3 Closing with handwritten signature

Comparison-and-Contrast Essay

To compare the two types of energy, we must first understand what energy is. Energy is the ability to do work. That doesn't just mean work as in homework or yard work. Energy comes in many forms, such as a rock falling off a cliff, a moving bicycle, or the stored energy in food. With all these forms, there are only two main types of energy, potential and kinetic. These are the energies of rest and motion.

1 Introduces the two subjects being compared and explains what they are

Potential energy is the energy an object has stored up based on how high up it is or how much it weighs. For instance, suppose two kids weigh the same and climb a tree. If they are on different branches, the kid on the higher branch has more potential energy than the kid on the lower branch. However, if one kid weighs more than the other, and they both sit at the same height, the heavier kid has more potential energy than the lighter kid.

2 Presents the first subject using a clear example to illustrate it

If the kids jump out of the tree, their potential energy becomes kinetic energy. This kind comes from the motion of an object. Kinetic energy increases with the speed of an object. When the kids jump, their speed increases as they fall. They have more kinetic energy when they are falling faster than they do when they first jump and are falling more slowly. Also, the larger an object is, the more kinetic energy it has. Even if both kids jump at the exact same time, the larger of the two will always have more kinetic energy.

3 Explains second subject using the same example to show how the two subjects relate

These two kids probably knew they were using a lot of energy, but they would probably be surprised to know how much work they had been doing.

4 Draws an interesting conclusion based on the comparison

Cause-and-Effect Essay

About 10,000 years ago, humans started to grow crops and to develop agriculture. The development of agriculture was one of the most important changes in human history. Farming caused the growth of villages and cities. Farming eventually made the kind of civilization we live in today possible.

❶ Gives a clear statement of the cause-effect relationship

The first effect of the switch to farming was that people didn't need to wander around in search of food. Farms gave people a constant food supply, so people began to build small villages around the farms. As people learned to be better farmers, these villages grew. Many of them became cities.

❷ States the first effect and provides an explanation for support

Another effect of farming was that for the first time there was more food than people needed. This meant that not all the people in a city or village had to be farmers. People became free to work at other things. They became specialists in things like religion, government, writing, and building or making things. Many specialists, like engineers, carpenters, and metalworkers, came together for projects like the building of irrigation systems. With all these different types of workers, differences between social classes began to form for the first time.

❸ Provides details to support ideas

The agricultural revolution <u>also</u> meant that people needed armies and weapons to defend their cities in times of conflict. The most common weapons were bronze spears made by metalworkers.

❹ Uses transitions to tie ideas together

All of these advances continued into the modern world. If it hadn't been for the discovery of agriculture, the world we live in today would be totally different.

❺ Summarizes the importance of this cause-effect relationship

Analyzing a Subject

This year I have read 23 books for our class's independent reading project. Most of the books I read were either science fiction or fantasy. Many people think that science fiction and fantasy are the same thing. Even book stores often put them in the same category. When you take a closer look, though, they are actually different.

Science fiction stories are about things like robots, space, time machines, and future technologies. Many things in science fiction are made up, but they can be explained in a scientific way. Even if they don't exist now, it's considered possible that they could exist some day. The best books I've read that would fit in the science fiction category are *2001: A Space Odyssey*, *Have Spacesuit—Will Travel*, and *The White Mountains*.

Fantasy books are about things like magic, ghosts, werewolves, talking animals, and other things. They tell about things that some people believe could exist but which can't be explained scientifically. These stories often take place hundreds of years ago or in other worlds. My favorite books in this category are *The Lion, the Witch and the Wardrobe*, *The Wizard of Oz*, and *Something Wicked This Way Comes*.

My favorite book all year, though, was *The Martian Chronicles*, which is hard to classify. It has a lot of science fiction ideas like space travel, colonizing another planet, and meeting aliens. But it's also fantasy because it has things like trees growing overnight and Martian ghost cities. Even if I can't classify it as one or the other it's still my favorite, maybe because it has elements of both.

❶ Introduces the topics for analysis

❷ Begins by defining the first topic and giving some examples

❸ Introduces the second topic and gives specific examples

❹ Ends with an example to show the close relationship of the two categories

Quick-Fix Spelling Machine

QUICK–FIX SPELLING MACHINE: PLURALS OF NOUNS

SINGULAR	RULE	PLURAL
skateboard painting ticket	Add -s to most nouns.	skateboards paintings tickets

WATCH OUT The exceptions to this rule are nouns whose plurals are formed in special ways, such as *man (men), woman (women),* and *child (children).*

SINGULAR	RULE	PLURAL
hiss dish ditch box buzz	Add -es to nouns that end in *s, sh, ch, x,* or *z.*	hisses dishes ditches boxes buzzes
auto igloo radio	Add -s to most nouns that end in *o.*	autos igloos radios
potato tomato mosquito	Add -es to a few nouns that end in *o.*	potatoes tomatoes mosquitoes
flurry deputy battery dairy	For most nouns ending in *y,* change the *y* to *i* and add -es.	flurries deputies batteries dairies
alley play turkey	Just add -s when a vowel comes before the *y.*	alleys plays turkeys
calf thief wife leaf knife	For most nouns ending in *f* or *fe,* change the *f* to *v* and add -es or -s.	calves thieves wives leaves knives
belief muff safe	Just add -s to a few nouns that end in *f* or *fe.*	beliefs muffs safes
series sheep species aircraft	Keep the same spelling for some nouns.	series sheep species aircraft

QUICK-FIX SPELLING MACHINE: POSSESSIVES

NOUN	RULE	POSSESSIVE
moon	Add an apostrophe and *-s* to a singular noun.	moon's light
student		student's locker
club		club's president
restaurant		restaurant's menu
school		school's teachers
bank		bank's assets
college		college's facilities
dog		dog's fur
garden		garden's scents
catalog		catalog's merchandise
museum		museum's exhibit
flower		flower's fragrance
book		book's cover
holiday		holiday's traditions
turkey		turkey's drumstick

 The exception to this rule is that the *s* after the apostrophe is dropped after *Jesus'*, *Moses'*, and certain names in classical mythology. Dropping the *-s* makes these possessive forms easier to pronounce.

x-rays	Add an apostrophe to a plural noun that ends in *s*.	x-rays' envelopes
organizations		organizations' budgets
teams		teams' coaches
buildings		buildings' windows
cities		cities' mayors
airports		airports' schedules
babies		babies' toys
groceries		groceries' prices
violets		violets' buds
necklaces		necklaces' clasps
butterflies		butterflies' wings

deer	Add an apostrophe and *-s* to a plural noun not ending in *s*.	deer's hoofs
oxen		oxen's load
salmon		salmon's gills
stepchildren		stepchildren's names
sheep		sheep's wool
mice		mice's nests
people		people's languages

QUICK–FIX SPELLING MACHINE: WORDS ENDING IN SILENT *e*

WORD	RULE	CHANGE
home engage hope tune shame state	Keep the silent *e* when a suffix beginning with a consonant is added to a word that ends in a silent *e*.	homeless engagement hopeful tuneless shameful statement

 Some words that are exceptions include *truly, awful, argument, ninth,* and *wholly.*

WORD	RULE	CHANGE
peace courage manage salvage outrage charge	Keep the silent *e* when a suffix beginning with *a* or *o* is added to a silent *e* word if the *e* follows a soft *c* or *g*.	peaceable courageous manageably salvageable outrageous chargeable

WORD	RULE	CHANGE
agree woe	Keep the silent *e* when a suffix beginning with a vowel is added to a word ending in *ee* or *oe*.	agreeable woeful

WORD	RULE	CHANGE
flake elevate haze institute shake create	Drop the silent *e* from the base word when you add a suffix beginning with *y* or a vowel.	flaky elevation hazy institution shaky creative

 Exceptions to this rule are such words as *changeable* and *courageous.*

QUICK–FIX SPELLING MACHINE: WORDS ENDING IN y

WORD	RULE	CHANGE
happy thirty merry greedy sneaky deputy	Change the *y* to *i* to add a suffix to a word ending in *y* if the *y* follows a consonant.	happiness thirtieth merriest greedily sneakier deputies
rally marry tally fry	Keep the *y* when adding *-ing* to a word ending in *y* if the *y* follows a consonant.	rallying marrying tallying frying
joy pay boy	Keep the *y* when adding a suffix to a word ending in a vowel and *y*.	joyous payable boyish

QUICK–FIX SPELLING MACHINE: WORDS ENDING IN A CONSONANT

WORD	RULE	CHANGE
mat slip hit dim	If a one-syllable word ends in a consonant preceded by a vowel, double the final consonant before adding a suffix beginning with a vowel.	matting slipped hitter dimmest
heap steal scoot meat	If a one-syllable word ends in a consonant preceded by two vowels, do not double the final consonant.	heaped stealing scooted meaty
transfer admit allot permit	Double the final consonant in a word of more than one syllable only if the word is accented on the last syllable.	transferring admitted allotting permitting

QUICK-FIX SPELLING MACHINE: ADVERBS

ADJECTIVE	RULE	ADVERB
sudden bad rapid	Add *-ly.*	suddenly badly rapidly
true	Drop *e,* add *-ly.*	truly
angry heavy steady	Change *y* to *i,* add *-ly.*	angrily heavily steadily

QUICK–FIX SPELLING MACHINE: COMPOUNDS

	SINGULAR	RULE	PLURAL
One word	dishcloth supermarket airport	Add *-s* to most words.	dishcloths supermarkets airports
Two or more words	feather bed atomic bomb attorney general	Make the main noun plural. The main noun is the noun that is modified.	feather beds atomic bombs attorneys general
Hyphenated words	son-in-law half-dollar vice-president	Make the main noun plural.	sons-in-law half-dollars vice-presidents

QUICK-FIX SPELLING MACHINE: OPEN AND CLOSED SYLLABLES

An *open syllable* ends in one vowel and has a long vowel sound.	baby labor fable cedar	ba by la bor fa ble ce dar
A *closed syllable* ends in a consonant and has a short vowel sound.	ladder mischief problem plunder	lad der mis chief prob lem plun der

QUICK-FIX SPELLING MACHINE: CONTRACTIONS

WORDS	RULE	CONTRACTION
I am	Combine a personal pronoun with a verb by adding an apostrophe in place of the missing letters.	I'm
you are		you're
he is		he's
she is		she's
it is		it's
we are		we're
they are		they're
I would		I'd
you would		you'd
he would		he'd
she would		she'd
we would		we'd
they would		they'd
I will		I'll
you will		you'll
he will		he'll
she will		she'll
it will		it'll
we will		we'll
they will		they'll
I have		I've
you have		you've
we have		we've
they have		they've
I had		I'd
you had		you'd
he had		he'd
she had		she'd
we had		we'd
they had		they'd
do not	Otherwise, combine two words into one by adding an apostrophe in place of the missing letters.	don't
where is		where's
there is		there's
could not		couldn't
would not		wouldn't
should not		shouldn't
is not		isn't
was not		wasn't
who is		who's

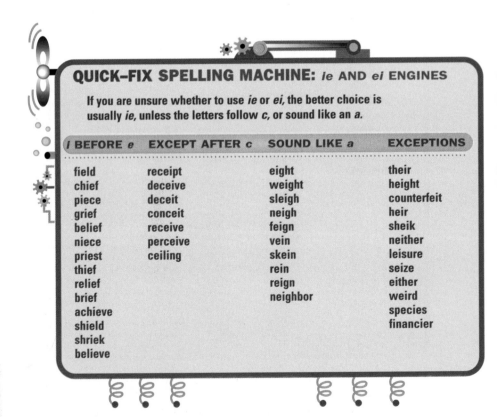

QUICK-FIX SPELLING MACHINE: SEED SORTER

Only one English word ends in *sede.*	supersede
Only three words end in *ceed.*	exceed
	proceed
	succeed
All other "seed" sound words end in *cede.*	accede
	concede
	precede
	recede
	secede

QUICK-FIX SPELLING MACHINE: *ie* AND *ei* ENGINES

If you are unsure whether to use *ie* or *ei,* the better choice is usually *ie,* unless the letters follow *c,* or sound like an *a.*

i BEFORE *e*	EXCEPT AFTER *c*	SOUND LIKE *a*	EXCEPTIONS
field	receipt	eight	their
chief	deceive	weight	height
piece	deceit	sleigh	counterfeit
grief	conceit	neigh	heir
belief	receive	feign	sheik
niece	perceive	vein	neither
priest	ceiling	skein	leisure
thief		rein	seize
relief		reign	either
brief		neighbor	weird
achieve			species
shield			financier
shriek			
believe			

QUICK-FIX SPELLING MACHINE: BORROWED WORDS

Over the centuries, as English speakers increased their contact with people from other lands, English speakers "borrowed" words from other languages. The English language began to grow in new directions and acquired new richness and flavor.

Spelling follows certain patterns in every language. For example, some letter patterns in French, Spanish, and Italian appear in words commonly used in English.

PATTERN	WORD

Some borrowed words keep their original spellings and pronunciations.

In many words taken from French, a final *t* is silent.	ballet beret buffet
In both English and French, a soft *g* is usually followed by *e, i,* or *y.*	mirage region energy
A hard *g* is followed by *a, o,* or *u.*	vague
Many words taken from the Dutch language have *oo* in their spellings.	cookie snoop hook caboose
Many words borrowed from Spanish end in *o.*	taco tornado rodeo bronco
Many words that were plural in Italian end in *i.*	spaghetti macaroni ravioli

Some words from other languages were changed to fit English rules of pronunciation and spelling.

Many words in Native American languages contain sound combinations unlike those in English words. English speakers found these words useful but difficult to pronounce, so they used more familiar sounds and letter combinations.	topaghan = toboggan tamahaac = tomahawk pakani = pecan squa = squaw wampumpeag = wampum qajaq = kayak

Commonly Misspelled Words

A
abbreviate
accidentally
achievement
analyze
anonymous
answer
apologize
appearance
appreciate
appropriate
argument
awkward

B
beautiful
because
beginning
believe
bicycle
brief
bulletin
business

C
calendar
campaign
candidate
caught
certain
changeable
characteristic
clothes
column

committee
courageous
courteous
criticize
curiosity

D
decision
definitely
dependent
description
desirable
despair
desperate
development
dictionary
different
disappear
disappoint
discipline
dissatisfied

E
eighth
eligible
eliminate
embarrass
enthusiastic
especially
essay
exaggerate
exceed
existence
experience

F
familiar
fascinating
favorite
February
foreign
fourth
fragile

G
generally
government
grammar
guarantee
guard

H
height
humorous

I
immediately
independent
irritable

J, K, L
judgment
knowledge
laboratory
library
license
lightning

literature
loneliness

M
mathematics
minimum
mischievous

N
necessary
nickel
ninety
noticeable
nuclear
nuisance

O
obstacle
occasionally
once
opinion
opportunity
outrageous

P
parallel
particularly
people
permanent
persuade
pleasant
pneumonia

possess
possibility
prejudice
principal
privilege
probably
psychology
pursue

R

realize
receipt
receive
recognize
recommend
reference
rehearse
repetition
restaurant
rhythm
ridiculous

S

sandwich
schedule
scissors
separate
sergeant
similar
sincerely
souvenir
specifically
strategy
success
surprise
syllable
sympathy
symptom

T

temperature
thorough
throughout
tomorrow
traffic
tragedy
transferred
truly
Tuesday
twelfth

U

unnecessary
usable

V

vacuum
vicinity
village

W

weird

Commonly Confused Words

Good writers master words that are easy to misuse and misspell. Study the following words, noting how their meanings differ.

accept, except *Accept* means "to agree to something" or "to receive something willingly." *Except* usually means "not including."
Did the teacher *accept* your report?
Everyone smiled for the photographer *except* Jody.

advice, advise *Advice* is a noun that means "counsel given to someone." *Advise* is a verb that means "to give counsel."
Jim should take some of his own *advice*.
The mechanic *advised* me to get new brakes for my car.

affect, effect *Affect* means "to move or influence" or "to wear or to pretend to have." *Effect* as a verb means "to bring about." As a noun, *effect* means "the result of an action."
The news from South Africa *affected* him deeply.
The band's singer *affects* a British accent.
The students tried to *effect* a change in school policy.
What *effect* did the acidic soil produce in the plants?

all ready, already *All ready* means "all are ready" or "completely prepared." *Already* means "previously."
The students were *all ready* for the field trip.
We had *already* pitched our tent before it started raining.

all right *All right* is the correct spelling. *Alright* is nonstandard and should not be used.

a lot *A lot* may be used in informal writing. *Alot* is incorrect.

borrow, lend *Borrow* means "to receive something on loan." *Lend* means "to give out temporarily."
Please *lend* me your book.
He *borrowed* five dollars from his sister.

bring, take *Bring* refers to movement toward or with. *Take* refers to movement away from.
I'll *bring* you a glass of water.
Would you please *take* these apples to Pam and John?

can, may *Can* means "to be able," or "to have the power to." *May* means "to have permission to." *May* can also mean "possibly will."

We *may* **not use pesticides on our community garden.**
Pesticides *may* **not be necessary, anyway.**
Vegetables *can* **grow nicely without pesticides.**

capital, capitol, **the Capitol**	*Capital* means "excellent," "most serious," or "most important." It also means "seat of government." A *capitol* is a building in which a state legislature meets. *The Capitol* is the building in Washington, D.C., in which the U.S. Congress meets. **Going to the beach is a** *capital* **idea.** **Is Madison the** *capital* **of Wisconsin?** **Protesters rallied at the state** *capitol.* **A subway connects the Senate and the House in** *the Capitol.*
desert, **dessert**	*Desert* (des´ ert) means "a dry, sandy, barren region." *Desert* (de sert´) means "to abandon." *Dessert* (des sert´) is a sweet, such as cake. **The Sahara in North Africa is the world's largest** *desert.* **The night guard did not** *desert* **his post.** **Alison's favorite** *dessert* **is chocolate cake.**
fewer, less	*Fewer* refers to numbers of things that can be counted. *Less* refers to amount, degree, or value. *Fewer* **than ten students camped out.** **We made** *less* **money this year on the walkathon than last year.**
good, well	*Good* is always an adjective. *Well* is usually an adverb that modifies an action verb. *Well* can also be an adjective meaning "in good health." **Dana felt** *good* **when she finished painting her room.** **Angela ran** *well* **in yesterday's race.** **I felt** *well* **when I left my house.**
its, it's	*Its* is a possessive pronoun. *It's* is a contraction for *it is* or *it has.* **Sanibel Island is known for** *its* **beautiful beaches.** *It's* **great weather for a picnic.**
lay, lie	*Lay* is a verb that means "to place." It takes a direct object. *Lie* is a verb that means "to be in a certain place." *Lie,* or its past form *lay,* never takes a direct object. **The carpenter will** *lay* **the planks on the bench.** **My cat likes to** *lie* **under the bed.**

lead, led	*Lead* can be a noun that means "a heavy metal" or a verb that means "to show the way." *Led* is the past tense form of the verb. **Lead is used in nuclear reactors.** **Raul always *leads* his team onto the field.** **She *led* the class as president of the student council.**
learn, teach	*Learn* means "to gain knowledge." *Teach* means "to instruct." **Enrique is *learning* about black holes in space.** **Marva *teaches* astronomy at a college in the city.**
leave, let	*Leave* means "to go away from" or "to allow to remain." *Leave* can be transitive or intransitive. *Let* is usually used with another verb. It means "to allow to." **Don't *leave* the refrigerator open.** **She *leaves* for Scotland tomorrow.** **Cyclops wouldn't *let* Odysseus' men *leave* the cave.**
like	*Like* used as a conjunction before a clause is incorrect. Use *as* or *as if.* **Ramon talked *as if* he had a cold.**
lose, loose	*Lose* means "to mislay or suffer the loss of something." *Loose* means "free" or "not fastened." **That tire will *lose* air unless you patch it.** **My little brother has three *loose* teeth.**
passed, past	*Passed* is the past tense of *pass* and means "went by." *Past* is an adjective that means "of a former time." *Past* is also a noun that means "time gone by." **We *passed* through the Florida Keys during our vacation.** **My *past* experiences have taught me to set my alarm.** **Ebenezer Scrooge is a character who relives his *past*.**
peace, piece	*Peace* means "a state of calm or quiet." *Piece* means "a section or part of something." **Sitting still can bring a sense of *peace*.** **Here's another *piece* of the puzzle.**
principal, principle	*Principal* means "of chief or central importance" or refers to the head of a school. *Principle* means "a basic truth, standard, or rule of behavior." **Lack of customers is the *principal* reason for closing the store.** **The *principal* of our school awarded the trophy.** **One of my *principles* is to be honest with others.**

raise, rise	*Raise* means "to lift" or "to make something go up." It takes a direct object. *Rise* means "to go upward." It does not take a direct object. **The maintenance workers *raise* the flag each morning.** **The city's population is expected to *rise* steadily.**
set, sit	*Set* means "to place" and takes a direct object. *Sit* means "to occupy a seat or a place" and does not take a direct object. **He *set* the box down outside the shed.** **We *sit* in the last row of the upper balcony.**
stationary, stationery	*Stationary* means "fixed or unmoving." *Stationery* means "fine paper for writing letters." **The wheel pivots, but the seat is *stationary*.** **Rex wrote on special *stationery* imprinted with his name.**
than, then	*Than* is used to introduce the second part of a comparison. *Then* means "next in order." **Ramon is stronger *than* Mark.** **Cut the grass and *then* trim the hedges.**
their, there, they're	*Their* means "belonging to them." *There* means "in that place." *They're* is the contraction for *they are*. **All the campers returned to *their* cabins.** **I keep my card collection *there* in those folders.** **Lisa and Beth run daily; *they're* on the track team.**
to, too, two	*To* means "toward" or "in the direction of." *Too* means "also" or "very." *Two* is the number 2. **We went *to* the mall.** **It's *too* risky riding without a helmet.** **_Two_ amusement parks are offering reduced rates for admission.**
whose, who's	*Whose* is the possessive form of *who*. *Who's* is a contraction of *who is* or *who has*. **_Whose_ parents will drive us to the movies?** **_Who's_ going to the recycling center?**
your, you're	*Your* is the possessive form of *you*. *You're* is a contraction of *you are*. **What was *your* record in the fifty-yard dash?** **_You're_ one of the winners of the essay contest.**

CONFUSED WORDS

MLA Citation Guidelines

Forms for Source Cards and Works Cited Entries

The following examples show some basic forms of bibliographic entries for research sources. Use these forms on source cards for your working bibliography and in the list of works cited at the end of your report.

Whole Books

The following models can also be used for citing reports and pamphlets.

A. One author

Blackwood, Gary. The Shakespeare Stealer. New York: Dutton, 1998.

B. Two authors

Cummings, Pat, and Linda Cummings. Talking with Adventurers. Washington: Natl. Geographic Soc., 1998.

C. Three authors

Silverstein, Alvin, Virginia Silverstein, and Laura Silverstein Nunn. The California Condor. Brookfield: Millbrook, 1998.

D. Four or more authors

The abbreviation *et al.* means "and others." Use *et al.* instead of listing all the authors.

Brown, Richard G., et al. Algebra 1: Explorations and Applications. Evanston: McDougal, 1998.

E. No author given

Webster's Word Histories. Springfield: Merriam, 1989.

F. An editor but no single author

Silverberg, Robert, ed. The Science Fiction Hall of Fame. Garden City: Doubleday, 1970.

G. Two or three editors

Colbert, Jan, and Ann McMillan Harms, eds. Dear Dr. King: Letters from Today's Children to Dr. Martin Luther King, Jr. New York: Hyperion, 1998.

H. An author and a translator

Pressler, Mirjam. Halinka. Trans. Elizabeth D. Crawford. New York: Holt, 1998.

I. An author, a translator, and an editor

Hugo, Victor. <u>The Hunchback of Notre-Dame</u>. Trans. Walter J.
Cobb. Ed. Robin Waterfield. London: Penguin, 1996.

J. An edition other than the first

Gibaldi, Joseph. <u>MLA Handbook for Writers of Research Papers</u>.
5th ed. New York: MLA, 1999.

K. A book or a monograph that is part of a series

Latta, Sara L. <u>Allergies</u>. Diseases and People. Springfield: Enslow,
1998.

L. A multivolume work

If you have used only one volume of a multivolume work, cite only
that volume.

Gonen, Amiram, ed. <u>Peoples of the World: Customs and Cultures</u>.
Vol. 3. Danbury: Grolier, 1998. 10 vols.

If you have used more than one volume of a multivolume work,
cite the entire work.

Gonen, Amiram, ed. <u>Peoples of the World: Customs and Cultures</u>.
10 vols. Danbury: Grolier, 1998.

M. A volume with its own title that is part of a multivolume work with a different title

Dué, Andrea, ed. <u>The Modern World</u>. Danbury: Grolier, 1999. Vol.
6 of <u>People and the Earth: An Environmental Atlas</u>. 6 vols.

N. A republished book or a literary work available in several editions

Give the date of the original publication after the title. Then give
complete publication information, including the date, for the
edition that you have used.

Lewis, C. S. <u>The Voyage of the Dawn Treader</u>. 1952. New York:
Harper, 1994.

O. A government publication

Give the name of the government (country or state). Then give the department if applicable, followed by the agency if applicable. Next give the title, followed by the author if known. Then give the publication information. The publisher of U.S. government documents is usually the Government Printing Office, or GPO.

United States. Dept. of Health and Human Services. Natl. Center for Health Statistics. <u>Health, United States, 1996–1997, and Injury Chartbook</u>. Washington: GPO, 1997.

Parts of Books

A. A poem, a short story, an essay, or a chapter in a collection of works by one author

Wilder, Laura Ingalls. "Whom Will You Marry?" <u>A Little House Reader: A Collection of Writings by Laura Ingalls Wilder</u>. Ed. William Anderson. New York: Harper, 1998. 130–43.

B. A poem, a short story, an essay, or a chapter in a collection of works by several authors

Angelou, Maya. "Still I Rise." <u>I, Too, Sing America: Three Centuries of African American Poetry</u>. Ed. Catherine Clinton. Boston: Houghton, 1998. 107–08.

C. A novel or a play in an anthology

Stone, Peter. <u>Titanic</u>. <u>The Best Plays of 1996–1997</u>. Ed. Otis L. Guernsey, Jr. New York: Limelight-Proscenium, 1997. 157–89.

D. An introduction, a preface, a foreword, or an afterword written by the author(s) of a work

Bradbury, Ray. Afterword. <u>Fahrenheit 451</u>. By Bradbury. New York: Ballantine, 1982. 167–73.

E. An introduction, a preface, a foreword, or an afterword written by someone other than the author(s) of a work

Allende, Isabel. Foreword. <u>Where Angels Glide at Dawn: New Stories from Latin America</u>. Ed. Lori M. Carlson and Cynthia L. Ventura. New York: Lippincott, 1990. ix–xii.

Magazines, Journals, Newspapers, and Encyclopedias

A. An article in a magazine, a journal, or a newspaper

Allen, Jodie. "Working Out Welfare." <u>Time</u> 29 July 1996: 53–54.

Abelson, Philip H. "Preparing Children for the Future." <u>Science</u> 13 Dec. 1996: 1819.

Voedisch, Lynn. "Have You Done Your Homework Yet?" <u>Chicago Tribune</u> 9 Oct. 1997, sec. 5: 5.

Fintor, Lou. "Cancer Control Efforts Reach Out to 'Culturally Isolated.'" <u>Journal of the National Cancer Institute</u> 90 (1998): 1424–27.

B. An article in an encyclopedia or other alphabetically organized reference work

Give the title of the article, the name of the reference work, and the year of the edition.

"Sioux Indians." <u>The World Book Encyclopedia</u>. 1999 ed.

C. A review

Crain, Caleb. "There but for Fortune." Rev. of <u>Hearts in Atlantis</u> by Stephen King. <u>New York Times Book Review</u> 12 Sept. 1999: 10.

Miscellaneous Print and Nonprint Sources

A. An interview you have conducted or a letter you have received

Sosa, Sammy. Letter to the author [*or* Personal interview]. 20 Oct. 1998.

B. A film

<u>Ever After</u>. Screenplay by Susannah Grant and Andy Tennant. Dir. Tennant. Perf. Drew Barrymore, Anjelica Huston, and Dougray Scott. 20th Century Fox, 1998.

C. A work of art (painting, photograph, sculpture)

Escher, M. C. <u>Sky and Water I</u>. National Gallery of Art, Washington.

D. A television or a radio program

Give the episode name (if applicable) and the series or program name. Include any information that you have about the program's writer and director. Then give the network, the local station, the city, and the date of the airing of the program.

"The Idol Maker." Narr. Vicki Mabrey. <u>60 Minutes II</u>. Prod. Aaron
    Wertheim. CBS. WBBM, Chicago. 29 Sept. 1999.

E. A musical composition

Mendelssohn, Felix. Symphony no. 4 in A major, op. 90.

F. A recording (compact disc, LP, or audiocassette)

If the recording is not a compact disc, include *LP* or *Audiocassette* before the manufacturer's name.

Johnson, James P. "Fascination." Perf. Marcus Roberts. <u>If I Could
    Be with You</u>. RCA, 1993.

Prado, Perez. "Mambo #8." <u>Que Rico Mambo</u>. Audiocassette.
    Rhino, 1989.

G. A lecture, a speech, or an address

Give the name of the speaker, followed by the name of the speech or the kind of speech (*Lecture, Introduction, Address*). Then give the event, the place, and the date.

Lowry, Lois. Speech. Newbery-Caldecott Awards Banquet.
    ALA Annual Conference. Convention Center, Miami Beach.
    26 June 1994.

Electronic Publications

The number of electronic information sources is great and increasing rapidly, so please refer to the most recent edition of the MLA Handbook for Writers of Research Papers *if you need more guidance. You can also refer to the page "MLA Style" at the Modern Language Association Web site <http://www.mla.org/>.*

Portable databases (CD-ROMs, DVDs, laser discs, diskettes, and videocassettes)

These products contain fixed information (information that cannot be changed unless a new version is produced and released). Citing them in a research paper is similar to citing printed sources. You should include the following information:

- Name of the author (if applicable)

- Title of the part of the work used (underlined or in quotation marks)
- Title of the product or the database (underlined)
- Publication medium (CD-ROM, DVD, laser disc, diskette, or videocassette)
- Edition, release, or version if applicable
- City of publication
- Name of publisher
- Year of publication

If you cannot find some of this information, cite what is available.

Burke, James. "Yesterday, Tomorrow and You." <u>Connections</u>. Video, Prod. BBC. Ambrose, 1978.

<u>Antarctica</u>. Dir. John Weiley. 1991. DVD. Slingshot, 1999.

"Boston Tea Party." <u>Encarta 98 Encyclopedia</u>. CD-ROM. 1998 ed. Redmond: Microsoft, 1998.

<u>Nerds 2.0.1: A Brief History of the Internet</u>. Prod. Oregon. 3 videocassettes. PBS, 1998.

Online Sources

Sources on the World Wide Web are numerous and include scholarly projects, reference databases, articles in periodicals, and professional and personal sites. Not all sites are equally reliable, and therefore material cited from the World Wide Web should be evaluated carefully. Entries for online sources in the Works Cited list should contain as much of the information listed below as is available.

- Name of the author, editor, compiler, or translator, followed by an abbreviation such as *ed., comp.,* or *trans.* if appropriate
- Title of the material accessed. Use quotation marks for titles of poems, short stories, articles, and similar short works. Underline the title of a book.
- Publication information for any print version of the source
- Title (underlined) of the scholarly project, database, periodical, or professional or personal site. For a professional or personal site with no title, add a description such as *Home page* (neither underlined nor in quotation marks).
- Name of the editor of the scholarly project or database

- For a journal, the volume number, issue number, or other identifying number
- Date of electronic publication, of the latest update, or of posting
- For a work from a subscription service, list the name of the service and—if a library is the subscriber—the name of the library and the town or state where it is located.
- Range or total number of pages, paragraphs, or other sections if they are numbered
- Name of any institution or organization that sponsors or is associated with the Web site
- Date the source was accessed
- Electronic address, or URL, of the source. For a subscription service, use the URL of the service's main page (if known) or the keyword assigned by the service.

Scholarly project

Donlan, Leni, and Kathleen Ferenz "student page." America Dreams Through the Decades. 21 Feb. 1999. Lib. of Congress American Memory Fellows Program. 6 Oct. 1999 <http://www.internet-catalyst.org/projects/amproject/student.html>.

Professional site

UNICEF. United Nations Children's Fund. 10 Oct. 1999 <http://www.unicef.org/>.

Personal site

Tomarkin, Craig. "World Series History." 6 Feb. 1998. BaseballGuru.com. 10 Oct. 1999 <http://members.aol.com/thebbguru/baseball/bbws1.html>.

Book

Twain, Mark. The Adventures of Tom Sawyer. New York: Harper, 1903. The Electronic Text Center. Ed. David Seaman. Aug. 1993. U of Virginia Lib. 10 Oct. 1999 <http://etext.lib.virginia.edu/ectbin/toccer-new?id=Twa2Tom&tag=public&images=images/modeng&data=/texts/english/modeng/parsed&part=0>.

Article in reference database

"Aztec." Encyclopedia.com. 1999. Infonautics Corp. 10 Oct. 1999 <http://www.encyclopedia.com/>.

Article in journal

Kientzler, Alesha Lynne. "Fifth- and Seventh-Grade Girls' Decisions about Participation in Physical Activity." <u>Elementary School Journal</u> 99.5 (1999): 391-414. 15 Oct. 1999 <http://www.journals.uchicago.edu/ESJ>.

Article in magazine

Warrick, Joby. "Death in the Gulf of Mexico." <u>National Wildlife</u> June/July 1999. 11 Oct. 1999 <http://www.nwf.org/nwf/natlwild/1999/mexico.html>.

Work from a subscription service

"Glasnost." <u>Merriam-Webster Collegiate Dictionary</u>. 1996. America Online. 7 Oct. 1999. Keyword: Collegiate.

Glossary for Writers

Alliteration : the repetition of beginning sounds of words in poetry or prose; for example, the "c" sound in "creeping cat"

Allusion : a reference to a historical or literary person, place, event, or aspect of culture

Analogy : a comparison used to explain an idea or support an argument. For example, an analogy for how a government works might be how a family works.

Analysis : a way of thinking that involves taking apart, examining, and explaining a subject or an idea

Anecdote : a brief story told as an example to illustrate a point

Argument : speaking or writing that expresses a position or states an opinion with supporting evidence. An argument often takes into account other points of view.

Audience : one's readers or listeners

Autobiography : a biography (life story) told by the person whose life it is

Bias : a leaning toward one side in an argument; to be unbiased is to be neutral

Bibliography : a list of sources (articles, books, encyclopedias) in a paper or report, used to document research or to recommend further study

Body : the main part of a composition, in which its ideas are developed

Brainstorming : a way of generating ideas that involves quickly listing ideas as they occur, without stopping to judge them

Cause and Effect : the relationship between an event (the cause) and an event it helps to bring about (the effect)

Characterization : the way people (characters) are portrayed by an author

Chronological : organized according to time sequence

Clarity : the quality of being clear and easy to understand

Classification	a way of organizing information by grouping or categorizing items according to some system or principle
Cliché	an overused expression, such as "quiet as a mouse"
Clustering	a brainstorming technique that involves creating an idea or topic map made up of circled groupings of related details
Coherence	connectedness; a sense that parts hold together. A paragraph has coherence when its sentences flow logically from one to the next. A composition has coherence when its paragraphs are connected logically and linked by transitional words and phrases.
Collaboration	the act of working with other people on projects or to problem solve
Comparison and Contrast	a pattern of organization in which two or more things are related on the basis of similarities and differences
Conclusion	a judgment or a decision that is based on evidence, experience, and logical reasoning; also, the final section of a composition, which summarizes an argument or main idea and points the reader toward action or further reflection
Connotation	an idea or feeling associated with a word, as opposed to the word's dictionary definition (denotation)
Context	the setting or situation in which something happens; the parts of a statement that occur just before and just after a specific word and help determine its meaning
Controversy	a disagreement, often one that has attracted public interest
Critical Thinking	what a writer *does* with information; thinking that goes beyond the facts to organize, analyze, evaluate, or draw conclusions about them
Criticism	an analysis (usually an essay) of something (usually a literary or artistic work) that evaluates how it does or does not succeed in communicating its meaning

Deductive Reasoning	the process of arriving at a specific conclusion by reasoning from a general premise or statement
Denotation	the dictionary definition of a word, as opposed to the ideas and feelings the word carries (connotation)
Descriptive Writing	an account of what it is like to experience some object, scene, or person; writing that usually gives one basic impression and emphasizes sensory detail
Dialect	a form of a language (usually regional) that has a distinctive pronunciation, vocabulary, and word order
Dialogue	spoken conversation of fictional characters or actual persons; the conversation in novels, stories, plays, poems, or essays
Documentation	the identification of documents or other sources used to support the information reported in an essay or other type of analysis; usually cited in footnotes or in parentheses
Editorial	an article in a publication or a commentary on radio or television expressing an opinion about a public issue
Elaboration	the support or development of a main idea with facts, statistics, sensory details, incidents, examples, quotations, or visual representations
Evaluation	writing that purposefully judges the worth, quality, or success of something
Expository Writing	writing that explains an idea or teaches a process; also called informative writing
Expressive	characterized by expression; refers to descriptive communication of ideas that are full of meaning or feeling, often used by writers in personal writing to explore ideas
Fiction	made-up or imaginary happenings as opposed to statements of fact or nonfiction. Short stories and novels are fiction, even though they may be based on real events; essays, scientific articles, biographies, and news stories are nonfiction.

Figurative Language	language that displays the imaginative and poetic use of words; writing that contains figures of speech such as simile, metaphor, and personification
Formal Language	language in which rules of grammar and vocabulary standards are carefully observed; used in textbooks, reports, and other formal communications
Freewriting	a way of exploring ideas, thoughts, or feelings that involves writing freely—without stopping or otherwise limiting the flow of ideas—for a specific length of time
Gender Free	refers to language that includes both men and women when making reference to a role or a group that consists of people of both sexes. "A medic uses his or her skills to save lives" and "Medics use their skills to save lives" are two gender-free ways of expressing the same idea.
Generalization	a statement expressing a principle or drawing a conclusion based on examples or instances
Graphic Device	a visual way of organizing information. Graphic devices include charts, graphs, outlines, and cluster diagrams.
Idea Tree	a graphic device in which main ideas are written on "branches" and related details are noted on "twigs"
Imagery	figurative language and descriptions used to produce mental images
Inductive Reasoning	a method of thinking or organizing in which a general conclusion is reached by reasoning from specific pieces of information
Inference	a logical guess that is based on observed facts and one's own knowledge and experience
Informative Writing	writing that explains an idea or teaches a process; also called expository writing
Interpretation	an explanation of the meaning of any text, set of facts, object, gesture, or event. To interpret something is to try to make sense of it.
Introduction	the opening section of a composition, which presents the main idea, grabs the reader's attention, and sets the tone

Invisible Writing writing done with a dimmed computer screen or with an empty ballpoint pen on two sheets of paper with carbon paper between them

Irony a figure of speech in which the intended meaning is the opposite of the stated meaning—saying one thing and meaning another

Jargon the special language and terminology used by people in the same profession or with specialized interests

Journal a record of thoughts and impressions, mainly for personal use

Learning Log a kind of journal used for recording and reflecting on what one has learned and for noting problems and questions

Literary Analysis critical thinking and writing about literature, presenting a personal perspective

Looping a repetitive process for discovering ideas on a topic through freewriting, stopping to find promising ideas, freewriting about those ideas, and repeating the loop several times

Media various forms of mass communication, such as newspapers, magazines, radio, television, and the Internet; the editorial voice and influence of all of these

Memoir an account of true events told by a narrator who witnessed or participated in the events; usually focuses on the personalities and actions of persons other than the writer

Metaphor a figure of speech that makes a comparison without using the word *like* or *as.* "All the world's a stage" is a metaphor.

Monologue a speech by one person without interruption by other voices. A dramatic monologue reveals the personality and experience of a person through a long speech.

Mood the feeling about a scene or a subject created by a writer's selection of words and details. The mood of a piece of writing may be suspenseful, mysterious, peaceful, fearful, and so on.

Narrative Writing	writing that tells a story—either made up or true. Some common types of narrative writing are biographies, short stories, and novels.
Onomatopoeia	the use of words (usually in poetry) to suggest sounds; examples are "the clinking of knives and forks," and "the hissing of the fans of the losing team."
Order of Degree	a pattern of organization in which ideas, people, places, or things are presented in rank order on the basis of quantity or extent. An example is listing items in order from most important to least important.
Paraphrase	a restatement in one's own words that stays true to the ideas, tone, and general length of the original passage
Parenthetical Documentation	the placement of citations or other documentation in parentheses within a report
Peer Response	suggestions and comments on a piece of writing, provided by peers or classmates
Personal Writing	writing that focuses on expressing the writer's own thoughts, experiences, and feelings
Personification	a figure of speech in which an object, event, abstract idea, or animal is given human characteristics
Persuasive Writing	writing that is intended to convince the reader to believe a particular point of view or to follow a course of action
Plagiarism	the act of dishonestly presenting someone else's words or ideas as one's own
Point of View	the angle from which a story is told, such as first-, second-, or third-person point of view
Portfolio	a container (usually a folder) for notes on work in progress, drafts and revisions, finished pieces, and peer responses
Proofreading	the act of checking work to discover typographical and other errors; usually the last stage of the revising or editing process
Propaganda	any form of communication aimed at persuading an audience, often containing false or misleading information; usually refers to manipulative political material

Prose	the usual language of speech and writing, lacking the characteristics of poetry; any language that is not poetry
Sensory Details	words that appeal to any of the five senses—the way something looks, sounds, smells, tastes, or feels
Sequential Order	a pattern of organization in which events are presented in the order in which they occur, as in telling a story chronologically or describing the sequence of steps in a process
Simile	a figure of speech that uses the word *like* or *as* to make a comparison. "Trees like pencil strokes" is a simile.
Spatial Order	a pattern of organization in which details are arranged in the order that they appear in space, such as from left to right
Style	the distinctive features of a literary or artistic work that collectively characterize a work of a particular individual, group, period, or school
Summary	a brief restatement of the main idea of a passage
Symbol	something (word, object, or action) that stands for or suggests something else. For example, a flag can stand for or symbolize a nation; a withered plant may suggest or symbolize a failing relationship.
Theme	the central idea or message of a work of literature
Thesis Statement	a statement in one or two sentences of the main idea or purpose of a piece of writing
Tone	a writer's attitude or manner of expression—detached, ironic, serious, or angry, for example
Topic Sentence	a sentence that expresses the main idea of a paragraph
Transition	a connecting word or phrase that clarifies relationships between details, sentences, or paragraphs
Tree Diagram	a graphic way of showing the relationships among ideas; particularly useful in generating ideas; also known as an idea tree or spider map
Trite Phrase	an overused phrase whose use suggests a lack of imagination on the part of the user

Unity	a quality of oneness. A paragraph has unity if all its sentences support the same main idea or purpose; a composition has unity if all its paragraphs support the thesis statement.
Venn Diagram	a way of visually representing the relationship between two items that are distinct but that have common or overlapping elements
Voice	an expression of a writer's personality through such stylistic elements as word choice and tone

Index

A

A, 123
Abbreviations
   capitalization of, 186
   periods in, 207
   for time, 196
About, 59, 148
Above, 148, 299
Across, 148, 299
Actions
   physical or mental, 88
   tenses of, 101–103
Action verbs, 10, 12, 88–89, 114, 115
   direct and indirect objects of, 33, 59,
     91–93
   to describe motion, 114
   transitive and intransitive, 92
Active listening, 482–484
Active reading, 453
A.D., capitalization of, 196
Addresses
   commas in, 212–213
   periods with abbreviations in, 207
Adjective phrases, 163
Adjectives, 120, 122–129, 144–145.
     See also Predicate adjectives.
   adverbs confused with, 136–137
   capitalization of, 188
   checklist for, 145
   commas between, 209, 230
   comparative and superlative forms of,
     144, 145
   for comparisons, 133–135, 247
   diagramming of, 233
   modifiers of, 130, 136, 144–145, 163
   nouns as, 127, 128, 129
   other words used as, 127–129
   pronouns as, 127
   proper, 123
   suffixes for, 525
   vivid, 140–141, 256
Adverb phrases, 163
Adverbs, 120, 130–132, 144–145
   adjectives confused with, 136–137
   checklist for, 145
   comparative and superlative forms of,
     144, 145
   for comparisons, 133–135, 247
   diagramming of, 233

   direct objects confused with, 92
   forming, 131
   intensifier, 130–131
   modifiers of, 130, 136, 144–145, 163
   prepositions confused with, 149
   suffixes for, 525
   vivid, 140–141, 256
Advertisements (ads), 272, 289, 335, 505
   emotional appeals in, 477
   target audiences of, 501
After, 148, 299, 309, 321
Against, 59, 148
Agreement
   indefinite-pronoun, 72–74
   pronoun-antecedent, 69–71, 72–74,
     85, 244
   subject-verb, 164–183, 242–243
Airplane names, capitalization of, 194
All, 72, 84, 127, 173, 174, 401
Alliteration, 411, 412
Almanac, 444
Almost, 131
Along, 148
Also, 293, 299, 309, 321, 471
Although, 283, 299, 321
Am, 12, 21, 57, 88, 89
A.M., capitalization of, 196
Among, 148, 149
An, 123
Analyzing
   of media, 502–504
   in test taking, 465
   of word parts, 517–519, 524
And, 14, 154–155, 282, 284
   in stringy sentences, 338
   subject-verb agreement and, 182
Anecdotes, 315, 320
Animation, 499
Announcements, writing, 208
Another, 72, 173
Antecedents, 54, 69–71
   indefinite pronouns and, 72–74
   pronoun, 85
   singular and plural, 85
Anthologies, 381
Antonyms, 523
Any, 72, 173, 174
Anybody, 72, 173
Anyone, 72, 84, 173
Anything, 72, 173

Apostrophes, 41, 51, 61, 62, 222–223, 230
Appear, 21, 88, 89
Appositives, 210
Are, 12, 21, 57, 88, 89
Arguments, 323, 329
Around, 148, 299, 309
Art works, titles of, 190
Articles, 123
    capitalization and, 190, 193
    definite and indefinite, 123
Article titles, 418. *See also* Titles; Works Cited list.
As, 148, 321
As a result, 299
As well, 471
At, 148
Atlas, 444
Attention, in listening, 483, 494
Audience, 265, 497
    for class newspaper, 506, 509
    for essays, 361
    for formal and informal language, 349
    listening and, 482
    for opinion statement, 401
    for personal experience essay, 361
    for place description, 369
    for poems, 413, 414
    for problem-solution essay, 393, 394
    for process description, 385
    for research report, 421
    for response to literature, 377
    for short story, 409, 410
    target, 501, 506, 508
    for World Wide Web, 504
Audio aids, for oral reports, 489, 490
Audiotapes, 438
Award names, capitalization of, 197, 202

B

Bad, badly, 136, 137, 145
Bandwagon appeal, 477
Barely, 138
Base words, 517, 518
B.C., capitalization of, 196
Be, 12, 21, 57, 88, 89, 99
    as helping verb, 89
    predicate adjectives and, 125
Because, 283, 293, 299, 321
Become, 88, 125
Been, 12, 21, 57, 88, 89
Before, 148, 309, 321
Behind, 148, 299
Being, 21, 88, 89
Being (verbs expressing), 88
Below, 148, 299, 309

Beneath, 148
Beside, 148
Better, 144
Between, 59, 78, 148, 149, 299
Beyond, 148, 299
Billboards, 498
Body
    of compositions, 312–313, 316–317
    of opinion statement, 401
    of problem-solution essay, 390, 393, 396
    of research report, 418, 426, 428, 432
    of response to literature, 374, 377, 380
    of short story, 416
Body language, 487, 494. *See also* Eye contact; Facial expressions; Gestures.
Books, 438, 498
    fiction, 439
    nonfiction, 439
    parts of, 445
    reference, 444–445
    source cards for, 423
    titles of, 190, 224
    titles of chapters in, 224
    Works Cited list of, 418
Both, 72, 127, 173
Brainstorming, 264, 361
    for sensory details, 326–327
Brand names, capitalization of, 194, 197
Bring, 91
Brochures, 498
Building names, capitalization of, 194
Bulletin boards, 272
Bumper stickers, 347, 353
Business letters, greetings in, 218
But, 14, 154–155, 282, 284, 306, 321
    as transition word, 293
By, 59, 148

C

Calendar items, capitalization of, 196, 202, 203
Call for action, 400
Can, 12, 89
Can be, 57
Can't, 138, 144
Capitalization, 184–203
    of A.D. and B.C., 196
    of airplane names, 194
    of A.M. and P.M., 196
    of award names, 197, 202
    in bar graphs, 198–199
    of brand names, 194, 197
    of building names, 194
    of calendar items, 196, 202, 203

INDEX

of car names, 194
checklist for, 203
of deities, 187
of first word of sentences, 189
of geographical names, 193
of historical items, 196
of holidays, 196, 197, 202
of languages, 188
in letters, 190, 192, 200, 203
of nationalities, 188
of objects of the universe, 193
of organization names, 196–197
in outlines, 190, 192
of people's names and initials, 186,
   202
of place names, 184, 193–195, 202
of plane names, 194
in poetry, 189, 202, 226
of proper adjectives, 123
of proper nouns, 36
in quotations, 189, 215
of races, 188
of religious terms, 187
rules for, 202–203
of seasons, 196, 197, 203
of ship names, 194
of spacecraft names, 194
of special events, 197
in tables, 198–199
of time abbreviations, 196
of titles, 186–187, 190, 202
of train names, 194
of vehicle names, 194
when not to use, 203
Captions, 45, 330–331
Card catalogs, 441
Car names, capitalization of, 194
Cartoons, 217, 504
Case, of pronoun, 54, 69, 77–79, 84, 245
Cause and effect, 469
Cause-and-effect order, 317, 321
Cause-and-effect reasoning, 399, 474
CD-ROMs, 438, 445, 499
CDs, 438
in oral reports, 490
titles of, 224
Chapter titles, 225
Charts
observation, 413
as visual aids, 331
for writing essays, 361
for writing opinion statement, 404
for writing poem, 413
for writing short story, 409
Choppy sentences, 341, 345
Chronological order, 302

in place descriptions, 367, 369
Circular reasoning, 474, 479
Cities, capitalization of, 193
Clarification, writing to ask for, 20
Clarity. See Sentences, clear; Thinking,
   clear; Writing, clear.
Clauses, independent, 237
Clichés, avoiding, 255, 352–353
Closer, sentence, 281, 286
Closing of a letter, 190
Clues
context, 514–516, 524
in examining media, 497
in listening, 483, 494
Cluster diagram, 265
Coherence, 317, 320
Collaboration. See Brainstorming;
   Publishing, working with other
   writers in.
Colons, 218–219
Columns, 505
Combining sentence parts, 284–285
Combining sentences, 14, 15, 155,
   282–285, 287.
commas in, 26, 282
in varying sentence length, 341
Comics, 505
Commands, sentences giving. See
   Imperative sentences.
Commas, 209–215, 230–231, 249
in addresses, 212–213
between adjectives, 209, 230
with appositives, 210
to avoid confusion, 210
between city and state, 212
in combining sentences, 26, 282
with conjunctions, 26, 155, 282
in dates, 212–213
with interrupters, 210, 230
with introductory words or phrases,
   210, 230
with items in series, 209
in letters, 212–213
misplaced or missing, 249
with nouns of direct address, 210
in place descriptions, 370
with quotation marks, 214–217, 231
in sentences, 209–211
Common nouns, 36, 50
adjectives and, 123
capitalization of, 203
Company names, capitalization of, 196
Comparative form, 133–135, 144, 145
in problem-solution essay, 394
Compare-and-contrast order, 306–307,
   308, 309

Comparisons, 133–135, 144, 145
  as context clues, 515, 524
  order of, 306–307, 321
  in problem-solution essay, 394
  in test taking, 465
Complements, 33, 45, 51. *See also*
    Direct objects; Indirect objects.
  of action verbs, 91
  diagramming of, 234–235
  direct objects as, 43
  indirect objects as, 43
  nouns as, 43
  objects of verbs as, 23–24
  predicate nouns as, 43
  subject, 21–22, 94
Complete predicates, 6–7, 9, 10, 32,
    278
Complete subjects, 6–7, 32, 278
Complex sentences, 283
Compositions, 311–321. *See also*
    Writing; Writing process.
  checklist for, 321
  coherence in, 317
  outlines for, 316
  summarizing in, 319, 321
  unity in, 316–317
Compound direct objects, diagramming
    of, 235
Compound numbers, 220
Compound objects, pronouns in, 77–79
Compound predicate pronouns, 77–79
Compound predicates, diagramming of,
    232–233
Compound sentences, 282
  diagramming of, 237
  semicolons in, 218
Compound subjects, 14–15, 33
  diagramming of, 232–233
  pronouns in, 57, 77–79, 85
  subject-verb agreement and,
    169–170, 178–179, 182–183
Compound verbs, 14–15, 33
Compound words, 220, 517
Computer catalogs, 440–441
Computer indexes, 443
Computers, 438
  spell checkers on, 62, 271
Conclusion (of a written work), 313,
    319, 321, 358, 360
  in opinion statement, 398, 400, 401
  in oral report, 489
  paragraphing for, 259
  in place description, 370
  in problem-solution essay, 390, 392,
    393, 396
  in research report, 418, 426, 432

in response to literature, 374, 376,
    377, 380
  in short story, 407, 416
Conclusion (of reasoning). *See* Drawing
    conclusions.
Condition (verb expressing), 88,
    101–103. *See also* Tenses of
    verbs
Conflict, in short story, 406, 408, 409,
    416
Conjunctions, 146, 154–156, 162–163,
    282
  capitalization and, 190
  checklist for, 163
  to combine choppy sentences, 341
  commas with, 26, 282
  for compound subjects, 14, 169–170
  coordinating, 237
  diagramming of, 232–233, 237
  between independent clauses, 237
  other than *and, but, or,* 283
  subject-verb agreement and, 182
Connecting words, 14, 282, 341. *See also*
    Conjunctions; Joining words and
    thoughts; Transition words or
    phrases.
Connotation, positive and negative, 351,
    354, 355
Consequently, 321
Content, 270
  of class newspaper, 509
  judging, 484
Context, 512, 514–516, 524
Continents, capitalization of, 193
Contractions
  in informal writing, 348
  possessive pronouns confused with,
    61–62, 66, 222–223
  subject-verb agreement and, 167
Contrast, 515, 524
  order of, 306–307, 317, 321
  in test taking, 465
Conventions, 269, 270
Conversation, 84. *See also* Dialogue.
Copyright date, 445
Could, 12, 89
Could be, 57
Countries, capitalization of, 193
Critical listening and thinking. *See*
    Analyzing; Listening; Thinking.

D

Dashes, 220–221
Dates
  capitalization of, 196, 202
  commas in, 212–213

Declarative sentences, 16–17, 28, 33, 343
  periods for, 206
  with subjects in unusual order, 18–20
Definite articles, 123
Definitions, 514, 524
  in informative paragraphs, 296
  in problem-solution essay, 394
  in process description, 384
Deities, capitalization of, 187
Delivery of a speech, 484, 489, 491
Demonstrative pronouns, 67–68, 84, 127
Denotation, 351
Describing a place, Writing Workshop for. See Place Description, Writing Workshop for.
Descriptive words, 8, 9, 120. See also Adjectives; Adverbs.
  action verbs as, 114
  in middle of sentences, 280
  subject complements as, 21
  in topic sentences, 291
Descriptive writing, 164, 294, 299. See also Metaphors, Similes.
  adjectives in, 120, 124
  adverbs in, 120
  in compositions, 313, 320
  elaboration and, 323, 325
  in essays, 358, 359, 361, 364
  figurative language in, 257
  imagery in, 352–353
  in introduction of compositions, 315, 320
  metaphoric, 95
  paragraphs in, 294
  photographs and, 305
  about places, 366–373
  plural nouns in, 40
  precise words in, 256
  predicate nouns in, 95
  prepositions in, 150
  in problem-solution essay, 391
  about processes, 382–389
  in short story, 409
  spatial order in, 304–305
  in test taking, 465
  about transportation, 86, 92
  verbs in, 86
Despite, 148
Details, 254. See also Sensory details.
  adjectives for, 124, 129
  adverbs for, 131
  complements for, 51
  as elaboration, 323
  in essays, 359, 361, 364
  to fix empty sentences, 336–337, 344

  nouns and, 44, 51
  in opinion statement, 398
  organization of, 369
  in place description, 369
  in poem, 413
  predicate adjectives for, 125
  in problem-solution essay, 390
  sentence length and, 340
  in short story, 406, 407, 409
  supporting, 254, 468
  types of, 325
  vocabulary building and, 516
Dewey Decimal System, 439, 448
Diagramming, 232–237
Diagrams, 333, 452, 454
  cluster, 265
  Venn, 306–307
Dialogue, 16, 17, 56, 84, 217
  in essays, 358, 359, 361
  paragraphs and, 317
  in place description, 366, 367, 368
  pronouns in, 80–81
  punctuation for, 216, 217, 410
  quotation marks with, 216, 217
  in short story, 406, 407, 410
Dictionaries, 444, 519, 522–523
Did, 12, 89
Direct address, nouns of, 210, 230
Directional phrases, 304–305
Directions, writing, 184, 194, 382–389
Direct objects, 23–24, 43, 51, 91–93, 119
  adverbs confused with, 92
  compound, 235
  diagramming of, 234–235
  personal pronouns as, 59
  pronouns as, 84
  whom as one, 66
Directories, 446–447
Direct quotations, 214
Discussion, 465, 488
Divided quotations, 215
Do, 12, 89
Documentaries, 499
Documentation, 428
Document names, capitalization of, 196
Does, 12, 89
Doesn't, 167
Don't, 138, 167
Double comparison, 144
Double negatives, 138–139, 144, 145
Down, 148
Drafts, 19, 26, 37, 264, 267–268
  combining sentences in, 284
  of compositions, 314
  before elaboration, 324
  for essays, 361

evaluating, 269–270
of opinion statement, 401
peer response and, 268
of place description, 369
of poem, 413
of problem-solution essay, 393
of process description, 385
of research report, 427
of response to literature, 377
of short story, 409
tips for, 274
Dramatic reading, 272, 417. *See also*
    Speaking.
Drawing conclusions, 472
Drawings, 454
    in oral reports, 490
    for process description, 385
Due to, 321
During, 148, 309

E

Each, 72, 84, 127, 173
East, capitalization of, 193, 194
Editing, 33, 239–262. *See also*
    Proofreading; Revising; Rewriting.
    to add supporting details, 254
    to avoid clichés and slang, 255
    to avoid wordiness, 251
    for capitalization, 200
    for comma usage, 249
    for comparison forms, 247
    of essays, 362
    for figurative language, 257
    to improve weak sentences, 250
    of opinion statement, 402
    of place description, 370
    of poem, 414
    for precision, 256
    of problem-solution essay, 394
    of process description, 386
    for pronoun case, 244–246
    for pronoun reference problems, 244
    proofreading marks in, 271
    of research report, 430
    of response to literature, 378
    of short story, 410
    as stage in writing process, 264, 271
    for subject-verb agreement, 242–243
    for verb forms and tenses, 110, 248
    for word choice, 256–257
Editorials, 404, 505, 506
Either, 72, 173
Either/or thinking, 475
Elaboration, 323–334
Electric Library, 443
Electronic bulletin boards, 272

Electronic encyclopedias, 445
Electronic games, 497
Electronic reference sources, 445
E-mail, 272, 348, 506
Emotions. *See also* Feelings.
    appeals to, 476–477
    interjections to express, 157, 162, 163
    in poems, 411
Encyclopedias, 423, 444, 445
End marks, 206–208, 214–217. *See*
    also Exclamation points; Periods;
    Question marks.
English, standard and nonstandard, 349
Especially, 131
Essay questions, on test, 463, 465
Essays
    checklist for, 365
    in class newspaper, 506
    paragraphing for, 259
    peer review of, 365
    personal experience, 358–365
    problem-solution, 390–397
    titles of, 224
Ethnic groups, capitalization of, 188
Evaluation
    of draft, 269
    in test taking, 465
Events, capitalization of, 196, 197, 202
Eventually, 299
Everybody, 72, 173
Everyone, 72, 173
Everything, 72, 173
Evidence. *See* Facts; Information;
    Reasons; Statistics.
Examples, 514–515, 524
    in informative paragraphs, 296
    in opinion statement, 398, 399
    in persuasive writing, 297
    in problem-solution essay, 390, 391,
        392, 394
Except, 148
Exclamation points, 16, 207, 214, 231
Exclamatory sentences, 16–17, 33, 343
    punctuation for, 207
    in quotations, 214
Explanations
    as elaboration, 323, 325
    listening and, 482
    in process description, 384
    in test taking, 465
Explanatory words or phrases, 214–217
Expository writing. *See* Writing Workshops,
    process description, problem-
    solution essay, research report.
Extremely, 131
Eye contact, 487, 491, 494

F

Facial expressions, 362, 489, 491, 493
Facts, 324, 328–329, 332
    in class newspaper, 506
    going beyond, 472–473
    in informative paragraphs, 296
    and opinions, 470–471
    in opinion statement, 398, 399, 401
    in persuasive writing, 297
    in problem-solution essay, 390
    unusual, 315, 320
Family histories, 438
Family relationships, capitalization for,
    187, 202, 203
Faulty reasoning, 474–475
Feature stories, 503, 505, 506
Feedback, 365.
    on class newspaper, 507
    on opinion statement, 405
    on place description, 373
    on poem, 417
    on problem-solution essay, 397
    on process description, 386
    on research report, 433
    on response to literature, 380
    on short story, 417
Feel, 21, 88, 125
Feelings. *See also* Emotions.
    in response to literature, 377
    sentences showing, 16, 20, 355
Feminine pronouns, 70–71, 244
Few, 72, 127, 173
Fiction, 439
Figurative language, 257, 352–353,
    354–355
    in place descriptions, 366, 367
    in poems, 411
Figure of speech, 257, 352
Films, 499, 502
Finally, 299, 309, 321
First, 299, 321
First person pronoun, 54–55, 69–70
Flyers, 498
Focus
    in essays, 358
    paragraphs and, 292–293
    in place description, 366, 367
    in poem, 411
    in process description, 382, 383
Followed by, 309
For, 59, 91, 148
For example, 299
Formal language, 348–349, 354
Formal outlines, 459
Formal speaking, 489–495

For this reason, 299, 321
Fractions, hyphens in spelling, 220
Fragments, 25–27, 33, 240, 250, 286
    checking for, 278
    in essays, 362
Freewriting
    for poem, 413
    for response to literature, 377
From, 59, 148, 321
Future perfect tense, 104–106, 109, 119
Future progressive tense, 101–103, 109
Future tense, 13, 101–103, 109
    simple, 101–102, 119

G

Games, 497, 499
    titles of, 190
    writing about, 459
Gender, of pronouns, 70, 85, 244
General context, 516
Geographical names, capitalization of,
    193
Gestures, 493. *See also* Body language.
Give, 91
Gods and godesses, capitalization of, 187
Good, well, 136, 137, 145
Grammar, 269, 270, 271
Graphics, 452, 453, 498
    for opinion statement, 404
    for organization, 372
    types of, 454–455
    on World Wide Web, 499
Graphs
    bar, 198–199
    for elaboration, 331, 333
    line, 333
    pie, 333
Greeting of a letter, 190, 218
Group discussion, 488
Group speaking, 487–488
Grow, 88

H

Had, 12, 89
Hand, 91
Hardly, 138, 144
Has, 12, 89
Has been, 57
Hasn't, 138
Have, 12, 89
Have been, 57
He, 54–55, 57, 84
    problems with, 77
Headings, for note cards, 457
Headlines, writing, 204, 227

Helping verbs, 12, 13, 114
  with present and past participle, 96
  subject-verb agreement and, 183
  verb phrases and, 89
Hemispheres, capitalization of, 193
Her, 55, 59, 61, 84, 127
  problems with, 77
Here, sentences beginning with, 19,
    176–179, 183
Hers, 61, 84
Herself, 64, 84
Him, 54–55, 59, 84
  problems with, 77
Himself, 64, 84
His, 54–55, 61, 84, 127
Historical items, capitalization of, 196
History, 131, 438
Holidays, capitalization of, 196, 197,
    202
However, 306, 309, 321
Hyperlinks, 499
Hyphens, 220–221

I

I, 54–55, 57, 84, 167, 187
  problems with, 77
Ideas. *See also* Brainstorming; Main
    ideas; Topics.
  categorizing, 361, 404, 409, 413, 501
  demonstrative pronouns and, 67
  for essays, 364
  in evaluating drafts, 269, 270
  finding, 264, 274
  in growing sentences, 280–281
  joining, 154, 283
  listening and, 482, 483
  nouns for, 34, 36, 38, 43
  for opinion statement, 401, 404
  order of, 267, 269, 270, 293, 358,
    361, 366, 367, 369, 385
  paragraphs containing too many, 258
  paragraphs for new, 317
  for place description, 372
  for poem, 413, 416
  for problem-solution essay, 393, 396
  for process description, 386
  pronouns for, 54
  related, 468–469, 471
  for research report, 418, 432, 433
  for response to literature, 377, 381
  sentences with too many, 250
  separating, 338–339
  sharing, 6–7, 467
  for short story, 409, 416
  similar, 33

similarities and differences in,
    306–307, 469, 471
thinking skills and, 467
topic sentences and, 290–291
Identifying nouns, pronouns with, 85
If, 321
Illustrations, 330, 333
Imagery, 352–353, 354, 355
  in essays, 359, 361
  in poems, 413
Images, in media, 498, 499
Imperative sentences, 16–17, 18, 28,
    33, 206, 343
In, 148
In addition, 321
In between, 299
In comparison, 471
In conclusion, 299
In contrast, 306, 321, 471
Indefinite articles, 123
Indefinite pronouns, 72–74, 80, 84, 127
  singular and plural, 72–74
  as subjects, 173–175
  subject-verb agreement and, 182–183
Independent clauses, diagramming of,
    237
Index, 442–443, 445
Index cards, 457
Indirect objects, 23–24, 43, 51, 91–93,
    119
  diagramming of, 235
  objects of prepositions confused
    with, 91
  personal pronouns as, 59
  pronouns as, 84
  whom as one, 66
Indirect questions, punctuation for, 206
Indirect quotations, 214
Inferences, 472, 473
Informal language, 348–349, 354
Informal outlines, 316, 459
Informal speaking, 487–488
Information, 437–450. *See also* Facts;
    Media; Reference materials;
    Sources of Information; Statistics.
  checklist for finding, 449
  conclusions and, 472–473
  documenting, 428
  elaboration and, 325
  in essays, 358
  finding and organizing, 266, 449
  in graphs and charts, 331
  inferences based on, 472, 473
  from interviewing, 485–486
  listening for, 482
  prewriting and, 264, 266

in problem-solution essay, 393
in process description, 382, 383, 385
reading for, 452–453
in research report, 418, 422–423
sentences giving, 20
sharing, 6–7
writing to ask for, 20
Informative paragraphs, 296, 299
Informative sentences, 20
Infotrac, 443
In front of, 309
Initials, periods with, 207
Inserting words or phrases, 284, 287
Inside, 148, 299
In spite of, 321
Instead, 299, 309, 321
Institution names, capitalization of, 196
Instructions, writing, 301, 303, 382–389
Intensifiers, 130–131
Intensive pronouns, 64–65, 84
Interjections, 146, 157, 162–163
checklist for, 163
punctuation for, 207
Internet. *See also* Online publishing
options; Web sites; World Wide
Web
class newspaper on, 506
source cards for, 423
writing contests on, 272
writing for, 272
Interpretation, 492–493
of maps and graphics, 453
Interrogative pronouns, 64, 80, 84
Interrogative sentences, 16–17, 18, 20,
28, 33, 206, 343
Interrupters, 210, 230
Interviewing, 485–486, 505, 506
letter for, 495
In the middle, 309
In the same way, 309, 321
Into, 148
Intransitive verbs, 92
Introduction. *See also* Openers.
in compositions, 312–313, 314–315,
320
in opinion statement, 399, 401
in oral reports, 489
paragraphing for, 258
in problem-solution essay, 390, 391,
393, 396
in research report, 418, 426, 432
in response to literature, 374, 375,
377, 378, 380
in short story, 407, 416
Introductory words or phrases, 210
colons following, 218

commas with, 230
Inverted sentences, 18–19
Irregular verbs, 97, 98–100, 116, 119
Is, 12, 21, 57, 88, 89
Islands, capitalization of, 193
It, 55, 57, 59, 84
Italics, 224, 230
It's, 61, 222
Its, 55, 61, 84, 127, 222
Itself, 64, 84

J

Joining words and thoughts, 154–155,
162–163. *See also* Connecting
words.
Journals, 438
Journal writing, 179
Judging content and delivery, 484
Just, 131
Just as, 321

K

Keywords, 440, 446, 448

L

Labels, 42, 330–331
Laid, 111
Lain, 111
Lakes, capitalization of, 193
Language, 355. *See also* Precise words;
Specific words.
effective, 347–357
exact, 350–351
formal and informal, 348–349, 354
loaded, 476
in opinion statement, 398, 401
positive and negative, 476
Languages, capitalization of, 188
Last, 321
Later, 293, 299, 309
Lay, 111, 119
Learn, 112, 119
Learned, 112
Lend, 91
Letters, 272
business, 218
capitalization in, 190, 192, 200, 203
commas in, 212–213
e-mail, 272, 348, 506
formal, 349
greetings and closings in, 190
to interviewee, 495
Libraries, 438–449, 471
catalogs in, 440–441
special services of, 438

Lie, 111, 119
Like, 148, 306, 309, 321
Likewise, 299, 321, 471
Line graphs, 333
Linking verbs, 10, 12, 21, 88–89, 114, 115
    predicate adjectives with, 21, 33, 94–95, 125
    predicate nouns with, 21, 33
    subject pronouns with, 57
Listening, 481–486, 494–495
    active, 482–484
    checklist for, 495
    informal speaking and, 487
    in interviewing, 485–486
Listings, 505
Lists, 451, 481
    or group discussion, 488
    for media product, 501
    periods in, 207
    in process description, 383, 385
    for research report, 418, 420, 429
    Works Cited, 420, 428, 429
Literature, response to. *See* Response to literature, Writing Workshop for.
Locations
    capitalization of, 194, 203
    prepositions for, 150
Logical order, 290, 293, 298
    coherence and, 317
    in process description, 382, 383, 385, 386
    in research report, 418, 420
Logical reasoning. *See also* Reasons.
    in opinion statement, 398, 399
    in problem-solution essay, 390, 392
Look, 21, 88, 125

M

Magazines, "zines," 272, 438, 497, 498, 501
    analyzing stories in, 503
    indexes of, 442–443
    in libraries, 442–443
    source cards for, 423
    titles of, 190, 224
    writing contests in, 272
Main ideas, 312–313, 320, 321
    in conclusion, 314–315, 316, 319, 320
    identifying, 468
    in introduction, 314–315, 320
    listening for, 483
Main verbs, 12, 89
Make, 91

Many, 72, 84, 173
Maps, 158, 159, 333, 452, 453, 455, 490
Masculine pronouns, 70–71, 244
Matching questions, 461
May, 12, 89
Me, 55, 59, 84
    problems with, 77
Meaning, 323
Meanwhile, 299
Mechanics, 271
Media, 497–509
    analyzing, 502–504
    checklist for learning about, 509
    elements of, 498–499
    library and, 438–439
    titles of different, 190
Media center, 438–439
Media literacy, 509
Media products, 500
Medium, definition of, 498
Message, 500–501
Metaphors, 95, 257, 352–353, 354, 355
    in essays, 364
    in poems, 411
Might, 12, 89
Mine, 55, 61, 84
Modifiers, 279, 286–287. *See also* Adjectives; Adverbs.
    adjective phrases as, 151, 163
    of adjectives, 136, 144–145, 163
    adverb phrases as, 151, 163
    of adverbs, 136, 144–145, 163
    adverbs as, 130–132
    common mistakes with, 136–137, 145
    in comparisons, 133–135, 144, 145
    diagramming of, 233, 235
    irregular, 134
    of more than one syllable, 134
    of nouns and pronouns, 122, 136, 144–145, 163
    nouns as, 127, 128
    one-syllable, 133
    precise, 256
    prepositional phrases as, 151, 235
    pronouns as, 127
    two-syllable, 133
    of verbs, 136, 144–145, 163
Mood of a sentence, 20
More, 133–135, 144, 394
Most, 72, 84, 127, 133–135, 144, 173, 174, 394
Mountains, capitalization of, 193
Movies, 497, 499
    titles of, 190, 224

INDEX

Multimedia, 499
Multiple choice questions, 461–462
Musical compositions, titles of, 190, 224
Musicals, titles of, 190
Music videos, 497, 499
Must, as helping verb, 89
My, 55, 61, 84, 127
Myself, 64, 84

N

Name calling, 401, 476–477
Names. *See also* Renaming.
   of bodies of the universe, 193
   of bridges, 194
   of buildings, 194
   of companies, 196
   geographical, 193
   initials for, 207
   of institutions, 196
   of landmarks, 194
   of monuments, 194
   nouns for, 34, 36, 38, 43
   of organizations, 196–197
   of people, 186
   of places, 184, 193–195
   proper, 8, 186–187, 194
   of stores, 196
   titles with, 186–187, 190
Narrative paragraphs, 295, 299
Nationalities, capitalization of, 188
Nations, capitalization of, 193
Near, 148, 309
Nearly, 131
Negative connotation, 351
Negative words, 138–139, 476
Neither, 72, 138, 173
Neuter pronouns, 70–71, 244
Never, 138, 144, 401
Newspapers, 272, 438, 498
   creating class, 505–507, 509
   features of, 505
   headlines in, 204, 207
   source cards for, 423
   stories in, 97, 505, 506
   titles of, 190
Next, 299, 309, 321
Next to, 309
No, 138
Nobody, 72, 138, 173
Nominative case, 84
None, 72, 84, 138, 173, 174
Nonfiction, 439, 441, 448
Nonstandard English, 349
No one, 72, 138, 173
Nor, 154–155
   with compound subject, 169

subject-verb agreement and, 182
North, capitalization of, 193, 194
Not, 138
Note cards, 266, 424, 456–458
Notes, 26
   drafting and, 267
   for oral report, 490
   organizing, 266
   for research report, 424, 427
Note taking, 266, 453, 456–458
   in group discussion, 488
   in interviewing, 506
   listening and, 483, 494
   for oral presentation, 492–493
   in reflecting, 370
   for research report, 424–425
Nothing, 72, 138, 173
Nouns, 34–50. *See also* Plural nouns;
    Singular nouns.
   as adjectives, 127, 128, 129
   adjectives and, 122, 123, 136
   antecedents and, 69
   appositives with, 210
   checklist for, 51
   common, 36, 50
   as complements, 43
   in diagrams, 46–47
   of direct address, 210, 230
   as direct objects, 91
   identifying, 85
   intensive pronouns and, 64
   modifiers of, 136, 144–145, 163
   as objects of prepositions, 44
   personal pronouns with, 75–79
   possessive, 41–42, 50, 51, 222–223
   predicate, 21, 22, 33, 43, 51, 94–95
   prepositions and, 148
   pronouns substituted for, 56
   proper, 36, 50
   in science, 46–47
   specific, 256
   spelling of possessive, 41, 51
   as subjects, 43
   suffixes for, 525
Now, 309
Nowhere, 138
Number (of pronoun), 54, 69, 85. *See also*
    Plural pronouns; Singular pronouns
Number (of subject), 166–168
Numbers
   apostrophes with, 223
   hyphens in spelling, 220

O

Objective case, 54–55, 84
Objective tests, 460–462

Object pronouns, 59–60, 80
Objects. *See also* Direct objects; Indirect
    objects.
    compound, 77–79
    personal pronouns with, 75
    pronouns as, 85
    whom as one, 66
Objects of prepositions, 44, 51, 59,
    149, 162
    diagramming of, 235
    indirect objects confused with, 91
    personal pronouns with, 75
    pronouns as, 84
    subject-verb agreement and, 172
    whom as one, 66
Objects of the universe, capitalization of,
    193
Observation charts, 413
Observations, writing, 131, 135
Oceans, capitalization of, 193
Of, 148
Off, 148
On, 148
One, 72, 173
Online publishing options
    for essays, 365
    for opinion statement, 405
    for place description, 373
    for problem-solution essay, 397
    for process description, 389
    for research report, 433
    for response to literature, 380
On the contrary, 321
On the other hand, 309, 321
On top of, 309
Openers. *See also* Introduction.
    in essays, 359
    in oral reports, 489
    sentence, 280, 286
Opinions, 313, 325, 328, 336
    elaboration and, 325
    and facts, 470–471
    in persuasive writing, 297
    in problem-solution essay, 390
Opinion statement, Writing Workshop for,
    398–405
Or, 14, 154–155, 282, 284
    with compound subject, 169
    subject-verb agreement and, 182
Oral communication, 489–495. *See also*
    Speaking.
    of demonstration, 387
    of essays, 363, 365
    of guided tour, 371
    of monologue, 363
    of opinion statement, 403, 405

of oral report, 431
of panel discussion, 403
of persuasive speech, 395
of place descriptions, 371, 373
of poem, 417
presentation of, 492–493
of problem-solution essay, 395, 397
of process description, 387, 389
of readers theater, 379
of research report, 431, 433
of response to literature, 379, 380
of short story, 415, 417
of skit, 415
Order. *See also* Logical order; Sequential
    order; Spatial order.
    cause-and-effect, 317, 321
    chronological, 302, 367, 369
    compare-and-contrast, 306–309,
        317, 321
    in essays, 358
    of subjects and verbs, 18–20, 33
Order of ideas, 267, 269, 270, 293,
    358, 361
    in place descriptions, 366, 367, 369
    in process description, 385
Organization. *See also* Order.
    checklist for, 309
    of compositions, 317
    of information, 266, 331
    of note cards, 266, 458
    paragraphing and, 301–309
    of place description, 369, 372
    of problem-solution essay, 393
    of research report, 426
    of response to literature, 377
    revising for, 269, 270
Organization names, capitalization of,
    196–197
Our, 61, 84, 127
Ours, 61, 84
Ourselves, 64, 84
Out, 148
Outlines, 316
    capitalization in, 190, 192
    creating, 459
    formal, 459
    informal, 316, 459
    parallelism in, 459
    periods in, 207
    for research report, 426, 427
    in test taking, 465
Outside, 299
Over, 148
Overgeneralizations, 474
Ownership, 84. *See also* Possessive case.

INDEX

P

Paragraphs, 258–259, 289–299
  checklist for, 299, 309
  in compositions, 312–321
  descriptive, 294, 299
  with dialogue, 410
  focusing, 292–293
  informative, 296, 299
  narrative, 295, 299
  organizing, 301–309
  persuasive, 297, 299
  in process description, 382
  in research report, 427
  in short story, 410
  topic sentences in, 290–291, 296, 297, 298
  transitions between, 318
  types of, 299
Parallelism, 459
Paraphrasing, 424, 457
Parentheses, 220–221
Parenthetical documentation, 428
Participles, 96–97, 98–100, 118
Parts of books, 445
Parts of compositions, 311
Parts of paragraphs, 292–293
Parts of sentences
  combining, 284–285
  diagramming of, 232–237
Parts of speech, 523
Parts of words, 517–519, 524
Past, 148
Past participle, 96–97, 98–100, 118
  perfect tenses and, 105
Past perfect, 104–106, 108, 119
Past progressive, 101–103, 108
Past tense, 13, 96–97, 101–103, 108, 118, 119
  simple, 101–102, 119
Peer response, 268
Peer review. *See also* Feedback.
  of essays, 365
  of place description, 373
Perfect tenses, 104–106, 107–109, 119
Periods, 16, 206–208
  in abbreviations, 207
  capitalization of historic, 196
  for initials, 207
  quotation marks with, 231
  with quotations, 214
Personal experience essay, Writing Workshop for, 358–365
Personal pronouns, 54–56
  agreement of antecedents with, 69–71, 72–74, 244

  in compounds, 77–79
  masculine, feminine, and neuter, 70–71, 244
  object pronouns as, 59–60
  possessive pronouns as, 61–62
  problems with, 75–79
Person (first, second, third), 54–55, 69–70. *See also* Person, of pronoun.
  as point of view in short story, 408
Person, of pronoun, 85
Persons
  adjectives and, 133
  adverbs and, 133
  articles and, 123
  capitalization of names of, 186–188, 202
  demonstrative pronouns and, 67
  initials for names of, 207
  nouns for, 34, 36, 38, 43
  predicate adjectives and, 125
  pronouns for, 54–56
  titles of, 186–187
Persuasive writing, 296, 297, 299, 393, 505. *See also* Writing Workshops, opinion statement.
Photographs, 330, 333, 438, 498
  captions for, 45, 330–331
  description of, 305
  in oral reports, 490
  for process description, 385
  writing about, 135
Phrases. *See also* Prepositional phrases; Transition words or phrases; Verb phrases.
  adjective, 163
  adverb, 163
  at beginning of sentence, 280
  directional, 304–305
  at end of sentence, 281
  inserting, 284, 287
  as interjections, 157
  in middle of sentence, 280
  rearranging, 342–343, 345
  between subjects and verbs, 171–172, 183
  that interfere, 77
Pictures, 330–331. *See also* Drawings; Illustrations; Photographs.
  word, 355, 411
Pie graphs, 333
Place description, Writing Workshop for, 366–373
Place names, 123
  capitalization of, 184, 193–195, 202
  demonstrative pronouns and names of, 67

descriptions of, 366–373
nouns for, 34, 36, 38, 43
pronouns for, 54
proper names for, 194
Plagiarism, 425, 457
Plane names
 capitalization of, 194
 italics and underlining of, 224
Planning
 for class newspaper, 506
 for interviewing, 485
 for research report, 421
Plays, titles of, 190, 224
Plural antecedents, 70–71, 85, 244
Plural forms, 223
 apostrophes with, 223
 of letters, 223
 of numerals, 223
Plural indefinite pronouns, 72–74,
 173–174
Plural nouns, 38–40, 50, 51
 agreement with, 166–168
 apostrophes with, 222–223
Plural pronouns, 54–55, 57, 69, 72–74,
 85
Plural subjects, 171–172
 agreement with, 166–168, 178–179,
 182–183
 with indefinite pronouns, 182–183
Plural verbs, 166–168, 171–172
 agreement with, 178–179, 182–183
 with compound subjects, 169
 with indefinite pronouns, 173–174,
 182–183
P.M., capitalization of, 196
Poem, Writing Workshop for, 411–417
Poetry
 capitalization in, 189, 202, 226
 checklist for, 417
 punctuation in, 226
 rhyme in, 411–414
 titles of, 190, 224
Point of view, 60, 408
Portfolios, 273
Positive connotation, 351
Positive language, 476
Possessive case, 54–55, 84
Possessive nouns, 41–42, 50, 222–223
Possessive pronouns, 61–63, 80, 127,
 222
Post cards, writing, 126
Posters, 129, 272, 498
Posture. See Delivery of speech.
Precise words, 256, 269, 270, 279,
 350–351, 354
 in describing places, 366, 367

in essays, 358
in poems, 411, 414
Predicate adjectives, 21, 22, 33, 125–126
 diagramming of, 234
 linking verbs and, 94–95
 well and *good* in, 145
Predicate nouns, 21, 22, 33, 43, 51
 for description, 95
 diagramming of, 234
 linking verbs and, 94–95
 personal pronouns with, 75
Predicate pronouns, 57, 84, 85
 compound, 77–79
 who used as one, 66
Predicates, 33
 complete, 6–7, 9, 10, 32, 278
 compound, 232–233
 diagramming of, 232–233
 joining, 154–155
 linking verbs and, 88
 simple, 10–11, 32
Prefixes, 517, 518, 524
Prepositional phrases, 149, 151–153,
 162–163
 diagramming of, 236
 placement of, 152
 subject-verb agreement and, 171,
 176–177, 183
Prepositions, 146, 148–153, 162–163.
 See also Objects of prepositions.
 adverbs confused with, 149
 capitalization and, 190, 193
 checklist for, 163
 to show location, 158–159
Presentation, 272–273, 490–491,
 492–493
Present participle, 96–97, 98–100, 118
Present perfect, 104–106, 107, 119
Present progressive, 101–103, 107
Present tense, 13, 101–103, 107, 118,
 119
 simple, 101–102, 119
Previewing, 452
Prewriting, 26, 264–266
 for essays, 361
 for opinion statement, 401
 for place description, 369
 for poem, 413
 for problem-solution essay, 393
 for process description, 385
 for response to literature, 377
 for short story, 409
Printing
 of class newspaper, 506, 509
 of essays, 365
 of opinion statement, 405

of place description, 373
of poem, 417
of process description, 389
of research report, 433
of response to literature, 380
of short story, 417
Print media, 498
Problem-solution essay, Writing
    Workshop for, 390–397
Problem solving
    groups for, 488
    listening for, 482
Process description, Writing Workshop
    for, 382–389
Pronoun-antecedent agreement, 85
Pronouns, 52–85. See also Indefinite
        pronouns; Personal pronouns;
        Plural pronouns; Singular pronouns.
    as adjectives, 127
    adjectives and, 122, 136
    antecedent agreement with, 69–71,
        72–74, 244
    as antecedents, 69, 72–74, 244
    appositives with, 210
    capitalization of, 187
    demonstrative, 67–68, 84, 127
    in dialogue, 80–81
    as direct objects, 91
    ending in self or selves, 64–65
    intensive, 64–65, 84
    interrogative, 64, 80, 84
    modifiers of, 136, 144–145, 163
    object, 59–60, 80
    as objects of prepositions, 44
    plural, 57
    possessive, 61–63, 80, 127, 222
    predicate, 57, 84
    prepositions and, 148
    problems with, 75–79, 85
    reflexive, 64–65, 80, 84
    subject, 57–58, 60, 77–79, 80
    types of, 84
Proofreading. See also Editing; Revising;
        Rewriting.
    for capitalization, 192, 200
    for contractions and possessive
        pronouns, 62, 63
    for double negatives, 139
    of essays, 362
    of letters, 192
    of opinion statement, 402
    of place description, 370
    for plural nouns, 39, 40
    of poem, 414
    for prepositional phrases, 153
    of problem-solution essay, 394

of process description, 386
for pronoun-antecedent agreement,
    70, 74
for pronoun errors, 79
of research report, 430
of response to literature, 378
of short story, 410
as stage in writing process, 264, 271
for subject-verb agreement, 168
tips for, 275
for troublesome verb pairs, 113
Proofreading marks, 271
Propaganda. See Media; Thinking.
Proper adjectives, capitalization of, 123
Proper names, 8
    in names of places, 194
    titles with, 186–187
Proper nouns, 36, 50, 202
    adjectives and, 123
    capitalization of, 36
    importance of, in writing, 36, 37
Publishing, 264, 272–273. See also
        Online publishing options; Printing.
    of class newspaper, 507, 509
    of essays, 365
    of place description, 373
    of poem, 417
    of problem-solution essay, 397
    of process description, 386
    of research report, 433
    of response to literature, 380
    of short story, 417
    working with other writers in, 272
Punctuation, 204–231, 269, 270, 271.
        See also Commas; Quotation
        marks.
    checklist for, 231
    colons, 218–219
    dashes, 220–221
    for dialogue, 216, 217, 410
    end marks, 206–208, 214–217
    hyphens, 220–221
    parentheses, 220–221
    periods, 206–208
    of poetry, 226
    of quotations, 214–217
    semicolons, 218–219
    of titles, 190, 224–225, 230–231
Purpose, 265
    of class newspaper, 506, 509
    of essay, 361
    in informal speaking, 488
    in listening, 482, 483, 494
    in the media, 500
    of opinion statement, 401
    of oral reports, 489

of place description, 366, 367, 369
of political cartoon, 504
of problem-solution essay, 393
of process description, 382, 383, 385
of research report, 421
of response to literature, 377
of short story, 409
in speaking, 494

Q

Question marks, 16, 206, 214
  with quotation marks, 231
Questionnaires, writing, 67
Questions. *See also* Interrogative
    sentences.
  elaboration and, 325
  in essays, 359
  in examining media, 497–501
  interrogative pronouns in, 16
  in interviewing, 486, 506
  in introduction of compositions, 315,
    320
  listening and, 483
  in poem, 412
  punctuation for, 206
  for research report, 421
  subjects in unusual positions in,
    176–177
  subject-verb agreement in, 183
  test, 460–462, 463
Quite, 131
Quotation marks, 214–217, 230–231,
    410
  with commas, 231
  for dialogue, 216, 217
  with exclamation points, 231
  for note cards, 457
  with periods, 231
  with question marks, 231
  in research report, 424, 425
  in short story, 410
Quotations, 214–217
  capitalization in, 189, 215
  direct, 214
  divided, 215
  indirect, 215
  in problem-solution essay, 391
  punctuation for, 214–217
  in response to literature, 374, 376,
    381

R

Races, capitalization of, 188
Raise, 111, 119
Raised, 111

Rather, 131
Readers, for peer response, 268
Reader's Guide, 442, 443
Reading aids, 452–453
Reading script, 493
Real, really 136, 137, 145
Reasoning
  cause-and-effect, 399, 474
  circular, 474, 479
  clear, 474–475
  faulty, 474–475
  logical, 390, 392, 398, 399
Reasons
  in opinion statement, 402
  in persuasive writing, 297
Recipes, writing, 301
Reference materials, 444–445, 522–523
Reference, unclear, 75, 76, 244
Reflecting, 264, 272–273.
  on essay, 362
  on opinion statement, 402
  on place description, 370
  on poem, 414
  on problem-solution essay, 394
  on process description, 386
  on research report, 430
  on response to literature, 378
  on short story, 410
Reflexive pronouns, 64–65, 80, 84
Regions, capitalization of, 193, 194
Regular verbs, principal parts of, 96–97,
    118
Rehearsing a speech, 493
Related ideas, 468–469, 478
Relationships, 84. *See also* Possessive
    case.
  conjunctions and, 155
  family, 187
  prepositions to show, 148, 162, 163
Religious terms, capitalization of, 187
Remain, 88
Renaming, 21, 43, 57
Reports
  notes for, 457
  oral, 489–495
  research, 418–433
  written, 489
Rereading, 377
Research. *See* Facts; Information;
    Libraries; Reference materials;
    Sources of information; Statistics.
Research report, Writing Workshop for,
    418–433
  checklist for, 433
  evaluating information sources for, 422
  notes for, 457

Response to literature, Writing Workshop for, 374–381
Restatements, 514, 524
Resulting from, 321
Reviewing, 453
Reviews, of media products, 471, 505
Revising, 19, 20, 37, 264, 269–270. *See also* Editing; Proofreading; Rewriting.
　to add facts, 329
　adding hyphens in, 221
　adjectives in, 129
　of capitalization, 195
　checklist for, 345
　complements in, 45
　of compositions, 314
　compound subjects in, 169, 170
　conjunctions in, 156
　for elaboration, 324
　of essays, 362
　for exact language, 350
　for formal language, 349
　of incorrect verb pairs, 116
　of letters, 349
　for more specific verbs, 350
　of opinion statement, 402
　of oral reports, 489–490
　peer response and, 268
　of place description, 370
　of poem, 414
　possessive nouns in, 42
　of problem-solution essay, 394
　of process description, 386
　for pronoun errors, 76
　pronouns in, 82
　by rearranging phrases, 342–343, 345
　of research report, 430
　of response to literature, 378
　of sentences, 335–345
　of short story, 410
　subject-verb agreement in, 167, 169, 170, 179, 180
　for verb tenses, 103
Rewriting. *See also* Editing; Proofreading; Revising
　for complete sentences, 278
　for pronoun-antecedent agreement, 74
　pronouns in, 56
　for subject-verb agreement, 177
　of topic sentences, 291
　for unity and coherence, 318
Rhyme, 411–414
Rhythm, 340
Riddles, writing, 126
Rise, 111, 119
Risen, 111

Rivers, capitalization of, 193
Roads, capitalization of, 193
Root words, 518–519, 524
Rose, 111
Route description, writing, 79
Rubric
　for opinion statement, 398–400
　for personal experience essay, 358–359
　for place description, 366–368
　for poem, 411–412
　for problem-solution essay, 390–392
　for process description, 382–384
　for research report, 418–420
　for response to literature, 374–376
　for short story, 406–408
Run-on sentences, 25–27, 33, 241

S

Sat, 112
Scarcely, 138
Science, writing about, 131, 152, 155, 281
Script, reading, 493
Search engines, 446–447
Seasons, capitalization of, 196, 197, 203
Second, 321
Second person pronoun, 54–55, 69–70
Sections, capitalization of, 194
Seem, 21, 88, 125
Semicolons, 218–219
Send, 91
Sensory details, 326–327, 332
　in essays, 358, 359, 360, 362, 364
　in place description, 366, 367
　in short story, 406, 409
Sentence closers, 281, 286
Sentence fragments. *See* Fragments.
Sentence middles, 280, 286
Sentence openers, 280, 286
Sentences, 269, 270. *See also* Declarative sentences; Exclamatory sentences; Imperative sentences; Interrogative sentences; Topic sentences.
　beginning with *Here* or *There,* 19, 176–179, 183
　building, 277–278
　capitalization of first word of, 202
　checklist for, 33, 287, 345
　choppy, 341, 345
　clear, 33, 73, 75, 210, 250
　commas in, 209–211
　complete, 4, 28
　complex, 283

compound, 218, 237, 282
diagramming, 232–237
editing, 33
expanding, 279, 286–287
fixing empty, 336–337, 344
fluency of, 269, 270
in formal writing, 349
fragments of, 25–27
growing, 280–281, 287
improving, 250, 278–279
in informal writing, 348
informative, 20
inverted, 18–19
kinds of, 4, 16–17, 33, 343
logical order of, 290, 293
modifiers for, 286
mood of, 20
nouns in, 43
overloaded, 338–339, 344
punctuation for different types of,
206–208
revising, 18, 20, 335–345
rhythm of, 340
run-on, 25–27, 33, 241
stringy, 338–339, 344
structure of, 6
subjects and predicates in, 6–7
too many ideas in, 250
tricky, 183
types of, 28–29
varying length of, 240–241, 252, 344
varying structure of, 252, 342–343,
344, 430
weak, 250
Sequence of events, 108, 109
Sequential order, 302–303, 308–309,
317, 321, 341
in process description, 386
in short story, 408
Series of items, commas with, 209, 218,
230
Set, 112, 119
Several, 72, 84, 173
Shall, 12, 89
Sharing ideas and information, 6–7, 467
Sharing your writing
for essays, 362
listening and, 482
for opinion statement, 402
for place description, 370
for poem, 414
for problem-solution essay, 394
for process description, 386
for research report, 430
for response to literature, 378
for short story, 410

She, 54–55, 57, 84
problems with, 77
Ship names, capitalization of, 194
Short-answer questions, 462
Short stories, 190, 224
checklist for, 417
Short story, writing workshop for,
406–410, 416–417
Should, 12, 89
Should be, 57
Show, 91
Similarly, 299, 306, 321, 471
Similes, 257, 352–353, 354, 355
in essays, 364
in poems, 411
Simple future tense, 101–102, 119
Simple past tense, 101–102, 119
Simple predicates, 10–11, 32. *See also*
Verbs.
Simple present tense, 101–102, 119
Simple subjects, 8–9, 32
diagramming of, 232
in unusual order, 20
Simple tenses, 101–103, 119
Since, 283, 299, 321
Singular antecedents, 70–71, 72–74,
85, 244
Singular indefinite pronouns, 72–74,
173–174
Singular nouns, 38–40, 50
agreement with, 166–168
apostrophe with, 222–223
Singular pronouns, 54–55, 57, 69,
72–74, 85
Singular subjects, 171–172
agreement with, 166–168, 178–179,
182–183
with indefinite pronouns, 182–183
Singular verbs, 166–168
agreement with, 178–179, 182–183
with indefinite pronouns, 173–174,
182–183
Sit, 112, 119
Skits, writing, 17, 365
Slang, 348
avoiding, 255, 349
in short story, 410
in speaking, 494
Slides, in oral reports, 490
Smell, 88
Snob appeal, 477
So, 131, 321
Some, 72, 127, 173, 174
Somebody, 72, 173
Someone, 72, 84, 173
Something, 72, 173

Songs, titles of, 190, 224
Sound, 21, 88
Sound devices
    in oral interpretations, 492
    in poems, 411
Sound, on World Wide Web, 499
Source cards, 422–423
Source line, 331, 425
Sources of information, 437–450
    evaluating, 422
    for research report, 418, 420,
        422–423
South, capitalization of, 193, 194
Spacecraft names, capitalization of, 194
Spatial order, 304–305, 308–309
    in describing places, 366, 367, 368,
        369
Speaking. *See also* Oral communication.
    checklist for, 495
    delivery in, 484, 489, 491
    dramatic, 272, 417
    formal, 489–495
    in groups, 487–488
    informal, 487–488
    listening and, 481
    occasions for, 349
    situations for, 487
    stage fright in, 491
Special events, capitalization of, 197
Specific words, 256, 350, 409, 523
Spell checkers, 62, 271
Spelling, 269, 270, 271
    of adverbs, 131
    of plural nouns, 38–40, 50, 51
    of possessive nouns, 41
Sports writing, 65, 505
Stage fright, 491
Standard English, 349
Statements. *See also* Declarative
    sentences.
    proving or disproving, 470
    thesis, 320, 418, 419, 432
States, capitalization of, 193, 194
Statistics
    in informative paragraphs, 296
    in opinion statement, 398, 399, 401
    in problem-solution essay, 390
Steps, in process description, 385, 386
Stores, capitalization of, 196
Stories
    feature, 503, 505, 506
    fiction and nonfiction, 439
    news, 505, 506
    titles of, 190, 224
    writing, 4–5
Streets, capitalization of, 193

Stringy sentences, 338–339, 344
Study skills, 451–466
    checklist for, 465
    notes and, 456–458
    outlines and, 459
Style, 269, 270, 509
Subject case, 54–55
Subject complements, 21–22, 94
    diagramming of, 234
Subject pronouns, 57–58, 60, 77–79,
    80, 84, 85
Subjects, 33. *See also* Compound
    subjects; Plural subjects; Singular
    subjects.
    complete, 6–7, 32, 278
    describing, 21
    indefinite pronouns as, 173–175
    joining, 154–155
    linking verbs and, 88
    nouns as, 43, 51
    order of verbs and, 18–20, 33
    personal pronouns with, 75
    phrases between verbs and,
        171–172, 183
    predicate adjectives and, 94–95, 125
    predicate nouns and, 94–95
    pronouns as, 57, 84, 85
    reflexive pronouns and, 64
    renaming, 21, 43, 57
    simple, 8–9, 20, 32, 232
    subject pronouns as, 58
    in unusual order, 18–20, 176–177
    who used as one, 66–67
Subject-verb agreement, 164–183,
    242–243
    checklist for, 183
    prepositional phrases and, 171,
        176–177, 183
    in response to literature, 378
Subtitles, 498
Suddenly, 299
Suffixes, 517, 518, 524, 525
Summarizing, 11. *See also* Conclusions
    (of a written work).
    in compositions, 319, 321
    in essays, 358
    information, 199
    in opinion statement, 400
    in oral reports, 490
    in response to literature, 374, 375,
        376, 377, 380
    in test taking, 465
Superlative form, 133–135, 144, 145
Supporting details, 254, 468
Supporting opinions, 471
Surveys, creating, 67

Suspense, revising sentences for, 20
Synonyms, 521, 523

T

Table of contents, 445
Target audience, 501, 506, 508
Taste, 21, 88, 125
Taught, 112
Teach, 91, 112, 119
Television (TV) shows, titles of, 190,
    224, 497, 499, 501
Tell, 91
Tenses of verbs, 13, 96–97, 107–110,
    118–119, 248
    in opinion statement, 402
    perfect, 104–106
    progressive forms of, 101–103,
      107–109
    in research report, 430
    simple, 101–103, 119
Test taking, 451–466
    checklist for, 465
    essay questions and, 463, 465
    objective tests and, 460–462
    writing in, 463
Text, 498, 499
That, 67–68, 84, 127
The, 123
Their, 55, 61, 84, 127, 222
Theirs, 55, 61, 84
Them, 55, 59, 84
    problems with, 77
Themselves, 64, 84
Then, 293, 299, 321
There, sentences beginning with, 19,
    176–179, 183
The same as, 309
Thesaurus, 444, 523
These, 67–68, 84, 127
Thesis statement, 320, 418, 419, 426,
    432
    drafting and, 427
They, 54–55, 57, 84
    problems with, 77
They're, 61, 222
Things
    adjectives and, 133
    adverbs and, 133
    articles and, 123
    capitalization of, 202
    demonstrative pronouns and, 67
    nouns for, 34, 36, 38, 43
    pronouns for, 54
Thinking, 467–480
    clear, 474, 475, 479
    conclusions in, 472–473

either/or, 475
    inferences in, 472, 473
    reasoning errors in, 474–475, 479
Third person pronoun, 54–55, 69–70
This, 67–68, 84, 127
Those, 67–68, 84, 127
Through, 148
Time
    abbreviations for, 196, 218
    capitalization of, 196
    colons in, 218
    tenses showing, 107, 108, 119
Timelines, 333, 455
Time order, 108, 109
Timing, in oral reports, 489
Titles, 224–225, 498
    of book chapters, 224
    of books, 190, 224
    capitalization of, 186–187, 190, 202
    of essays, 224
    italics or underlining for, 224
    of people and cultures, 186–188
    of plays, 224
    of poems, 224
    punctuation of, 190, 224–225,
      230–231
    quotation marks for, 224
    as reading aid, 452
    reading, for overview, 498
    of short story, 190, 224
    of songs, 224
    and subtitles, 498
    of written works, 190, 224
To, 59, 91, 131, 148
Too, 309
Topics, 264–265. *See also* Ideas.
    for essays, 361
    for opinion statement, 401
    for oral reports, 489
    for problem-solution essay, 393
    for process description, 385
    for research report, 421
    for response to literature, 377
Topic sentence, 290–291, 296, 298
    in body of compositions, 313
    facts in, 329
    in informative paragraphs, 297
    in persuasive paragraphs, 297
Totally, 401
Toward, 148
Towns, capitalization of, 193
Train names, capitalization of, 194
Transition ideas, for research report, 418
Transition words or phrases, 293, 298,
    299, 302, 309
    coherence and, 318

for comparison or contrast, 306–307
in essays, 359
in opinion statement, 400
in process description, 382, 383, 385
in research report, 420
types of, 321
Transitive verbs, 92
Transportation, writing about, 86, 92
True-false questions, 460
TV. *See* Television (TV) shows, titles of.

U

Under, 148
Underlining, 224, 225
Underneath, 309
Unity, 290, 292, 298, 316, 320
Unlike, 309, 321, 471
Until, 148
Up, 148
Us, 55, 59, 84
  problems with, 75, 77, 85
  and *we,* 75, 85
Usually, 131

V

Vague words, 401
Variety in sentences, 19–20, 33, 344
  length, 240–241, 253, 344
  in research report, 430
  structure, 252, 342–343, 344
Vehicle names, capitalization of, 194
Venn diagram, 306–307
Verb forms, 101–103, 107–109, 248
Verb phrases, 12–13, 89, 114
  agreement with subject by, 166–168
  with subjects in unusual order, 18–20
Verbs, 10–11, 86–119. *See also* Action
    verbs; Helping verbs; Linking
    verbs; Plural verbs; Singular verbs;
    Tenses of verbs.
  checklist for, 119
  complements to, 91
  in complete predicates, 6
  compound, 14–15, 33
  diagramming of, 232–233
  direct objects of, 59
  exact, 256
  in instructions, 115
  intransitive, 92
  irregular, 97, 98–100, 116, 119
  main, 12, 89
  missing, 18
  modifiers of, 130, 136, 144–145, 163
  objects of, 23–24
  order of subjects and, 18–20, 33

phrases between subjects and,
    171–172, 183
in a play-by-play, 115
principal parts of, 96–97, 118, 119
reflexive pronouns and, 64
regular, 96–97, 118
simple predicates, 10–11, 32
strong, 256
with subjects in unusual order, 18–20
suffixes for, 525
transitive, 92
troublesome pairs of, 111–113
Very, 131
Videos, 438, 499
Visuals, 324, 330–331, 332–333
  in magazines, 443
  for oral reports, 489, 490
  for process description, 385
  understanding, 454–455
Vocabulary
  building your, 511–525
  checklist for, 525
  in formal writing, 349
Voice
  and kinds of sentences, 33
  in reading essay, 362
  as writing style, 269, 270

W

Was, 12, 21, 57, 88, 89
We, 54–55, 57, 84
  problems with, 75, 77, 85
  and *us,* 75, 85
Web sites, 272, 445. *See also* Internet;
    Online publishing options; World
    Wide Web
Well, good, 136, 137, 145
Were, 12, 21, 57, 88, 89
West, capitalization of, 193, 194
What, 66–68, 84
Which, 66–68, 84
While, 321
Who, 66–68, 84, 246
  problems with, 85
Whom, 66–68, 84, 246
  problems with, 85
Who's, 222
Whose, 84, 222
Will, 12, 89
Will be, 57
With, 148
Within, 148
Without, 148
Word families, 520–521
Wordiness, 15, 251

Word parts, analyzing, 517–519, 524
Words. *See also* Descriptive words;
    Transition words or phrases;
    Vocabulary.
  base, 517, 518
  changing form of, 285, 287
  choice of, 269, 270
  compound, 517
  connecting, 14, 282, 341
  connotation of, 351, 354, 355
  context of, 512, 514–516, 524
  definitions of, 514, 524
  denotation of, 351
  exact, 350–351, 354
  inserting, 284, 287
  as interjections, 157
  joining, 154, 162–163
  negative, 138–139
  precise, 256, 270, 279, 350–351,
    354
  root, 518–519, 524
  specific, 256, 350, 409, 523
  unnecessary, 14, 251, 292, 413
  vague, 401
Word traps, 275
Works Cited list, 418, 420, 429
World regions, capitalization of, 193
World Wide Web, 446–447, 449, 499.
    See also Internet; Online
    publishing options; Web sites
  analyzing information on, 504
  searching, 446–447
Would, 12, 89
Write, 91
Writing. *See also* Compositions;
    Descriptive writing; Prewriting;
    Rewriting; Writing process; Writing
    Workshops.
  about games, 459
  about history, 131
  about media, 497
  about observations, 131, 135
  about photographs, 135
  about science, 131, 152, 155, 281
  about the future, 109
  about the past, 108
  about the present, 107
  adjectives in, 129, 134, 135, 137
  of ads, 289, 335
  adverbs in, 131, 132, 134, 135, 137
  of announcements, 208
  arguments made in, 323, 329
  audiotape or videotape and, 272
  building compositions in, 311–321
  building sentences in, 277
  for bulletin boards, 272

  for bumper stickers, 347, 353
  of captions, 45, 330–331
  of cartoons, 217
  checklist for, 275, 321
  clear, 92, 336–337
  combining sentences in, 284
  of communication schedule, 481
  comparative and superlative forms in,
    134, 135
  comparisons in, 134, 135
  complete sentences in, 7, 9
  compound subjects in, 14, 15, 169
  compound verbs in, 14, 15
  conjunctions in, 146, 155
  contractions in, 62, 223
  details in, 323
  of dialogue, 16, 17, 56, 217
  of directions, 184
  direct objects in, 24, 92
  double negatives in, 138–139
  for dramatic reading, 272
  elaboration in, 323–334
  in e-mail, 272, 348, 509
  emotions expressed in, 146, 157
  facts in, 328
  feelings and attitudes expressed in,
    16, 17, 355
  figurative language in, 257, 352–353
  focusing on a topic in, 265
  fragments in, 26, 27
  freewriting, 377, 413
  of headlines, 204, 227
  here and *there* in, 177
  ideas and topics for, 264, 265, 468
  indefinite-pronoun agreement in, 73,
    74
  indefinite pronouns in, 174, 175
  indirect objects in, 24
  information and, 437
  informative paragraphs in, 296
  of instructions, 301, 303
  interjections in, 146, 157
  for Internet journal, 272
  interrogative pronouns in, 67, 68
  of introductions, 315
  irregular verbs in, 100
  of journal entry, 179
  kinds of sentences in, 16, 17
  of labels, 330–331
  for magazines, "zines", 272
  main ideas in, 468
  method of, 274
  mood expressed in, 20
  narrative paragraphs in, 295
  for newspaper, 272
  of news report, 97

nouns in, 44
opinions expressed in, 313, 325, 328, 336
outlines in, 190, 192, 459
peer response to improve, 268
perfect tenses in, 105, 106
periods in, 208
personal pronouns in, 55, 56, 60, 73, 74, 76, 79
persuasive, 296, 505
planning in, 267–268
plural nouns in, 39, 40
point of view in, 60
portfolios for, 273
possessives in, 41, 62, 223
of post cards, 126
of posters, 129
precise words in, 256
predicate adjectives in, 125, 126
predicate nouns in, 95
prepositional phrases in, 152, 172, 177
prepositions in, 146, 150
presentation of, 272–273
pronoun-antecedent agreement in, 70, 73, 74
pronouns in, 52, 58, 60
proper nouns in, 37
publishing, 272–273
of quizzes, 68
quotation marks in, 217, 225
of recipes, 301
reflecting on, 272–273
of riddles, 126
of route description, 79
run-ons in, 26, 27
semicolons and colons in, 219
sensory details in, 327
"show, don't tell" in, 325
to show similarities and differences, 306–307, 469, 471
similes and metaphors in, 352–353
simple predicates in, 11
six traits of good, 269–270, 275
of skits, 17
"sound" of words in, 58, 78, 137
speaking and, 489–491
specific words in, 523
sports, 65, 505
steps in, 264
of stories, 4–5
style of, 269, 270
subject complements in, 22
subject pronouns in, 58
with subjects in unusual order, 19, 20, 177

subject-verb agreement in, 164, 167, 172, 174, 177
suggestions made in, 319, 321
summarizing in, 11
of television or radio show, 272
in test taking, 463, 465
thinking clearly and, 467
titles in, 225
underlining in, 225
using dictionary and thesaurus in, 523
variety in, 19–20, 33
verbs in, 86, 90, 97, 100
verb tenses in, 102, 105, 107–109, 116
vocabulary and, 511
for Web site, 272
what and *which* in, 68
who and *whom* in, 67, 68
of yearbook message, 52
Writing Process, 263–275. *See also* Writing.
drafting, 267–268, 274
editing, 271, 275
prewriting, 264–266, 274
proofreading, 271, 274. 275
publishing, 272, 274
reflecting, 273
revising, 269–270, 274
Writing Workshops
opinion statement, 398–405
personal experience essay, 358–365
place description, 366–373
poem, 411–417
problem-solution essay, 390–397
process description, 382–389
research report, 418–433
response to literature, 374–381
short story, 406–410, 416–417

Y

Yearbook message, writing, 52
Yesterday, 309
Yet, 309
You, 54–55, 57, 59, 84, 167
   as subject of imperative sentences, 18
You and *I,* common mistake with, 78
Your, 55, 61, 84, 127, 222
You're, 61, 222
Yours, 55, 61, 84
Yourself, 64, 84
Yourselves, 64

Z

"Zines." See Magazines, "zines."
ZIP codes, 212

Acknowledgments

For Literature and Text

Bilingual Press/Editorial Bilingüe: Excerpt from "The Sand Castle," from *Weeping Woman: La Llorona and Other Stories* by Alma Luz Villanueva. Copyright © 1994 by Alma Luz Villanueva. / Excerpt from "The Scholarship Jacket" by Marta Salinas, from *Nosotras: Latina Literature Today* (1986), edited by María del Carmen Boza, Beverly Silva, and Carmen Valle. / Reprinted by permission of Bilingual Press/Editorial Bilingüe, Arizona State University, Tempe, Ariz.

Don Congdon Associates: Excerpt from "All Summer in a Day" by Ray Bradbury, published in *Magazine of Fantasy and Science Fiction,* March 1954. Copyright © 1954, renewed 1982 by Ray Bradbury. Reprinted by permission of Don Congdon Associates, Inc.

Doubleday: Excerpt from "Night Journey" by Theodore Roethke, from *The Collected Poems of Theodore Roethke.* Copyright 1940 by Theodore Roethke. Used by permission of Doubleday, a division of Random House, Inc.

Lynnette Michelle Fisher: "Who" by Lynnette Michelle Fisher, from *Signatures from Big Sky: Montana Student Literary/Art Magazine,* Vol. 7 (1977). Copyright © 1997 by *Signatures from Big Sky.* Reprinted by permission of Lynnette Michelle Fisher.

Greenwillow Books: Excerpt from "The Boy Who Flew," from *The Robber Baby: Stories from the Greek Myths* by Anne Rockwell. Copyright © 1994 by Anne Rockwell. Reprinted by permission of Greenwillow Books, a division of William Morrow & Company, Inc.

Virginia Hamilton: Excerpt from "Under the Back Porch" by Virginia Hamilton. Copyright © 1992, 1999 by Virginia Hamilton Adoff. Used by permission of the author.

Henry Holt and Company: Excerpt from "Questioning Faces" by Robert Frost, from *The Poetry of Robert Frost,* edited by Edward Connery Lathem. Copyright © 1962 by Robert Frost, © 1969 by Henry Holt and Company, Inc. Reprinted by permission of Henry Holt and Company, Inc.

Houghton Mifflin Company and HarperCollins Publishers, London: Excerpt from "All That Is Gold," from *The Fellowship of the Ring* by J.R.R. Tolkien. Copyright © 1954, 1965 by J.R.R. Tolkien, copyright © renewed 1982 by Christopher R. Tolkien, Michael H. R. Tolkien, John F. R. Tolkien, and Priscilla M.A.R. Tolkien. Reprinted by permission of Houghton Mifflin Company and HarperCollins Publishers, London. All rights reserved.

Francisco Jiménez: Excerpt from "The Circuit" by Francisco Jiménez, *Arizona Quarterly,* Autumn 1973. Reprinted by permission of Francisco Jiménez.

Keith Ross Leckie: Excerpt from *Words on a Page* by Keith Ross Leckie. Reprinted by permission of the author.

Little, Brown and Company: Excerpt from "My First Dive with the Dolphins," from *The Dolphins and Me* by Don C. Reed. Text copyright © 1988 by Don C. Reed. Illustrations © 1988 by Pamela & Walter Carroll. Reprinted by permission of Little, Brown and Company.

McIntosh and Otis: Excerpt from "Scout's Honor" by Avi, from *When I Was Your Age,* edited by Amy Ehrlich, published by Candlewick Press. Copyright © 1996 by Avi Wortis. Reprinted by permission of McIntosh and Otis, Inc.

Scott Meredith Literary Agency: Excerpt from "Ghost of the Lagoon" by Armstrong Sperry. Copyright © 1980 by Armstrong Sperry. Reprinted by permission of the author and the author's agents, Scott Meredith Literary Agency, L.P.

Professional Publishing Services: Excerpt from "The Dog of Pompeii," from *The Donkey of God* by Louis Untermeyer. Published by arrangement with the Estate of Louis Untermeyer, Norma Anchin Untermeyer, c/o Professional Publishing Services Company. This permission is expressly granted by Laurence S. Untermeyer.

Reader's Digest Association: Excerpt from *Reader's Digest Book of Facts.* Copyright © 1987 by The Reader's Digest Association, Inc. Used by permission of Reader's Digest, Pleasantville, N.Y. (www.readersdigest.com).

Scholastic: Excerpt from "Why Monkeys Live in Trees," from *How Many Spots Does a Leopard Have? and Other Tales* by Julius Lester. Copyright © 1989 by Julius Lester. Reprinted by permission of Scholastic Inc.

Simon & Schuster Books for Young Readers: Excerpts from "Oh Broom, Get to Work," from *The Invisible Thread* by Yoshiko Uchida. Copyright © 1991 by Yoshiko Uchida. / Excerpt from *The House of Dies Drear* by Virginia Hamilton. Copyright © 1968 by Virginia Hamilton. / Reprinted with the permission of Simon & Schuster Books for Young Readers, an imprint of Simon & Schuster Children's Publishing Division.

Timed Resources and Lydia Eickstaedt: "Lion and the Peculiar Purple Peach" by Lydia Eickstaedt, from *The Children's Magazine,* Fall 1997. Copyright © 1997 by Timed Resources, Inc. Reprinted by permission of Timed Resources, Inc., and Lydia Eickstaedt.

Heidi Wiedenheft: "Theater" by Heidi Wiedenheft, from *Signatures from Big Sky: Montana Student Literary/Art Magazine,* Vol. 6 (1996). Copyright © 1996 by *Signatures from Big Sky.* Reprinted by permission of Heidi Wiedenheft.

Table of Contents

viii *top* Illustration by Todd Graveline; *bottom* Photo by Sharon Hoogstraten; **ix** Copyright © 1999 PhotoDisc, Inc.; **x, xi** Illustrations by Todd Graveline; **xii** Copyright © 1999 PhotoDisc, Inc.; **xiii** *top* Illustration by Todd Graveline; *bottom* Copyright © Kenneth W. Fink/Bruce Coleman, Inc.; **xv** Karl Weatherly/Corbis; **xvi, xvii, xviii, xix** Illustrations by Todd Graveline; **xx** Photo by Sharon Hoogstraten; **xxi** Illustration by Todd Graveline; **xxii** Photo by Sharon Hoogstraten; **xxiii** Illustration by Todd Graveline; **xxiv** Photo by Sharon Hoogstraten; **xxv** Illustration by Todd Graveline; **xxvi** Photo by Sharon Hoogstraten; **xxvii** Copyright © Stockbyte; **xxviii** *top* Illustration by Todd Graveline; *bottom* Photo by Sharon Hoogstraten; **xxix** *left, right* Copyright © 1999 PhotoDisc; **xxx** Illustration by Todd Graveline; **xxxi** Courtesy of Habitat For Humanity; **1** Illustration by Todd Graveline.

Illustrations by Todd Graveline

8, 17, 27, 32, 33, 38, 50, 51, 56, 64, 67, 84, 85, 112, 119, 131, 145, 148, 152, 163, 182 *top, bottom,* **188, 202, 203, 231, 232, 238, 240, 265, 268, 272** *top, center, bottom,* **274** *center, bottom,* **275** *top, center,* **284, 286, 287, 298** *center, bottom,* **305** *top,* **308, 309, 315, 317, 320, 321, 323** *center foreground,* **327** *top,* **328** *bottom,* **332, 335, 339, 342** *center,* **344** *top, bottom,* **345, 348** *bottom,* **350, 355, 372, 373** *top, center,* **442, 443, 448, 464, 467** *foreground,* **471, 472, 478** *top, bottom,* **479, 508, 509, 519, 524, 525.**

Art Credits

COVER *center* Photo by Sharon Hoogstraten; *center right* Copyright © 1997 Jim Karageorge/FPG International; *bottom left* Copyright © Myrleen Ferguson/PhotoEdit.

CHAPTER 1 **2–3** Copyright © Darren Robb/Tony Stone Images; **4** *background* Copyright © Tony Freeman/PhotoEdit; *foreground* Photo by Sharon Hoogstraten; **8, 9** Copyright © Lawrence Migdale; **11** Copyright © Pallas de Velletri/SuperStock; **15** The Granger Collection, New York; **25, 27** Copyright © Giraudon/Art Resource, NY; **28** Illustration by Arvis Stewart, from *The Macmillan Book of Greek Gods and Heroes* by Alice Low. Copyright © 1985 Macmillan Publishing Company, reprinted with the permission of Simon & Schuster Books for Young Readers, an imprint of Simon & Schuster Children's Publishing Division.

CHAPTER 2 **34** Gail Mooney/Corbis; **36** Photography by D. R. Baston, courtesy of the Center for American Archaeology, Kampsville, Illinois; **40** *left, right* Richard T. Nowitz/Corbis; **42** Copyright © Richard Pasley/Stock, Boston/PNI; **45** Nik Wheeler/Corbis; **47** *left* Copyright © Arthur Gurmankin/Phototake/PNI; *right* Eric and David Hosking/Corbis; **48** *The Far Side* copyright © 1985 FarWorks, Inc. All rights reserved.

CHAPTER 3 **52** Photo by Sharon Hoogstraten; **55** Copyright © SuperStock; **58** AP/Wide World Photos; **60** Copyright © Photo Researchers, Inc.; **62** AP/Wide World Photos; **68** The Gorilla Foundation/Ron Cohn; **71** From *Number the Stars* by Lois Lowry. Copyright © 1989 by Lois Lowry. Used by permission of Random House Children's Books, a division of Random House, Inc.; **73** Copyright © Royal Geographical Society; **79** Brown Brothers; **82** British Museum.

CHAPTER 4 **86** Copyright © Jeremy Walker/Tony Stone Images; **93** Schenectady Museum; Hall of Electrical History Foundation/Corbis; **95** Copyright © Stamp Design *2001 U.S. Postal Service. Reproduced with permission. All rights reserved. Reproduced courtesy of Marion Coleman.; **101** Copyright © Lester Lefkowitz / The Stock Market; **103** U.S. Patent Office; **104** Copyright © James Randklev / Stock Connection/PNI; **107** Dean Conger/Corbis; **108** Corbis; **116** NASA.

CHAPTER 5 **120** *background* Copyright © Vern Clevenger/Adventure Photo & Film; **122** Corbis; **127** *top* Copyright © 1999 PhotoDisc, Inc.; *bottom* Copyright © 1991 Matthew Borkoski/Stock Boston; **128** Jay Syverson/Corbis; **129** Copyright © 1999 PhotoDisc, Inc.; **135** *left, right* Copyright © James D. Watt /www.norbertwu.com; *center* Copyright © Stuart Westmorland/Tony Stone Images; **138** Catherine Karnow/Corbis.

CHAPTER 6 **146** Copyright © ILM/Photofest; **149** Douglas Peebles/Corbis; **153** Copyright © Kenneth W. Fink/Bruce Coleman, Inc.; **154** Copyright © Wolfgang Baver/Bruce Coleman, Inc.; **156** Copyright © Roy Morsch/Bruce Coleman Inc.; **157** The Far Side copyright © 1991 FarWorks, Inc. All rights reserved.; **158, 159** Illustrations by Daniel Guidera.

CHAPTER 7 **164** Copyright © David Madison/Tony Stone Images; **167** Copyright © Michael Newman/PhotoEdit; **171** AP/Wide World Photos; **173** Jonathan Blair/ Corbis; **174** Copyright © Paul Souders/Tony Stone Images; Photo by Sharon Hoogstraten; **180** Copyright © SuperStock.

CHAPTER 8 **184** Copyright © Kindra Clineff/AllStock/PNI; **187** Andrew Cowin; Travel Ink/Corbis; **189** Photo, By Permission of the Folger Shakespeare Library; **191** *top* Corbis/Bettmann; *bottom* Kennan Ward/Corbis; **193** Copyright © 1999 PhotoDisc, Inc.; **195** Map illustration by David Fuller, DLF Group; **197** Copyright © 1999 PhotoDisc, Inc.

CHAPTER 9 **204** *background* Corbis; *foreground* Photo by Sharon Hoogstraten; **206** Copyright © Manuela Hoefer/Tony Stone Images; **214** Illustration by Ken Marshall © 1998 from Madison Publishing Inc., a Scholastic/Madison Press Book.; **217** Calvin and Hobbes copyright © 1989 Watterson. Dist. by Universal Press Syndicate. Reprinted with permission. All rights reserved.; **221** Corbis/Bettmann.

CHAPTER 10 **260–261** Copyright © Laurence Dutton/Tony Stone Images; **262** *background* Copyright © Tom Brakefield/Stock Connection/PNI; *foreground* Copyright © 1999 PhotoDisc, Inc.; **263** Copyright © Bob Daemmrich/Stock, Boston/PNI; **266** Calvin and Hobbes copyright © 1989 Watterson. Dist. by Universal Press Syndicate. Reprinted with permission. All rights reserved.; **267** Copyright © David T. Roberts/Nature's Images, Inc./Photo Researchers, Inc.

CHAPTER 11 **276** *background, foreground* Copyright © 1999 PhotoDisc, Inc.; **277** *background* Copyright © 1999 PhotoDisc, Inc.; *left, right* George Lepp/Corbis; **279** Copyright © Miro Vintoniv/Stock Boston/PNI; **280** National Archives.

CHAPTER 12 **288** Copyright © 1999 PhotoDisc, Inc.; **289** Photo by Sharon Hoogstraten; **291** Copyright © Chuck Carlton/Index Stock Imagery/PNI; **292** Corbis; **293** Corbis/Bettmann; 294 Photograph by Cox Studios; **296** Copyright © S. J. Krasemann/Peter Arnold, Inc.

CHAPTER 13 **300, 301** Copyright © 1999 PhotoDisc, Inc.; **302** Peanuts reprinted by permission of United Feature Syndicate, Inc.; **305** *bottom* AP/Wide World Photos; **307** *left, right* Copyright © 1999 PhotoDisc, Inc.

CHAPTER 14 **310** Copyright © 1999 PhotoDisc, Inc.; **311** Courtesy of Habitat For Humanity; **313, 318** Corbis.

CHAPTER 15 **322, 323** Photos copyright © 1999 PhotoDisc, Inc; **325** Photo by Sharon Hoogstraten; **327** *bottom* Calvin and Hobbes copyright © 1987 Bill Watterson. Dist. by Universal Press Syndicate. Reprinted with permission. All rights reserved.; **328** *top* Stephen Frink/Corbis, *center* Copyright © Stuart Westmorland/Natural Selection; **330** *center* Larry Lee/Corbis; **333** *top left* Illustration Copyright © 1999 by Matt Zumbo.

CHAPTER 16 **334** Copyright © Joe Cornish/Tony Stone Images; **337** Copyright © Glen & Rebecca Gramb/Natural Selection; **342** *bottom left* Copyright © 1998 David Young-Wolff/PNI; *bottom center* Copyright © Terje Rakke/Image Bank;

bottom right Copyright © Arthur Grace/Stock Boston/PNI.

CHAPTER 17   346 Copyright © Phil Schermeister/AllStock/PNI; **347** Dewitt Jones/Corbis; **348** *top* Luann reprinted by permission of United Feature Syndicate, Inc.; **351** Copyright © 1999 PhotoDisc, Inc.; **352** By permission of Mell Lazarus and Creators Syndicate; **353** Paul A. Souders/Corbis.

CHAPTER 18   356, 357 Copyright © John Rizzo/Photonica; **363** *top, bottom* Photos by Sharon Hoogstraten.

CHAPTER 19   371 *top, center foreground, bottom* Photos by Sharon Hoogstraten; *center background* Copyright © Darrell Gulin/Tony Stone Images.

CHAPTERS 20 (379), 21 (387), 22 (395), 23 (403), 24 (415): Photos by Sharon Hoogstraten.

CHAPTER 25   431 *center* Photo by Sharon Hoogstraten; *center left* Arte & Immagini srl/Corbis; *bottom center* Adam Woolfitt/Corbis.

CHAPTER 26   434–435 Copyright © 1997 VCG/FPG International; **436** Copyright © 1999 PhotoDisc, Inc.; **437** Copyright © 1993 Ron Lowery/ The Stock Market; **439** *top, bottom* Corbis; **445** Copyright © Stockbyte.

CHAPTER 27   450 Copyright © 1999 PhotoDisc, Inc.; **451** *top left* Wolfgang Kaehler/Corbis; *top right* Copyright © Dr. Dan P. Cole; *center right* Giraudon/Art Resource, NY; *bottom right* Copyright © Dr. Dan P. Cole; *bottom center* Gail Mooney/Corbis; *bottom left* Exekias (6th BCE). Dionysos in his ship. Attic wine cup. 540 BCE. Museo Archeologico Nazionale, Naples, Italy. Staatliche Antikensammlung, Munich, Germany. Copyright © Eric Lessing/Art Resource; *center foreground* Photo by Allan Landau; **452–453** Copyright © Houghton Mifflin; **452** *inset* Scala/Art Resource, NY; **453** *top inset* Copyright © Michael Kuh/Photo Researchers, Inc.; **454, 455, 464** *top center* Copyright © Houghton Mifflin; **464** *top left* Copyright © 1999 PhotoDisc, Inc.

CHAPTER 28   466 Philadelphia Museum of Art/Corbis; **467** *background* Photo by Sharon Hoogstraten; **470** Copyright © The New Yorker Collection 1972, Frank Modell from cartoonbank.com. All Rights Reserved.; **473** Calvin and Hobbes copyright © 1990 Watterson. Dist. by Universal Press Syndicate. Reprinted with permission. All rights reserved.; **475** Copyright © 1999 PhotoDisc, Inc.; **476** Copyright © John Shaw/Photo Researchers Inc.; **477** Copyright © 1999 PhotoDisc, Inc.

CHAPTER 29   480 Copyright © Phil Banko/Tony Stone Images; **481** *background* Copyright © 1999 PhotoDisc, Inc.; *left, right* Copyright © 1999 PhotoDisc; *center foreground* Peanuts reprinted by permission of United Feature Syndicate, Inc.; **482** Skjold Photographs; **483** Copyright © 1997 Tom Stewart/The Stock Market; **484, 490** Photos by Sharon Hoogstraten; **491** Copyright © James L. Shaffer; **493** Photo by Sharon Hoogstraten; **494** *left, right* Copyright © 1999 PhotoDisc.

CHAPTER 30   496 Copyright © Stephen Johnson/Tony Stone Images; **497** *left* Copyright © Buena Vista Pictures Distribution, Inc./Photofest; *center left* Photograph by Renee Stockdale. Copyright © Cat Fancy Magazine; *center right* Copyright © Tribune Media Services, Inc. All Rights Reserved. Reprinted with permission.; *right* Minnesota 4–H Project Homepage Template designed by Roger J. Reinert, Extension Educator and Assistant Professor, Univerity of Minnesota Extension Service, 1997; **498** Copyright © 9 August 1999, U.S. News & World Report; **499** *top* Copyright © UPN/Photofest; *bottom* Copyright © Russ Finley/Finley–Holiday Film Corp.; **501** Karl Weatherly/Corbis; **502** Photofest; **503** *They Asked For the Moon,* Copyright © 1999 Time Inc. Reprinted by permission. Photo courtesy of NASA; **504** *top* NASA; *bottom* Cartoonists & Writers Syndicate, http://CartoonWeb.com; **507** Copyright © 1999 PhotoDisc, Inc.; **508** *top* Copyright © 1999 PhotoDisc, Inc.; *bottom* Copyright © The New Yorker Collection 1987 Warren Miller from cartoonbank.com. All Rights Reserved.

CHAPTER 31   510 Copyright © Suzanne & Nick Geary/Tony Stone Images; **511** Copyright © 1999 PhotoDisc, Inc.; **513** Copyright © 1999 Zits Partnership. Reprinted with special permission of King Features Syndicate; **515** *left, center, right* Copyright © 1999 PhotoDisc, Inc.

McDougal Littell Inc. has made every effort to locate the copyright holders of all copyrighted material in this book and to make full acknowledgment for its use.